Course	Senior Capstone Seminar
Course Number	**HD 4714**
	Mary Ellen Verdu
	VIRGINIA TECH
	HUMAN DEVELOPMENT

D1306114

http://create.mheducation.com

ISBN-10: 1308830351   ISBN-13: 9781308830353

Contents

Credits

Leadership Is a Process, Not a Position

Part 1

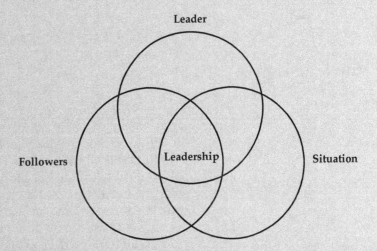

If any single idea is central to this book, it is that leadership is a process, not a position. The entire first part of this book explores that idea. One is not a leader—except perhaps in name only—merely because one holds a title or position. Leadership involves something happening as a result of the interaction between a leader and followers.

In Chapter 1 we define leadership and explore its relationship to concepts such as management and followership, and we also introduce the interactional framework. The interactional framework is based on the idea that leadership involves complex interactions between the leader, the followers, and the situations they are in. That framework provides the organizing principle for the rest of the book. Chapter 2 looks at how we can become better leaders by profiting more fully from our experiences, which is not to say that either the study or the practice of leadership is simple. Part 1 concludes with a chapter focusing on basic leadership skills. There also will be a corresponding skills chapter at the conclusion of each of the other three parts in this book.

Chapter 1

What Do We Mean by Leadership?

Introduction

In the spring of 1972, an airplane flew across the Andes mountains carrying its crew and 40 passengers. Most of the passengers were members of an amateur Uruguayan rugby team en route to a game in Chile. The plane never arrived. It crashed in snow-covered mountains, breaking into several pieces on impact. The main part of the fuselage slid like a toboggan down a steep valley, coming to rest in waist-deep snow. Although a number of people died immediately or within a day of the impact, the picture for the 28 survivors was not much better. The fuselage offered little protection from the extreme cold, food supplies were scant, and a number of passengers had serious injuries from the crash. Over the next few days, several surviving passengers became psychotic and several others died from their injuries. The passengers who were relatively uninjured set out to do what they could to improve their chances of survival.

Several worked on "weatherproofing" the wreckage; others found ways to get water; and those with medical training took care of the injured. Although shaken by the crash, the survivors initially were confident they would be found. These feelings gradually gave way to despair as search and rescue teams failed to find the wreckage. With the passing of several weeks and no sign of rescue in sight, the remaining passengers decided to mount expeditions to determine the best way to escape. The most physically fit were chosen to go on the expeditions because the thin mountain air and the deep snow made the trips difficult. The results of the trips were both frustrating and demoralizing: the expedition members determined they were in the middle of the Andes mountains, and walking out to find help was believed to be impossible. Just when the survivors thought nothing worse could possibly happen, an avalanche hit the wreckage and killed several more of them.

The remaining survivors concluded they would not be rescued, and their only hope was for someone to leave the wreckage and find help. Three of the fittest passengers were chosen for the final expedition, and everyone else's work was directed toward improving the expedition's chances of success. The three expedition members were given more food and were exempted from routine survival activities; the rest spent most of their energies securing supplies for the trip. Two months after the plane crash, the expedition members set out on their final attempt to find help. After hiking for 10 days through some of the most rugged terrain in the world, the expedition stumbled across a group of Chilean peasants tending cattle. One of the expedition members stated, "I come from a plane that fell in the mountains. I am Uruguayan . . ." Eventually 14 other survivors were rescued.

When the full account of their survival became known, it was not without controversy. It had required extreme and unsettling measures: the survivors had lived only by eating the flesh of their deceased comrades. Nonetheless, their story is one of the most moving survival dramas of all time, magnificently told by Piers Paul Read in *Alive*.[1] It is a story of tragedy and courage, and it is a story of leadership.

Perhaps a story of survival in the Andes is so far removed from everyday experience that it does not seem to hold any relevant lessons about leadership for you personally. But consider some of the basic issues the Andes survivors faced: tension between individual and group goals, dealing with the different needs and personalities of group members, and keeping hope alive in the face of adversity. These issues are not so different from those facing many groups we're a part of. We can also look at the Andes experience for examples of the emergence of informal leaders in groups. Before the flight, a boy named Parrado was awkward and shy, a "second-stringer" both athletically and socially. Nonetheless, this unlikely hero became the best loved and most respected among the survivors for his courage, optimism, fairness, and emotional support. Persuasiveness in group decision making also was an important part of leadership among the Andes survivors. During the difficult discussions preceding the agonizing decision to survive on the flesh of their deceased comrades, one of the rugby players made his reasoning clear: "I know that if my dead body could help you stay alive, then I would want you to use it. In fact, if I do die and you don't eat me, then I'll come back from wherever I am and give you a good kick in the ass."[2]

*Lives of great men all remind us
We can make our lives sublime
And, departing, leave behind us
Footprints on the sands of time.*
Henry Wadsworth Longfellow

What Is Leadership?

The Andes story and the experiences of many other leaders we'll introduce to you in a series of profiles sprinkled throughout the chapters provide numerous examples of leadership. But just what *is* leadership?

4   Part One   *Leadership Is a Process, Not a Position*

People who do research on leadership disagree more than you might think about what leadership really is. Most of this disagreement stems from the fact that **leadership** is a complex phenomenon involving the leader, the followers, and the situation. Some leadership researchers have focused on the personality, physical traits, or behaviors of the leader; others have studied the relationships between leaders and followers; still others have studied how aspects of the situation affect how leaders act. Some have extended the latter viewpoint so far as to suggest there is no such thing as leadership; they argue that organizational successes and failures often get falsely attributed to the leader, but the situation may have a much greater impact on how the organization functions than does any individual, including the leader.[3]

Perhaps the best way for you to begin to understand the complexities of leadership is to see some of the ways leadership has been defined. Leadership researchers have defined leadership in many different ways:

- The process by which an agent induces a subordinate to behave in a desired manner.[4]
- Directing and coordinating the work of group members.[5]
- An interpersonal relation in which others comply because they want to, not because they have to.[6]
- The process of influencing an organized group toward accomplishing its goals.[7]
- Actions that focus resources to create desirable opportunities.[8]
- Creating conditions for a team to be effective.[9]
- The ability to get results and the ability to build teams; these represent the what and the how of leadership.[10]
- A complex form of social problem solving.[11]

As you can see, definitions of leadership differ in many ways, and these differences have resulted in various researchers exploring disparate aspects of leadership. For example, if we were to apply these definitions to the Andes survival scenario described earlier, some researchers would focus on the behaviors Parrado used to keep up the morale of the survivors. Researchers who define leadership as influencing an organized group toward accomplishing its goals would examine how Parrado managed to convince the group to stage and support the final expedition. One's definition of leadership might also influence just *who* is considered an appropriate leader for study. Thus each group of researchers might focus on a different aspect of leadership, and each would tell a different story regarding the leader, the followers, and the situation.

Although having many leadership definitions may seem confusing, it is important to understand that there is no single correct definition. The various definitions can help us appreciate the multitude of factors that affect leadership, as well as different perspectives from which to view it. For example, in the first definition just listed, the word *subordinate* seems to confine leadership to downward influence in hierarchical relationships; it seems to exclude informal leadership. The second definition emphasizes the directing and controlling aspects of leadership, and thereby may deemphasize emotional aspects of leadership. The emphasis placed in the third definition on subordinates' "wanting to" comply with a leader's wishes seems to exclude any kind of coercion as a leadership tool. Further, it becomes problematic to identify ways in which a leader's actions are really leadership if subordinates voluntarily comply when a leader with considerable potential coercive power merely asks others to do something without explicitly threatening them. Similarly, a key reason behind using the phrase *desirable opportunities* in one of the definitions was precisely to distinguish between leadership and tyranny. And partly because there are many different definitions of leadership, there is also a wide range of individuals we consider leaders. In addition to stories about leaders and leadership we will sprinkle through this book, we will highlight several in each chapter in a series of Profiles in Leadership. The first of these is Profiles in Leadership 1.1, which highlights Peter Jackson.

All considered, we find that defining leadership as "the process of influencing an organized group toward accomplishing its goals" is fairly comprehensive and helpful. Several implications of this definition are worth further examination.

Leadership Is Both a Science and an Art

Saying leadership is both a science and an art emphasizes the subject of leadership as a field of scholarly inquiry, as well as certain aspects of the practice of leadership. The scope of the science of leadership is reflected in the number of studies—approximately 8,000—cited in an authoritative reference work, *Bass & Stogdill's Handbook of Leadership: Theory, Research, and Managerial Applications.*[12] However, being an expert on leadership research is neither necessary nor sufficient for being a good leader. Some managers may be effective leaders without ever having taken a course or training program in leadership, and some scholars in the field of leadership may be relatively poor leaders themselves.

However, knowing something about leadership research is relevant to leadership effectiveness. Scholarship may not be a prerequisite for leadership effectiveness, but understanding some of the major research findings can help individuals better analyze situations using a variety of perspectives. That, in turn, can tell leaders how to be more effective. Even so, because skills in analyzing and responding to situations vary greatly across leaders, leadership will always remain partly an art as well as a science.

Any fool can keep a rule. God gave him a brain to know when to break the rule.
General Willard W. Scott

Peter Jackson

PROFILES IN LEADERSHIP 1.1

When Peter Jackson read *The Lord of the Rings* trilogy at the age of 18, he couldn't wait until it was made into a movie; 20 years later he made that movie himself. In 2004 *The Lord of the Rings: The Return of the King* took home 11 Academy Awards, winning the Oscar in every category for which it was nominated. This tied the record for the most Oscars ever earned by one motion picture. Such an achievement might seem unlikely for a producer/director whose film debut was titled *Bad Taste,* which it and subsequent works exemplified in spades. Peter Jackson made horror movies so grisly and revolting that his fans nicknamed him the "Sultan of Splatter." Nonetheless, his talent was evident to discerning eyes—at least among horror film aficionados. *Bad Taste* was hailed as a cult classic at the Cannes Film Festival, and horror fans tabbed Jackson as a talent to follow.

When screenwriter Costa Botes heard that *The Lord of the Rings* would be made into a live action film, he thought those responsible were crazy. Prevailing wisdom was that the fantastic and complex trilogy simply could not be believably translated onto the screen. But he also believed that "there was no other director on earth who could do it justice" (Botes, 2004). And do it justice he obviously did. What was it about the "Sultan of Splatter's" leadership that gave others such confidence in his ability to make one of the biggest and best movies of all time? What gave him the confidence to even try? And what made others want to share in his vision?

Peter Jackson's effectiveness as a leader has been due in large part to a unique combination of personal qualities and talents. One associate, for example, called him "one of the smartest people I know," as well as a maverick willing to buck the establishment. Jackson is also a tireless worker whose early successes were due in no small part to the combination of his ambition and dogged perseverance (Botes, 2004). His initial success was driven largely by his budding genius in making films on a low budget and with virtually no other staff. In reading others' comments who worked with him on the *LOTR* project, however, it's clear that his leadership continued to develop over the years. It was his ability to communicate a shared vision and inspire such extraordinary work from an incredibly large staff that made *LOTR* so spectacularly successful.

Not one to rest on his laurels, in 2012 Jackson released the first installment of *The Hobbit,* another technologically standard-breaking and popular film trilogy.

Source: Adapted from Costa Botes, *Made in New Zealand: The Cinema of Peter Jackson,* NZEDGE.com, May 2004.

Highlight 1.1 provides further perspective on how the art and science of leadership are represented in somewhat distinctive research traditions.

Leadership Is Both Rational and Emotional

Leadership involves both the rational and emotional sides of human experience. Leadership includes actions and influences based on reason and logic as well as those based on inspiration and passion. We do not want to cultivate merely intellectualized leaders who respond with only logical predictability. Because people differ in their thoughts and feelings, hopes and dreams, needs and fears, goals and ambitions, and strengths and weaknesses, leadership situations can be complex. People are both rational and emotional, so leaders can use rational techniques and emotional appeals to influence followers, but they must also weigh the rational and emotional consequences of their actions.

A democracy cannot follow a leader unless he is dramatized. A man to be a hero must not content himself with heroic virtues and anonymous action. He must talk and explain as he acts—drama.

William Allen White, American writer and editor, *Emporia Gazette*

The Academic and Troubadour Traditions of Leadership Research

HIGHLIGHT 1.1

On a practical level, leadership is a topic that almost everyone is interested in at one time or another. People have a vested interest in who is running their government, schools, company, or church, and because of this interest thousands of books and articles have been written about the topic of leadership. Curphy and Hogan believe these works can be divided into two major camps. The **academic tradition** consists of articles that use data and statistical techniques to make inferences about effective leadership. Because the academic tradition is research based, for the most part these findings are written for other leadership researchers and are virtually uninterpretable to leadership *practitioners*. As such, leadership practitioners are often unfamiliar with the research findings of the academic tradition.

The second camp of leadership literature is the **troubadour tradition.** These books and articles often consist of nothing more than the opinions or score-settling reminiscences of former leaders. Books in the troubadour tradition, such as *Who Moved My Cheese?, What the CEO Wants You to Know, Winning,* and *Lead Like Jesus: Lessons from the Greatest Leadership Role Model of all Time,* are wildly popular, but it is difficult to separate fact from fiction or determine whether these opinions translate to other settings. People who are unfamiliar with the findings of the academic tradition and the limitations of the troubadour tradition find it difficult to differentiate research findings from opinion.

Perhaps the biggest challenge to improving the practice of leadership is to give practitioners timely, easily digestible, research-grounded advice on how to effectively lead others. The knowledge accumulated from 90 years of leadership research is of tremendous value, yet scientists have paid little attention to the ultimate consumers of their work—leaders and leaders-to-be. Leadership practitioners often want fast answers about how to be more effective or successful and understandably turn to popular books and articles that *appear* to provide timely answers to their practical concerns. Unfortunately, however, the claims in the popular literature are rarely based on sound research; they oversimplify the complexities of the leadership process; and many times they actually offer bad advice. Relatively little weight is given to well-researched leadership studies, primarily because the arcane requirements of publishing articles in scholarly journals make their content virtually unreadable (and certainly uninteresting) to actual leadership practitioners. One of the primary objectives of this book is to make the results of leadership research more usable for leaders and leaders-to-be.

Sources: G. J. Curphy, M. J. Benson, A. Baldrica, and R. T. Hogan, *Managerial Incompetence* (unpublished manuscript, 2007); G. J. Curphy, "*What We Really Know about Leadership (But Seem Unwilling to Implement)*" (presentation given to the Minnesota Professionals for Psychology and Applied Work, Minneapolis, MN, January 2004); R. T. Hogan, *Personality and the Fate of Organizations* (Mahwah, NJ: Lawrence Erlbaum Associates, 2007).

A full appreciation of leadership involves looking at both these sides of human nature. Good leadership is more than just calculation and planning, or following a checklist, even though rational analysis can enhance good leadership. Good leadership also involves touching others' feelings; emotions play an important role in leadership too. Just one example of this is the civil rights movement of the 1960s, which was based on emotions as well as on principles. Dr. Martin Luther King Jr. inspired many people to action; he touched people's hearts as well as their heads.

Aroused feelings, however, can be used either positively or negatively, constructively or destructively. Some leaders have been able to inspire others to deeds of great purpose and courage. On the other hand, as images of Adolf Hitler's mass rallies or present-day angry mobs attest, group frenzy can readily become group mindlessness. As another example, emotional appeals by the Reverend Jim Jones resulted in approximately 800 of his followers volitionally committing suicide.

The mere presence of a group (even without heightened emotional levels) can also cause people to act differently than when they are alone. For example, in airline cockpit crews, there are clear lines of authority from the captain down to the first officer (second in command) and so on. So strong are the norms surrounding the authority of the captain that some first officers will not take control of the airplane from the captain even in the event of impending disaster. Foushee[13] reported a study wherein airline captains in simulator training intentionally feigned incapacitation so the response of the rest of the crew could be observed. The feigned incapacitations occurred at a predetermined point during the plane's final approach in landing, and the simulation involved conditions of poor weather and visibility. Approximately 25 percent of the first officers in these simulated flights allowed the plane to crash. For some reason, the first officers did not take control even when it was clear the captain was allowing the aircraft to deviate from the parameters of a safe approach. This example demonstrates how group dynamics can influence the behavior of group members even when emotional levels are *not* high. (Believe it or not, airline crews are so well trained that this is *not* an emotional situation.) In sum, it should be apparent that leadership involves followers' feelings and nonrational behavior as well as rational behavior. Leaders need to consider *both* the rational and the emotional consequences of their actions.

Leadership and Management

In trying to answer "What is leadership?" it is natural to look at the relationship between leadership and management. To many, the word **management** suggests words like *efficiency, planning, paperwork, procedures, regulations, control,* and *consistency.* Leadership is often more associated with words like *risk taking, dynamic, creativity, change,* and *vision.* Some say leadership is fundamentally a value-choosing, and thus a value-laden, activity, whereas management is not. Leaders are thought to *do the right things,* whereas managers are thought to *do things right.*[14,15] Here are some other distinctions between managers and leaders:[16]

- Managers administer; leaders innovate.
- Managers maintain; leaders develop.
- Managers control; leaders inspire.

If you want some ham, you gotta go into the smokehouse.

Huey Long, governor of Louisiana, 1928–1932

- Managers have a short-term view; leaders, a long-term view.
- Managers ask how and when; leaders ask what and why.
- Managers imitate; leaders originate.
- Managers accept the status quo; leaders challenge it.

Zaleznik[17] goes so far as to say these differences reflect fundamentally different personality types: leaders and managers are basically different kinds of people. He says some people are managers *by nature;* other people are leaders *by nature.* One is not better than the other; they are just different. Their differences, in fact, can be useful because organizations typically need both functions performed well. For example, consider again the U.S. civil rights movement in the 1960s. Dr. Martin Luther King Jr. gave life and direction to the civil rights movement in America. He gave dignity and hope of freer participation in national life to people who before had little reason to expect it. He inspired the world with his vision and eloquence, and he changed the way we live together. America is a different nation today because of him. Was Dr. Martin Luther King Jr. a leader? Of course. Was he a manager? Somehow that does not seem to fit, and the civil rights movement might have failed if it had not been for the managerial talents of his supporting staff. Leadership and management complement each other, and both are vital to organizational success.

With regard to the issue of leadership versus management, the authors of this book take a middle-of-the-road position. We think of leadership and management as closely related but distinguishable functions. Our view of the relationship is depicted in Figure 1.1, which shows leadership and management as two overlapping functions. Although some functions performed by leaders and managers may be unique, there is also an area of overlap. In reading Highlight 1.2, do you see more good management in the response to the 1906 San Francisco earthquake, more good leadership, or both?

FIGURE 1.1
Leadership and Management Overlap

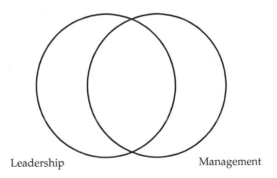

Leadership   Management

The Response of Leadership to a Natural Disaster

HIGHLIGHT 1.2

Much has been written about the inadequate response of local, state, and federal agencies to Hurricane Katrina. It may be instructive to compare the response of government agencies to a natural disaster on a different coast a century earlier: the San Francisco earthquake and fire of 1906.

While the precipitant disaster was the earthquake itself, much destruction resulted from the consequent fire, one disaster aggravating the impact of the other. Because of the earthquake, utility poles throughout the city fell, taking the high-tension wires they were carrying with them. Gas pipes broke; chimneys fell, dropping hot coals into thousands of gallons of gas spilled by broken fuel tanks; stoves and heaters in homes toppled over; and in moments fires erupted across the city. And because the earthquake's first tremors also broke water pipes throughout the city, fire hydrants everywhere suddenly went dry, making fighting the fires virtually impossible. In objective terms, the disaster is estimated to have killed as many as 3,000 people, rendered more than 200,000 homeless, and by some measures caused $195 billion in property loss as measured by today's dollars.

How did authorities respond to the crisis when there were far fewer agencies with presumed response plans to combat disasters, and when high-tech communication methods were unheard of? Consider these two examples:

- The ranking officer assigned to a U.S. Army post in San Francisco was away when the earthquake struck, so it was up to his deputy to help organize the army's and federal government's response. The deputy immediately cabled Washington, D.C., requesting tents, rations, and medicine. Secretary of War William Howard Taft, who would become the next U.S. president, responded by immediately dispatching 200,000 rations from Washington State. In a matter of days, every tent in the U.S. Army had been sent to San Francisco, and the longest hospital train in history was dispatched from Virginia.

- Perhaps the most impressive example of leadership initiative in the face of the 1906 disaster was that of the U.S. Post Office. It recovered its ability to function in short order without losing a single item that was being handled when the earthquake struck. And because the earthquake had effectively destroyed the city's telegraphic connection (telegrams inside the city were temporarily being delivered by the post office), a critical question arose: How could people struck by the disaster communicate with their families elsewhere? The city postmaster immediately announced that all citizens of San Francisco could use the post office to inform their families and loved ones of their condition and needs. He further stipulated that for outgoing private letters *it would not matter whether the envelopes bore stamps.* This was what was needed: Circumstances demanded that people be able to communicate with friends and family whether or not they could find or pay for stamps.

Perhaps this should remind us that modern leadership is not necessarily better leadership, and that leadership in government is not always bureaucratic and can be both humane and innovative.

Source: Adapted from S. Winchester, *A Crack in the Edge of the World: America and the Great California Earthquake of 1906* (New York: Harper Perennial, 2006).

The Romance of Leadership

HIGHLIGHT 1.3

This text is predicated on the idea that leaders can make a difference. Interestingly, though, while businesspeople generally agree, not all scholars do.

People in the business world attribute much of a company's success or failure to its leadership. One study counted the number of articles appearing in *The Wall Street Journal* that dealt with leadership and found nearly 10 percent of the articles about representative target companies addressed that company's leadership. Furthermore, there was a significant positive relationship between company performance and the number of articles about its leadership; the more a company's leadership was emphasized in *The Wall Street Journal,* the better the company was doing. This might mean the more a company takes leadership seriously (as reflected by the emphasis in *The Wall Street Journal*), the better it does.

However, the study authors were skeptical about the real utility of leadership as a concept.

They suggested leadership is merely a romanticized notion—an obsession people want and need to believe in. Belief in the potency of leadership may be a cultural myth that has utility primarily insofar as it affects how people create meaning about causal events in complex social systems. The behavior of leaders, the authors contend, does not account for much of the variance in an organization's performance. Nonetheless, people seem strongly committed to a basic faith that individual leaders shape organizational destiny for good or ill.

As you read this book and come to appreciate how many factors affect a group's success *besides* the talents of the individual leader, you might pay a price for that understanding. As you appreciate the *complexity* of leadership more, the *romance* of leadership might slightly diminish.

Source: J. R. Meindl, S. B. Ehrlich, and J. M. Dukerich, "The Romance of Leadership," *Administrative Science Quarterly* 30 (1985), pp. 78–102.

Leadership Myths

Few things pose a greater obstacle to leadership development than certain unsubstantiated and self-limiting beliefs about leadership. Therefore, before we begin examining leadership and leadership development in more detail, we will consider what they are not. We will examine several beliefs (we call them myths) that stand in the way of fully understanding and developing leadership.

Myth: Good Leadership Is All Common Sense

At face value, this myth says one needs only common sense to be a good leader. It also implies, however, that most if not all of the studies of leadership reported in scholarly journals and books only confirm what anyone with common sense already knows.

The problem, of course, is with the ambiguous term *common sense*. It implies a common body of practical knowledge about life that virtually any reasonable person with moderate experience has acquired. A simple experiment, however, may convince you that common sense may be less common than you think. Ask a few friends or acquaintances whether the old folk wisdom "Absence makes the heart grow fonder" is true or false. Most will say it is true. After that ask a different group whether the old folk wisdom "Out of sight, out of mind" is true or false. Most of that group will answer true as well, even though the two proverbs are contradictory.

A similar thing sometimes happens when people hear about the results of studies concerning human behavior. On hearing the results, people may say, "Who needed a study to learn that? I knew it all the time." However, several experiments[18,19] showed that events were much more surprising when subjects had to guess the outcome of an experiment than when subjects were told the outcome. What seems obvious after you know the results and what you (or anyone else) would have predicted beforehand are not the same thing. Hindsight is always 20/20.

The point might become clearer with a specific example; read the following paragraph:

> After World War II, the U.S. Army spent enormous sums of money on studies only to reach conclusions that, many believed, should have been apparent at the outset. One, for example, was that southern soldiers were better able to stand the climate in the hot South Sea islands than northern soldiers were.

This sounds reasonable, but there is a problem: the statement here is exactly contrary to the actual findings. Southerners were no better than northerners in adapting to tropical climates.[20] Common sense can often play tricks on us.

Put a little differently, one challenge of understanding leadership may be to know when common sense applies and when it does not. Do leaders need to act confidently? Of course. But they also need to be humble enough to recognize that others' views are useful, too. Do leaders need to persevere when times get tough? Yes. But they also need to recognize when times change and a new direction is called for. If leadership were nothing more than common sense, there should be few, if any, problems in the workplace. However, we venture to guess you have noticed more than a few problems between leaders and followers. Effective leadership must be something more than just common sense.

Myth: Leaders Are Born, Not Made

Some people believe being a leader is either in one's genes or not; others believe that life experiences mold the individual and that no one is born a leader. Which view is right? In a sense, both and neither. Both views are right in that innate factors as well as formative experiences influence many sorts of behavior, including leadership. Yet both views are wrong to the extent they imply leadership is *either* innate *or* acquired; what matters more is how these factors *interact*. It does not seem useful,

If you miss seven balls out of ten, you're batting three hundred and that's good enough for the Hall of Fame. You can't score if you keep the bat on your shoulder.
Walter B. Wriston, chairman of Citicorp, 1970–1984

we believe, to think of the world as composed of two mutually exclusive types of people, leaders and nonleaders. It is more useful to address how each person can make the most of leadership opportunities he or she faces.

It may be easier to see the pointlessness of asking whether leaders are born or made by looking at an alternative question of far less popular interest: Are *college professors* born or made? Conceptually the issues are the same, and here too the answer is that every college professor is both born *and* made. It seems clear enough that college professors are partly "born" because (among other factors) there is a genetic component to intelligence, and intelligence surely plays some part in becoming a college professor (well, at least a *minor* part!). But every college professor is also partly "made." One obvious way is that college professors must have advanced education in specialized fields; even with the right genes one could not become a college professor without certain requisite experiences. Becoming a college professor depends partly on what one is born with and partly on how that inheritance is shaped through experience. The same is true of leadership.

More specifically, research indicates that many cognitive abilities and personality traits are at least partly innate.[21] Thus natural talents or characteristics may offer certain advantages or disadvantages to a leader. Consider physical characteristics: A man's above-average height may increase others' tendency to think of him as a leader; it may also boost his own self-confidence. But it doesn't make him a leader. The same holds true for psychological characteristics that seem related to leadership. The stability of certain characteristics over long periods (for example, at school reunions people seem to have kept the same personalities we remember them as having years earlier) may reinforce the impression that our basic natures are fixed, but different environments nonetheless may nurture or suppress different leadership qualities.

Myth: The Only School You Learn Leadership from Is the School of Hard Knocks

Some people skeptically question whether leadership can develop through formal study, believing instead it can be acquired only through actual experience. It is a mistake, however, to think of formal study and learning from experience as mutually exclusive or antagonistic. In fact, they complement each other. Rather than ask whether leadership develops from formal study or from real-life experience, it is better to ask what kind of study will help students learn to discern critical lessons about leadership from their own experience. Approaching the issue in such a way recognizes the vital role of experience in leadership development, but it also admits that certain kinds of study and training can improve a person's ability to discern important lessons about leadership

Never reveal all of yourself to other people; hold back something in reserve so that people are never quite sure if they really know you.
Michael Korda, author, editor

Progress always involves risks. You can't steal second base and keep your foot on first.
Frederick B. Wilcox

from experience. It can, in other words, accelerate the process of learning from experience.

We argue that one advantage of formally studying leadership is that formal study provides students with a variety of ways of examining a particular leadership situation. By studying the different ways researchers have defined and examined leadership, students can use these definitions and theories to better understand what is going on in any leadership situation. For example, earlier in this chapter we used three different leadership definitions as a framework for describing or analyzing the situation facing Parrado and the survivors of the plane crash, and each definition focused on a different aspect of leadership. These frameworks can similarly be applied to better understand the experiences one has as both a leader and a follower. We think it is difficult for leaders, particularly novice leaders, to examine leadership situations from multiple perspectives; but we also believe developing this skill can help you become a better leader. Being able to analyze your experiences from multiple perspectives may be the greatest single contribution a formal course in leadership can give you. Maybe you can reflect on your own leadership over a cup of coffee in Starbucks as you read about the origins of that company in Profiles in Leadership 1.2.

Howard Schultz

PROFILES IN LEADERSHIP 1.2

Starbucks began in 1971 as a very different company than we know it as today. The difference is due in large part to the way its former CEO, Howard Schultz, reframed the kind of business Starbucks should be. Schultz joined Starbucks in 1981 to head its marketing and retail store operations. While on a trip to Italy in 1983, Schultz was amazed by the number and variety of espresso bars there—1,500 in the city of Turin alone. He concluded that the Starbucks stores in Seattle had missed the point: *Starbucks should be not just a store but an experience—a gathering place.*

Everything looks clearer in hindsight, of course, but the Starbucks owners resisted Schultz's vision; Starbucks was a retailer, they insisted, not a restaurant or bar. Schultz's strategic reframing of the Starbucks opportunity was ultimately vindicated when—after having departed Starbucks to pursue the same idea with another company—Schultz had the opportunity to purchase the whole Starbucks operation in Seattle, including its name.

Despite today's pervasiveness of Starbucks across the world, however, and the seeming obviousness of Schultz's exemplary leadership, the Starbucks story has not been one of completely consistent success. After Schultz retired as Starbucks CEO when it was a global megabrand, the company's performance suffered to the point Schultz complained that it was "losing its soul." He was asked to return as CEO in 2008 and has tried to resurrect Starbucks by bringing new attention to the company's operating efficiency and by admitting, in effect, that some of his own earlier instinctive approach to company strategy and management would no longer be sufficient for the new global scale of Starbucks operation. In fact, Schultz discovered the challenges and the road to recovery even more daunting than he expected. Leadership—even for one with a proven track record—is never easy.

The Interactional Framework for Analyzing Leadership

Perhaps the first researcher to formally recognize the importance of the leader, follower, and situation in the leadership process was Fred Fiedler.[22] Fiedler used these three components to develop his contingency model of leadership, a theory of leadership that will be discussed in more detail in Chapter 13. Although we recognize Fiedler's contributions, we owe perhaps even more to Hollander's[23] transactional approach to leadership. We call our approach the **interactional framework.**

Several aspects of this derivative of Hollander's approach are worthy of additional comment. First, as shown in Figure 1.2, the framework depicts leadership as a function of three elements—the **leader,** the **followers,** and the **situation.** Second, a particular leadership scenario can be examined using each level of analysis separately. Although this is a useful way to understand the leadership process, we can understand the process even better if we also examine the **interactions** among the three elements, or lenses, represented by the overlapping areas in the figure. For example, we can better understand the leadership process if we not only look at the leaders and the followers but also examine how leaders and followers affect each other in the leadership process. Similarly, we can examine the leader and the situation separately, but we can gain even further understanding of the leadership process by looking at how the situation can constrain or facilitate a leader's actions and how the leader can change different aspects of the situation to be more effective. Thus a final important aspect of the framework is that leadership is the result of a complex set of interactions among the leader, the followers, and the situation. These complex interactions may be why broad generalizations about leadership are problematic: many factors influence the leadership process (see Highlight 1.3 on page 11).

FIGURE 1.2
An Interactional Framework for Analyzing Leadership

Source: Adapted from E. P. Hollander, *Leadership Dynamics: A Practical Guide to Effective Relationships* (New York: Free Press, 1978).

An example of one such complex interaction between leaders and followers is evident in what have been called in-groups and out-groups. Sometimes there is a high degree of mutual influence and attraction between the leader and a few subordinates. These subordinates belong to the **in-group** and can be distinguished by their high degree of loyalty, commitment, and trust felt toward the leader. Other subordinates belong to the **out-group.** Leaders have considerably more influence with in-group followers than with out-group followers. However, this greater degree of influence has a price. If leaders rely primarily on their formal authority to influence their followers (especially if they punish them), then leaders risk losing the high levels of loyalty and commitment followers feel toward them.[24]

The Leader

This element examines primarily what the leader brings *as an individual* to the leadership equation. This can include unique personal history, interests, character traits, and motivation.

Leaders are *not* all alike, but they tend to share many characteristics. Research has shown that leaders differ from their followers, and effective leaders differ from ineffective leaders, on various personality traits, cognitive abilities, skills, and values.[25-30] Another way personality can affect leadership is through temperament, by which we mean whether a leader is generally calm or is instead prone to emotional outbursts. Leaders who have calm dispositions and do not attack or belittle others for bringing bad news are more likely to get complete and timely information from subordinates than are bosses who have explosive tempers and a reputation for killing the messenger.

Another important aspect of the leader is how he or she achieved leader status. Leaders who are appointed by superiors may have less credibility with subordinates and get less loyalty from them than leaders who are elected or emerge by consensus from the ranks of followers. Often emergent or elected officials are better able to influence a group toward goal achievement because of the power conferred on them by their followers. However, both elected and emergent leaders need to be sensitive to their constituencies if they wish to remain in power.

More generally, a leader's experience or history in a particular organization is usually important to her or his effectiveness. For example, leaders promoted from within an organization, by virtue of being familiar with its culture and policies, may be ready to "hit the job running." In addition, leaders selected from within an organization are typically better known by others in the organization than are leaders selected from the outside. That is likely to affect, for better or worse, the latitude others in the organization are willing to give the leader; if the leader is widely respected for a history of accomplishment, she may be given more latitude than a newcomer whose track record is less well known. On the other hand, many people tend to give new leaders a fair chance to succeed, and newcomers to an organization often take time to learn the organization's informal rules, norms, and "ropes" before they make any radical or potentially controversial decisions.

A leader's legitimacy also may be affected by the extent to which followers participated in the leader's selection. When followers have had a say in the selection or election of a leader, they tend to have a heightened sense of psychological identification with her, but they also may have higher expectations and make more demands on her.[31] We also might wonder what kind of support a leader has from his own boss. If followers sense their boss has a lot of influence with the higher-ups, subordinates

"I'll be blunt, coach. I'm having a problem with this 'take a lap' thing of yours . . ."

> *I must follow the people. Am I not their leader?*
>
> **Benjamin Disraeli, 19th-century British prime minister**

may be reluctant to take their complaints to higher levels. On the other hand, if the boss has little influence with higher-ups, subordinates may be more likely to make complaints to these levels.

The foregoing examples highlight the sorts of insights we can gain about leadership by focusing on the individual leader as a level of analysis. Even if we were to examine the individual leader completely, however, our understanding of the leadership process would be incomplete.

The Followers

> *The crowd will follow a leader who marches twenty steps in advance; but if he is a thousand steps in front of them, they do not see and do not follow him.*
>
> **Georg Brandes**

Followers are a critical part of the leadership equation, but their role has not always been appreciated, at least in empirical research (but read Highlight 1.4 to see how the role of followers has been recognized in literature). For a long time, in fact, "the common view of leadership was that leaders actively led and subordinates, later called followers, passively and obediently followed."[32] Over time, especially in the last century, social change shaped people's views of followers, and leadership theories gradually recognized the active and important role that followers play in the leadership process.[33] Today it seems natural to accept the important role

---

The *First* Band of Brothers

HIGHLIGHT 1.4

Many of you probably have seen, or at least heard of, the award-winning series *Band of Brothers* that followed a company of the famous 101st Airborne division during World War II. You may not be aware that an earlier band of brothers was made famous by William Shakespeare in his play *Henry V*.

In one of the most famous speeches by any of Shakespeare's characters, the young Henry V tried to unify his followers when their daring expedition to conquer France was failing. French soldiers followed Henry's army along the rivers, daring them to cross over and engage the French in battle. Just before the battle of Agincourt, Henry's rousing words rallied his vastly outnumbered, weary, and tattered troops to victory. Few words of oratory have ever better bonded a leader with his followers than Henry's call for unity among "we few, we happy few, we band of brothers."

Hundreds of years later, Henry's speech is still a powerful illustration of a leader who emphasized the importance of his followers. Modern leadership concepts like vision, charisma, relationship orientation, and empowerment are readily evident

in Henry's interactions with his followers. Here are the closing lines of Henry's famous speech:

> *From this day to the ending of the world,*
> *But we in it shall be remembered—*
> *We few, we happy few, we band of brothers;*
> *For he today that sheds his blood with me*
> *Shall be my brother; be he ne'er so vile,*
> *This day shall gentle his condition;*
> *And gentlemen in England now-a-bed*
> *Shall think themselves accurs'd they were not here,*
> *And hold their manhoods cheap whiles any speaks*
> *That fought with us upon Saint Crispin's day.*

Shakespeare's insights into the complexities of leadership should remind us that while modern research helps enlighten our understanding, it does not represent the only, and certainly not the most moving, perspective on leadership to which we should pay attention.

Source: N. Warner, "Screening Leadership through Shakespeare: Paradoxes of Leader–Follower Relations in *Henry V* on Film," *The Leadership Quarterly* 18 (2007), pp. 1–15.

A Student's Perspective on Leadership and Followership

HIGHLIGHT 1.5

Krista Kleiner, a student at Claremont-McKenna College and active in its Kravis Leadership Institute, has offered these reflections on the importance for both students and college administrators of taking seriously the opportunities provided in the classroom for developing leadership and followership skills.

She notes that the admissions process to college (as well, we might add, as postcollege job searches) typically places significant emphasis on a person's leadership experience and abilities. Usually this is reflected in something like a list of "leadership positions held." Unfortunately, however, this system tends to overemphasize the mere acquisition of leadership titles and pays insufficient attention to the domain that is the most central and common element of student life: the classroom learning environment. Outstanding learning, she argues, is to a significant degree a collaborative experience between the formal leader (the teacher) and the informal followers (the students). The learning experience is directly enhanced by the degree to which effective participation by students contributes to their classroom groups, and this requires good leadership and good followership. The quality of one's contribution to the group could be

assessed via peer surveys, the results of which would be made available to the teacher. The surveys would assess dimensions of student contributions like these:

- Which students displayed particularly helpful leadership in work groups you participated in, and what did they do that was effective?

- Which students displayed particularly helpful followership in work groups you participated in that supported or balanced the leadership that emerged in the group or that was helpful to fellow group members?

- How have you contributed to the learning experience of your peers through your leadership–followership role in the classroom? How have you grown as a constructive leader and constructive follower through these experiences?

We hope these ideas challenge you to be a leader in your own student life and especially in this leadership course.

Source: K. Kleiner, "Rethinking Leadership and Followership: A Student's Perspective," in R. Riggio, I. Chaleff, and J. Lipman-Blumen (eds.), *The Art of Followership: How Great Followers Create Great Leaders and Organizations* (San Francisco: Jossey-Bass, 2008), pp. 89–93.

All men have some weak points, and the more vigorous and brilliant a person may be, the more strongly these weak points stand out. It is highly desirable, even essential, therefore, for the more influential members of a general's staff not to be too much like the general.

Major General Hugo Baron von Freytag-Loringhoven, anti-Hitler conspirator

followers play. Highlight 1.5 suggests some interesting interactions between leadership and followership in an arena familiar to you.

One aspect of our text's definition of leadership is particularly worth noting in this regard: Leadership is a social influence process shared among *all* members of a group. Leadership is not restricted to the influence exerted by someone in a particular position or role; followers are part of the leadership process, too. In recent years both practitioners and scholars have emphasized the relatedness of leadership and **followership.** As Burns[34] observed, the idea of "one-man leadership" is a contradiction in terms.

Obvious as this point may seem, it is also clear that early leadership researchers paid relatively little attention to the roles followers play in the leadership process.[35,36] However, we know that the followers' expectations, personality traits, maturity levels, levels of competence, and motivation affect the leadership process too. Highlight 1.6 describes a systematic approach to classifying different kinds of followers that has had a major impact on research.[37-40]

20   Part One   *Leadership Is a Process, Not a Position*

Followership Styles

HIGHLIGHT 1.6

The concept of different styles of leadership is reasonably familiar, but the idea of different styles of followership is relatively new. The very word *follower* has a negative connotation to many, evoking ideas of people who behave like sheep and need to be told what to do. Robert Kelley, however, believes that followers, rather than representing the antithesis of leadership, are best viewed as collaborators with leaders in the work of organizations.

Kelley believes that different types of followers can be described in terms of two broad dimensions. One of them ranges from **independent, critical thinking** at one end to **dependent, uncritical thinking** on the other end. According to Kelley, the best followers think for themselves and offer constructive advice or even creative solutions. The worst followers need to be told what to do. Kelley's other dimension ranges from whether people are **active followers** or **passive followers** in the extent to which they are engaged in work. According to Kelley, the best followers are self-starters who take initiative for themselves, whereas the worst followers are passive, may even dodge responsibility, and need constant supervision.

Using these two dimensions, Kelley has suggested five basic styles of followership:

1. *Alienated followers* habitually point out all the negative aspects of the organization to others. While alienated followers may see themselves as mavericks who have a healthy skepticism of the organization, leaders often see them as cynical, negative, and adversarial.

2. *Conformist followers* are the "yes people" of organizations. While very active at doing the organization's work, they can be dangerous if their orders contradict societal standards of behavior or organizational policy. Often this style is the result of either the demanding and authoritarian style of the leader or the overly rigid structure of the organization.

3. *Pragmatist followers* are rarely committed to their group's work goals, but they have learned not to make waves. Because they do not like to stick out, pragmatists tend to be mediocre performers who can clog the arteries of many organizations. Because it can be difficult to discern just where they stand on issues, they present an ambiguous image with both positive and negative characteristics. In organizational settings, pragmatists may become experts in mastering the bureaucratic rules which can be used to protect them.

4. *Passive followers* display none of the characteristics of the exemplary follower (discussed next). They rely on the leader to do all the thinking. Furthermore, their work lacks enthusiasm. Lacking initiative and a sense of responsibility, passive followers require constant direction. Leaders may see them as lazy, incompetent, or even stupid. Sometimes, however, passive followers adopt this style to help them cope with a leader who expects followers to behave that way.

5. *Exemplary followers* present a consistent picture to both leaders and co-workers of being independent, innovative, and willing to stand up to superiors. They apply their talents for the benefit of the organization even when confronted with bureaucratic stumbling blocks or passive or pragmatist co-workers. Effective leaders appreciate the value of exemplary followers. When one of the authors was serving in a follower role in a staff position, he was introduced by his leader to a conference as "my favorite subordinate because he's a loyal 'No-Man.' "

Exemplary followers—high on both critical dimensions of followership—are essential to organizational success.

Leaders, therefore, would be well advised to select people who have these characteristics and, perhaps even more importantly, *create the conditions that encourage these behaviors.*

Source: Adapted from R. Kelley, *The Power of Followership* (New York: Doubleday Currency, 1992).

The nature of followers' motivation to do their work is also important. Workers who share a leader's goals and values, and who feel intrinsically rewarded for performing a job well, might be more likely to work extra hours on a time-critical project than those whose motivation is solely monetary.

Even the number of followers reporting to a leader can have significant implications. For example, a store manager with three clerks working for him can spend more time with each of them (or on other things) than can a manager responsible for eight clerks and a separate delivery service; chairing a task force with 5 members is a different leadership activity than chairing a task force with 18 members. Still other relevant variables include followers' trust in the leader and their degree of confidence that he or she is interested in their well-being. Another aspect of followers' relations to a leader is described in Profiles in Leadership 1.3.

Paul Revere

PROFILES IN LEADERSHIP 1.3

A fabled story of American history is that of Paul Revere's ride through the countryside surrounding Boston, warning towns that the British were coming so local militia could be ready to meet them. As a result, when the British did march toward Lexington on the following day, they faced unexpectedly fierce resistance. At Concord the British were beaten by a ragtag group of locals, and so began the American Revolutionary War.

It has been taken for granted by generations of Americans that the success of Paul Revere's ride lay in his heroism *and* in the self-evident importance of the news itself. A little-known fact, however, is that Paul Revere was not the only rider that night. A fellow revolutionary by the name of William Dawes had the same mission: to ride simultaneously through a separate set of towns surrounding Boston to warn them that the British were coming. He did so, carrying the news through just as many towns as Revere did. But his ride was not successful; those local militia leaders weren't aroused and did not rise up to confront the British. If they had been, Dawes would be as famous today as Paul Revere.

Why was Revere's ride successful when Dawes's ride was not? Paul Revere started a word-of-mouth epidemic, and Dawes did not, *because of differing kinds of relationships the two men had with others.* It wasn't, after all, the nature of the news itself that proved ultimately important so much as the nature of the men who carried it. Paul Revere was a gregarious and social person—what Malcolm Gladwell calls a *connector*. Gladwell writes that Revere was "a fisherman and a hunter, a cardplayer and a theaterlover, a frequenter of pubs and a successful businessman. He was active in the local Masonic Lodge and was a member of several select social clubs." He was a man with a knack for always being at the center of things. So when he began his ride that night, it was Revere's nature to stop and share the news with anyone he saw on the road, and he would have known who the key players were in each town to notify.

Dawes was not by nature so gregarious as Revere, and he did not have Revere's extended social network. It's likely he *wouldn't* have known whom to share the news with in each town and whose doors to knock on. Dawes did notify some people, but not enough to create the kind of impact that Revere did. Another way of saying this is simply to note that the people Dawes notified didn't know *him* the way that Revere was known by those *he* notified.

It isn't just the information or the ideas you have as a leader that make a difference. It's also whom you know, and how many you know—and what they know about you.

Source: Adapted from Malcolm Gladwell, *The Tipping Point* (New York: Little, Brown and Company, 2002).

Never try to teach a pig to sing; it wastes your time and it annoys the pig.

Paul Dickson, baseball writer

In the context of the interactional framework, the question "What is leadership?" cannot be separated from the question "What is followership?" There is no simple line dividing them; they merge. The relationship between leadership and followership can be represented by borrowing a concept from topographical mathematics: the Möbius strip. You are probably familiar with the curious properties of the Möbius strip: when a strip of paper is twisted and connected in the manner

Source: © *Tribune Media Services, Inc. All Rights Reserved. Reprinted with permission.*

FIGURE 1.3
The Leadership/
Followership
Möbius Strip

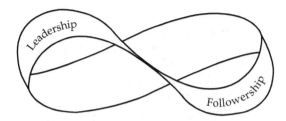

depicted in Figure 1.3, it has only one side. You can prove this to your-self by putting a pencil to any point on the strip and tracing continu-ously. Your pencil will cover the entire strip (that is, both "sides"), eventually returning to the point at which you started. To demonstrate the relevance of this curiosity to leadership, cut a strip of paper. On one side write *leadership,* and on the other side write *followership.* Then twist the strip and connect the two ends in the manner of the figure. You will have created a leadership/followership Möbius strip wherein the two concepts merge, just as leadership and followership can become indis-tinguishable in organizations.[41]

This does not mean leadership and followership are the same thing. When top-level executives were asked to list qualities they most look for and admire in leaders and followers, the lists were similar but not identical.[42] Ideal leaders were characterized as honest, competent, forward-looking, and inspiring; ideal followers were described as honest, competent, independent, and cooperative. The differences could become critical in certain situations, as when a forward-looking and inspiring sub-ordinate perceives a significant conflict between his own goals or ethics and those of his superiors. Such a situation could become a crisis for the individual and the organization, demanding a choice between leading and following.

As the complexity of the leadership process has become better under-stood, the importance placed on the leader–follower relationship itself has undergone dynamic change.[43,44] One reason for this is an increasing pressure on all kinds of organizations to function with reduced resources. Reduced resources and company downsizing have reduced the number of managers and increased their span of control, which in turn leaves follow-ers to pick up many of the functions traditionally performed by leaders. Another reason is a trend toward greater power sharing and decentral-ized authority in organizations, which create greater interdependence among organizational subunits and increase the need for collaboration among them. Furthermore, the nature of problems faced by many organi-zations is becoming so complex and the changes are becoming so rapid that more and more people are required to solve them.

These trends suggest several different ways in which followers can take on new leadership roles and responsibilities in the future. For one thing, followers can become much more proactive in their stance toward organizational problems. When facing the discrepancy between the way things are in an organization and the way they could or should be, followers can play an active and constructive role collaborating with leaders in solving problems. In general, making organizations better is a task that needs to be "owned" by followers as well as by leaders. With these changing roles for followers, it should not be surprising to find that qualities of good followership are statistically correlated with qualities typically associated with good leadership. One recent study found positive correlations between the followership qualities of active engagement and independent thinking and the leadership qualities of dominance, sociability, achievement orientation, and steadiness.[45]

In addition to helping solve organizational problems, followers can contribute to the leadership process by becoming skilled at "influencing upward." Because followers are often at the levels where many organizational problems occur, they can give leaders relevant information so good solutions are implemented. Although it is true that some leaders need to become better listeners, it is also true that many followers need training in expressing ideas to superiors clearly and positively. Still another way followers can assume a greater share of the leadership challenge in the future is by staying flexible and open to opportunities. The future portends more change, not less, and followers who face change with positive anticipation and an openness to self-development will be particularly valued and rewarded.[46]

Thus, to an ever-increasing degree, leadership must be understood in terms of both leader variables and follower variables, as well as the interactions among them. But even that is not enough—we must also understand the particular situations in which leaders and followers find themselves.

The Situation

The situation is the third critical part of the leadership equation. Even if we knew all we could know about a given leader and a given set of followers, leadership often makes sense only in the context of how the leader and followers interact in a particular situation (see Profiles in Leadership 1.4 and 1.5).

This view of leadership as a complex interaction among leader, follower, and situational variables was not always taken for granted. To the contrary, most early research on leadership was based on the assumption that leadership is a general personal trait expressed independently of the situation in which the leadership is manifested. This view, commonly known as the **heroic theory,** has been largely discredited

You've got to give loyalty down, if you want loyalty up.

Donald T. Regan, former CEO and White House chief of staff

Aung San Suu Kyi

PROFILES IN LEADERSHIP 1.4

In 1991 Aung San Suu Kyi already had spent two years under house arrest in Burma for "endangering the state." That same year she won the Nobel Peace Prize. She was not released from house arrest until 2010, and in 2012 was elected to Parliament. Like Nelson Mandela, Suu Kyi is an international symbol of heroic and peaceful resistance to government oppression.

Until the age of 43, Suu Kyi led a relatively quiet existence in England as a professional working mother. Her life changed dramatically in 1988 when she returned to her native country of Burma to visit her sick mother. That visit occurred during a time of considerable political unrest in Burma. Riot police had recently shot to death hundreds of demonstrators in the capital city of Rangoon (the demonstrators had been protesting government repression). Over the next several months, police killed nearly 3,000 people who had been protesting government policies.

When hundreds of thousands of pro-democracy demonstrators staged a protest rally at a prominent pagoda in Rangoon, Suu Kyi spoke to the crowd. Overnight she became the leading voice for freedom and democracy in Burma.

Today she is the most popular and influential leader in her country.

What prepared this woman, whose life was once relatively simple and contented, to risk her life by challenging an oppressive government? What made her such a magnet for popular support? Impressive as Aung San Suu Kyi is as a populist leader, it is impossible to understand her effectiveness purely in terms of her own personal characteristics. It is impossible to understand it independent of her followers—the people of Burma. Her rapid rise to prominence as the leading voice for democracy and freedom in Burma must be understood in terms of the living link she represented to the country's greatest modern hero—her father. He was something of a George Washington figure in that he founded the Burmese Army in 1941 and later made a successful transition from military leadership to political leadership. At the height of his influence, when he was the universal choice to be Burma's first president, he was assassinated. Suu Kyi was two years old. Stories about his life and principles indelibly shaped Suu Kyi's own life, but his life and memory also created a readiness among the Burmese people for Suu Kyi to take up her father's mantle of leadership.

but for a long time represented the dominant way of conceptualizing leadership.[47]

In the 1950s and 1960s a different approach to conceptualizing leadership dominated research and scholarship. It involved the search for effective leader *behaviors* rather than the search for universal *traits* of leadership. That approach proved too narrow because it neglected important contextual, or situational, factors in which presumably effective or ineffective behaviors occur. Over time, the complexities of interactions among leader, follower, and situational variables increasingly have been the focus of leadership research.[48] (See Chapters 6, 7, and 13 for more detailed discussions of leader attributes, leader behaviors, and formal theories of leadership that examine complex interdependencies between leader, follower, and situational variables.) Adding the situation to the mix of variables that make up leadership is complicated. The

Bill Gates's Head Start

PROFILES IN LEADERSHIP 1.5

Belief in an individual's potential to overcome great odds and achieve success through talent, strength, and perseverance is common in America, but usually there is more than meets the eye in such success stories. Malcolm Gladwell's best seller *Outliers* presents a fascinating exploration of how situational factors contribute to success in addition to the kinds of individual qualities we often assume are all-important. Have you ever thought, for example, that Bill Gates was able to create Microsoft because he's just brilliant and visionary?

Well, let's take for granted he *is* brilliant and visionary—there's plenty of evidence of that. The point here, however, is that's not always enough (and maybe it's *never* enough). Here are some of the things that placed Bill Gates, with all his intelligence and vision, at the right time in the right place:

- Gates was born to a wealthy family in Seattle that placed him in a private school for seventh grade. In 1968, his second year there, the school started a computer club—even before most *colleges* had computer clubs.

- In the 1960s virtually everyone who was learning about computers used computer cards, a tedious and mind-numbing process. The computer at Gates's school, however, was linked to a mainframe in downtown Seattle. Thus in 1968 Bill Gates was practicing computer programming via time-sharing as an eighth grader; few others in the world then had such opportunity, whatever their age.

- Even at a wealthy private school like the one Gates attended, however, funds ran out to cover the high costs of buying time on a mainframe computer. Fortunately, at about the same time, a group called the Computer Center Corporation was formed at the University of Washington to lease computer time. One of its founders, coincidentally a parent at Gates's own school, thought the school's computer club could get time on the computer in exchange for testing the company's new software programs. Gates then started a regular schedule of taking the bus after school to the company's offices, where he programmed long into the evening. During one seven-month period, Gates and his fellow computer club members averaged eight hours a day, seven days a week, of computer time.

- When Gates was a high school senior, another extraordinary opportunity presented itself. A major national company (TRW) needed programmers with specialized experience—exactly, as it turned out, the kind of experience the kids at Gates's school had been getting. Gates successfully lobbied his teachers to let him spend a spring doing this work in another part of the state for independent study credit.

- By the time Gates dropped out of Harvard after his sophomore year, he had accumulated more than *10,000 hours* of programming experience. It was, he's said, a better exposure to software development than anyone else at a young age could have had—and all because of a lucky series of events.

It appears that Gates's success is at least partly an example of the right person being in the right place at just the right time.

Source: Malcolm Gladwell, *Outliers: The Story of Success* (New York: Little, Brown and Company, 2008).

situation may be the most ambiguous aspect of the leadership framework; it can refer to anything from the specific task a group is engaged in to broad situational contexts such as the remote predicament of the Andes survivors. One facet of the complexity of the situation's role in leadership is examined in Highlight 1.7.

Decision Making in a Complex World

HIGHLIGHT 1.7

Decision making is a good example of how leaders need to behave differently in various situations. Until late in the 20th century, decision making in government and business was largely based on an implicit assumption that the world was orderly and predictable enough for virtually all decision making to involve a series of specifiable steps: assessing the facts of a situation, categorizing those facts, and then responding based on established practice. To put that more simply, decision making required managers to *sense, categorize*, and *respond*.

The Situation	The Leader's Job
Simple: predictable and orderly; right answers exist.	Ensure that proper processes are in place, follow best practices, and communicate in clear and direct ways.
Complex: flux, unpredictability, ambiguity, many competing ideas, lots of unknowns.	Create environments and experiments that allow patterns to emerge; increase levels of interaction and communication; use methods that generate new ideas and ways of thinking among everyone.

That process is actually still effective in simple contexts characterized by stability and clear cause-and-effect relationships that are readily apparent. Not all situations in the world, however, are so simple, and new approaches to decision making are needed for situations that have the elements of what we might call complex systems: large numbers of interacting elements, nonlinear interactions among those elements by which small changes can produce huge effects, and interdependence among the elements so that the whole is more than the sum of the parts. The challenges of dealing with the threat of terrorism are one example of the way complexity affects decision making, but it's impacting how we think about decision making in business as well as government. To describe this change succinctly, the decision-making process in complex contexts must change from sense, categorize, and respond to probe, sense, and respond.

In other words, making good decisions is about both *what* decisions one makes and understanding the role of the situation in affecting *how* one makes decisions.

Source: D.F. Snowden and M.E. Boone, "A Leader's Framework for Decision Making," *Harvard Business Review*, November 2007, pp. 69–76.

Illustrating the Interactional Framework: Women in Leadership Roles

Not long ago if people were asked to name a leader they admired, most of the names on the resulting list could be characterized as "old white guys." Today the names on that same list would be considerably more heterogeneous. That change—which we certainly consider progress—represents a useful illustration of the power of using the interactional framework to understand the complexities of the leadership process.

A specific example is women in leadership roles, and in this section we'll examine the extent to which women have been taking on new leadership roles, whether there are differences in the effectiveness of men and women in leadership roles, and what explanations have been offered for differences between men and women in being selected for and succeeding in positions of leadership. This is an area of considerable academic research and popular polemics, as evident in many recent articles in the popular press that claim a distinct advantage for women in leadership roles.[49]

It is clear that women are taking on leadership roles in greater numbers than ever before. On the other hand, the actual percentage of women in leadership positions has stayed relatively stable. For example, a report released in 2010 by the U.S. Government Accountability Office indicated that women comprised an estimated 40 percent of managers in the U.S. workforce in 2007 compared with 39 percent in 2000.[50] And the percentage of women in top executive positions is considerably less encouraging. In a 2009 study by the nonprofit organization Catalyst, women made up only 13.5 percent of senior executive positions; almost 30 percent of companies in the Fortune 500 had no women in those top positions.[51]

Although these statistics are important and promising, problems still exist that constrain the opportunity for capable women to rise to the highest leadership roles in organizations. Many studies have considered this problem, a few of which we'll examine here.

One recent study reported that a higher percentage of women executives now receive on-the-job mentoring than men. The same study, however, found that the mentors of those women executives had less organizational influence and clout than did the mentors of their male counterparts. While such mentoring can still provide invaluable psychosocial support for personal and professional development, it does not seem sufficient to assure promotion to higher level jobs (mentoring will be explored in greater detail in the next chapter).[52] Another recent study examined differences in the networking patterns of men and women. Compared to men, women's trust in each other tends to decrease when work situations become more professionally risky. Such a pattern of behavior could potentially become a kind of self-imposed promotion disadvantage by women on themselves.[53]

In a classic study of sex roles, Schein[54,55] demonstrated how bias in sex role stereotypes created problems for women moving up through managerial roles. Schein asked male and female middle managers to complete a survey in which they rated various items on a five-point scale in terms of how characteristic they were of men in general, women in general, or successful managers. Schein found a high correlation between the ways both male and female respondents perceived "males" and "managers," but no correlation between the ways the respondents perceived "females" and "managers." It was as though being a manager was defined by attributes thought of as masculine.

Furthermore, it does not appear that the situation has changed much over the past two decades. In 1990 management students in the United

States, Germany, and Great Britain, for example, still perceived successful middle managers in terms of characteristics more commonly ascribed to men than to women.[56] A 2011 meta-analysis of studies of gender stereotyping continued to find strong evidence of a tendency for leadership to be viewed as culturally masculine. It involved sophisticated statistical analyses of the results of 40 separate studies similar to Schein's paradigm of *think manager–think male*; of 22 other studies that looked at gender stereotyping in an *agency–communion* paradigm; and of a third group of 7 studies that looked at stereotyping through the lens of occupational stereotyping. The study concluded that a strong masculine stereotype of leadership continues to exist in the workplace and that it will continue to challenge women for some time to come.[57] One area where views *do* seem to have changed over time involves women's perceptions of their own roles. In contrast to the earlier studies, women today see as much similarity between "female" and "manager" as between "male" and "manager."[58] To women, at least, being a woman and being a manager are not contradictory.

There have been many other studies of the role of women in management. In one of these, *Breaking the Glass Ceiling*,[59] researchers documented the lives and careers of 78 of the highest-level women in corporate America. A few years later the researchers followed up with a small sample of those women to discuss any changes that had taken place in their leadership paths. The researchers were struck by the fact that the women were much like the senior men they had worked with in other studies. Qualitatively, they had the same fears: They wanted the best for themselves and for their families. They wanted their companies to succeed. And not surprisingly, they still had a drive to succeed. In some cases (also true for the men) they were beginning to ask questions about life balance—was all the sacrifice and hard work worth it? Were 60-hour workweeks worth the cost to family and self?

More quantitatively, however, the researchers expected to find significant differences between the women who had broken the glass ceiling and the men who were already in leadership positions. After all, the popular literature and some social scientific literature had conditioned them to expect that there is a feminine versus a masculine style of leadership, the feminine style being an outgrowth of a consensus/team-oriented leadership approach. Women, in this view, are depicted as leaders who, when compared to men, are better listeners, more empathic, less analytical, more people oriented, and less aggressive in pursuit of goals.

In examining women in leadership positions, the researchers collected behavioral data, including ratings by both self and others, assessment center data, and their scores on the California Psychological Inventory. Contrary to the stereotypes and popular views, however, there were no statistically significant differences between men's and women's leadership styles. Women and men were equally analytical, people oriented, forceful, goal oriented, empathic, and skilled at listening. There were other differences between the men and women, however, beyond the question of leadership styles. The researchers did find (and these results must be interpreted cautiously because of the relatively small numbers involved) that women had significantly lower well-being scores, their commitment to the organizations they worked for was more guarded than that of their male counterparts, and the women were much more likely to be willing to take career risks associated with going to new or unfamiliar areas of the company where women had not been before.

Continued work with women in corporate leadership positions has both reinforced and clarified these findings. For example, the lower scores for women in general well-being may reflect the inadequacy of their support system for dealing with day-to-day issues of living. This is tied to the reality for many women that in addition to having roles in their companies they remain chief caretakers for their families. Further, there may be additional pressures of being visibly identified as proof that the organization has women at the top.

Other types of differences—particularly those around "people issues"—are still not evident. In fact, the hypothesis is that such supposed differences may hinder the opportunities for leadership development of women in the future. For example, turning around a business that is in trouble or starting a new business are two of the most exciting opportunities a developing leader has to test her leadership abilities. If we apply the "women are different" hypothesis, the type of leadership skills needed for successful completion of either of these assignments may leave women off the list of candidates. However, if we accept the hypothesis that women and men are more alike as leaders than they are different, women will be found in equal numbers on the candidate list.

Research on women leaders from medium-sized, nontraditional organizations has shown that successful leaders don't all come from the same mold. Such women tended to be successful by drawing on their shared experience as women, rather than by adhering to the "rules of conduct" by which men in larger and more traditional organizations have been successful.[60] Survey research by Judith Rosener identified several differences in how men and women described their leadership experiences. Men tended to describe themselves in somewhat transactional terms, viewing leadership as an exchange with subordinates for services rendered. They influenced others primarily through their organizational position and authority. The women, on the other hand, tended to describe themselves in transformational terms. They helped subordinates develop commitment to broader goals than their own self-interest, and they described their influence more in terms of personal characteristics like charisma and interpersonal skill than mere organizational position.

According to Rosener, such women leaders encouraged participation and shared power and information, but went far beyond what is commonly thought of as participative management. She called it **interactive leadership.** Their leadership self-descriptions reflected an approach based on enhancing others' self-worth and believing that the best performance results when people are excited about their work and feel good about themselves.

How did this interactive leadership style develop? Rosener concluded it was due to these women's socialization experiences and career paths. As we have indicated, the social role expected of women has emphasized that they be cooperative, supportive, understanding, gentle, and service-oriented. As they entered the business world, they still found themselves in roles emphasizing these same behaviors. They found themselves in staff, rather than line, positions, and in roles lacking formal authority over others so that they had to accomplish their work without reliance on formal power. What they had to do, in other words, was employ their socially acceptable behavioral repertoire to survive organizationally.

What came easily to women turned out to be a survival tactic. Although leaders often begin their careers doing what comes naturally and what fits

"That's what they all say, honey."

Source: © Tom Cheney, *The New Yorker Collection, www.cartoonbank.com.*

Neither shall you allege the example of the many as an excuse for doing wrong.

Exodus 23.2

within the constraints of the job, they also develop their skills and styles over time. The women's use of interactive leadership has its roots in socialization, and the women interviewees believe that it benefits their organizations. Through the course of their careers, they have gained conviction that their style is effective. In fact, for some it was their own success that caused them to formulate their philosophies about what motivates people, how to make good decisions, and what it takes to maximize business performance.

Rosener has called for organizations to expand their definitions of effective leadership—to create a *wider* band of acceptable behavior so both men and women will be freer to lead in ways that take advantage of their true talents. There is further discussion of stereotype-based "bands of acceptable behavior" in Highlight 1.8.

The Narrow Band of Acceptable Behavior

HIGHLIGHT 1.8

One of the most important factors that seems to impede the advance of women and other minorities into leadership roles is bias. A bias that might be labeled "the narrow band of acceptable behavior" is depicted below.

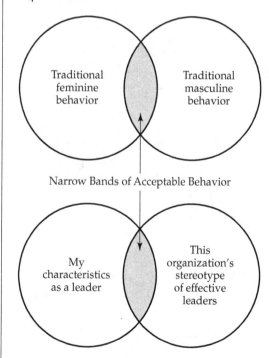

Narrow Bands of Acceptable Behavior

The characteristics and behaviors in the right-hand circle are those associated with traditional masculine behavior, and the characteristics and behaviors in the left-hand circle are those associated with traditional feminine behavior. The narrow band of overlap between the two circles can be thought of as a "hoop" women executives need to pass through.

The concept of a narrow band of acceptable behavior is not limited to women. It may be applied to any individual's deviation from organizationally defined standards. The more a person looks like, acts like, dresses like, and talks like other leaders in the organization, the wider the band of acceptable behavior (the greater the overlap of the two circles). The less one looks like, acts like, dresses like, and talks like other leaders in the organization (some aspects of which, such as gender and race, are beyond a person's control) the narrower the band of acceptable behavior. One implication of this view is that an individual who differs in obvious ways from the prototypical image of a leader (as with gender) has less "wiggle room" available; it's as though there are already one or two strikes against that person. It's like walking a tightrope.

Source: Adapted from A. M. Morrison, R.P. White, and E. Van Velsor, *Breaking the Glass Ceiling* (Reading, MA: Addison-Wesley, 1987).

A more recent study sheds additional light on factors that affect the rise of women in leadership positions.[61] It identifies four general factors that explain the shift toward more women leaders.

The first of these is that *women themselves have changed*. That's evident in the ways women's aspirations and attitudes have become more similar to those of men over time. This is illustrated in findings about the career aspirations of female university students;[62] in women's self-reports of traits such as assertiveness, dominance, and masculinity;[63,64] and in the value that women place on characteristics of work such as freedom, challenge, leadership, prestige, and power.[65] The second factor is that *leadership roles have changed*, particularly with regard to a trend toward less stereotypically masculine characterizations of leadership. Third, *organizational practices have changed*. A large part of this can be attributed to legislation prohibiting gender-based discrimination at work, as well as changes in organizational norms that put a higher priority on results than on an "old boy" network. Finally, the *culture has changed*. This is evident, for example, in the symbolic message often intended by appointment of women to important leadership positions, one representing a departure from past practices and signaling commitment to progressive change.

Finally, in addition to the glass ceiling, another recently identified challenge for women is called the **glass cliff**. The glass cliff refers to the intriguing finding that female candidates for an executive position are *more* likely to be hired than equally qualified male candidates when an organization's performance is declining. At first that may seem like good news for women, but the picture is not quite so positive. When an organization's performance is declining, there is inherently an increased risk of failure. The increased likelihood of women being selected in those situations may actually reflect a greater willingness to put women in precarious positions;[66] it could also, of course, represent an increased willingness to take some chances when nothing else seems to be working.

There Is No Simple Recipe for Effective Leadership

To fill the gaps between leadership research and practice, this book will critically review major findings about the nature of leadership as well as provide practical advice for improving leadership. As our first step in that journey, the next chapter of the book will describe how leadership develops through experience. The remainder of the book uses the leader–follower–situation interaction model as a framework for organizing and discussing various theories and research findings related to leadership. In this study, it will become clear that while there is no simple recipe for effective leadership, there *are* many different paths to effective leadership.

Little things affect little minds.

Benjamin Disraeli, British prime minister, 1874–1880

As noted previously, it is important to understand how the three domains of leadership interact—how the leader, the followers, and the situation are all part of the leadership process. Understanding their interaction is necessary before you can draw valid conclusions from the leadership you observe around you. When you see a leader's behavior (even when it may appear obviously effective or ineffective to you), you should not automatically conclude something good or bad about the leader, or what is the right way or wrong way leaders should act. You need to think about the effectiveness of that behavior in *that* context with *those* followers.

As obvious as this advice sounds, we often ignore it. Too frequently we look at just the leader's behavior and conclude that he or she is a good leader or a bad leader apart from the context. For example, suppose you observe a leader soliciting advice from subordinates. Obviously it seems unreasonable to conclude that good leaders always ask for advice or that leaders who do not frequently ask for advice are not good leaders. The appropriateness of seeking input from subordinates depends on many factors, such as the nature of the problem or the subordinates' familiarity with the problem. Perhaps the subordinates have a lot more experience with this particular problem, and soliciting their input is the correct action to take in this situation.

Consider another example. Suppose you hear that a leader did not approve a subordinate's request to take time off to attend to family matters. Was this bad leadership because the leader did not appear to be taking care of her people? Was it good leadership because she did not let personal matters interfere with the mission? Again, you cannot make an intelligent decision about the leader's actions by looking at the behavior itself. You must always assess leadership in the context of the leader, the followers, and the situation.

The following statements about leaders, followers, and the situation make these points a bit more systematically:

- A leader may need to respond to various followers differently in the same situation.
- A leader may need to respond to the same follower differently in different situations.
- Followers may respond to various leaders quite differently.
- Followers may respond to each other differently with different leaders.
- Two leaders may have different perceptions of the same followers or situations.

All of these points lead to one conclusion: the right behavior in one situation is not necessarily the right behavior in another situation. It does *not* follow, however, that any behavior is appropriate in any situation. Although we may not be able to agree on the one best behavior in a given situation, we often can agree on some clearly inappropriate behaviors.

Saying that the right behavior for a leader depends on the situation is not the same thing as saying it does not matter what the leader does. It merely recognizes the complexity among leaders, followers, and situations. This recognition is a helpful first step in drawing meaningful lessons about leadership from experience.

Summary

We have defined leadership as the process of influencing an organized group toward achieving its goals. The chapter also looked at the idea that leadership is both a science and an art. Because leadership is an immature science, researchers are still struggling to find out what the important questions in leadership are; we are far from finding conclusive answers to them. Even individuals with extensive knowledge of leadership research may be poor leaders. Knowing what to do is not the same as knowing when, where, and how to do it. The art of leadership concerns the skill of understanding leadership situations and influencing others to accomplish group goals. Formal leadership education may give individuals the skills to better understand leadership situations, and mentorships and experience may give individuals the skills to better influence others. Leaders must also weigh both rational and emotional considerations when attempting to influence others. Leadership sometimes can be accomplished through relatively rational, explicit, rule-based methods of assessing situations and determining actions.

Nevertheless, the emotional side of human nature must also be acknowledged. Leaders are often most effective when they affect people at both the emotional level and the rational level. The idea of leadership as a whole-person process can also be applied to the distinction often made between leaders and managers. Although leadership and management can be distinguished as separate functions, there is considerable overlap between them in practice.

Leadership is a process in which leaders and followers interact dynamically in a particular situation or environment. Leadership is a broader concept than that of leaders, and the study of leadership must involve more than just the study of leaders as individuals. The study of leadership must also include two other areas: the followers and the situation. In addition, the interactive nature of these three domains has become increasingly important in recent years and can help us to better understand the changing nature of leader–follower relationships and the increasing complexity of situations leaders and followers face. Because of this complexity, now, more than ever before, effective leadership cannot be boiled down to a simple recipe. It is still true, however, that good leadership makes a difference, and it can be enhanced through greater awareness of the important factors influencing the leadership process.

Key Terms

leadership, 4
academic tradition, 7
troubadour
  tradition, 7
management, 8
interactional
  framework, 15
leader, 15

followers, 15
situation, 15
interactions, 15
in-group, 16
out-group, 16
followership, 19
independent, critical
  thinking, 20

dependent, uncritical
  thinking, 20
active followers, 20
passive followers, 20
heroic theory, 24
interactive
  leadership, 30
glass cliff, 33

Questions

1. We say leadership involves influencing organized groups toward goals. Do you see any disadvantages to restricting the definition to organized groups?

2. How would you define *leadership*?

3. Are some people the "leader type" and others not the "leader type"? If so, what in your judgment distinguishes them?

4. Identify several "commonsense" notions about leadership that, to you, are self-evident.

5. Does every successful leader have a valid theory of leadership?

6. Would you consider it a greater compliment for someone to call you a good manager or a good leader? Why? Do you believe you can be both?

7. Do you believe leadership can be studied scientifically? Why or why not?

8. To the extent that leadership is an art, what methods come to mind for improving one's "art of leadership"?

9. According to the interactional framework, effective leader behavior depends on many variables. It follows that there is no simple prescription for effective leader behavior. Does this mean effective leadership is merely a matter of opinion or subjective preference?

10. Generally leaders get most of the credit for a group's or an organization's success. Do you believe this is warranted or fair?

11. What are some other characteristics of leaders, followers, and situations you could add to those listed in Figure 1.2?

Activities

1. Describe the best leader you have personally known or a favorite leader from history, a novel, or a movie.

2. In this activity you will explore connotations of the words *leadership* and *management*. Divide yourselves into small groups and have each group brainstorm different word associations to the terms *leader* and *leadership* or *manager* and *management*. In addition, each group should discuss whether they would prefer to work for a manager or for a leader, and why. Then the whole group should discuss similarities and differences among the respective perceptions and feelings about the two concepts.

Minicase

Richard Branson Shoots for the Moon

The Virgin Group is the umbrella for a variety of business ventures ranging from air travel to entertainment. With close to 200 companies in over 30 countries, it is one of the largest companies in the world. At the head of this huge organization is Richard Branson. Branson founded Virgin over 30 years ago and has built the organization from a small student magazine to the multibillion-dollar enterprise it is today.

Branson is not your typical CEO. Branson's dyslexia made school a struggle and sabotaged his performance on standard IQ tests. His teachers and tests had no way of measuring his greatest strengths—his uncanny knack for uncovering lucrative business ideas and his ability to energize the ambitions of others so that they, like he, could rise to the level of their dreams.

Richard Branson's true talents began to show themselves in his late teens. While a student at Stowe School in England in 1968, Branson decided to start his own magazine, *Student*. Branson was inspired by the student activism on his campus in the 1960s and decided to try something different. *Student* differed from most college newspapers or magazines; it focused on the students and their interests. Branson sold advertising to major corporations to support his magazine. He included articles by ministers of Parliament, rock stars, intellectuals, and celebrities. *Student* grew to become a commercial success.

In 1970 Branson saw an opportunity for *Student* to offer records cheaply by running ads for mail-order delivery. The subscribers to *Student* flooded the magazine with so many orders that his spin-off discount music venture proved more lucrative than the magazine subscriptions. Branson recruited the staff of *Student* for his discount music business. He built a small recording studio and signed his first artist. Mike Oldfield recorded "Tubular Bells" at Virgin in 1973; the album sold 5 million copies, and Virgin Records and the Virgin brand name were born. Branson has gone on to start his own airline (Virgin Atlantic Airlines was launched in 1984), build hotels (Virgin Hotels started in 1988), get into the personal finance business (Virgin Direct Personal Finance Services was launched in 1995), and even enter the cola wars (Virgin Cola was introduced in 1994). And those are just a few highlights of the Virgin Group—all this while Branson has attempted to break world speed records for crossing the Atlantic Ocean by boat and by hot air balloon.

As you might guess, Branson's approach is nontraditional—he has no giant corporate office or staff and few if any board meetings. Instead he keeps each enterprise small and relies on his skills of empowering people's ideas to fuel success. When a flight attendant from Virgin Airlines approached him with her vision of a wedding business, Richard told her to go do it. He even put on a wedding dress himself to help launch the publicity. Virgin Brides was born. Branson relies heavily on the creativity of his staff; he is more a supporter of new ideas than a creator of them. He encourages searches for new business ideas everywhere he goes and even has a spot on the Virgin website called "Got a Big Idea?"

In December 1999 Richard Branson was awarded a knighthood in the Queen's Millennium New Year's Honours List for "services to entrepreneurship." What's next on Branson's list? It's Virgin Galactic, Branson's company designed in part to make space tourism available to private citizens. He has announced that the company's first space flight will take place in 2013 on its *Spaceship Two* traveling 62 miles above the earth. The first passengers will be Branson himself and his two adult sons; you can take a later flight yourself for a mere $200,000 for a two-hour trip. Not everyone is convinced that space tourism can become a fully fledged part of the travel industry, but with Branson behind the idea it just might fly.

1. Would you classify Richard Branson as a manager or a leader? What qualities distinguish him as one or the other?

2. As mentioned earlier in this chapter, followers are part of the leadership process. Describe the relationship between Branson and his followers.

3. Identify the myths of leadership development that Richard Branson's success helps to disprove.

Sources: http://www.johnshepler.com/articles/branson.html; http://www.wma.com/richard_branson/summary/; http://www.virgin.com/aboutvirgin/allaboutvirgin/thewholestory/; http://www.virgin.com/aboutvirgin/allaboutvirgin/whosrichardbranson/; http://www.qksrv.net/click-310374-35140; http://www.guardian.co.uk/space/article/0,14493,1235926,00.html.

End Notes

1. P. P. Read, *Alive* (New York: J. B. Lippincott, 1974).
2. Ibid., p. 77.
3. J. R. Meindl and S. B. Ehrlich, "The Romance of Leadership and the Evaluation of Organizational Performance," *Academy of Management Journal* 30 (1987), pp. 90–109.
4. W. G. Bennis, "Leadership Theory and Administrative Behavior: The Problem of Authority," *Administrative Science Quarterly* 4 (1959), pp. 259–60.
5. F. Fiedler, *A Theory of Leadership Effectiveness* (New York: McGraw-Hill, 1967).
6. R. K. Merton, *Social Theory and Social Structure* (New York: Free Press, 1957).
7. C. F. Roach and O. Behling, "Functionalism: Basis for an Alternate Approach to the Study of Leadership," in *Leaders and Managers: International Perspectives on Managerial Behavior and Leadership,* eds. J. G. Hunt, D. M. Hosking, C. A. Schriesheim, and R. Stewar (Elmsford, NY: Pergamon, 1984).

8. D. P. Campbell, *Campbell Leadership Index Manual* (Minneapolis: National Computer Systems, 1991).

9. R. C. Ginnett, "Team Effectiveness Leadership Model: Identifying Leverage Points for Change," *Proceedings of the 1996 National Leadership Institute Conference* (College Park, MD: National Leadership Institute, 1996).

10. G. J. Curphy and R. T. Hogan, *The Rocket Model: Practical Advice for Building High Performing Teams* (Tulsa, OK: Hogan Press, 2012).

11. M. D. Mumford, S. J. Zaccaro, F. D. Harding, T. O. Jacobs, and E. A. Fleishman, "Leadership Skills for a Changing World," *Leadership Quarterly* 11, no. 1 (2000), pp. 11–35.

12. B. M. Bass, *Bass and Stogdill's Handbook of Leadership,* 3rd ed. (New York: Free Press, 1990).

13. H. C. Foushee, "Dyads and Triads at 35,000 Feet: Factors Affecting Group Process and Aircrew Performance," *American Psychologist* 39 (1984), pp. 885–93.

14. W. G. Bennis and B. Nanus, *Leaders: The Strategies for Taking Charge* (New York: Harper & Row, 1985).

15. A. Zaleznik, "The Leadership Gap," *Washington Quarterly* 6, no. 1 (1983), pp. 32–39.

16. W. G. Bennis, *On Becoming a Leader* (Reading, MA: Addison-Wesley, 1989).

17. Zaleznik, "The Leadership Gap."

18. P. Slovic and B. Fischoff, "On the Psychology of Experimental Surprises," *Journal of Experimental Social Psychology* 22 (1977), pp. 544–51.

19. G. Wood, "The Knew-It-All-Along Effect," *Journal of Experimental Psychology: Human Perception and Performance* 4 (1979), pp. 345–53.

20. P. E. Lazarsfeld, "The American Soldier: An Expository Review," *Public Opinion Quarterly* 13 (1949), pp. 377–404.

21. For example, A. Tellegen, D. T. Lykken, T. J. Bouchard, K. J. Wilcox, N. L. Segal, and S. Rich, "Personality Similarity in Twins Reared Apart and Together," *Journal of Personality and Social Psychology* 54 (1988), pp. 1031–39.

22. Fiedler, *A Theory of Leadership Effectiveness.*

23. E. P. Hollander, *Leadership Dynamics: A Practical Guide to Effective Relationships* (New York: Free Press, 1978).

24. G. B. Graen and J. F. Cashman, "A Role-Making Model of Leadership in Formal Organizations: A Developmental Approach," in *Leadership Frontiers,* eds. J. G. Hunt and L. L. Larson (Kent, OH: Kent State University Press, 1975).

25. R. M. Stogdill, "Personal Factors Associated with Leadership: A Review of the Literature," *Journal of Psychology* 25 (1948), pp. 35–71.

26. R. M. Stogdill, *Handbook of Leadership* (New York: Free Press, 1974).

27. R. T. Hogan, G. J. Curphy, and J. Hogan, "What We Know about Personality: Leadership and Effectiveness," *American Psychologist* 49 (1994), pp. 493–504.

28. R. G. Lord, C. L. DeVader, and G. M. Allinger, "A Meta-Analysis of the Relationship between Personality Traits and Leadership Perceptions: An Application of Validity Generalization Procedures," *Journal of Applied Psychology* 71 (1986), pp. 402–10.

29. R. M. Kanter, *The Change Masters* (New York: Simon & Schuster, 1983).

30. E. D. Baltzell, *Puritan Boston and Quaker Philadelphia* (New York: Free Press, 1980).

31. E. P. Hollander and L. R. Offermann, "Power and Leadership in Organizations," *American Psychologist* 45 (1990), pp. 179–89.

32. S. D. Baker, "Followership: The Theoretical Foundation of a Contemporary Construct," *Journal of Leadership & Organizational Studies* 14, no. 1 (2007), p. 51.

33. Baker, "Followership."

34. J. M. Burns, *Leadership* (New York: Harper & Row, 1978).

35. B. M. Bass, *Bass and Stogdill's Handbook of Leadership,* 3rd ed. (New York: Free Press, 1990).

36. Stogdill, *Handbook of Leadership.*

37. C. D. Sutton and R. W. Woodman, "Pygmalion Goes to Work: The Effects of Supervisor Expectations in the Retail Setting," *Journal of Applied Psychology* 74 (1989), pp. 943–50.

38. L. I. Moore, "The FMI: Dimensions of Follower Maturity," *Group and Organizational Studies* 1 (1976), pp. 203–22.

39. T. A. Scandura, G. B. Graen, and M. A. Novak, "When Managers Decide Not to Decide Autocratically: An Investigation of Leader-Member Exchange and Decision Influence," *Journal of Applied Psychology* 52 (1986), pp. 135–47.

40. C. A. Sales, E. Levanoni, and D. H. Saleh, "Satisfaction and Stress as a Function of Job Orientation, Style of Supervision, and the Nature of the Task," *Engineering Management International* 2 (1984), pp. 145–53.

41. Adapted from K. Macrorie, *Twenty Teachers* (Oxford: Oxford University Press, 1984).

42. J. M. Kouzes and B. Z. Posner, *The Leadership Challenge: How to Get Extraordinary Things Done in Organizations* (San Francisco: Jossey-Bass, 1987).

43. R. Lippitt, "The Changing Leader–Follower Relationships of the 1980s," *Journal of Applied Behavioral Science* 18 (1982), pp. 395–403.

44. P. Block, *Stewardship* (San Francisco: Berrett-Koehler, 1992).

45. G. F. Tanoff and C. B. Barlow, "Leadership and Followership: Same Animal, Different Spots?" *Consulting Psychology Journal: Practice and Research,* Summer 2002, pp. 157–65.

46. P. M. Senge, *The Fifth Discipline: The Art and Practice of the Learning Organization* (New York: Doubleday/Currency, 1990).

47. V. Vroom and A. G. Jago, "The Role of the Situation in Leadership," *American Psychologist* 62, no. 1 (2007), pp. 17–24.

48. Vroom and Jago, "The Role of the Situation in Leadership."

49. For example, M. Conlin, "The New Gender Gap: From Kindergarten to Grad School, Boys Are Becoming the Second Sex," *BusinessWeek,* May 26, 2003.

50. GAO, Women in Management: Female Managers' Representation, Characteristics, and Pay, GAO-10-1064T (Washington, D.C.: September 28, 2010).

51. http://catalyst.org/press-release/161/2009-catalyst-census-of-the-fortune-500-reveals-women-missing-from-critical-business-leadership. 10/05/2010.

52. H. Ibarra, N. M. Carter, and C. Silva, "Why Men Still Get More Promotions Than Women," *Harvard Business Review,* September 2010, pp. 80–85.

53. D. Bevelander and M. J. Page, "Ms. Trust: Gender, Networks and Trust—Implications for Management and Education," *Academy of Management Learning & Education* 10, no. 4 (2011), pp. 623–42.

54. V. Schein, "The Relationship between Sex Role Stereotypes and Requisite Management Characteristics," *Journal of Applied Psychology* 57 (1973), pp. 95–100.

55. V. Schein, "Relationships between Sex Role Stereotypes and Requisite Management Characteristics among Female Managers, *Journal of Applied Psychology* 60 (1975), pp. 340–44.

56. V. Schein and R. Mueller, "Sex Role Stereotyping and Requisite Management Characteristics: A Cross Cultural Look," *Journal of Organizational Behavior* 13 (1992), pp. 439–47.

57. A. M. Koenig, A. H. Eagly, A. A. Mitchell, and T. Ristikari, "Are Leader Stereotypes Masculine? A Meta-analysis of Three Research Paradigms," *Psychological Bulletin* 137, no. 4, (2011), pp. 616–42.

58. O. C. Brenner, J. Tomkiewicz, and V. E. Schein, "The Relationship between Sex Role Stereotypes and Requisite Management Characteristics Revisited," *Academy of Management Journal* 32 (1989), pp. 662–69.

59. A. M. Morrison, R. P. White, and E. Van Velsor, *Breaking the Glass Ceiling* (Reading, MA: Addison-Wesley, 1987).

60. J. B. Rosener, "Ways Women Lead," *Harvard Business Review* 68 (1990), pp. 119–25.

61. A. H. Eagly and L. L. Carli, "The Female Leadership Advantage: An Evaluation of the Evidence," *The Leadership Quarterly* 14 (2003), pp. 807–34.

62. A. W. Astin, S. A. Parrrott, W. S. Korn, and L. J. Sax, *The American Freshman: Thirty Year Trends* (Los Angeles: Higher Education Research Institute, University of California, 1997).

63. J. M. Twenge, "Changes in Masculine and Feminine Traits over Time: A Meta-analysis," *Sex Roles* 36 (1997), pp. 305–25.

64. J. M. Twenge, "Changes in Women's Assertiveness in Response to Status and Roles: A Cross-Temporal Meta-analysis, 1931–1993," *Journal of Personality and Social Psychology* 81 (2001), pp. 133–45.

65. A. M. Konrad, J. E. Ritchie, Jr., P. Lieb, and E. Corrigall, "Sex Differences and Similarities in Job Attribute Preferences: A Meta-analysis," *Psychological Bulletin* 126 (2000), pp. 593–641.

66. S. A. Haslam and M. K. Ryan, "The Road to the Glass Cliff: Differences in the Perceived Suitability of Men and Women for Leadership Positions in Succeeding and Failing Organizations," *The Leadership Quarterly* 19 (2008), pp. 530–46.

Chapter 2

Leader Development

Introduction

In Chapter 1 we discussed the importance of using multiple perspectives to analyze various leadership situations. It's also true that there are multiple paths by which one's own leadership is developed. That's what this chapter is about: how to become a better leader. This is not a mere "academic" matter without practical import. In fact, the enterprise of leadership development has grown into a $60 billion industry in the United States alone. At the same time, public confidence in leadership has declined 30 percent since 1995, and most corporations report having inadequate leadership capacity to meet their challenges.[1]

As an overview, we begin this chapter by presenting a general model that describes how we learn from experience. Next we describe how perceptions can affect a leader's interpretation of, and actions in response to, a particular leadership situation and why reflection is important to leadership development. The chapter also examines several specific mechanisms often used to help leaders become *better* leaders.

Perhaps a word here might be useful about titling this chapter *leader development*. We have done so deliberately to distinguish the phrase from *leadership development*. Although the two may seem synonymous to the reader, they have come to be treated by scholars and practitioners in the field as having distinct meanings. That wasn't always the case. Until a decade or so ago, scholars and practitioners, too, considered them essentially synonymous. Gradually, however, it became useful to use *leader development* when referring to methods intended to facilitate growth in an *individual's* perspectives or skills. For example, training designed to develop one's skill in giving feedback to another person would be considered leader development. Over the past decade, though, the term *leadership* has taken on a somewhat richer meaning transcending a focus on individual-level characteristics and skills even when the focus is on developing such qualities in *many* individuals. Paralleling a gradual shift in understanding that leadership is a process in which many people in an organization share in complex and interdependent ways (as we discussed in Chapter 1), the term *leadership development* has come to designate a focus on developing shared properties of whole groups or social systems such as the degree of trust among all the members of a team or department, or on enhancing the reward systems in an organization to better encourage collaborative behavior.[2] Although such things are frequently addressed throughout this text, the focus of this chapter will be on processes and methods designed to foster individual-level growth—hence the choice of chapter title.

And one more thing before we get into those substantive parts of the chapter: it might be useful to start with a fundamental question about the value of an academic course in leadership. Before the authors wrote this textbook, we and other colleagues taught an undergraduate course in leadership required of all cadets at the U.S. Air Force Academy. Undergraduate courses in leadership are fairly common now, but they weren't in the 1980s. For many decades the U.S. Air Force Academy and the U.S. Military Academy were among the few undergraduate schools offering such courses.

Because undergraduate leadership courses were somewhat uncommon then, the idea of an academic course in leadership was a novel idea to many faculty members from other departments. Some were openly skeptical that leadership was an appropriate course for an academic department to offer. It was a common experience for us to be asked, "Do you really think you can *teach* leadership?" Usually this was asked in a tone of voice that made it clear the questioner took it for granted that leadership couldn't be taught. Colleagues teaching leadership courses at other institutions have found themselves in similar situations.

Over time, we formulated our own response to this question, and it still reflects a core belief we continue to hold. Not coincidentally, that belief has been hinted at in the subtitle to every edition of our text: *Enhancing the Lessons of Experience*. Let us describe how that idea represents the answer to those skeptical questioners, and also how reflecting on their questions shaped these authors' thinking about one important objective of an academic course in leadership.

Just to be clear, we *don't* disagree completely with the premise of those skeptical questioners. We don't believe that merely taking a one-semester college course in leadership will make one a better leader. However, we believe strongly that it can lay a valuable foundation to becoming a better leader over time.

Here's our reasoning. If you accept that leadership can be learned (rather than just "being born" in a person), and if you also believe that the most powerful lessons about leadership come from one's own experience, then the matter boils down to the process of how we learn from experience. If one important factor in learning from experience pertains to how complex or multifaceted your conceptual lenses are for construing experience, then it's no big stretch to claim that becoming familiar with the complex variables that affect leadership gives you a greater variety of ways to make sense of the leadership situations you confront in your own life. In that way, completing a college course in leadership may not make you a better leader directly and immediately, but actively mastering the concepts in the course can nonetheless *accelerate the rate at which you learn from the natural experiences you have* during and subsequent to your course.

For efficiency, organizations that value developing their leaders usually create intentional pathways for doing so. In other words, leader development in most large organizations is not left to osmosis. There typically are structured and planned approaches to developing internal leaders or leaders-to-be. Formal training is the most common approach to developing leaders, even when research consistently shows that it's not the most effective method. It should not be surprising, then, that organizational members are often not satisfied with the opportunities generally provided within their organizations for developing as leaders. A recent study of more than 4,500 leaders from over 900 organizations found that only half were satisfied with their developmental opportunities.[3]

Findings like that do not prove that leader development opportunities are inherently inadequate or poorly designed. It must be remembered, for example, that developmental opportunities by their nature typically are not free despite whatever long-term advantages might accrue from them for both the individual and the organization. It would seem desirable, then, to ensure that developmental opportunities are provided based on our best understanding of leader development processes. Morgan McCall has summarized some of the key things we've learned about leader development over the last several decades in these seven general points:[4]

- To the extent that leadership is learned at all, it is learned from experience. In fact, about 70 percent of variance in a person's effectiveness in a leadership role is due to the results of her experience; only 30 percent is due to heredity.
- Certain experiences have greater developmental impact than others in shaping a person's effectiveness as a leader.
- What makes such experiences valuable are the challenges they present to the person.
- Different types of experience teach different leadership lessons.
- Some of the most useful experiences for learning leadership come in the jobs we're assigned to, and they can be designed to better enhance their developmental richness.
- Obstacles exist to getting all the developmental experiences we may desire, but we can still get many of them through our own diligence and with some organizational support.
- Learning to be a better leader is a lifelong pursuit with many twists and turns.

Leadership, like swimming, cannot be learned by reading about it.
Henry Mintzberg, scholar

Leadership and learning are indispensable to each other.
John F. Kennedy

The Action–Observation–Reflection Model

Consider for a moment what a young person might learn from spending a year working in two very different environments: as a staff assistant in the U.S. Congress or as a carpenter on a house construction crew. Each activity offers a rich store of leadership lessons. Working in Congress, for example, would provide opportunities to observe political leaders both onstage in the public eye and backstage in more private moments. It would provide opportunities to see members of Congress interacting with different constituencies, to see them in political defeat and political victory, and to see a range of leadership styles. A young person could also learn a lot by working on a building crew as it turned plans and materials into the reality of a finished house: watching the coordination with subcontractors, watching skilled craftspeople train younger ones, watching the leader's reactions to problems and delays, watching the leader set standards and ensure quality work. At the same time, a person could work in either environment and *not* grow much if he or she were not disposed to. Making the most of experience is key to developing one's leadership ability. In other words, leadership development depends not just on the kinds of experiences one has but also on how one uses them to foster growth. A study of successful executives found that a key quality that characterized them was an "extraordinary tenacity in extracting something worthwhile from their experience and in seeking experiences rich in opportunities for growth."[5]

But how does one do that? Is someone really more likely to get the lessons of experience by looking for them? Why is it not enough just to be there? Experiential learning theorists, such as Kolb,[6] believe people learn more from their experiences when they spend time thinking about them. These ideas are extended to leadership in the **action–observation–reflection (A-O-R) model**, depicted in Figure 2.1, which shows that leadership development is enhanced when the experience involves three different processes: action, observation, and reflection. If a person acts but does not observe the consequences of her actions or reflect on their significance and meaning, then it makes little sense to say she has learned from an experience. Because some people neither observe the consequences of their actions nor reflect on how they could change their actions to become better leaders, leadership development through experience may be better understood as the growth resulting from repeated movements through all three phases rather than merely in terms of some objective dimension like time (such as how long one has been on the job). We believe the most productive way to develop as a leader is to travel along the **spiral of experience** depicted in Figure 2.1.

Perhaps an example from Colin Powell's life will clarify how the spiral of experience pertains to leadership development. Powell held positions at the highest levels of U.S. military and civilian leadership as Chairman

FIGURE 2.1
The Spiral of Experience

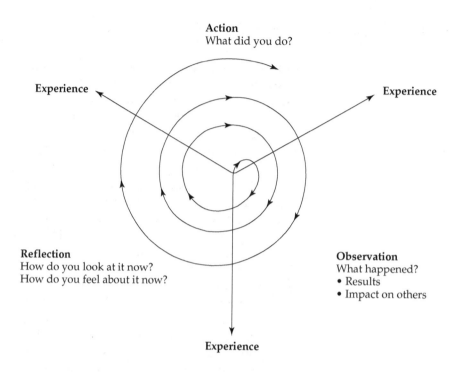

of the Joint Chiefs of Staff and U.S. Secretary of State, but in 1963 he was a 26-year-old officer who had just returned to the United States from a combat tour in Vietnam. His next assignment would be to attend a month-long advanced airborne Ranger course. Near the end of the course, he was to parachute with other troops from a helicopter. As the senior officer on the helicopter, Powell had responsibility for ensuring it went well. Early in the flight he shouted for everyone to make sure their static lines were secure—these are the cables that automatically pull the parachutes open when people jump. Nearing the jump site, he yelled for the men to check their hookups one more time. Here are his words describing what happened next:

> Then, like a fussy old woman, I started checking each line myself, pushing my way through the crowded bodies, running my hand along the cable and up to each man's chute. To my alarm, one hook belonging to a sergeant was loose. I shoved the dangling line in his face, and he gasped. . . . This man would have stepped out of the door of the helo and dropped like a rock.[7]

What did Powell learn from this experience?

Moments of stress, confusion, and fatigue are exactly when mistakes happen. And when everyone else's mind is dulled or distracted the leader must be doubly vigilant. "Always check small things" was becoming another one of my rules.[8]

We shall not cease from exploration And the end of all our exploring Will be to arrive where we started And know the place for the first time.

T. S. Eliot

Let us examine this incident in light of the A-O-R model. *Action* refers to Powell's multiple calls for the parachutists to check their lines. We might speculate from his self-description ("like a fussy old woman") that Powell might have felt slightly uncomfortable with such repeated emphasis on checking the lines, even though he persisted in the behavior. Perhaps you, too, sometimes have acted in a certain manner (or were forced to by your parents) despite feeling a little embarrassed about it, and then, if it was successful, felt more comfortable the next time acting the same way. That seems to be what happened with Powell here. The *observation* phase refers to Powell's shocked realization of the potentially fatal accident that would have occurred had he *not* double-checked the static lines. And the *reflection* phase refers to the lesson Powell drew from the experience: "Always check the small things." Even though this was not a totally new insight, its importance was strongly reinforced by this experience. In a real sense Powell was "spiraling" through a lesson he'd learned from other experiences too, but embracing it even more this time, making it part of his style.

We also should note that Powell himself described his learning in a manner consistent with our interactional framework. He emphasized the situational importance of the leader's attention to detail, especially during moments of stress, confusion, and fatigue, when mistakes may be most likely to happen. Finally, it's worth noting that throughout Powell's autobiography he discusses many lessons he learned from experience. A key to his success was his ability to keep learning throughout his career.

The Key Role of Perception in the Spiral of Experience

Experience is not just a matter of what events happen to you; it also depends on how you perceive those events. Perception affects all three phases of the action–observation–reflection model and thus plays an important role in what anyone will extract from a leadership course or from any leadership situation. Human beings are not passive recorders of experiences that happen to them; rather, people actively shape and construct their experiences. To better understand how perception affects experience, we will examine its role in each part of the action–observation–reflection model. We will begin with the stage that seems to correspond most directly with perception—the observation phase.

Perception and Observation

Observation and perception both deal with attending to events around us. Both seem to take place spontaneously and effortlessly, so it is easy to regard them as passive processes. Our usual mental images of the perceptual process reflect this implicit view. For example, it is a common misconception that the eye operates essentially like the film in a continuously running camera. The fallacy of this passive view of perception is that it assumes we attend to all aspects of a situation equally. However, we do not see everything that happens in a particular leadership situation, nor do we hear everything. Instead we are selective in what we attend to and what we, in turn, perceive. One phenomenon that demonstrates this selectivity is called **perceptual set.** Perceptual sets can influence any of our senses, and they are the tendency or bias to perceive one thing and not another. Many factors can trigger a perceptual set, such as feelings, needs, prior experience, and expectations. Its role in distorting what we hear proved a costly lesson when a sympathetic airline pilot told his depressed copilot, "Cheer up!" The copilot thought the pilot had said, "Gear up," and raised the wheels while the plane was still on the ground.[9] Try your own ability to overcome perceptual set with the following exercise. Read through this narrative passage several times:

FINISHED FILES ARE THE RESULT OF YEARS OF SCIENTIFIC STUDY COMBINED WITH THE EXPERIENCE OF MANY YEARS.

Make sure you have read it to yourself several times *before going any further.* Now go back to the text and count the number of times the letter *F* appears.

How many did you count? Three? Four? Five? Six? Most people do not get the correct answer (six) the first time. The most frequent count is three; perhaps that was how many you saw. If you did not find six, go back and try again. The most common error in this seemingly trivial task is overlooking the three times the word *of* appears. People easily overlook it because the word *of* has a *v* sound, not an *f* sound. Most people unconsciously make the task an auditory search task and listen for the sound of *F* rather than look for the shape of *F*; hence they find three *F*s rather than six. Listening for the sound constitutes a counterproductive perceptual set for this task, and having read the passage several times before counting the *F*s only exaggerates this tendency. Another reason people overlook the word *of* in this passage is that the first task was to *read* the passage several times. Because most of us are accomplished readers, we tend to ignore small words like *of*—they disappear from our perceptual set. Then, when we are asked to count the number of *F*s, we have already defined the passage as a reading task, so the word *of* is really not there for us to count. See Highlight 2.1 to learn about other factors that can affect our observational effectiveness.

There are strong parallels between this example of a perceptual set and the perceptual sets that come into play when we are enrolled in a leadership course or observe a leadership situation. For example, your instructor for this class may dress unstylishly, and you may be prejudiced in thinking that poor dressers generally do not make good leaders. Because of your biases, you may discount or not attend to some things your instructor has to say about leadership. This would be unfortunate because your instructor's taste in clothes has little to do with his or her ability to teach (which is, after all, a kind of leadership).

It's not what we don't know that hurts, it's what we know that ain't so.

Will Rogers

On Being Observant and Lucky and Learning from Experience

HIGHLIGHT 2.1

It's often said that some people have all the luck. Do you think that's true—are some people luckier than others? Richard Wiseman, a professor at the University of Hertfordshire, has written a book about just that question, and his findings are relevant to the role observation plays in our spiral of experience.

In one of his experiments, Wiseman placed advertisements in national newspapers asking for people to contact him who felt either consistently lucky or consistently unlucky. In one experiment, he gave both self-described lucky and unlucky people a newspaper to read and asked them to look it over and tell him how many photographs were inside.

Halfway through the paper he'd put a half-page message with two-inch lettering saying, "Tell the experimenter you have seen this and win $250."

The advertisement was staring everyone in the face, but the unlucky people tended to miss it whereas the lucky people tended to notice it. One reason may be related to the fact that Wiseman claims unlucky people are somewhat more anxious than lucky people, and that might disrupt their ability to notice things that are unexpected.

How observant are *you*, and might developing your own observation skills help you learn from experience more effectively?

Source: Adapted from Richard Wiseman, *The Luck Factor* (New York: Miramax Books, 2003).

A similar phenomenon takes place when one expects to find mostly negative things about another person (such as a problem employee). Such an expectation becomes a perceptual set to look for the negative and look past the positive things in the process. Stereotypes about gender, race, and the like represent powerful impediments to learning because they function as filters that distort one's observations. For example, if you do not believe women or minorities are as successful as white males in influencing others, you may be biased to identify or remember only instances where a woman or minority leader failed, and discount or forget instances where women or minority members succeeded as leaders. Unfortunately we all have similar biases, although we are usually unaware of them. Often we become aware of our perceptual sets only when we spend time reflecting about the content of a leadership training program or a particular leadership situation.

Perception and Reflection

Perceptual sets influence what we attend to and what we observe. In addition, perception also influences the next stage of the spiral of experience—reflection—because reflection is how we interpret our observations. Perception is inherently an interpretive, or a meaning-making, activity. One important aspect of this is a process called **attribution.**

Attributions are the explanations we develop for the behaviors or actions we attend to. For example, if you see Julie fail in an attempt to get others to form a study group, you are likely to attribute the cause of the

Success is a lousy teacher. It seduces smart people into thinking they can't lose.
Bill Gates

failure to dispositional factors within Julie. In other words, you are likely to attribute the failure to form a study group to Julie's intelligence, personality, physical appearance, or some other factor even though factors beyond her control could have played a major part. This tendency to overestimate the dispositional causes of behavior and underestimate the environmental causes when others fail is called the **fundamental attribution error.**[10] People prefer to explain others' behavior on the basis of personal attributions even when obvious situational factors may fully account for the behavior.

On the other hand, if *you* attempted to get others to form a study group and failed, you would be more likely to blame factors in the situation for the failure (there was not enough time, or the others were not interested, or they would not be good to study with). This reflects a **self-serving bias**[11]—the tendency to make external attributions (blame the situation) for one's own failures yet make internal attributions (take credit) for one's successes. A third factor that affects the attribution process is called the **actor/observer difference.**[12] This refers to the fact that people who are observing an action are much more likely than the actor to make the fundamental attribution error. Consider, for example, a student who gets a bad score on an exam. The person sitting next to her (an observer) would tend to attribute the bad score to *internal* characteristics (not very bright, weak in this subject) whereas the student herself would be more likely to attribute the bad score to *external* factors (the professor graded unfairly). Putting these factors together, each of us tends to see our own success as due to our intelligence, personality, or physical abilities, but others' success as more attributable to situational factors or to luck.

We note in concluding this section that reflection also involves higher functions like evaluation and judgment, not just perception and attribution. We will address these broader aspects of reflection, which are crucial to learning from experience, just ahead.

Perception and Action

We have seen how perception influences both the observation and reflection stages in the spiral of experience. It also affects the actions we take. For example, Mitchell and his associates[13–15] have examined how perceptions and biases affect supervisors' actions in response to poorly performing subordinates. In general, these researchers found that supervisors were biased toward making dispositional attributions about a subordinate's substandard performance and, as a result of these attributions, often recommended that punishment be used to remedy performance deficits.

Another perceptual variable that can affect our actions is the **self-fulfilling prophecy,** which occurs when our expectations or predictions play a causal role in bringing about the events we predict. It is not difficult to see how certain large-scale social phenomena may be affected this

Common sense is the collection of prejudices acquired by age 18.
Albert Einstein

FIGURE 2.2
The Role of Expectations in Social Interaction

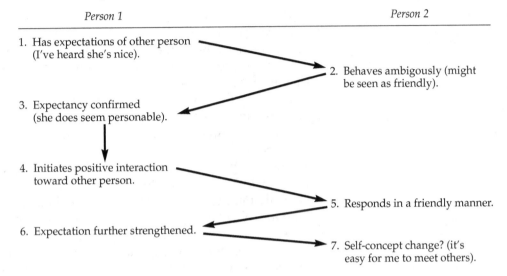

Source: *From Edward E. Jones, "Interpreting Interpersonal Behavior: The Effects of Expectancies," Science 234, 3, October 1986, p. 43. Reprinted with permission from AAAS.*

way. For example, economists' predictions of an economic downturn may, via the consequent decreased investor confidence, precipitate an economic crisis. But the self-fulfilling prophecy occurs at the interpersonal level, too. A person's expectations about another may influence how he acts toward her, and in reaction to his behavior she may act in a way that confirms his expectations.[16] An illustrative interaction sequence is shown in Figure 2.2.

Some of the best evidence to support the effects of self-fulfilling prophecies on leadership training was collected by Eden and Shani in the context of military boot camp.[17] They conducted a field experiment in which they told leadership instructors their students had unknown, regular, or high command potential. However, the students' actual command potential was never assessed, and unknown to the instructors, the students were actually randomly assigned to the unknown, regular, or high command potential conditions. Nevertheless, students in the high-potential condition had significantly better objective test scores and attitudes than the students in the unknown- or regular-potential conditions, even though instructors simultaneously taught all three types of students. Somehow the students picked up on their instructor's expectations and responded accordingly. Thus merely having expectations (positive or negative) about others can subtly influence our actions, and these actions can, in turn, affect the way others behave.

Reflection and Leadership Development

Perhaps the most important yet most neglected component of the action–observation–reflection model is reflection. Reflection is important because it can provide leaders with a variety of insights into how to frame problems differently, look at situations from multiple perspectives, or better understand subordinates. However, most managers spend relatively little time on this activity, even though the time spent reflecting about leadership can be fruitful. The importance of reflection in developing executive competence continues to be a major element of advancing scholarly thought and practice.[18]

One reason the reflection component is often neglected is because of the implicit or taken-for-granted beliefs about leadership that many people have. By their unrecognized and untested nature, implicit beliefs can inadvertently insulate a person from seeing things in new ways and from potential learning. Leadership development can be enhanced by raising such implicit beliefs to conscious awareness and thereby more to thoughtful reflection. One approach, for example, used a variety of art prints to stimulate personal and group reflection on ideal forms of leadership. The prints were used to evoke *metaphors* of leadership, and ultimately five fundamental archetypes of leadership were identified:

- **Teacher-Mentor**, who cares about developing others and works beside them as a role model.
- **Father-Judge**, who provides oversight, control, moral guidance, and caring protectiveness.
- **Warrior-Knight**, who takes risks and action in a crisis.
- **Revolutionary-Crusader**, who challenges the status quo and guides adaptation.
- **Visionary-Alchemist**, who imagines possibilities that can benefit all members and brings them into reality.

This overall process helped participants to articulate their tacit knowledge of leadership, to see similarities and differences between their own views and others, and to better understand the complexities of leadership.[19] That the process of forming implicit beliefs about leadership can begin very early in life is evident in Highlight 2.2.

Another reason the reflection component is often neglected may be time pressure at work. Leaders are usually busy working in pressure-filled situations and often do not have time to ponder all the possible consequences of their actions or reflect on how they could have accomplished a particular action better. Sometimes it takes an out-of-the-ordinary experience to focus one's attention on developmental challenges. In addition, some leaders may not be aware of the value of reflection in leadership development. Intentional reflection might even prompt one to see potential benefits in

Being ignorant is not so much a shame as being unwilling to learn.
Benjamin Franklin

What Do Children Believe about Leadership? "Wut Do Ldrs Do?"

HIGHLIGHT 2.2

A 5-year-old girl wrote and illustrated an un-prompted "book" for her grandfather, a friend of the authors. We've included a few of the pages here. They convey what at least some young children believe are important qualities of leaders. You might ask yourself how valid this characterization is . . . and in what ways it is likely to be shaped by experiences between kindergarten and adulthood. The words are written entirely with a 5-year-old's phonetic spelling, so you'll need to be creative in interpreting the qualities!

If we were to apply our A-O-R model here, would you say this 5-year-old was learning from her experience?

By Hailey Bemis Age 5

Translation Frame A: What do leaders do?

Translation Frame B: They call 911 if someone gets hurt.

Translation Frame C: They get people excited to learn.

Translation Frame D: They be nice to people.

Translation Frame E: They help people.

experience not initially considered relevant to leadership in organizational settings. We hope this section will clarify the value of reflection and, in so doing, complement the emphasis, throughout the remainder of the book, on looking at leadership from different perspectives.

Single- and Double-Loop Learning

It is difficult for leaders to fundamentally change their leadership style without engaging in some kind of reflection. Along these lines, Argyris[20] described an intensive effort with a group of successful chief executive officers who became even better leaders through increased self-awareness. His model for conceptualizing this growth is applicable to any level of leader and is worth considering in more detail.

Argyris said that most people interact with others and the environment on the basis of a belief system geared to manipulate or control others, and to minimize one's own emotionality and the negative feelings elicited from others. This belief system also tends to create defensive interpersonal relationships and limits risk taking. People "programmed" with this view of life (as most of us are, according to Argyris) produce group and organizational dynamics characterized by avoidance of conflict, mistrust, conformity, intergroup rivalry, misperceptions of and miscommunications with others, ineffective problem solving, and poor decision making.

Most important for our purposes here, this belief system generates a certain kind of learning that Argyris called **single-loop learning.** Single-loop learning describes a kind of learning between the individual and the environment in which learners seek relatively little feedback that may significantly confront their fundamental ideas or actions. There is relatively little public testing of ideas against valid information. Consequently, an actor's belief system becomes self-sealing and self-fulfilling, and little time is spent reflecting about the beliefs. Argyris used the term *single-loop learning* because it operates somewhat like a thermostat: individuals learn only about subjects within the comfort zone of their belief systems. They might, for example, learn how well they are achieving a designated goal. They are far less likely, however, to question the validity of the goal or the values implicit in the situation, just as a thermostat does not question its temperature setting. That kind of self-confrontation would involve double-loop learning.

Double-loop learning involves a willingness to confront one's own views and an invitation to others to do so, too. It springs from an appreciation that openness to information and power sharing with others can lead to better recognition and definition of problems, improved communication, and increased decision-making effectiveness. Mastering double-loop learning can be thought of as learning how to learn. With considerable collective work, including the difficult task of working through personal blind spots, Argyris's group of leaders did move to this stage. In other words, through reflection they learned how to change their leadership styles by questioning their assumptions about others, their roles in the organization, and their underlying assumptions about the importance of their own goals and those of the organization.

What makes double-loop learning so difficult? By their very nature, leadership experiences are often ambiguous; they typically involve multiple stakeholders having multiple perspectives and interests; and emotional stakes can be high. Such ambiguity, complexity, and emotionality can make it difficult for a leader to determine causal relationships between his or her behavior and specific outcomes, or whether different behavior would have led to different outcomes. Learning about leadership from one's raw experience is *not* easy, not even for those deeply committed to doing so. A recent study sheds further light on how it can be enhanced.

It turns out that while *unaided* learning from experience is difficult for all the reasons just noted, it can be enhanced through a practice of systematic reflection or **after event reviews** (AERs).[21] These AERs involved reflection and facilitated discussion on personal leadership experiences such as what the potential impact of alternative leadership behaviors might have been and how individuals believe they might behave differently in the future. The study found that individuals who participated in these AERs improved the effectiveness of their leadership over time whereas little or no development occurred *from the same experiences* among those who did not participate in the AER process.

Making the Most of Your Leadership Experiences: Learning to Learn from Experience

This section builds on the ideas previously introduced in this chapter by giving leadership practitioners a few suggestions to enhance learning from experience. For decades, researchers have been studying the role of learning from experience as an important developmental behavior for people in executive positions. Although this research has contributed a great deal to *what* people need to learn to be successful (see Highlight 2.3 for a comparison of lessons men and women managers learn from experience), less is known about the process of learning or *how* we learn to be successful.

Bunker and Webb[22] asked successful executives to list adjectives describing how they felt while working through powerful learning events and potent developmental experiences. Their typical responses were a combination of both positive and negative feelings:

Negatives	Positives		Negatives	Positives
Pained	Challenged		Overwhelmed	Exhilarated
Fearful	Successful		Uncertain	Talented
Frustrated	Proud		Angry	Resourceful
Stressed	Capable		Hurt	Learning
Anxious	Growing			

What Do Men and Women Managers Learn from Experience?

HIGHLIGHT 2.3

For a quarter century or so, significant numbers of women have been represented in the management ranks of companies. During that period companies have promoted large pools of high-potential women, but relatively few of them have achieved truly top-level positions. Several factors probably account for this, but one possibility is that men and women learn differently from their work experiences. Researchers have studied how male and female executives describe the important lessons they've learned from their career experiences, and there are some interesting differences between the genders as well as significant overlap.

Most Frequent Lessons for Men and Women	For Men Only	For Women Only
Directing and motivating employees.	Technical/professional skills.	Personal limits and blind spots.
Self-confidence.	All about the business.	Taking charge of career.
Basic management values.	Coping with ambiguous situations.	Recognizing and seizing opportunities.
How to work with executives.	Shouldering full responsibility.	Coping with situations beyond your control.
Understanding other people's perspective.	Persevering through adversity.	Knowing what excites you.
Dealing with people over whom you have no authority.		
Handling political situations.		

Why would there be any learning differences between the genders? One hypothesis is that men and women managers tend to have different career patterns. For example, there is some evidence that women receive fewer truly challenging developmental opportunities. Do you believe there is any difference at your school between the opportunities provided to male and female students?

Source: Adapted from E. Van Velsor and M. W. Hughes, *Gender Differences in the Development of Managers: How Women Managers Learn from Experience* (Technical Report No. 145) (Greensboro, NC: Center for Creative Leadership, 1990).

This pattern strongly supports the long-hypothesized notion of a meaningful link between stress and learning.[23] The learning events and developmental experiences that punctuate one's life are usually—perhaps always—stressful.[24–27]

Bunker and Webb note that executives try to be successful without experiencing stress. They are most comfortable when they can draw on a proven repertoire of operating skills to tackle a challenge they have conquered in the past. Combined with the organizational pressure to have "proven performers" in important positions, there is a tremendous initial pressure to "continue to do what we've always done." In stressful situations, this tendency may become even more powerful. What results is

Oprah Winfrey

PROFILES IN LEADERSHIP 2.1

In January 2007 doors opened for the first class of girls at the Oprah Winfrey Leadership Academy near Johannesburg, South Africa. The first admissions included about 150 seventh and eighth grade girls, with plans to expand to more than 400 girls in the seventh through twelfth grades by 2011. Winfrey's vision is that the academy will help develop the future women leaders of South Africa. This will be one more accomplishment for a woman whose television show received the highest ratings for a talk show in television history, publishes two different magazines, was nominated for an Academy Award for acting in *The Color Purple,* made Dr. Phil famous, and whose recommendation can virtually guarantee a book's commercial success. She may be the most influential woman in the world.

No one would have predicted this from the poor and troubled family conditions she was born into. Her Grandmother Hattie Mae, however, who raised Oprah during her first six years, saw something special in her from the beginning. She taught Oprah to read before the age of 3, and at church Oprah was known as "the preacher" because of her ability to recite Bible verses. As a teenager in school she was voted "most popular girl," and she placed second in a national competition for dramatic interpretation. At 18 she won the Miss Black Tennessee beauty pageant.

Even from an early age there were glimpses of the direction Oprah's life would take. As a child she played games "interviewing" everything from her corncob doll to crows on the fence, but her true start in broadcasting came at the age of 17 when she worked part-time at a local radio station while attending college. She became the youngest news anchor and the first black female news anchor at WLAC-TV in Nashville. In 1976 she moved to anchor the news in Baltimore, and in 1978 she became co-host of a local TV talk show. She moved to Chicago to host a talk show there, first airing in 1984; months later it was renamed *The Oprah Winfrey Show.* Its first national broadcast was in 1986, and the rest, as they say, is history. But Oprah is still making history—not only in virtually every facet of media but also in her philanthropic efforts to develop a generation of women leaders in South Africa. Oh - and she's also moved on from having her own television show to having her own TV network!

Teach a highly educated person that it is not a disgrace to fail and that he must analyze every failure to find its cause. He must learn how to fail intelligently, for failing is one of the greatest arts in the world.

Charles F. Kettering, inventor, automotive pioneer, and corporate leader

one of the great challenges of adult development: the times when people most need to break out of the mold created by past learning patterns are the times when they are most unwilling to do so. Being able to *go against the grain* of one's personal historical success requires an unwavering commitment to learning and a relentless willingness to let go of the fear of failure and the unknown.

To be successful, learning must continue throughout life, beyond the completion of one's formal education. The end of extrinsically applied education should be the start of an education that is motivated intrinsically. At that point the goal of studying is no longer to make the grade, earn a diploma, and find a good job. Rather, it is to understand what is happening around one, to develop a personally meaningful sense of what one's experience is about.[28]

This applies to the specific challenge of *becoming* and *remaining* an effective leader, too. People who lead in modern organizations need to be engaged in a never-ending learning process.[29] Ron Riggio of the Kravis

Leadership Institute characterized this challenge well in observing that organizational leaders are practitioners of leadership at the same time they must continue to be students of leadership. "The practice of leadership, just like the practice of medicine, or law, or any other profession, is a continual learning process. The complexity of these professions means that one can always improve and learn how to do it better. The wise leader accepts this and goes through the sometimes painful process of personal leader development."[30]

Leader Development in College

Virtually everyone using this text is taking a college course in leadership for academic credit. But one academic course in leadership is only part of what at some schools is an entire curriculum of leadership studies. Riggio, Ciulla, and Sorenson, representing three different institutions, have described the rise and key elements of leadership studies programs in liberal arts colleges, and note that there are now nearly 1,000 recognized leadership development programs in institutions of higher education.[31] Few, of them, though, are curriculum-based programs that offer academic credit in the form of, for example, an academic minor. As such programs continue to increase in number, several features should guide their design.

At liberal arts institutions, leadership studies programs should be multidisciplinary. As you will notice in this text, the field of leadership encompasses a broad range of disciplines including psychology, organizational behavior, history, education, management, and political science, to name just a few. Also, leadership studies need to be academically authorized courses of study (obvious as this may seem, one challenge to it was evident in the anecdote shared in the introduction to this chapter). Another important feature is that leadership programs need to deliberately cultivate values represented in the broader field, especially those that are particularly salient at each local institution. These values could include social responsibility and the expectation to become engaged in one's community; in such cases **service learning** is a common part of the programs. In other programs, global awareness is another guiding value. Finally, consistent with requirements across higher education, leadership studies programs should focus on expected developmental outcomes, with associated assessment and evaluation to determine program effectiveness.[32]

Some key curricular components of college-based leadership studies programs include coursework examining foundational theories and concepts in leadership (the kind this textbook is intended to support). In addition, coursework in ethics is vital to leadership studies. As just mentioned, service learning and other experiential learning opportunities should be provided and integrated with the classroom elements of the program. An understanding of group dynamics is critical to effective

Steve Jobs

PROFILES IN LEADERSHIP 2.2

Steve Jobs was one of the most famous and successful business leaders in the world, even if also known as having a temperamental, aggressive, and demanding style with others. At the age of 20, with partner Steve Wozniak, he helped launch the personal computer revolution with Apple Computer and ultimately through its premier PC, the Macintosh. After leaving Apple, he founded another company, NeXT Computer, and in 1986 he bought a computer animation company called Pixar. The company's first film, *Toy Story,* made history by being the first entirely computer-animated feature film. After returning to Apple, Jobs created even further revolutions in consumer technology products with the iPod, iPhone, and iPad.

In 2005 Jobs delivered the commencement address at Stanford. In that address he talked about one of the most difficult and yet most valuable experiences of his life: getting fired from Apple, the company that he had helped found. He and Wozniak started Apple, he said, in 1970 in his parents' garage. In 10 years it had grown into a $2 billion company. He could not believe it, amid that success, when he was fired by Apple's board of directors. "How can you get fired from a company you started? What had been the focus of my entire adult life was gone, and it was devastating." Yet now, reflecting on the opportunities that he was able to take advantage of because he left Apple, Jobs said to the graduating class, "I didn't see it then, but it turned out that getting fired from Apple was the best thing that ever could have happened to me."

Jobs believed that leadership meant creating an environment where excellence is expected and innovation flourishes. But he also had a dark side that punctuated and colored his success and genius as a business leader. Walter Isaacson pulled no punches in depicting both sides of Jobs's character in his gripping 2011 biography.

For example, Jobs had a mercurial personality and might change mood in minutes, crying or throwing tantrums, for example, over things that others would take more in stride. His tyrannical interpersonal style caused him to be banished off the night shift at Atari. He tended to categorize his own staff as either "gods" or "s___heads," yet even the "gods" knew they might fall of that pedestal at any moment. He perfected the art of silence and staring in order to intimidate others and could behave in incredibly mean and demeaning ways toward others. He was a consummate con man who seemed able to convince anyone of anything. He took to heart Picasso's observation that "Good artists borrow, great artists steal;" he shamelessly stole ideas from other companies and others within his own company. He simply believed that the laws and rules of conduct that governed others did not apply to him. He created his own idiosyncratic perceptions of reality that, to everyone else, had no basis in fact; Jobs, nonetheless, was absolutely convinced his view alone was correct despite all evidence to the contrary. Others even gave this "flying in the face of reality" characteristic a name—his "reality distortion field."

So what do you think: Was Steve Jobs as successful as he was because of these dark side qualities, or might he have been even more successful without them?

Source: W. Isaacson, *Steve Jobs* (New York: Simon and Schuster, 2011).

Tell me and I'll forget; show me and I may remember; involve me and I'll understand.
Chinese proverb

leadership, and its development requires student experiences interacting with others; leadership studies inherently require a social dimension of experience. Finally, as implied by the interdisciplinary nature of leadership studies, a variety of faculty from many different departments and disciplines should be involved in the program.[33]

How few there are who have the courage to own their own faults, or resolution enough to mend them!

Benjamin Franklin

Within leadership studies programs, various leader development methods may be used beyond service learning. Some courses or program elements might involve **individualized feedback** to students in the form of personality, intelligence, values, or interest test scores or leadership behavior ratings. **Case studies** describe leadership situations and are used as a vehicle for leadership discussions. **Role playing** is also a popular methodology. In role playing, participants are assigned parts to play (such as a supervisor and an unmotivated subordinate) in a job-related scenario. Role playing has the advantage of letting trainees actually practice relevant skills and thus has greater transferability to the workplace than do didactic lectures or abstract discussions about leadership. **Simulations** and **games** are other methods of leader development. These are relatively structured activities designed to mirror some of the challenges or decisions commonly faced in the work environment. A newer approach puts participants in relatively unfamiliar territory (such as outdoors rather than offices) and presents them physical, emotionally arousing, and often team-oriented challenges.

All these sorts of methods likely contribute to development in a variety of ways, including providing opportunities for self-discovery, practice, and generalization of behaviors to multiple contexts and groups. As methodologies they share a capability to move learning from the purely cognitive domain to affective, social, and behavioral ones as well. Recent research suggests that development as a leader may most authentically and enduringly occur when the context and design of the experiences afford learners the opportunity to deeply *personalize* their lessons of experience. This might be, for example, through structured and psychologically safe opportunities to reflect on development experiences that students might have found personally disturbing or confusing.[34]

Leader Development in Organizational Settings

The title of this section does not imply that colleges and universities are not organizations; obviously they are. Nonetheless, college-based leadership studies differ in some significant ways from leader development programs one finds in the corporate sector or in the military. Most obvious, perhaps, is the fact that the essential purpose of college-based programs is to prepare students for their ultimate productive service as citizens, including in their own vocations. Our focus in this section is on methods of leader development provided in organizations not just for the individual's personal development but also (and maybe primarily) for the organization's benefit. Although all of the relatively short-term development methods just mentioned are used routinely in organizational programs, some of the most potent work-based leader development methods are longer-term in nature.

In light of the considerable amount spent on leadership development noted at the beginning of this chapter, it is reasonable to ask, "Is it worth it?" Until recently, there has been little basis for answering that question beyond the obvious fact that countless people must have *believed* it was worth it or else the money wouldn't have been spent. Nonetheless, leadership development has only recently been subjected to the same kind of rigorous analysis that other business decisions, especially capital investments, routinely face. That kind of analysis is used to determine **return on investment**, or ROI. The logic is rather straightforward. To illustrate a simple case, suppose that a leadership development program for one manager cost the company $2,000. The company would have a positive ROI, or a positive return on that investment, if after the training the increase in that manager's productivity was greater than $2,000. Such enhanced productivity might result from improved decision making, more motivated and better-managed direct reports, and more. What matters is that there is demonstrably improved leader behavior by the person who went through the development program. And, in fact, recent research indicates that, on average, the ROI for investments in leadership development is both positive and substantial.[35]

There are numerous leadership training programs aimed particularly toward leaders and supervisors in industry or public service. In many ways these have strong parallels to both the content and techniques used in university-level courses on leadership. However, these programs tend to be more focused than a university course that typically lasts an entire semester. The content of industry programs also depends on the organizational level of the recipients; programs for first-level supervisors focus on developing supervisory skills such as training, monitoring, giving feedback, and conducting performance reviews with subordinates. Generally these programs use lectures, case studies, and role-playing exercises to improve leadership skills. The programs for midlevel managers often focus on improving interpersonal, oral communication, and written communication skills, as well as giving tips on time management, planning, and goal setting. These programs rely more heavily on individualized feedback, case studies, presentations, role playing, simulations, and **in-basket exercises** to help leaders develop. With in-basket exercises, participants are given a limited amount of time to prioritize and respond to a number of notes, letters, and phone messages from a fictitious manager's in-basket. This technique is particularly useful in assessing and improving a manager's planning and time management skills. In leaderless group discussions, facilitators and observers rate participants on the degree of persuasiveness, leadership, followership, or conflict each member manifests in a group that has no appointed leader. These ratings are used to give managers feedback about their interpersonal and oral communication skills.

In reviewing the general field of leadership development and training, Conger offered this assessment: "Leadership programs can work, and work well, if they use a multi-tiered approach. Effective training depends on the combined use of four different teaching methods which I call personal growth, skill building, feedback, and conceptual awareness."[36] Some programs seek to stimulate leadership development by means of emotionally intense personal growth experiences such as river rafting, wilderness survival, and so forth. Leadership development through skill building involves structured activities focusing on the sorts of leadership skills featured in the final section of this book. Some approaches to leadership development emphasize individualized feedback about each person's strengths and weaknesses, typically based on standardized assessment methods. Feedback-based approaches can help identify "blind spots" an individual may be unaware of, as well as help prioritize which aspects of leadership development represent the highest priorities for development focus. Still other sorts of programs develop leadership by emphasizing its conceptual or intellectual components. An example of this approach would be an emphasis on theory and the use of case studies, common in many MBA programs. There are merits in each of these approaches, but Conger was on solid ground when he emphasized the value of combining elements of each. Highlight 2.4 can give you a more detailed look at leadership development in a company highly regarded for its work in this area.

In a related vein, others have emphasized that leader development in the 21st century must occur in more lifelike situations and contexts.[37] Toward that end, they have advocated creating better practice fields for leadership development analogous to the practice fields whereon skills in competitive sports are honed, or practice sessions analogous to those in music training wherein those skills are sharpened. Increasingly leadership development is occurring in the context of work itself.[38]

Leadership programs for senior executives and CEOs tend to focus on strategic planning, developing and communicating a vision, public relations, and interpersonal skills. Many times the entire senior leadership of a company will go through a leadership program at the same time. One goal of such a group might be to learn how to develop a strategic plan for their organization. To improve public relations skills, some programs have CEOs undergo simulated, unannounced interviews with television reporters and receive feedback on how they could have done better.

In the following sections we discuss research surrounding four popular and increasingly common methods of leader development: action learning, development planning, coaching, and mentoring. Some less well-established approaches to leadership development are described in Highlight 2.5.

Action Learning

Perhaps the best way to appreciate the nature of **action learning** is to contrast it with more traditional **training programs**. The latter term refers to leadership development activities that typically involve personnel attending a class, often for several days or even a week. In such classes, many of

Leadership Development in the Private Sector: 3M

HIGHLIGHT 2.4

3M is a science and product company that generates approximately $30 billion in annual revenues and consists of 85,000 employees located in more than 70 countries. Headquartered in St. Paul, Minnesota, the 65,000 products in 3M's portfolio include adhesives, abrasives, nanotechnology, electronics and software, lighting management, microreplication, and nonwoven materials and some 40 other technological platforms. Many of these products, such as Post-It notes, are highly recognizable. 3M has always put a premium on innovation, and to date its 8,000 research scientists have generated over 3,100 U.S. patents. Because of the success of its products, 3M has consistently been ranked as a top 10 Most Admired Company by *Fortune* magazine.

In 2006 the company noticed that the costs for getting new products to the market were rising at an alarming rate. 3M did not want to focus exclusively on reducing costs, however, as this could negatively impact the development of new products. Company managers believed that the key to improving both efficiency and innovation was employee engagement, which it defined as, "An individual's sense of purpose and focused energy, evident to others in the display of personal initiative, effort, and persistence directed towards organizational goals." 3M management felt that the more people who were engaged with their work, the more likely they would be to offer and execute ideas to improve innovation and reduce costs.

3M had been measuring employee satisfaction and attitudes toward work since the early 1950s and redesigned these companywide surveys as part of the focus on employee engagement. The data were collected in such a way that individual first-line supervisors, mid-level managers, country managers, regional executives, and functional managers could see the average engagement levels of their respective employees. At the same time, the Leadership Development function at 3M supplemented its offerings in order to educate leaders on what employee engagement is, how it can be a competitive advantage, and what they can do to improve it.

3M's Leadership Development function has been recognized as one of the best in the world and makes extensive use of leaders teaching leaders (i.e., the CEO and executive leadership team all spend time teaching leadership courses to fellow 3M leaders). The function's action learning programs are offered to some of the best and brightest in the company and consist of temporary teams that are tasked with developing ideas and business plans to generate an additional $25 million in sales or significant revenue and cost improvements within a geographic region. The function also offers traditional classroom training and hundreds of e-learning modules for leaders in first-line, mid-level, and executive-level leadership positions. Social media, do-it-yourself YouTube-type videos, blogs, wikis, and the like are also used extensively to teach leaders how to promote employee engagement. As a result of these leadership development efforts, overall employee engagement has improved dramatically to 4.8/5.0, new products are being released, revenues are growing, and costs are being managed more effectively.

3M's new CEO Inge Thulin, himself a product of this well-established company widely known for its innovation and leadership development, is also now bringing an even greater focus on people development. Within a week of his appointment as CEO, he announced a new vision for the company and six major business strategies, one of which was aimed directly at raising the bar even higher for "building high-performing and diverse global talent" at 3M. Certainly, many companies *think* leadership effectiveness at all levels is critical to driving an aggressive growth strategy: Thulin, however, has operationalized this, making development of all talent, including leaders, a core business strategy.

Sources: K. B. Paul and C. J. Johnson, "Engagement at 3M: A Case Study," in K. Oakes and P. Galagan (eds.), *The Executive Guide to Integrated Talent Management* (Alexandria, VA: American Society for Training and Development Press, 2011); http://money.cnn.com/magazines/fortune/most-admired/2012/full_list/; www.3M.com

Innovative Approaches to Leader Development

HIGHLIGHT 2.5

Several well-established methods of leader development are highlighted in this chapter such as coaching and mentoring, but many innovative or nontraditional approaches are also worth noting. We've listed a few of them here, grouped into three broad categories: arts-based approaches, technology-based approaches, and adventure-based approaches.

ARTS-BASED APPROACHES

Some arts-based approaches may be described as "projective" because they involve some form of artistic creation or interpretation that allows participants to reveal inner thoughts and feelings (the name *projective* was originally associated with the Rorschach Inkblot test, a projective psychological test). For example, visual images (such as photographs or artwork) can provide a stimulus for a person to elaborate on in describing some leadership theme (the best team I've ever been on, what it feels like to work in this company, or the like). It's striking how rich and candid a person's reflections typically are when made in response to something tangible like an evocative image. Another projective technique would be to use simple building materials (like Legos) and instruct participants to create some depiction (perhaps of their organizational structure or strategy). Critical skills such as demonstrating empathy can be learned with dramatic and theatrical training (especially valuable for medical personnel). And films, which often have high emotional impact, can be used to facilitate rich discussions of various leadership issues.

TECHNOLOGY-BASED APPROACHES

Video games and virtual reality simulations also open new doors for leadership development because they share several distinctly advantageous characteristics for training and development. For one thing, they require speedy thought and action. Actions that might take weeks or longer to unfold in real life can be compressed into hours or minutes, and thus the pace of leadership can be heightened. These venues also encourage risk taking, and leadership roles in gaming or virtual reality contexts are often temporary, involving frequent swapping of roles. Even the U.S. Air Force has developed virtual reality simulations for leadership development in situations that are complex, ambiguous, and highly interdependent.

What kinds of experiences at your college might be untapped leadership laboratories?

ADVENTURE-BASED APPROACHES

Organizations such as the National Outdoor Leadership School and Outward Bound use the unfamiliarity and inherent challenges of outdoor wilderness experience as a laboratory for leadership development. Learning to work effectively with diverse strangers while navigating difficult terrain, forging rivers, setting up tents, and fixing meals in foul-weather conditions creates countless opportunities to learn about oneself and how to work with others in novel and often stressful situations. It's not just the wilderness, though, that can provide a challenging environment for leadership development. Urban environments can too. The New York City Fire Department (FDNY) offers a program called the Firefighter for a Day Team Challenge, and the FDNY has partnered with the Wharton Business School in adapting the program for executive education. The program immerses participants in realistic firefighting scenarios such as a terrorist bus-bombing incident. The philosophy underlying most adventure-based approaches is that deeper levels of personal and interpersonal insight can occur when the context of learning is unfamiliar and one's customary repertoire of "office" survival skills and roles are inadequate and maybe even irrelevant.

Sources: S. S. Taylor and D. Ladkin, "Understanding Arts-Based Methods in Managerial Development," *Academy of Management Learning & Education* 8, no. 1 (2009), pp. 55–69; B. Reeves, T. W. Malone, and T. O'Driscoll, "Leadership's Online Labs," *Harvard Business Review,* May 2008, pp. 59–66; R. L. Hughes, and A. Stricker, "Outside-in and Inside-out Approaches to Transformation," in D. Neal, H. Friman, R. Doughty, and L. Wells (eds.), *Crosscutting Issues in International Transformation: Interactions and Innovations among People, Organizations, Processes, and Technology* (Washington, DC: Center for Technology and National Security Policy, National Defense University, 2009); J. Kanengieter and A. Rajagopal-Durbin, "Wilderness Leadership—On the Job," *Harvard Business Review,* April 2012, pp. 127–31; G. Peifer, "Soapbox: Learn to Take the Heat," trainingmag.com.

the kinds of developmental activities already mentioned might be included such as exercises, instrument-based feedback, and various presentations on different aspects of leadership. The key point is that attendance at a training program inherently involves time away from immediate job responsibilities. And while the various exercises presumably address many common leadership issues such as communication, conflict, feedback, and planning, the inevitably artificial nature of such activities make transfer back to the actual work situation more difficult.

Action learning, on the other hand, is the use of actual work issues and challenges as the developmental activity itself. The basic philosophy of action learning is that for adults in particular, the best learning is *learning by doing*. Furthermore, action learning often is conducted in teams of work colleagues who are addressing actual company challenges; the members of action learning teams are placed into problem-solving roles and are expected to reach team decisions concerning the challenge or problem, and formally present their analysis and recommendations to others (often senior executives in their own company). Importantly, action learning also involves built-in opportunities for feedback and reflection for the participants about the perceived quality of their analysis and recommendations as well as, ideally, about aspects of their respective individual strengths and weaknesses as leaders working on the collaborative project together.

In the past 15 years or so, action learning has gone from being a relatively rare development vehicle to being found in many companies' internal portfolios of leader development opportunities. Unfortunately, however, its demonstrated effectiveness for leader development, as distinguished from its use in generating fresh ideas for thorny company problems, has not kept pace with its increasing popularity and widespread use.

There are many reasons for this—not the least of which is that the links between a particular action learning project and its leadership challenges may be tenuous. Too often personnel are assigned to action learning teams assuming that they'll inevitably learn critical leadership lessons along the way; it usually doesn't happen so easily. If it were easy and automatic, we should expect more "leadership learning" from the experience of one's primary job and not need action learning at all. Furthermore, the very time-critical, high-visibility, and all-too-real elements that can make action learning problems so engaging and popular also often require a work pace that does not allow the kind of reflection we know is an important part of leader development. A final reason we'll mention here for why action learning projects may not achieve their desired leader development outcomes is because teams at work often fall prey to the same kinds of problems that you probably have experienced in team-based projects in your own academic coursework. It's one thing to *call* something a project requiring teamwork; it's quite another thing for the actual work on that project to truly *reflect* good teamwork. In poorly designed and supported action learning projects, the work might be dominated by one person or

When you're in a new job where you're stretched, your focus should be on learning, not getting an A.
**Mary Dee Hicks,
consultant**

by just one perspective within the organization. Action learning holds great promise but has not yet delivered uniform results.[39]

Development Planning

How many times have you resolved to change a habit, only to discover two months later that you are still exhibiting the same behaviors? This is often the fate of well-intentioned New Year's resolutions. Most people do not even make such resolutions because the failure rate is so high. Given this track record, you might wonder if it is possible to change one's behavior, particularly if an existing pattern has been reinforced over time and is exhibited almost automatically. Fortunately, however, it *is* possible to change behavior, even long-standing habits. For example, many people permanently quit smoking or drinking without any type of formal program. Others may change after they gain insight into how their behavior affects others. Some will need support to maintain a behavioral change over time, whereas others seem destined to never change.[40–42]

Managers seem to fall into the same categories; some managers change once they gain insight, others change with social and organizational support, and others may not ever change. But do people just fall into one of these groups by accident? Is there any way to stack the odds in favor of driving behavioral change? Research provides several suggestions that leaders can take to accelerate the development of their own leadership skills.[43–48] These include five critical behavioral change questions, and leaders must provide positive answers to all five questions if they want to maximize the odds of enduring behavior change taking place.

Question 1: Do leaders know which of their behaviors need to change? Leaders are capable of exhibiting hundreds of different behaviors, but do they precisely know which behaviors they need to start, stop, or keep doing to build effective teams or achieve better results? The insight component of the development pipeline is concerned with giving leaders accurate feedback on their strengths and development needs, and 360-degree feedback can provide useful information in this regard. Other sources of information about development needs can come from the results of an assessment center, a performance appraisal, or direct feedback from others.

Question 2: Is the leader motivated to change these behaviors? The next step in developing one's own leadership skills is working on development goals that matter. No leader has all of the knowledge and skills necessary to be successful; as a result most leaders have multiple development needs. Leaders need to determine which new skills will have the highest personal and organizational payoffs and build development plans that address these needs. The development plan should be focused on only one or two needs; plans addressing more than this tend to be overwhelming and unachievable. If leaders have more than two development needs, they should first work to acquire one or two skills before moving on to the next set of development needs.

Question 3: Do leaders have plans in place for changing targeted behaviors? For leaders, this means creating a written **development plan** that capitalizes on available books, seminars, college courses, e-learning modules, and so forth to acquire the knowledge underlying a particular development need (see Figure 2.3). For example, you can either learn how to delegate through the

FIGURE 2.3
Sample Individual Development Plan

Individual Development Plan (IDP)

Name: Mark McMurray   Supervisor: Steve Tolley   Planning Period: Apr–Dec 2014

Development Goals	Action Plans – Developmental Activities & Resources (What, Who, & How)	Time Line (Target Dates)	Criteria for Success (What will successful outcomes be?)
• Control reactions in stressful situations.	1. Set up a regular exercise routine (at least 5 times per week). 2. Exercise at least 5 times per week for at least 45 minutes. 3. Identify triggers and situations most likely to cause me to lose my temper. 4. Work with Steve Tolley to develop strategies to either avoid or cope with stressful situations.	NLT 30 April 2014 Review each week until end of year NLT 30 April 2014 Begin 30 April 2014	Boss does not receive any reports of emotional outbursts from now until Dec 2014. Higher manager ratings on end-of-year employee survey.

• Develop more patience when dealing with others.	1. Identify those people or situations that cause me to lose patience.
	2. Develop listening skills through consistent practice. Work with peers and direct reports to practice and demonstrate skills.
	   a) Wait my turn in conversation: work on not interrupting conversations.
	   b) Take notes in meetings to capture key messages and refer back to notes later.
	   c) Practice asking clarifying questions to probe issues and gain full understanding.
	3. Engage in two-way dialogue on a consistent basis. End conversations with a clear understanding of the purpose, discussion points, and resulting action items.
		NLT 15 May 2014
		
		Begin 15 May 2014
		
		Begin 15 May 2014
			Be viewed as approachable and responsive by all staff – Manager, Peers, and Associates.
			
			Have a better understanding of key issues, role responsibilities, and resulting actions. As a result, achieve better results on the job.
			
			Higher manager ratings on end of year employee survey.

• Improve team building skills.	1. Work with key direct reports to develop a common set of assumptions, vision, and goals for the team. 2. Work with Steve Tolley to review and upgrade team bench strength in light of team goals. 3. Work with team to develop common meeting, communication, decision-making, and accountability norms. 4. Work with Steve Tolley to develop strategies for motivating team members or acquiring the resources needed to achieve team goals. 5. Review progress on team goals with team members and Steve Tolley.	30 May 2014 30 June 2014 30 July 2014 30 July 2014 Monthly	Team assumptions, vision, and goals submitted to Steve Tolley for approval. Team consists of only A and B players as reviewed with Steve Tolley. New norms written up, sent to all team members, and reviewed on a regular basis with the team. Team results.

Source: G. J. Curphy, *Personal Insights and Development Planning Training Manual* (North Oaks, MN: Curphy Consulting Corporation, 2007).

The more you crash, the more you learn.
David B. Peterson, Personnel Decisions International

The only thing more painful than learning from experience is not learning from experience.
Archibald MacLeish, Librarian of Congress

school of hard knocks or take a seminar to learn the best delegation skills. As we will see, knowledge alone is not enough to develop a new skill, but relevant books and courses can accelerate the learning process.[49] In addition, it is important not to underestimate the power of a written development plan. Leaders (and followers) who have a written plan seem more likely to keep development on their radar screens and take the actions necessary to acquire new skills.

Question 4: Do leaders have opportunities to practice new skills? Taking courses and reading books are good ways for leaders to acquire foundational knowledge, but new skills will be acquired only when they are practiced on the job. Just as surgeons can read about and watch a surgery but will perfect a surgical technique only through repeated practice, so too will leaders acquire needed skills only if they practice them on the job. Therefore, good development plans use on-the-job experiences to hone needed leadership skills. Peterson maintains that most leadership positions offer ample opportunities to develop new skills, provided that leaders leverage all the experiences available to them. These on-the-job activities are so important to development that 70 to 80 percent of the action steps in a development plan should be job related.

Question 5: Are leaders held accountable for changing targeted behaviors? The last step in acquiring new skills is accountability, and there are several ways to make this happen with a development plan. One way to build in accountability is to have different people provide ongoing feedback on the action steps taken to develop a skill. For example, leaders could ask for feedback from a peer or direct report on their listening skills immediately after staff meetings. Another way to build accountability is to periodically review progress on development plans with the boss. This way the boss can look for opportunities to help the leader further practice developing skills and determine when it is time to add new development needs to the plan.

Development planning is more than a plan—it is really a process. Good development plans are constantly being revised as new skills are learned or new opportunities to develop skills become available. Leaders who take the time to write out and execute best-practice development plans usually report the most improvement in later 360-degree feedback ratings. Development planning provides a methodology for leaders to improve their behavior, and much of this development can occur as they go about their daily work activities.

Coaching

Development plans tend to be self-focused; leaders and followers use them as a road map for changing their own behaviors. When trying to change the behavior of followers, however, leaders can often do more than review followers' development plans or provide ongoing feedback. The next step in followers' development often involves coaching.

TABLE 2.1
The Five Steps of Informal Coaching

Source: D. B. Peterson and M. D. Hicks, *Leader as Coach: Strategies for Coaching and Developing Others* (Minneapolis, MN: Personnel Decisions International, 1996).

Forge a partnership: Coaching works only if there is a trusting relationship between the leader and his or her followers. In this step leaders also determine what drives their followers and where they want to go with their careers.
Inspire commitment: In this step leaders help followers determine which skills or behaviors will have the biggest payoff if developed. Usually this step involves reviewing the results of performance appraisals, 360-degree feedback, values, personality assessment reports, and so on.
Grow skills: Leaders work with followers to build development plans that capitalize on on-the-job experiences and create coaching plans to support their followers' development.
Promote persistence: Leaders meet periodically with followers to provide feedback, help followers keep development on their radar screens, and provide followers with new tasks or projects to develop needed skills.
Shape the environment: Leaders need to periodically review how they are role-modeling development and what they are doing to foster development in the workplace. Because most people want to be successful, doing this step well will help attract and retain followers to the work group.

The best executive is one who has enough sense to pick good men to do what he wants done, and the self-restraint to keep from meddling while they do it.

Theodore Roosevelt, U.S. president

Coaching is a key leadership skill that can help leaders improve the bench strength of the group, which in turn should help the group accomplish its goals. Because of its role in development, coaching can also help to retain high-quality followers.[50] Because of these outcomes, coaching is a popular topic these days, but it is also frequently misunderstood.

Coaching is the "process of equipping people with the tools, knowledge, and opportunities they need to develop and become more successful."[51] In general, there are two types of coaching: informal and formal. **Informal coaching** takes place whenever a leader helps followers to change their behaviors. According to Peterson and Hicks, the best informal coaching generally consists of five steps:[52] forging a partnership, inspiring commitment, growing skills, promoting persistence, and shaping the environment (see Table 2.1).

Several points about informal coaching are worth additional comment. First, the five-step process identified by Peterson and Hicks can be used by leadership practitioners to diagnose why behavioral change is *not* occurring and what can be done about it. For example, followers may not be developing new skills because they do not trust their leader, the skills have not been clearly identified or are not important to them, or they do not have a plan to acquire these skills. Second, informal coaching can and does occur anywhere in the organization. Senior executives can use this model to develop their staffs, peers can use it to help each other, and so forth. Third, this process is just as effective for high-performing followers as it is for low-performing followers. Leadership practitioners have a tendency to forget to coach their solid or top followers, yet these individuals are often making the greatest contributions to team or organizational success. Moreover, research has shown that the top performers in a job often

FIGURE 2.4
What Were the Most Useful Factors in the Coaching You Received?

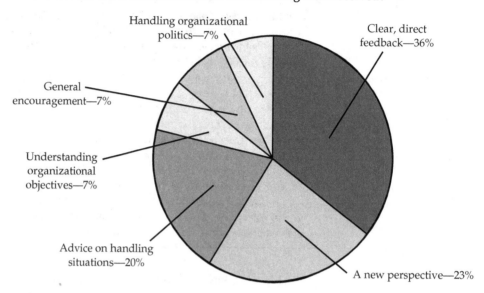

Handling organizational politics—7%

Clear, direct feedback—36%

General encouragement—7%

Understanding organizational objectives—7%

Advice on handling situations—20%

A new perspective—23%

Source: "The Business Leader as Development Coach," *PDI Portfolio,* Winter 1996, p. 6.

produce 20–50 percent more than the average performer, depending on the complexity of the job.[53] So if leaders would focus on moving their solid performers into the highest-performing ranks and making their top performers even better, chances are their teams might be substantially more effective than if they focused only on coaching those doing most poorly. It would also behoove coaches to be mindful of the kinds of coaching that coachees themselves regard as most helpful (see Figure 2.4).

Fourth, both "remote" coaching of people and coaching of individuals from other cultures can be particularly difficult.[54-55] It is more difficult for leaders to build trusting relationships with followers when they are physically separated by great distances. The same may be true with followers from other cultures—what may be important to, say, a Kenyan follower and how this person views the world may be very different from what his or her Dutch or Singaporean leader believes. For example, cultures vary in the extent to which members are receptive to feedback. The importance of "saving face" in certain cultures makes it correspondingly more challenging when coaching individuals from such cultures to give feedback (especially negative feedback) in ways that do not seem like an attack on the coachee.[56]

Most people are familiar with the idea of a personal fitness trainer—a person who helps design a fitness program tailored to a specific individual's needs and goals. **Formal coaching** programs provide a similar kind of service for executives and managers in leadership positions. Approximately 65 percent of the Global 1,000 companies use some form of formal coaching.[57] Formal coaching programs are individualized by their nature, but several common features deserve mention. There is a one-on-one relationship between the manager and the coach (that is, an internal or external consultant) that lasts from six months to more than a year. The process usually begins with the manager's completion of extensive tests of personality, intelligence, interests, and value; 360-degree feedback instruments; and interviews by the coach of other individuals in the manager's world of work. As the result of the assessment phase of this process, both the manager and the coach have a clear picture of development needs. The coach and the manager then meet regularly (roughly monthly) to review the results of the feedback instruments and work on building skills and practicing target behaviors. Role plays and videotape are used extensively during these sessions, and coaches provide immediate feedback to clients practicing new behaviors in realistic work situations. Another valuable outcome of coaching programs can involve clarification of managers' values, identification of discrepancies between their espoused values and their actual behaviors, and devising strategies to better align their behaviors with their values.

A formal coaching program can cost more than $100,000, and it is reasonable to ask if this money is well spent. A solid body of research shows that well-designed and well-executed coaching programs do in fact change behavior if, as Highlight 2.6 points out, certain conditions are met.[58–61] Figure 2.5 shows that coaching may be more effective at changing behavior than more traditional learning and training approaches. Moreover, the behavioral changes appear to be in place one year after the termination of a coaching program, indicating permanent behavioral change.[62] Such changes can be particularly important if the person making them—that is, the leader being coached—is highly placed or in a very responsible position. Most coaching candidates have hundreds, if not thousands, of subordinates, and usually oversee multimillion- or multibillion-dollar budgets. Thus the money spent on a coaching program can be relatively small in comparison to the budgets and resources the candidates control and as a result turn out to have a good return on investment.

Mentoring

In an organization, you also can gain valuable perspectives and insights through close association with an experienced person willing to take you under her or his wing. Such an individual is often called a **mentor,** after the character in Greek mythology whom Odysseus trusted to run his household and see to his son's education when Odysseus went off to fight the Trojans. Now, 3,000 years later, Mentor's name is used to describe the process by which an older and more experienced person helps to socialize and encourage younger organizational colleagues.[63]

Mentoring is a personal relationship in which a more experienced mentor (usually someone two to four levels higher in an organization)

No man is so foolish but he may sometimes give another good counsel, and no man so wise that he may not easily err if he takes no other counsel than his own. He that is taught only by himself has a fool for a master.

Ben Jonson

Parents are the first leadership trainers in life.

Bruce Avolio, leadership researcher

Some Critical Lessons Learned from Formal Coaching

HIGHLIGHT 2.6

1. **The person being coached must want to change.** It is difficult to get someone to change their behavior unless they want to change. Coaches need to ensure that coachees clearly understand the benefits of changing their behavior and the consequences if they do not change. Often it is much easier to get people to change when coaches link the new behaviors to coachees' values and career goals.

2. **Assessments are important.** Formal assessments involving personality, values, mental abilities, and multirater feedback are essential to understanding what behaviors coachees need to change, what is driving these needed changes, and how easy or difficult it will be to change targeted behaviors.

3. **Some behaviors cannot be changed.** Some behaviors are so ingrained or unethical that the best option may be termination. For example, one of the authors was asked to coach a married vice president who got two of his executive assistants pregnant in less than a year. Given that the coach was not an expert in birth control, the coach turned down the engagement.

4. **Practice is critical.** Good coaches not only discuss what needs to change, but also make coachees practice targeted behaviors. Often the initial practice takes place during coaching sessions, where the coach may play the role of another party and give the coachee feedback and suggestions for improvement. These practices are then extended to work, where the coachee must use these newly acquired behaviors in real-world situations.

5. **There is no substitute for accountability.** Superiors must be kept in the loop about coachees' progress and must hold them accountable for on-the-job changes. If coaches are working with potential derailment candidates, superiors must be willing to let coachees go if they do not make needed changes. Although fear and threats are not the best way to get people to change, some derailment candidates are in so much denial about their problems that it is only by fear of losing their high-status jobs that they are motivated to change.

As you read through this list of coaching "best practices," how might you distinguish good coaching from giving advice?

Sources: S. Berglas, "The Very Real Dangers of Executive Coaching," *Harvard Business Review,* June 2002, pp. 86–93; G. J. Curphy, "What Role Should I/O Psychologists Play in Executive Education?" in *Models of Executive Education,* R. T. Hogan (chair), presentation at the 17th Annual Society for Industrial and Organizational Psychology, Toronto, Canada, April 2002.

acts as a guide, role model, and sponsor of a less experienced protégé. Mentors provide protégés with knowledge, advice, challenge, counsel, and support about career opportunities, organizational strategy and policy, office politics, and so forth. Although mentoring has a strong developmental component, it is not the same as coaching. One key difference is that mentoring may not target specific development needs. Protégés often meet with their mentors to get a different perspective on the organization or for advice on potential committee and task force assignments or promotion opportunities. Another difference is that this guidance is not coming from the protégé's immediate supervisor, but rather from someone several leadership levels higher in the organization. Protégés often do receive informal coaching from their bosses but may be

FIGURE 2.5
The Power of Coaching

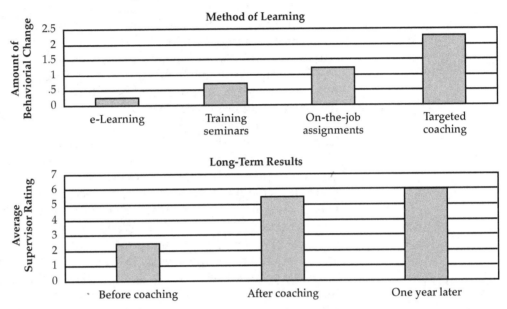

Source: D. B. Peterson, *Individual Coaching Services: Coaching That Makes a Difference* (Minneapolis, MN: Personnel Decisions International, 1999).

more apt to seek career guidance and personal advice from their mentors. Another difference is that the mentor may not even be part of the organization. A mentor may have retired from the organization or may have been someone for whom the protégé worked a number of years earlier.

As in coaching, there are both formal and informal mentoring programs. *Informal mentoring* occurs when a protégé and mentor build a long-term relationship based on friendship, similar interests, and mutual respect. These relationships often begin with the protégé working in some part of the mentor's organization or on a high-visibility project for the mentor. *Formal mentoring* programs occur when the organization assigns a relatively inexperienced but high-potential leader to one of the top executives in the company. The protégé and mentor get together on a regular basis so the protégé can gain exposure and learn more about how decisions are made at the top of the organization. Often organizations implement formal mentoring programs to accelerate the development of female or minority protégés.[64–66]

Mentoring is quite prevalent in many organizations today. Researchers reported that 74 percent of the noncommissioned officers and officers in the U.S. Army had mentors and 67 percent of all U.S. Navy admirals had mentors sometime in their careers. Moreover, many admirals reported having an average of 3.5 mentors by the time they retired.[67–69] Other researchers have reported positive relationships between mentoring, personal learning, career satisfaction, pay, promotions, and retention.[70-74] But some of this research also found that formal mentoring programs were better than no mentoring programs but less effective than informal mentoring for protégé compensation and promotion.[75-77] The reason for these diminished results may be that most formal mentoring programs have a difficult time replicating the strong emotional bonds found in informal programs. In addition, most formal mentoring programs last only a year, whereas many informal mentoring relationships can last a lifetime.

Thomas examined the role mentoring played in the careers of minority leaders. He reported that minority leaders at the top of their organizations often had two key qualities. First, successful minority executives were concerned with getting the right experiences and developing the right foundation of leadership skills when they first joined the organization. Their focus was more on personal growth at each leadership level than with titles and rewards. Second, they had an extensive set of mentors and corporate sponsors who provided guidance and support over their careers. These mentors and sponsors helped the executives to develop the "three Cs" critical to advancement: confidence, competence, and credibility. Thomas also stated that the most successful white mentor–minority protégé relationships recognized that race was a potential barrier to advancement but were still able to bring up and work through touchy issues. Less successful white mentor–minority protégé relationships engaged in "protective hesitation," in which race or sensitive issues were avoided, ignored, or discounted.[78] Because of the benefits of informal mentoring, leadership practitioners should look for opportunities to build mentoring relationships with senior leaders whenever possible. However, it is important to realize that protégés cannot make these relationships happen by themselves. In many cases mentors seek out protégés, or mentors and protégés seek out each other to build relationships. But leaders and leaders-to-be can do a couple of things to improve the odds of finding a mentor. The first step is to do one's current job extremely well. Mentors are always looking for talent, and they are unlikely to take someone under their wing who appears unmotivated or incompetent. The second step is to look for opportunities to gain visibility and build social relationships with potential mentors. Working on a key task force, doing presentations for the executive committee, or signing up for community activities sponsored by a top executive are just a few pathways one could take to gain the attention of potential mentors.

Building Your Own Leadership Self-Image

This chapter has explored various aspects of how leadership develops, but we must acknowledge that not everyone *wants* to be a leader or believes he or she can be. John Gardner has argued that many of our best and brightest young people actually have been immunized against, and dissuaded from, seeking leadership opportunities and responsibilities.[79] Other young people, even if they want to be leaders, may not believe they have what it takes. Both groups, we believe, are selling themselves short.

For those who merely want to avoid the responsibilities of leadership, we encourage an openness of mind about leadership's importance and pervasiveness. We hope this book offers ways of thinking about leadership that make it at once more immediate, more relevant, and more interesting than it may have seemed before. For others, we encourage flexibility in self-image. Do not stay out of the leadership arena based on some self-defeating generalization such as "I am not the leader type." Experiment and take a few risks with different leadership roles. This will help you appreciate new facets of yourself as well as broaden your leadership self-image. It would be wise, in fact, to build your leadership self-image through carefully selected developmental experiences that don't necessarily have the words "leadership development" emblazoned across them. See, for example, the kind of developmental experience described in Highlight 2.7.

Being Intentional about Your Own Development

HIGHLIGHT 2.7

We subtitled this book "Enhancing the Lessons of Experience" to underscore that people can strengthen their leadership effectiveness by "mining" the developmental value of their own life experiences. Internships are one popular form of developmental experience, and this highlight describes how a young woman named Tierney Ducharme was impressively intentional in both choosing her internship and in learning from it.

Tierney graduated from Furman University in South Carolina in 2008 with a degree in communications. After graduation she explored various post-graduate internship opportunities to further broaden and enrich her experience before jumping into regular career employment. Her ideal internship would offer international travel and cross-cultural experience, contribute in some way to the broad field of human rights, and entail actual responsibilities that could translate directly into a follow-on job in her chosen field of communications.

Tierney was selected for and accepted a year-long internship with International Justice Mission (IJM), a global human rights organization headquartered in Washington, D.C. IJM's mission is to bring rescue to victims of slavery, sexual exploitation, and other forms of violent oppression. As Tierney discovered first-hand, human slavery today is a scourge grossly underestimated and misunderstood by most people: There are, unbelievably, more slaves being held today than during the 400-year-long transatlantic slave trade.

Tierney was selected to serve as an intern in one of IJM's field offices in India, and she was among the very first interns in IJM history to serve in an overseas position with responsibilities specifically focused in the communications arena. In that role she helped pioneer a new model of embedding "reporters" in IJM's overseas field offices. As an embedded reporter, Tierney's role was to help tell the story about IJM's slave rescue operations in India to both IJM staff and concerned citizens around the

continued

continued

world. She did this by writing articles about rescue operations and by preparing training presentations and materials for professional staff and local community leaders. In order to let the field office's staff of lawyers, social workers, and investigators focus their energy and expertise for maximum impact, she also helped in more administrative ways like setting up paper and electronic record-keeping systems.

Tierney credits her internship experience with providing powerful developmental lessons. By working in a cross-cultural context she learned the importance of not letting her perceptions and behavior be limited by naive expectations. She said, in fact, that the fewer expectations she brought into a situation, the more she could relax, enjoy it, and pay attention to what was actually happening around her. She also learned the importance of active and continuous learning, especially in unfamiliar environments. She learned to listen and pay attention to local norms before speaking up too quickly or taking immediate action; it took longer,

but this more deliberate approach proved more effective in the long run. She learned that doing mundane things with humility was a good way to earn the trust and respect of others. She became more aware of herself as a global citizen.

Perhaps most importantly, Tierney says it was "hugely impactful and inspiring to work alongside Indian colleagues and leaders who were so passionate about changing conditions and ending slavery in India." It did, in fact, crystallize the kind of career she wanted to pursue when her internship ended. As a result, Tierney continues to work at IJM, but her role now is supporting and equipping *all* of the communications interns in the organization's now even larger internship program. She is the person at IJM headquarters who manages and edits all the stories from IJM's global field offices about their ongoing worldwide educational efforts and rescue operations.

It seems fair to say that Tierney was intentional about her own development, and so masterful in it that she impressed her organization that they couldn't do without her!

Summary

This chapter reviewed several major points regarding how leadership can be developed through both formal education and experience. One way to get more out of your leadership courses and experiences is through the application of the action–observation–reflection model. This model provides a framework for better understanding of leadership situations. In addition, being aware of the role perception plays in leadership development is important because it affects what you observe, how you interpret your observations, and what actions you take as a leader. Finally, remember that both education and experience can contribute to your development as a leader by enhancing your ability to reflect on and analyze leadership situations. Exposure to formal leadership education programs can help you develop multiple perspectives to analyze leadership situations, and the people you work with and the task itself can also provide you with insights on how to be a better leader. However, what you gain from any leadership program or experience is a function of what you make of it. Successful leaders are those who have "an extraordinary tenacity in extracting something worthwhile from their experience and in seeking experiences rich in opportunities for growth."[80] If you want to become a better leader, you must seek challenges and try to get all you can from any leadership situation or opportunity.

The chapter also examined several specific ways of changing behavior and developing leadership. For most people, behavior change efforts will be most successful if some formal system or process of behavioral change is put into place; these systems include development planning, informal and formal coaching programs, and mentorships. Development planning is the process of pinpointing development needs, creating development plans, implementing plans, and reflecting on and revising plans regularly. Good development plans focus on one or two development needs, capitalize upon on-the-job experiences, and specify sources of feedback. Organizations with formal development systems are likely to realize greater behavioral changes from more managers than organizations having no system or only an informal one.

Leaders can create development plans for themselves, and they can also help their followers with behavioral change through coaching or mentoring programs. Informal coaching programs often consist of a series of steps designed to create permanent behavioral changes in followers, and both leaders and followers play active roles in informal coaching programs. Formal coaching typically involves a formal assessment process and a series of one-on-one coaching sessions over a 6- to 12-month period. These sessions target specific development needs and capitalize on practice and feedback to acquire needed skills. Mentoring programs have many of the same objectives as coaching programs but take place between an individual (the protégé) and a leader several levels higher in the organization (the mentor).

Key Terms

action–observation–reflection model, *45*
spiral of experience, *45*
perceptual set, *48*
attribution, *49*
fundamental attribution error, *50*
self-serving bias, *50*
actor/observer difference, *50*
self-fulfilling prophecy, *50*

single-loop learning, *54*
double-loop learning, *54*
after event reviews, *55*
service learning, *58*
individualized feedback, *60*
case studies, *60*
role playing, *60*
simulations, *60*
games, *60*
return on investment, *61*

in-basket exercises, *61*
action learning, *62*
training programs, *62*
development plan, *67*
development planning, *68*
coaching, *69*
informal coaching, *69*
formal coaching, *70*
mentor, *71*
mentoring, *71*

Questions

1. Not all effective leaders seem to be reflective by nature. How do you reconcile that with the concept of the spiral of experience and its role in leadership development?

2. Explain how you can use knowledge about each of the following to enrich the benefits of your own present leadership experiences:

    a. The action–observation–reflection model.

    b. The people you interact and work with.

    c. The activities you're involved in.

3. Using the role of teacher as a specific instance of leadership, discuss how a teacher's perceptual set, expectations of students, and attributions may affect student motivation and performance. Do you think some teachers could become more effective by becoming more aware of these processes? Would that be true for leaders in general?

4. If you were to design the perfect leadership development experience for yourself, how would you do so and what would it include? How would you know whether it was effective?

5. Do you think people have a need for growth and development?

6. One important aspect of learning from experience is observing the consequences of one's actions. Sometimes, however, the most significant consequences of a leader's actions do not occur for several years (for example, the ultimate impact of certain personnel decisions or a strategic decision to change a product line). Is there any way individuals can learn from the consequences of those actions in a way to modify their behavior? If consequences are so delayed, is there a danger they might draw the wrong lessons from their experiences?

7. What would a development plan for student leaders look like? How could you capitalize on school experiences as part of a development plan?

8. What would a leadership coaching or mentoring program for students look like? How could you tell whether the program worked?

Activities

1. Divide yourselves into groups, and in each group contrast what attributions you might make about the leadership style of two different individuals. All you know about them is the following:

	Person A	Person B
Favorite TV Show	*60 Minutes*	*Survivor*
Car	Ford Mustang	Volkswagen Beetle
Favorite Sport	American football	Mountain biking
Political Leaning	Conservative Republican	Liberal Democrat
Favorite Music	Country and western	New age

2. Read the development planning material in Chapter 11 of this book. Complete a GAPS analysis and create a development plan for yourself. Share your development plan with someone else in your class. Check with your partner in two to four weeks to review progress on your plans.

Minicase

Developing Leaders at UPS

UPS is the nation's fourth-largest employer with 357,000 employees worldwide and operations in more than 200 countries. UPS is consistently recognized as one of the "top companies to work for" and was recently recognized by *Fortune* as one of the 50 best companies for minorities. A major reason for UPS's success is the company's commitment to its employees. UPS understands the importance of providing both education and experience for its next generation of leaders—spending $300 million annually on education programs for employees and encouraging promotion from within. All employees are offered equal opportunities to build the skills and knowledge they need to succeed. A perfect example of this is Jovita Carranza.

Jovita Carranza joined UPS in 1976 as a part-time clerk in Los Angeles. Carranza demonstrated a strong work ethic and a commitment to UPS, and UPS rewarded her with opportunities—opportunities Carranza was not shy about taking advantage of. By 1985 Carranza was the workforce planning manager in metropolitan Los Angeles. By 1987 she was district human resources manager based in Central Texas. By 1990 she had accepted a move to district human resources manager in Illinois. She received her first operations assignment, as division manager for hub, package, and feeder operations, in Illinois in 1991. Two years later, she said yes to becoming district operations manager in Miami. In 1996 she accepted the same role in Wisconsin. By 1999 Carranza's progressive successes led UPS to promote her to president of the Americas Region. From there she moved into her current position as vice president of UPS Air Operations, based in Louisville, Kentucky.

The $1.1 billion air hub she currently oversees sprawls across the equivalent of more than 80 football fields. It can handle 304,000 packages an hour, its computers process nearly 1 million transactions per minute, and it serves as the lynchpin for the $33 billion business that has become the world's largest package delivery company.

Carranza attributes much of her success to her eagerness to take on new challenges: "The one error that people make early on in their careers is that they're very selective about opportunities so they avoid some, prefer others," she says. "I always accepted all opportunities that presented themselves because from each one you can learn something, and they serve as a platform for future endeavors."

It has also been important, she says, to surround herself with capable, skilled employees who are loyal to the company and committed to results. After nearly 30 years with UPS, Carranza says teamwork, interaction, and staff development are the achievements of which she is proudest: "Because that takes focus, determination, and sincerity to perpetuate the UPS culture and enhance it through people."

Carranza's corporate achievements, determination, drive, innovation, and leadership in business have earned her the distinction of being named *Hispanic Business Magazine*'s Woman of the Year. She credits her parents, both of Mexican descent, with teaching her "the importance of being committed, of working hard, and doing so with a positive outlook"—principles she says continue to guide her personal and professional life. These principles mirror those of the company whose corporate ladder she has climbed nonstop, an organization she says values diversity and encourages quality, integrity, commitment, fairness, loyalty, and social responsibility.

Among Carranza's words of wisdom: "Sit back and listen and observe," she says. "You learn more by not speaking. Intelligent people learn from their own experiences; with wisdom, you learn from other people's mistakes. I'm very methodical about that."

1. What are the major skills Jovita Carranza has demonstrated in her career at UPS that have made her a successful leader?

2. Consider the spiral of experience that Jovita Carranza has traveled. How has her experience affected her ability as a leader?

3. Do you think Jovita Carranza's performance and rise in UPS would have been similarly impressive if she worked in the corporate sector rather than the government?

Sources: http://www.ups.com; http://www.hispaniconline.com/vista/febhisp.htm; http://www.hispanicbusiness.com/news/newsbyid.asp?id=15535&page=3; http://www.socialfunds.com/csr/profile.cgi/1841.html.

End Notes

1. Kaiser, R.B. (2013, April). *Why is the Leadership Industry Failing?* Symposium presented at the 28th Annual Conference of the Society for Industrial and Organizational Psychology, Houston, TX.

2. D. V. Day, "Leadership Development: A Review in Context," *Leadership Quarterly* 11, no. 4 (2000), pp. 581–613.

3. P. Bernthal and R. Wellins, "Trends in Leader Development and Succession," *Human Resource Planning* 29, no. 2 (2006), pp. 31–40.

4. M. McCall, "Recasting Leadership Development," *Industrial and Organizational Psychology* 3 (2010), pp. 3–19.

5. M. W. McCall Jr., M. M. Lombardo, and A. M. Morrison, *The Lessons of Experience: How Successful Executives Develop on the Job* (Lexington, MA: Lexington Books, 1988), p. 122.

6. D. Kolb, *Experiential Learning: Experience as the Source of Learning and Development* (Englewood Cliffs, NJ: Prentice Hall, 1983).

7. C. Powell, with Joe Pirsico, *My American Journey* (New York: Random House, 1995), p. 109.

8. Ibid.

9. J. Reason and K. Mycielska, *Absent-Minded? The Psychology of Mental Lapses and Everyday Errors* (Englewood Cliffs, NJ: Prentice Hall, 1982), p. 183.

10. L. Ross, "The Intuitive Psychologist and His Shortcomings: Distortions in the Attribution Process," in *Advances in Experimental Social Psychology* 10, ed. L. Berkowitz (New York: Academic Press, 1977), pp. 173–220.

11. D. T. Millerand M. Ross, "Self-Serving Biases in the Attribution of Causality: Fact or Fiction?" *Psychological Bulletin* 82 (1975), pp. 213–25.

12. E. E. Jones and R. E. Nisbett, "The Actor and the Observer: Divergent Perceptions of the Causes of Behavior," in *Attribution: Perceiving the Causes of Behavior,* eds. E. E. Jones, D. E. Kanouse, H. H. Kelley, R. E. Nisbett, S. Valins, and B. Weiner (Morristown, NJ: General Learning Press, 1972).

13. S. G. Green and T. R. Mitchell, "Attributional Processes of Leaders in Leader–Member Interactions," *Organizational Behavior and Human Performances* 23 (1979), pp. 429–58.

14. T. R. Mitchell, S. G. Green, and R. E. Wood, "An Attributional Model of Leadership and the Poor Performing Subordinate: Development and Validation," in *Research in Organizational Behavior,* eds. B. M. Staw and L. L. Cummings (Greenwich, CN: JAI, 1981), pp. 197–234.

15. T. R. Mitchell and R. E. Wood, "Supervisors Responses to Subordinate Poor Performance: A Test of an Attributional Model," *Organizational Behavior and Human Performance* 25 (1980), pp. 123–38.

16. E. E. Jones, "Interpreting Interpersonal Behavior: The Effects of Expectancies," *Science* 234, no. 3 (October 1986), pp. 41–46.

17. D. Eden and A. B. Shani, "Pygmalion Goes to Boot Camp: Expectancy, Leadership, and Trainee Performance," *Journal of Applied Psychology* 67 (1982), pp. 194–99.

18. K. D. Roglio and G. Light, "Executive MBA Programs: The Development of the Reflective Executive," *Academy of Management Learning & Education* 8, no. 2 (2009), pp. 156–73.

19. J. L. Lindsey, "Fine Art Metaphors Reveal Leader Archetypes," *Journal of Leadership & Organizational Studies* 18 (2011), 56–63.

20. C. Argyris, *Increasing Leadership Effectiveness* (New York: John Wiley, 1976).

21. S. S. DeRue, J. D. Nahrgang, J. R. Hollenbeck, and K. Workman, "A Quasi-Experimental Study of After-Event Reviews and Leadership Development," *Journal of Applied Psychology* 97, no. 5 (2012), 997–1015.

22. K. A. Bunker and A. Webb, *Learning How to Learn from Experience: Impact of Stress and Coping,* Report No. 154 (Greensboro, NC: Center for Creative Leadership, 1992).

23. I. L. Janis, *Stress and Frustration* (New York: Harcourt Brace Jovanovich, 1971).

24. R. J. Grey and G. G. Gordon, "Risk-Taking Managers: Who Gets the Top Jobs?" *Management Review* 67 (1978), pp. 8–13.

25. D. C. Hambrick, "Environment, Strategy and Power within Top Management Teams," *Administrative Science Quarterly* 26 (1981), pp. 253–75.

26. G. Jennings, *The Mobile Manager* (New York: McGraw-Hill, 1971).

27. E. Schein, *Career Dynamics: Matching Individual and Organizational Needs* (Reading, MA: Addison-Wesley, 1978).

28. M. Csikszentmihalyi, *Flow: The Psychology of Optimal Experience* (New York: Harper & Row, 1990), p. 142.

29. R. T. Hogan and R. Warrenfelz, "Educating the Modern Manager," *Academy of Management Learning and Education* 2, no. 1 (2003), pp. 74–84.

30. R. E. Riggio, "Leadership Development: The Current State and Future Expectations," *Consulting Psychology Journal: Practice and Research* 60, no. 4 (2008), pp. 383–92.

31. R. E. Riggio, J. B. Ciulla, and G. J. Sorenson, "Leadership Education at the Undergraduate Level: A Liberal Arts Approach to Leadership Development," in S. E. Murphy and R. E. Riggio (eds.), *The Future of Leadership Development*, pp. 223–36 (Mahwah, NJ: Lawrence Erlbaum Associates).

32. Ibid.

33. Ibid.

34. G. P. Insed, J. D. Wood, and J. L. Petriglieri, "Up Close and Personal: Building Foundations for Leaders' Development through the Personalization of Management Learning," *Academy of Management Learning & Education*, 10, no. 3 (2011), 430–50.

35. B.J. Avolio, J.B. Avey and D. Quisenberry, "Estimating Return on Leadership Development Investment," *The Leadership Quarterly* 21 (2010), 633–44.

36. J. Conger, "Can We Really Train Leadership?" *Strategy, Management, Competition*, Winter 1996, pp. 52–65.

37. M. Nevins and S. Stumpf, "21st-Century Leadership: Redefining Management Education," *Strategy, Management, Competition*, 3rd quarter (1999), pp. 41–51.

38. G. Hernez-Broome and R. L. Hughes, "Leadership Development: Past, Present and Future," *Human Resource Planning* 27, no. 1 (2004), pp. 24–32.

39. J. A. Conger and G. Toegel, "Action Learning and Multirater Feedback: Pathways to Leadership Development?" in *The Future of Leadership Development*, eds. S. E. Murphy and R. E. Riggio, pp. 107–125 (Mahwah, NJ: Lawrence Erlbaum Associates, 2003).

40. W. R. Miller, and S. Rollnick, *Motivational Interviewing: Preparing People to Change Addictive Behavior* (New York: Guilford Press, 1991).

41. J. Polivy and C. P. Herman, "If at First You Don't Succeed: False Hopes of Self-Change," *American Psychologist* 57, no. 9 (2002), pp. 677–89.

42. M. D. Peterson and M. D. Hicks, *Development FIRST: Strategies for Self-Development* (Minneapolis, MN: Personnel Decisions International, 1995).

43. J. F. Hazucha, S. A. Hezlett, and R. J. Schneider, "The Impact of 360-Degree Feedback on Management Skills Development," *Human Resource Management* 32 (1993), pp. 325–51.

44. C. D. McCauley, M. N. Ruderman, P. J. Ohlott, and J. E. Morrow, "Assessing the Developmental Components of Managerial Jobs," *Journal of Applied Psychology* 79, no. 4 (1994), pp. 544–60.

45. D. B. Peterson and M. D. Hicks, *Leader as Coach: Strategies for Coaching and Developing Others* (Minneapolis, MN: Personnel Decisions International, 1996).

46. K. Behar, D. Arvidson, W. Omilusik, B. Ellsworth, and B. Morrow, *Developing Husky Oil Leaders: A Strategic Investment* (Calgary, Canada: Husky Energy, 2000).

47. D. B. Peterson, *The Science and Art of Self-Development.* Paper presented at the Arabian States Human Resource Management Society Annual Conference, Bahrain, October 2001.

48. G. J. Curphy, "Good Leadership Is Hard to Find," *JobDig,* August 21–28 (2006), pp. 23–24.

49. W. Arthur, Jr., W. Bennett, Jr., P. S. Edens, and S. T. Bell. "Effectiveness of Training in Organizations: A Meta-analysis of Design and Evaluation Features," *Journal of Applied Psychology* 88, no. 2 (2003), pp. 234–45.

50. K. M. Wasylyshyn, B. Gronsky, and J. W. Hass, "Tigers, Stripes, and Behavior Change: Survey Results of a Commissioned Coaching Program," *Consulting Psychology Journal* 58, no. 2 (2006), pp. 65–81.

51. Peterson and Hicks, *Leader as Coach: Strategies for Coaching and Developing Others.*

52. Ibid.

53. J. E. Hunter, F. L. Schmidt, and M. K. Judiesch, "Individual Differences in Output Variability as a Function of Job Complexity," *Journal of Applied Psychology* 74 (1990), pp. 28–42.

54. G. J. Curphy, *The Accelerated Coaching Program Training Manual* (North Oaks, MN: Curphy Consulting Corporation, 2003).

55. D. B. Peterson and M. D. Hicks, *Professional Coaching: State of the Art, State of the Practice* (Minneapolis, MN: Personnel Decisions International, 1998).

56. C. W. Coultas, W. L. Bedwell, C. S. Burke, and E. Salas, "Values Sensitive Coaching: The Delta Approach to Coaching Culturally Diverse Executives," *Consulting Psychology Journal: Practice and Research* 63, no. 3 (2011), pp. 149–61.

57. Peterson and Hicks, *Professional Coaching: State of the Art, State of the Practice.*

58. K. M. Wasylyshyn, B. Gronsky, and J. W. Hass, "Tigers, Stripes, and Behavior Change: Survey Results of a Commissioned Coaching Program," *Consulting Psychology Journal* 58, no. 2 (2006), pp. 65–81.

59. W. J. G. Evers, A. Brouwers, and W. Tomic. "A Quasi-Experimental Study on Management Coaching Effectiveness." *Consulting Psychology Journal* 58, no. 3 (2006), pp. 174–82.

60. D. B. Peterson and J. Millier, "The Alchemy of Coaching: You're Good, Jennifer, But You Could Be Really Good," *Consulting Psychology Journal* 57 no. 1 (2005), pp. 14–40.

61. S. V. Bowles and J. J. Picano, "Dimensions of Coaching Related to Productivity and Quality of Life," *Consulting Psychology Journal* 58, no. 4 (2006), pp. 232–39.

62. D. B. Peterson, *Individual Coaching Services: Coaching That Makes a Difference* (Minneapolis, MN: Personnel Decisions International, 1999).

63. J. A. Wilson and N. S. Elman, "Organizational Benefits of Mentoring," *Academy of Management Executive* 4 (1990), pp. 88–93.

64. Ragins, B. R., J. L. Cotton, and J. S. Miller. "Marginal Mentoring: The Effects of Types of Mentor, Quality of Relationship, and Program Design of Work and Career Attitudes," *Academy of Management Journal* 43, no. 6 (2000), pp. 1177–94.

65. D. A. Thomas, "The Truth about Mentoring Minorities: Race Matters," *Harvard Business Review,* April (2001), pp. 98–111.

66. Menttium. *Menttium 100: Cross-Company Mentoring for High Potential Women.* Minneapolis, MN: The Menttium Corporation, 2007.

67. A. G. Steinberg and D. M. Foley, "Mentoring in the Army: From Buzzword to Practice," *Military Psychology* 11, no. 4 (1999), pp. 365–80.

68. R. Lall, "Mentoring Experiences of Retired Navy Admirals," paper presented at Personnel Decisions International, Denver, CO, May 6, 1999.

69. S. C. De Janasz, S. E. Sullivan, and V. Whiting, "Mentor Networks and Career Success: Lessons for Turbulent Times," *Academy of Management Executive* 17, no. 3 (2003), pp. 78–88.

70. Menttium. *Menttium 100: Cross-Company Mentoring for High Potential Women* (Minneapolis, MN: The Menttium Corporation, 2007).

71. T. D. Allen, L. T. Eby, M. L. Poteet, E. Lentz, and L. Lima, "Career Benefits Associated with Mentoring for Protégés: A Meta-analysis," *Journal of Applied Psychology* 89, no. 1 (2004), pp. 127–36.

72. T. D. Allen, L. T. Eby, and E. Lentz. "The Relationship between Formal Mentoring Program Characteristics and Perceived Program Effectiveness," *Personnel Psychology* 59 (2006), pp. 125–53.

73. L. T. Eby, M. Butts, A. Lockwood, and S. A. Simon, "Protégés' Negative Mentoring Experiences: Construct Development and Nomological Validation," *Personnel Psychology* 57, no. 2 (2004), pp. 411–48.

74. M. Abrahams, "Making Mentoring Pay," *Harvard Business Review,* June 2006, p. 21.

75. B. R. Ragins, J. L. Cotton, and J. S. Miller, "Marginal Mentoring: The Effects of Types of Mentor, Quality of Relationship, and Program Design of Work and Career Attitudes," *Academy of Management Journal* 43, no. 6 (2000), pp. 1177–94.

76. T. D Allen, L. T. Eby, and E. Lentz, "Mentorship Behaviors and Mentorship Quality Associated with Formal Mentoring Programs: Closing the Gap between Research and Practice," *Journal of Applied Psychology* 91, no. 3 (2006), pp. 567–78.

77. Allen, Eby, and Lentz, "The Relationship between Formal Mentoring Program Characteristics."

78. Thomas, "The Truth about Mentoring Minorities."

79. J. W. Gardner, "The Antileadership Vaccine," essay in the Carnegie Corporation of New York annual report, 1965.

80. McCall Jr., Lombardo, and Morrison, *The Lessons of Experience.*

Chapter 4

Power and Influence

Introduction

We begin Part 2 by examining the phenomenon of power. Some of history's earliest characterizations of leaders concerned their use of power. Shakespeare's plays were concerned with the acquisition and failing of power,[1] and Machiavelli's *The Prince* has been described as the "classic handbook on power politics."[2] Current scholars have also emphasized the need to conceptualize leadership as a power phenomenon.[3,4] Power may be the single most important concept in all the social sciences,[5] though scholars today disagree over precisely how to define power or influence. But it's not just scholars who have different ideas about power. The concept of power is so pervasive and complex that each of us probably thinks about it a little differently.

What comes to *your* mind when you think about power? Do you think of a person wielding enormous authority over others? Do you think of high office? Do you think of making others do things against their will? Is power ethically neutral, or is it inherently dangerous as Lord Acton said? ("Power corrupts, and absolute power corrupts absolutely.") Do you think a leader's real power is always obvious to others? What sorts of things might enhance or detract from a leader's power? What are the pros and cons of different ways of trying to influence people? These are the kinds of issues we will explore in this chapter.

Some Important Distinctions

Power has been defined as the capacity to produce effects on others[6] or the potential to influence others.[7] Although we usually think of power as belonging to the leader, it is actually a function of the leader, the followers, and the situation. Leaders have the potential to influence their followers' behaviors and attitudes. However, followers also can affect the leader's behavior and attitudes. Even the situation itself can affect a leader's capacity to influence followers (and vice versa). For example, leaders who can reward and punish followers may have a greater capacity to influence followers than leaders who cannot use rewards or punishments. Similarly, follower or situational characteristics may diminish a leader's potential to influence followers, such as when the latter belong to a strong, active union.

The fact that power is not merely a function of leaders is reflected in the continuing research on the use of power in organizations. Not only has there been ongoing research to examine the negotiation of power dynamics within and across organizations,[8] but also research examining power relationships between shareholders and governance boards[9] and power related to gender (a topic we will examine in more detail later in this chapter) in entrepreneurial relationships.[10]

Several other aspects of power also are worth noting. Gardner has made an important point about the exercise of power and its effects.[11] He stated that "power does not need to be exercised in order to have its effect—as any hold-up man can tell you."[12] Thus merely having the capacity to exert influence can often bring about intended effects, even though the leader may not take any action to influence his or her followers. For example, some months after the end of his term, Eisenhower was asked if leaving the White House had affected his golf game. "Yes," he replied, "a lot more people beat me now." Alternatively, power represents an inference or attribution made on the basis of an agent's observable acts of influence.[13] From this perspective, power is never directly observed but rather attributed to others on the basis and frequency of influence tactics they use and on their outcomes.

Many people use the terms *power, influence,* and *influence tactics* synonymously,[14] but it is useful to distinguish among them. **Influence** can be defined as the change in a target agent's attitudes, values, beliefs, or behaviors as the result of influence tactics. **Influence tactics** refer to one person's actual behaviors designed to change another person's attitudes, beliefs, values, or behaviors. Although these concepts are typically examined from the leader's perspective (such as how a leader influences followers), we should remember that followers can also wield power and influence over leaders as well as over each other. Leadership practitioners can improve their effectiveness by reflecting on the types of power they and their followers have and the types of influence tactics that they may use or that may be used on them.

Whereas power is the *capacity* to cause change, influence is the degree of actual change in a target person's attitudes, values, beliefs, or behaviors. Influence can be measured by the behaviors or attitudes manifested by followers as the result of a leader's *influence tactics*. For example, a leader may ask a follower to accomplish a particular task, and whether or not the task is accomplished is partly a function of the leader's request. (The follower's ability and skill as well as access to the necessary equipment and resources are also important factors.) Such things as subordinates' satisfaction or motivation, group cohesiveness and climate, or unit performance measures

The true leader must submerge himself in the fountain of the people.
V. I. Lenin

can be used to assess the effectiveness of leaders' influence attempts. The degree to which leaders can change the level of satisfaction, motivation, or cohesiveness among followers is a function of the amount of power available to both leaders and followers. On one hand, leaders with relatively high amounts of power can cause fairly substantial changes in subordinates' attitudes and behaviors; for example, a new and respected leader who uses rewards and punishments judiciously may cause a dramatic change in followers' perceptions about organizational climate and the amount of time followers spend on work-related behaviors. On the other hand, the amount of power followers have in work situations can also vary dramatically, and in some situations particular followers may exert relatively more influence over the rest of the group than the leader does. For example, a follower with a high level of knowledge and experience may have more influence on the attitudes, opinions, and behaviors of the rest of the followers than a brand-new leader. Thus the amount of change in the attitudes or behaviors of the targets of influence is a function of the agent's capacity to exert influence and the targets' capacity to resist this influence.

Leaders and followers typically use a variety of tactics to influence each other's attitudes or behaviors (see Highlight 4.1 for a description of some nonverbal power cues common to humans). Influence tactics are the overt behaviors exhibited by one person to influence another. They range from emotional appeals, to the exchange of favors, to threats. The particular tactic used in a leadership situation is probably a function of the power possessed by both parties. Individuals with a relatively large amount of power may successfully employ a wider variety of influence tactics than individuals with little power. For example, a well-respected leader could make an emotional appeal, a rational appeal, a personal appeal, a legitimate request, or a threat to try to modify a follower's behavior. The follower in this situation may be able to use only ingratiation or personal appeals to change the leader's attitude or behavior.

At the same time, because the formal leader is not always the person who possesses the most power in a leadership situation, followers often can use a wider variety of influence tactics than the leader to modify the attitudes and behaviors of others. This would be the case if a new leader were brought into an organization in which one of his or her subordinates was extremely well liked and respected. In this situation, the subordinate may be able to make personal appeals, emotional appeals, or even threats to change the attitudes or behaviors of the leader, whereas the new leader may be limited to making only legitimate requests to change the attitudes and behaviors of the followers. And finally, as if figuring out relative status isn't enough of a problem, when working globally, the various rules and customs of cultures often clash. Mrs. Obama discovered this in 2009 when attending a social function at Buckingham Palace for the G20 conference. While posing for pictures, Mrs. Obama reached out and patted Queen Elizabeth on the back, a nonverbal message that was unheard of and apparently inappropriate to many.

Gestures of Power and Dominance

HIGHLIGHT 4.1

We can often get clues about relative power just by paying attention to behaviors between two people. There are a number of nonverbal cues we might want to pay attention to. The phrase **pecking order** refers to the status differential between members of a group. It reminds us that many aspects of human social organization have roots, or at least parallels, in the behavior of other species. The animal kingdom presents diverse and fascinating examples of stylized behaviors by which one member of a species shows its relative dominance or submissiveness to another. There is adaptive significance to such behavioral mechanisms because they tend to minimize actual physical struggle and maintain a stable social order. For example, lower-ranking baboons step aside to let a higher-status male pass; they become nervous if he stares at them. The highest-status male can choose where he wants to sleep and whom he wants to mate with. Baboons "know their place." As with humans, rank has its privileges.

Our own stylized power rituals are usually so ingrained that we aren't conscious of them. Yet there is a "dance" of power relations among humans just as among other animals. The following are some of the ways power is expressed nonverbally in humans:

Staring: In American society, it is disrespectful for a person of lower status to stare at a superior, though superiors are not bound by a similar restriction. Children, for example, are taught not to stare at parents. And it's an interesting comment on the power relationship between sexes that women are more likely to avert their gaze from men than vice versa.

Pointing: Children are also taught that it's not nice to point. However, adults rarely correct each other for pointing because, more than mere etiquette, pointing seems to be a behavior that is acceptable for high-status figures or those attempting to assert dominance. An angry boss may point an index finger accusingly at an employee; few employees who wanted to keep their jobs would respond in kind. The same restrictions apply to frowning.

Touching: Invading another person's space by touching the person without invitation is acceptable when one is of superior status but not when one is of subordinate status. It's acceptable, for example, for bosses or teachers to put a hand on an employee's or a student's shoulder, respectively, but not vice versa. The disparity also applies to socioeconomic status; someone with higher socioeconomic status is more likely to touch a person of lower socioeconomic status than vice versa.

Interrupting: Virtually all of us have interrupted others, and we have all been interrupted ourselves. Again, however, the issue is who interrupted whom. Higher-power or status persons interrupt; lower-power or status persons are interrupted. A vast difference in the frequency of this behavior also exists between the sexes in American society. Men interrupt much more frequently than women do.

Source: D. A. Karp and W. C. Yoels, *Symbols, Selves, and Society* (New York: Lippincott, 1979).

Power and Leadership

And when we think we lead, we are most led.
    Lord Byron

We began this chapter by noting how an understanding of power has long been seen as an integral part of leadership. Several perspectives and theories have been developed to explain the acquisition and exercise of power. In this section we will first examine various *sources* of power. Then we will look at how individuals vary in their personal *need* for power.

Sources of Leader Power

Where does a leader's power come from? Do leaders *have* it, or do followers *give* it to them? As we will see, the answer may be both . . . and more.

Something as seemingly trivial as the arrangement of furniture in an office can affect perceptions of another person's power. One vivid example comes from John Ehrlichman's book *Witness to Power.*[15] Ehrlichman described his first visit to J. Edgar Hoover's office at the Department of Justice. The legendary director of the FBI had long been one of the most powerful men in Washington, DC, and as Ehrlichman's impressions reveal, Hoover used every opportunity to reinforce that image. Ehrlichman was first led through double doors into a room replete with plaques, citations, trophies, medals, and certificates jamming every wall. He was then led through a second similarly decorated room into a third trophy room, and finally to a large but bare desk backed by several flags and still no J. Edgar Hoover. The guide opened a door behind the desk, and Ehrlichman went into a smaller office, which Hoover dominated from an impressive chair and desk that stood on a dais about six inches high. Erhlichman was instructed to take a seat on a lower couch, and Hoover peered down on Ehrlichman from his own loftier and intimidating place.

On a more mundane level, many people have experienced a time when they were called in to talk to a boss and left standing while the boss sat behind the desk. Probably few people in that situation misunderstand the power message there. In addition to the factors just described, other aspects of office arrangements also can affect a leader's or follower's power. One factor is the shape of the table used for meetings. Individuals sitting at the ends of rectangular tables often wield more power, whereas circular tables facilitate communication and minimize status differentials. However, specific seating arrangements even at circular tables can affect participants' interactions; often individuals belonging to the same cliques and coalitions will sit next to each other. By sitting next to each other, members of the same coalition may exert more power as a collective group than they would sitting apart from each other. Also, having a private or more open office may not only *reflect* but also *affect* power differentials between people. Individuals with private offices can dictate to a greater degree when they want to interact with others by opening or closing their doors or by giving instructions about interruptions. Individuals with more open offices have much less power to control access to them. By being aware of dynamics like these, leaders can somewhat influence others' perceptions of their power relationship.

Prominently displaying symbols like diplomas, awards, and titles also can increase one's power. This was shown in an experiment in a college setting where a guest lecturer to several different classes was introduced in a different way to each. To one group he was introduced as a student; to other groups he was introduced as a lecturer, senior lecturer, or professor, respectively. After the presentation, when he was no longer in the room, the class estimated his height. Interestingly, the same man was perceived by different groups as increasingly taller with each increase in academic status. The "professor" was remembered as being several inches taller than the "student."[16]

This finding demonstrates the generalized impact a seemingly minor matter like one's title can have on others. Another study points out more dramatically how dangerous it can be when followers are overly responsive to the *appearances* of title and authority. This study took place in a medical setting and arose from concern among medical staff that nurses were responding mechanically to doctors' orders. A researcher made telephone calls to nurses' stations in numerous different medical wards. In each, he identified himself as a hospital physician and directed the nurse answering the phone to administer a particular medication to a patient in that ward. Many nurses complied with the request despite the fact it was against hospital policy to transmit prescriptions by phone. Many did so despite never even having talked to the particular "physician" before the call—and despite the fact that the prescribed medication was dangerously excessive, not to mention unauthorized. In fact, 95 percent of the nurses complied with the request made by the most easily falsifiable symbol of authority, a bare title.[17] (See also Highlight 4.2.)

Even choice of clothing can affect one's power and influence. Uniforms and other specialized clothing have long been associated with authority and status, including their use by the military, police, hospital staffs, clergy, and so on. In one experiment, people walking along a city sidewalk were stopped by someone dressed either in regular clothes or in the uniform of a security guard and told this: "You see that guy over there by the meter? He's overparked but doesn't have any change. Give him a dime!" Whereas fewer than half complied when the requestor was dressed in regular clothes, over 90 percent did when he was in uniform.[18]

This same rationale is given for having personnel in certain occupations (such as airline crew members) wear uniforms. Besides identifying them to others, the uniforms increase the likelihood that in emergency situations their instructions will be followed. Similarly, even the presence of something as trivial as tattoos can affect the amount of power wielded in a group. One of the authors of this text had a friend named Del who was a manager in an international book publishing company. Del was a former merchant marine whose forearms were adorned with tattoos. Del would often take off his suit coat and roll up his sleeves when meetings were not going his way, and he often exerted considerably more influence by merely exposing his tattoos to the rest of the group.

A final situational factor that can affect one's potential to influence others is the presence or absence of a crisis. Leaders usually can exert more power during a crisis than during periods of relative calm. Perhaps this is because during a crisis leaders are willing to draw on bases of power they

He who has great power should use it lightly.
Seneca

The Milgram Studies

HIGHLIGHT 4.2

One intriguing way to understand power, influence, and influence tactics is to read a synopsis of Stanley Milgram's classic work on obedience and to think about how this work relates to the concepts and theories discussed in this chapter. Milgram's research explored how far people will go when directed by an authority figure to do something that might injure another person. More specifically, Milgram wanted to know what happens when the dictates of authority and the dictates of one's conscience seem incompatible.

The participants were men from the communities surrounding Yale University. They were led to believe they were helping in a study concerning the effect of punishment on learning; the study's legitimacy was enhanced by the study being conducted on the Yale campus. Two subjects at a time participated in the study—one as a teacher and the other as a learner. The roles apparently were assigned randomly. The teacher's task was to help the learner memorize a set of word pairs by providing electric shocks whenever the learner (who would be in an adjacent room) made a mistake.

A stern experimenter described procedures and showed participants the equipment for administering punishment. This "shock generator" looked ominous, with rows of switches, lights, and warnings labeled in 15-volt increments all the way to 450 volts. Various points along the array were marked with increasingly dire warnings such as *extreme intensity* and *danger: severe*. The switch at the highest level of shock was simply marked *XXX*. Every time the learner made a mistake, the teacher was ordered by the experimenter to administer the next higher level of electric shock.

In actuality, there was only one true subject in the experiment—the teacher. The learner was really a confederate of the experimenter. The supposed random assignment of participants to teacher and learner conditions had been rigged in advance. The real purpose of the experiment was to assess how much electric shock the teachers would administer to the learners in the face of the latter's increasingly adamant protestations to stop. This included numerous realistic cries of agony and complaints of a heart condition—all standardized, predetermined, tape-recorded messages delivered via the intercom from the learner's room to the teacher's room. If the subject (that is, the teacher) refused to deliver any further shocks, the experimenter prodded him with comments such as "The experiment requires that you go on" and "You have no other choice; you must go on."

Before Milgram conducted his experiment, he asked mental health professionals what proportion of the subjects would administer apparently dangerous levels of shock. The consensus was that only a negligible percentage would do so—perhaps 1 or 2 percent of the population. Milgram's actual results were dramatically inconsistent with what any experts had predicted. Fully 70 percent of the subjects carried through with their orders, albeit sometimes with great personal anguish, and delivered the maximum shock possible—450 volts!

Source: S. Milgram, "Behavioral Study of Obedience," *Journal of Abnormal and Social Psychology* 67 (1963), pp. 371–78.

normally forgo. For example, a leader who has developed close interpersonal relationships with followers generally uses her referent power to influence them. During crises or emergency situations, however, leaders may be more apt to draw on their legitimate and coercive bases of power to influence subordinates. That was precisely the finding in a study of bank managers' actions; the bank managers were more apt to use legitimate and coercive power during crises than during noncrisis situations.[19] This same phenomenon is observable in many dramatizations. In the television series *Star Trek, the Next Generation,* for example, Captain Picard normally uses his referent and expert power to influence subordinates. During emergencies, however, he will often rely on his legitimate and coercive power. Another factor may be that during crises followers are more willing to accept greater direction, control, and structure from leaders, whatever power base may be involved.

A Taxonomy of Social Power

French and Raven identified five sources, or bases, of power by which an individual can potentially influence others.[20] As shown in Figure 4.1, these five sources include one that is primarily a function of the leader; one that is a function of the relationship between leaders and followers; one that is primarily a function of the leader and the situation; one that is primarily a function of the situation; and finally, one that involves aspects of all three elements. Understanding these bases of power can give leadership practitioners greater insight about the predictable effects—positive or negative—of various sorts of influence attempts. Following is a more detailed discussion of French and Raven's five bases of social power.[21]

Expert Power

Expert power is the power of knowledge. Some people can influence others through their relative expertise in particular areas. A surgeon may wield considerable influence in a hospital because others depend on her knowledge, skill, and judgment, even though she may have no formal authority over them. A mechanic may be influential among his peers because he is widely recognized as the best in the city. A longtime employee may be influential because her corporate memory provides a useful historical perspective to newer personnel. Legislators who are experts in the

FIGURE 4.1
Sources of Leader Power in the Leader–Follower–Situation Framework

intricacies of parliamentary procedure, athletes who have played in championship games, and soldiers who have been in combat are valued for the lessons learned and the wisdom they can share with others.

Because expert power is a function of the amount of knowledge one possesses relative to the rest of the members of the group, it is possible for followers to have considerably more expert power than leaders in certain situations. For example, new leaders often know less about the jobs and tasks performed in a particular work unit than the followers do, and in this case the followers can potentially wield considerable influence when decisions are made regarding work procedures, new equipment, or the hiring of additional workers. Probably the best advice for leaders in this situation is to ask a lot of questions and perhaps seek additional training to help fill this knowledge gap. So long as different followers have considerably greater amounts of expert power, it will be difficult for a leader to influence the work unit on the basis of expert power alone.

Referent Power

One way to counteract the problems stemming from a lack of expertise is to build strong interpersonal ties with subordinates. **Referent power** refers to the potential influence one has due to the strength of the relationship between the leader and the followers. When people admire a leader and see her as a role model, we say she has referent power. For example, students may respond positively to advice or requests from teachers who are well liked and respected, while the same students might be unresponsive to less popular teachers. This relative degree of responsiveness is primarily a function of the strength of the relationship between the students and the different teachers. We knew one young lieutenant who had enormous referent power with the military security guards working for him due to his selfless concern for them, evident in such habits as bringing them hot chocolate and homemade cookies on their late-night shifts. The guards, sometimes taken for granted by other superiors, understood and valued the extra effort and sacrifice this young supervisor put forth for them. When Buddy Ryan was fired as head coach of the Philadelphia Eagles football team, many of the players expressed fierce loyalty to him. One said, "We'd do things for Buddy that we wouldn't do for another coach. I'd sell my body for Buddy."[22] That is referent power.

Another way to look at referent power is in terms of the role friendships play in making things happen. It is frequently said, for example, that many people get jobs based on whom they know, not what they know. This is true. But we think the best perspective on this issue was offered by David Campbell, who said, "It's not who you know that counts. It's what who you know *knows about you* that counts!" (personal communication).

Referent power often takes time to develop, but it can be lost quickly—just ask Tiger Woods. Furthermore, it can have a downside in that a desire to *maintain* referent power may limit a leader's actions in particular situations.

Power in an organization is the capacity generated by relationships.
Margaret A. Wheatley, futurist

For example, a leader who has developed a strong relationship with a follower may be reluctant to discipline the follower for poor work or chronic tardiness because such actions could disrupt the nature of the relationship between the leader and the follower. Thus referent power is a two-way street; the stronger the relationship, the more influence leaders and followers exert over each other. Moreover, just as it is possible for leaders to develop strong relationships with followers and, in turn, acquire more referent power, it is also possible for followers to develop strong relationships with

Michael Dell

PROFILES IN LEADERSHIP 4.1

The problem of having power you didn't know you had and might not even want.

It's hard to imagine anyone not recognizing the name Michael Dell. As founder of the computer company Dell, Inc., he created one of the most profitable computer companies in the world, with annual sales of up to $50 billion. Michael Dell has also become one of the wealthiest people in the world with a 25th place listing on the *Forbes* rich Americans list in 2013 and an estimated worth of $15.9 billion. In July 2007 *USA Today* published its ranking of the 25 most influential business leaders in the last 25 years. Number 17 on this list was Michael Dell.

With just $1,000 in his pocket, Dell started PC's Limited in 1984. From his university dorm room Dell started building and selling personal computers from stock computer parts. In 1988 PC's Limited changed its name to Dell Computer Corporation and had an initial public offering (IPO) that valued the company at roughly $80 million. By 1992 Dell Computer Corporation was listed on the *Fortune* 500 list of the largest companies in the world, making Dell the youngest CEO ever to head a *Fortune* 500 company.

One of this book's authors worked with Michael Dell in the early 1990s (and wishes he had bought stock). He was chatting with Michael and describing the problems that can happen in large organizations when the leader has a lot of personal or referent power. Michael said, "Oh, I'm learning about that. We've even got a name for that problem. We call them, 'Michael saids.'"

Here's an example of a "Michael said." One afternoon, Michael was walking around the plant and stopped to ask one of the assembly employees how things were going and what could be done to make things better. The assembler said that things were great but that occasionally there was some confusion with a particular electronic component (let's call it a resistor). Sometimes the resistors were red and sometimes they were green, and the red ones looked like another component. The assembler suggested that this problem could be eliminated if this particular resistor came only in green. Michael said that seemed like a reasonable solution and passed that information along to the people who bought resistors from the suppliers.

Six months later, Michael was having a meeting in his office when someone knocked on the door. It was a frazzled person who said he was terribly sorry to interrupt but there was a crisis down in manufacturing and production was about to stop. "Why?" asked Michael. The messenger said that the supplier of green resistors had a problem and the only resistors they could get were red and they couldn't use the red resistors. "Why not?" asked Michael. The messenger looked sheepishly at his feet and passed along the bad news. They couldn't use the red ones because "Michael said we could only use green resistors."

While referent and expert power may be good to use, as Dell and others have found out, there can be a potential downside of which you might not even be aware.

other followers and acquire more referent power. Followers with relatively more referent power than their peers are often the spokespersons for their work units and generally have more latitude to deviate from work unit norms. Followers with little referent power have little opportunity to deviate from group norms. For example, in an episode of the television show *The Simpsons*, Homer Simpson was fired for wearing a pink shirt to work (everybody else at the Springfield nuclear power plant had always worn white shirts). Homer was fired partly because he "was not popular enough to be different."

Legitimate Power

Legitimate power depends on a person's organizational role. It can be thought of as one's formal or official authority. Some people make things happen because they have the power or authority to do so. The boss assigns projects; the coach decides who plays; the colonel orders compliance with uniform standards; the teacher assigns homework and awards grades. Individuals with legitimate power exert influence through requests or demands deemed appropriate by virtue of their role and position. In other words, legitimate power means a leader has authority because she or he has been assigned a particular role in an organization. Note that the leader has this authority only while occupying that position and operating within the proper bounds of that role.

Legitimate authority and leadership are not the same thing. Holding a position and being a leader are not synonymous, despite the relatively common practice of calling position holders in bureaucracies the leaders. The head of an organization may be a true leader, but he or she also may not be. Effective leaders often intuitively realize they need more than legitimate power to be successful. Before he became president, Dwight Eisenhower commanded all Allied troops in Europe during World War II. In a meeting with his staff before the Normandy invasion, Eisenhower pulled a string across a table to make a point about leadership. He was demonstrating that just as you can pull a string, not push it, officers must lead soldiers and not push them from the rear.

It is also possible for followers to use their legitimate power to influence leaders. In these cases, followers can actively resist a leader's influence attempt by doing only work specifically prescribed in job descriptions, bureaucratic rules, or union policies. For example, many organizations have job descriptions that limit both the time spent at work and the types of tasks and activities performed. Similarly, bureaucratic rules and union policies can be invoked by followers to resist a leader's influence attempts. Often the leader will need to change the nature of his or her request or find another way to resolve the problem if these rules and policies are invoked by followers. If this is the case, the followers will have successfully used legitimate power to influence their leader.

Reward Power

Reward power involves the potential to influence others due to one's control over desired resources. This can include the power to give raises, bonuses, and promotions; to grant tenure; to select people for special assignments or desirable activities; to distribute desired resources like computers, offices, parking places, or travel money; to intercede positively on another's behalf; to recognize with awards and praise; and so on. Many corporations use rewards extensively to motivate employees. At McDonald's, for example, great status is accorded the All-American Hamburger Maker—the cook who makes the fastest, highest-quality hamburgers in the country. At individual fast-food restaurants, managers may reward salespeople who handle the most customers during rush periods. Tupperware holds rallies for its salespeople. Almost everyone wins something, ranging from pins and badges to lucrative prizes for top performers.[23] Schools pick teachers of the year, and professional athletes are rewarded by selection to all-star teams for their superior performance.

The potential to influence others through the ability to administer rewards is a joint function of the leader, the followers, and the situation. Leaders vary considerably in the types and frequency with which they give rewards, but the position they fill also helps determine the frequency and types of rewards administered. For example, employees of the month at Kentucky Fried Chicken are not given new cars; the managers of these franchises do not have the resources to offer such awards. Similarly, leaders in other organizations are limited to some extent in the types of awards they can administer and the frequency with which they can do so. Nevertheless, leaders can enhance their reward power by spending some time reflecting on the followers and the situation. Often a number of alternative or innovative rewards can be created, and these rewards, along with ample doses of praise, can help a leader overcome the constraints his or her position puts on reward power.

Although using reward power can be an effective way to change the attitudes and behaviors of others, in several situations it can be problematic. For example, the perception that a company's monetary bonus policy is handled equitably may be as important in motivating good work (or avoiding morale problems) as the amounts of the bonuses. Moreover, a superior may mistakenly assume that a particular reward is valued when it is not. This would be the case if a particular subordinate were publicly recognized for her good work when she actually disliked public recognition. Leadership practitioners can avoid the latter problem by developing good relationships with subordinates and administering rewards that they, not the leader, value. Another potential problem with reward power is that it may produce compliance but not other desirable outcomes like commitment.[24] In other words, subordinates may perform only at the level necessary to receive a reward and may not be willing to put forth the extra effort needed to make the

Unreviewable power is the most likely to self-indulge itself and the least likely to engage in dispassionate self-analysis.

Warren E. Burger, U.S. Supreme Court, Chief Justice, 1969–1986

organization better. An overemphasis on rewards as payoff for performance may also lead to resentment and feelings by workers of being manipulated, especially if it occurs in the context of relatively cold and distant superior–subordinate relationships. Extrinsic rewards like praise, compensation, promotion, privileges, and time off may not have the same effects on behavior as intrinsic rewards such as feelings of accomplishment, personal growth, and development. There is evidence that under some conditions extrinsic rewards can decrease intrinsic motivation toward a task and make the desired behavior less likely to persist when extrinsic rewards are not available.[25,26] Overemphasis on extrinsic rewards may instill an essentially contractual or economic relationship between superiors and subordinates, diluting important aspects of the relationship like mutual loyalty or shared commitment to higher ideals.[27] These cautions about reward power should not cloud its real usefulness and effectiveness. As noted previously, top organizations make extensive use of both tangible and symbolic rewards in motivating their workers. Furthermore, all leaders can use some of the most important rewards—sincere praise and thanks to others for their loyalty and work. The bottom line is that leaders can enhance their ability to influence others based on reward power if they determine what rewards are available, determine what rewards are valued by their subordinates, and establish clear policies for the equitable and consistent administration of rewards for good performance.

Finally, because reward power is partly determined by one's position in the organization, some people may believe followers have little, if any, reward power. This may not be the case. If followers control scarce resources, they may use the administration of these resources to get leaders to act as they want. Moreover, followers may reward their leader by putting out a high level of effort when they feel their leader is doing a good job, and they may put forth less effort when they feel their leader is doing a poor job. By modifying their level of effort, followers may in turn modify a leader's attitudes and behaviors. And when followers compliment their leader (such as for running a constructive meeting), it is no less an example of reward power than when a leader compliments a follower. Thus leadership practitioners should be aware that followers can also use reward power to influence leaders.

Coercive Power

You do not lead by hitting people over the head—that's assault, not leadership.

Dwight D. Eisenhower

Coercive power, the opposite of reward power, is the potential to influence others through the administration of negative sanctions or the removal of positive events. In other words, it is the ability to control others through the fear of punishment or the loss of valued outcomes. Like reward power, coercive power is partly a function of the leader, but the situation often limits or enhances the coercive actions a leader can take (see Highlight 4.3). Examples of coercive power include police giving tickets

Leadership Lessons from the Stanford Prison Experiment

HIGHLIGHT 4.3

Almost nowhere is power as unequally distributed as in a prison. The administration and guards have both freedom and control while the prisoners have neither, at least officially. But there are important leadership lessons to be learned here as well.

A short review of the history of leadership might be helpful. If your grandparents happened to study leadership anytime from 1900 until about 1950, they would have read case studies of famous leaders. This "great man" theory of leadership hoped to unearth the traits that differentiated great leaders from lesser leaders. For the most part, this quest for the underlying innate leadership abilities stopped in the late 1940s when Ralph Stogdill published his findings that there was no clear set of traits responsible for great leaders.

From the 1950s to the 1980s, we decided that because leadership could not be comprehended by focusing solely on the leader, we should look at the relationship between the leader and the followers. As you will learn in Part 3 of this book, as the maturity and skills of the followers change, so should the behavior of the leader.

In the mid-1980s we started to consider the leadership implications of research done about 25 years earlier. We began to acknowledge that even if it were possible to know everything about a leader and everything about her or his followers, another variable powerfully affected leadership and performance: the situation (the focus of Part 4).

Two troubling studies clearly demonstrated this situational impact. The first, conducted by Stanley Milgram, was described in Highlight 4.2. The lesson learned was that reasonable, normal people, when put in a situation where authority told them to behave in a nefarious manner, for the most part did just that.

Ten years after Milgram's research, Phillip Zimbardo at Stanford University recruited students to serve as either "prisoners" or "guards" in a "prison" that was simulated in the basement of a campus building. Neither the guards nor the prisoners were given any instructions about how to behave. The experiment was to have lasted for approximately two weeks but was canceled after only six days because the "guards" were abusing their fellow student "prisoners" both physically and emotionally. It's not that the student guards were bad people; rather, they were put in a power situation that overcame their own beliefs and values. Fortunately an occasional noble hero rises to stand on higher moral ground. But as leaders, we cannot rely on that. For the masses, the situation is a powerful determinant of behavior. Incidentally, the Stanford Prison Experiment has its own website at www.prisonexp.org should you care to learn more about it, and the experiment will be described in more detail in Chapter 10.

Knowing what Milgram and Zimbardo demonstrated, it is at least possible to comprehend how someone like Pfc. Lynndie England, who according to her family would not even shoot a deer, could have become caught up in clearly inappropriate behavior in her role as a U.S. Army guard in the notorious Abu Ghraib prison debacle in Iraq. This is not to excuse her behavior but to help us understand it. And if we should not excuse the behavior of an undertrained soldier, we should be even less willing to excuse the leadership that put her and others in this situation without clear behavioral guidelines. After all, we've known about these studies for over 50 years!

Whether under the direction of authority as in the Milgram study, or under role assignments as in the Zimbardo study, the Abu Ghraib case showed a leadership vacuum that should not be tolerated.

And what about the business world? Leaders cannot claim they want and expect teamwork and collaboration from their subordinates if they place them in a situation that fosters competition and enmity. Neither can leaders claim that they want creativity from their subordinates if they have created a situation where the slightest deviation from rigid rules brings punishment. And perhaps most importantly, leaders can not expect egalitarian behaviors if people are put in highly differentiated power situations. People in organizations are smart. They are less likely to give you the behaviors you espouse in your speeches and more likely to give you the behavior demanded by the situation in which you place them. The leader's job is to create the conditions for the team to be successful, and the situation is one of the most important variables. What to consider in the situation will be discussed in more detail in Chapter 12.

for speeding, the army court-martialing AWOL soldiers, a teacher detaining disruptive students after school, employers firing lazy workers, and parents reprimanding children.[28] Even presidents resort to their coercive powers. Historian Arthur Schlesinger Jr., for example, described Lyndon Johnson as having a "devastating instinct for the weaknesses of others." Lyndon Johnson was familiar and comfortable with the use of coercion; he once told a White House staff member, "Just you remember this. There's only two kinds at the White House. There's elephants and there's ants. And I'm the only elephant."[29]

Nearly all men can stand adversity, but if you want to test a man's character, give him power.

Abraham Lincoln

Coercive power, like reward power, can be used appropriately or inappropriately. It is carried to its extreme in repressive totalitarian societies. One of the most tragic instances of coercive power was the cult led by Jim Jones, which unbelievably self-exterminated in an incident known as the Jonestown massacre.[30] Virtually all of the 912 people who died there drank, at Jones's direction, from large vats of a flavored drink containing cyanide. The submissiveness and suicidal obedience of Jones's followers during the massacre were due largely to the long history of rule by fear that Jones had practiced. For example, teenagers caught holding hands were beaten, and adults judged slacking in their work were forced to box for hours in marathon public matches against as many as three or four bigger and stronger opponents. Jim Jones ruled by fear, and his followers became self-destructively compliant.

Perhaps the preceding example is so extreme that we can dismiss its relevance to our own lives and leadership activities. Yet abuses of power, especially abuses of coercive power, continue to make the news, whether we are seeing reports of U.S. military abuse in Iraq or Taliban abuse in Afghanistan. On the other hand, such examples provide a dramatic reminder that reliance on coercive power has inherent limitations and drawbacks. But this is not to say disciplinary sanctions are never necessary; sometimes they are. Informal coercion, as opposed to the threat of formal punishment, can also change the attitudes and behaviors of others. Informal coercion is usually expressed implicitly, and often nonverbally, rather than explicitly. It may be the pressure employees feel to donate to the boss's favorite charity, or it may be his or her glare when they bring up an unpopular idea. One of the most common forms of coercion is simply a superior's temperamental outbursts. The intimidation caused by a leader's poorly controlled anger is usually, in its long-term effects, a dysfunctional style of behavior for leaders.

It is also possible for followers to use coercive power to influence their leader's behavior. For example, a leader may be hesitant to take disciplinary action against a large, emotionally unstable follower. Followers can threaten leaders with physical assaults, industrial sabotage, or work slowdowns and strikes, and these threats can modify a leader's behavior. Followers are more likely to use coercive power to change their leader's behavior if they have a relatively high amount of referent power with their fellow co-workers. This may be particularly true for threats of work slowdowns or strikes.

Concluding Thoughts about French and Raven's Power Taxonomy

Can we reach any conclusions about what base of power is best for a leader to use? As you might have anticipated, we must say that's an unanswerable question without knowing more facts about a particular situation. For example, consider the single factor of whether a group is facing a crisis. This might affect the leader's exercise of power simply because leaders usually can exert more power during crises than during periods of relative calm. Furthermore, during crises followers may be more eager to receive direction and control from leaders.

Can we make any generalizations about using various sources of power? Actually, considerable research has examined French and Raven's ideas, and generally the findings indicate that leaders who rely primarily on referent and expert power have subordinates who are more motivated and satisfied, are absent less, and perform better.[31] However, Yukl[32] and Podsakoff and Schriesheim[33] have criticized these findings, and much of their criticism centers on the instrument used to assess a leader's bases of power. Hinkin and Schriesheim[34] developed an instrument that overcomes many of the criticisms, and future research should more clearly delineate the relationship between the five bases of power and various leadership effectiveness criteria.

Four generalizations about power and influence seem warranted. First, effective leaders typically take advantage of *all* their sources of power. Effective leaders understand the relative advantages and disadvantages of different sources of power, and they selectively emphasize one or another depending on their objectives in a given situation. Second, whereas leaders in well-functioning organizations have strong influence over their subordinates, *they are also open to being influenced by them.* High degrees of reciprocal influence between leaders and followers characterize the most effective organizations.[35] Third, leaders vary in the extent to which they share power with subordinates. Some leaders seem to view their power as a fixed resource that, when shared with others (like cutting a pie into pieces), reduces their own portion. They see power in zero-sum terms. Other leaders see power as an expandable pie. They see the possibility of increasing a subordinate's power without reducing their own. Needless to say, which view a leader subscribes to can have a major impact on the leader's support for power-sharing activities like delegation and participative management. A leader's support for power-sharing activities (or in today's popular language, *empowerment*) is also affected by the practice of holding leaders responsible for subordinates' decisions and actions as well as their own. It is, after all, the coach or manager who often gets fired when the team loses.[36,37] Fourth, effective leaders generally work to increase their various power bases (whether expert, referent, reward, or legitimate) or become more willing to use their coercive power.

Leader Motives

Thus far we have been looking at how different *sources* of power can affect others, but that's only one perspective. Another way of looking at the relationship between power and leadership involves focusing on the individual leader's personality. We will look most closely at the role personality plays in leadership in an upcoming chapter, but it will be nonetheless useful now to briefly examine how all people (including leaders) vary in their personal motivation to have or wield power.

People vary in their motivation to influence or control others. McClelland[38] called this the **need for power,** and individuals with a high need for power derive psychological satisfaction from influencing others. They seek positions where they can influence others, and they are often involved concurrently in influencing people in many different organizations or decision-making bodies. In such activities they readily offer ideas, suggestions, and opinions, and also seek information they can use in influencing others. They are often astute at building trusting relationships and assessing power networks, though they can also be quite outspoken and forceful. They value the tangible signs of their authority and status as well as the more intangible indications of others' deference to them. Two different ways of expressing the need for power have been identified: **personalized power** and **socialized power.** Individuals who have a high need for personalized power are relatively selfish, impulsive, uninhibited, and lacking in self-control. These individuals exercise power for their own needs, not for the good of the group or the organization. Socialized power, on the other hand, implies a more emotionally mature expression of the motive. Socialized power is exercised in the service of higher goals to others or organizations and often involves self-sacrifice toward those ends. It often involves an empowering, rather than an autocratic, style of management and leadership.

Although the need for power has been measured using questionnaires and more traditional personality inventories, McClelland and his associates have used the Thematic Apperception Test (TAT) to assess need for power. The TAT is a **projective personality test** consisting of pictures such as a woman staring out a window or a boy holding a violin. Subjects are asked to make up a story about each picture, and the stories are then interpreted in terms of the strengths of various needs imputed to the characters, one of which is the need for power. Because the pictures are somewhat ambiguous, the sorts of needs projected onto the characters are presumed to reflect needs (perhaps at an unconscious level) of the storyteller. Stories concerned with influencing or controlling others would receive high scores for the need for power.

The need for power is positively related to various leadership effectiveness criteria. For example, McClelland and Boyatzis[39] found the need for power to be positively related to success for nontechnical managers at AT&T, and Stahl[40] found that the need for power was positively related to managers' performance ratings and promotion rates. In addition, Fodor[41] reported that small groups of ROTC students were more likely to successfully solve a subarctic survival situation if their leader had a strong need for power. Although these findings appear promising, several cautions should be kept in mind. First, McClelland and Boyatzis[42] also reported that the need for power was unrelated to the success of technical managers at AT&T. Apparently the level of knowledge (that is, expert power) played a more important role in the success of the technical managers versus that of the nontechnical managers. Second, McClelland[43] concluded that although some need for power was necessary for leadership potential, successful leaders also have the ability to inhibit their manifestation of this need. Leaders who are relatively uninhibited in their need for power will act like dictators; such individuals use power impulsively, to manipulate or control others, or to achieve at another's expense. Leaders with a high need for power but low activity inhibition may be successful in the short term, but their followers, as well as the remainder of the organization, may pay high costs for this success. Some of these costs may include perceptions by fellow members of the organization that they are untrustworthy, uncooperative, overly competitive, and looking out primarily for themselves. Finally, some followers have a high need for power too. This can lead to tension between leader and follower when a follower with a high need for power is directed to do something.

Individuals vary in their motivation to manage, just as in their need for power. Miner[44] described the **motivation to manage** in terms of six composites:

- Maintaining good relationships with authority figures.
- Wanting to compete for recognition and advancement.
- Being active and assertive.
- Wanting to exercise influence over subordinates.
- Being visibly different from followers.
- Being willing to do routine administrative tasks.

Like McClelland, Miner also used a projective test to measure a person's motivation to manage. Miner's Sentence Completion Scale (MSCS) consists of a series of incomplete sentences dealing with the six components just described (such as "My relationship with my boss . . . "). Respondents are asked to complete the sentences, which are scored according to established criteria. The overall composite MSCS score (though not component scores) has consistently been found to predict leadership success in hierarchical or bureaucratic organizations.[45] Thus individuals who maintained respect for authority figures, wanted to be recognized, acted assertively, actively influenced subordinates, maintained "psychological distance" between themselves and their followers, and readily took on routine administrative tasks were more apt to be successful in bureaucratic organizations. However, Miner claimed that different qualities were needed in flatter, nonbureaucratic organizations, and his review of the MSCS[46] supports this view.

Findings concerning both the need for power and the motivation to manage have several implications for leadership practitioners. First, not all individuals like being leaders. One reason may be that some have a relatively low need for power or motivation to manage. Because these scores are relatively stable and fairly difficult to change, leaders who do not enjoy their role may want to seek positions where they have fewer supervisory responsibilities.

Second, a high need for power or motivation to manage does not guarantee leadership success. The situation can play a crucial role in determining whether the need for power or the motivation to manage is related to leadership success. For example, McClelland and Boyatzis[47] found the need for power to be related to leadership success for nontechnical managers only, and Miner[48] found that motivation to manage was related to leadership success only in hierarchical or bureaucratic organizations.

Third, to be successful in the long term, leaders may require both a high need for socialized power and a high level of activity inhibition. Leaders who impulsively exercise power merely to satisfy their own selfish needs will probably be ineffective in the long term. Finally, it is important to remember that followers, as well as leaders, differ in the need for power, activity inhibition, and motivation to manage. Certain followers may have stronger needs or motives in this area. Leaders may need to behave differently toward these followers than they might toward followers having a low need for power or motivation to manage.

Two recent studies offer a fitting conclusion to this section about power and the individual's motives and a transition to our next topic. Magee and Galinsky[49] not only have presented a comprehensive review of the nature of power in hierarchical settings but also have noted that the acquisition and application of power induce transformation of individual psychological process, with the result being manifested by actions to further increase power! This is not the first time this phenomenon has been observed (recall Lord Acton's words about power and corruption). That power actually transforms individual psychological processes as an underlying cause of this phenomenon is fascinating.

But just having power, by either situation or individual transformation, does not guarantee success. Treadway and colleagues[50] have presented research showing that while past work performance is a source of personal reputation and can increase an individual's power, this increase does not necessarily translate into influence over others. Many fail to achieve this increased influence due to their lack of political skills for influence, and the application of influence is our next topic.

Influence Tactics

Whereas power is the capacity or potential to influence others, influence tactics are the actual behaviors used by an agent to change the attitudes, opinions, or behaviors of a target person. Kipnis and his associates accomplished much of the early work on the types of influence tactics one person uses to influence another.[51] Various instruments have been developed to study influence tactics, but the Influence Behavior Questionnaire, or IBQ,[52] seems to be the most promising. Here is a detailed discussion of the different influence tactics assessed by the IBQ.

Types of Influence Tactics

The IBQ is designed to assess nine types of influence tactics, and its scales give us a convenient overview of various methods of influencing others. **Rational persuasion** occurs when an agent uses logical arguments or factual evidence to influence others. An example of rational persuasion would be when a politician's adviser explains how demographic changes in the politician's district make it important for the politician to spend relatively more time in the district seeing constituents than she has in the recent past. Agents make **inspirational appeals** when they make a request or proposal designed to arouse enthusiasm or emotions in targets. An example here might be a minister's impassioned plea to members of a congregation about the good works that could be accomplished if a proposed addition to the church were built. **Consultation** occurs when agents ask targets to participate in planning an activity. An example of consultation would be if a minister established a committee of church members to help plan the layout and use of a new church addition. In this case the consultative work might not only lead to a better building plan but also *strengthen member commitment* to the idea of a new addition. **Ingratiation** occurs when an agent attempts to get you in a good mood before making a request. A familiar example here would be a salesperson's good-natured or flattering banter with you before you make a decision about purchasing a product. Agents use **personal appeals** when they ask another to do a favor out of friendship. A sentence that opens with, "Bill, we've known each other a long time and I've never asked anything of you before" represents the beginning of a personal appeal, whereas influencing a target through the exchange of favors is labeled **exchange.** If two politicians agree to vote for each other's pet legislation despite minor misgivings about each other's bills, that is exchange. **Coalition tactics** differ from consultation in that they are used when agents seek the aid or support of others to influence the target. A dramatic example of coalition tactics occurs when several significant people in an alcoholic's life (such as spouse, children, employer, or neighbor) agree to confront the alcoholic in unison about the many dimensions of his or her problem. Threats or persistent reminders used to influence targets are known as **pressure tactics.** A judge who

A leader is like a shepherd. He stays behind the flock, letting the most nimble go out ahead, whereupon the others follow, not realising that all along they are being directed from behind.

Nelson Mandela

gives a convicted prisoner a suspended sentence but tells him to consider the suspension a "sword hanging over his head" if he breaks the law again is using pressure tactics. Finally, **legitimizing tactics** occur when agents make requests based on their position or authority. A principal may ask a teacher to be on the school's curriculum committee, and the teacher may accede to the request despite reservations because it is the principal's prerogative to appoint any teacher to that role. In practice, of course, actual tactics often combine these approaches. Rarely, for example, is an effective appeal purely inspirational without any rational elements.

Influence Tactics and Power

As alluded to throughout this chapter, a strong relationship exists between the relative power of agents and targets and the types of influence tactics used. Because leaders with high amounts of referent power have built close relationships with followers, they may be more able to use a wide variety of influence tactics to modify the attitudes and behaviors of their followers. For example, leaders with referent power could use inspirational appeals, consultations, ingratiation, personal appeals, exchanges, and even coalition tactics to increase the amount of time a particular follower spends doing work-related activities. Note, however, that leaders with high referent power generally do not use legitimizing or pressure tactics to influence followers because, by threatening followers, leaders risk some loss of referent power. Leaders who have only coercive or legitimate power may be able to use only coalition, legitimizing, or pressure tactics to influence followers. In fact, influence tactics can be so effective, Cialdini[53] refers to them as "Weapons of Influence."

Other factors also can affect the choice of influence tactics.[54] People typically use hard tactics (that is, legitimizing or pressure tactics) when an influencer has the upper hand, when they anticipate resistance, or when the other person's behavior violates important norms. People typically use soft tactics (such as ingratiation) when they are at a disadvantage (see Highlight 4.4 comparing football and judo for an example of using a disadvantage to your advantage), when they expect resistance, or when they will personally benefit if the attempt is successful. People tend to use rational tactics (the exchange and rational appeals) when parties are relatively equal in power, when resistance is not anticipated, and when the benefits are organizational as well as personal. Studies have shown that influence attempts based on factual, logical analyses are the most frequently reported method by which middle managers exert lateral influence[55] and upward influence.[56] Other important components of successful influence of one's superiors include thoroughly preparing beforehand, involving others for support (coalition tactics), and persisting through a combination of approaches.[57]

Findings about who uses different tactics, and when, provide interesting insights into the influence process. It is clear that one's influence tactic of choice depends on many factors, including intended outcomes and one's

Don't threaten. I know it's done by some of our people, but I don't go for it. If people are running scared, they're not going to make the right decisions. They'll make decisions to please the boss rather than recommend what has to be done.

Charles Pilliod

Power and Influence (or Football and Judo)

HIGHLIGHT 4.4

While great leaders use both power and influence effectively (see Highlight 4.7 for perhaps the quintessential example of using both techniques effectively), it can also be instructive to compare and contrast the two at their most obvious polarities. At least for one of your authors, football and judo are cases in point.

Football, and by that I mean what is known in Europe as "American football," is a game about power. Of course, influence can also be used and often is quite effectively. But overwhelmingly, football is a game about size, strength, and speed. If one combines those three concepts and then searches for a single word to describe then, I would submit that "power" might work. If you have ever been around professional football players, you will discover this for yourself. They are a powerful group of men. Quite a while back, my brother-in-law was a professional football player. He played as an offensive end in college but was converted to a linebacker as a pro. I remember back in college that I thought he was about the largest human being I had ever known; if he was in a room with normal-sized, non-football-playing people, he readily stood out, and above, everyone else. As a result of these experiences, the first time I attended a game in which he was playing as a pro, I expected to be able to pick him out easily. But on the field with other powerful pro football players, he was indistinguishable except for his jersey number.

This notion of the importance of power to the game of football was summed up once by one of my coaches who repeatedly informed us that "a good big man is always better than a good small man."

Contrast this with judo, or its cousin, jujitsu (see Robert Cialdini's excellent book entitled Influence: Science and Practice* for more details on using jujitsu as "a weapon"). Again, your author's experience is cited as but one example. After a not-so-great experience as an undersized high school football player, I tended to blame my lack of power (size, strength, and speed) for my results. That notion changed later in life. Having been selected to be part of a covert operations group during the Vietnam War, I was sent to a number of preparatory courses, and one of these was a course

in judo. I remember quite vividly my first day in the *dojo*, as we stood around in our ill-fitting *gis*. I had the sense that most of us were engaged in the same mental activity; we were sizing up our classmates hoping to avoid the most "powerful" of our peers. In this search for the most powerful among us, there was one small person meekly sitting over against the wall who received no consideration as a threat and for whom I almost felt sorry. He appeared more timid than the rest of us and was not even prone to make eye contact with anyone. Clearly possessing the smallest and "least powerful" body in the room, he just sat quietly, thumbing through some sort of notebook.

As the minute hand moved to the top of the clock, we all kept an eye on the door watched for our instructor to enter the room at any moment. We didn't even notice when the small fellow put down his notebook and stood quietly against the wall. Then he spoke, saying that his name was Tze Lang Chen, and he would be our *sensei*. Really? This was the instructor? I was sure he was going to be crushed, especially by some of our larger classmates. Let me assure you, that notion was rapidly and completely dispelled.

In judo, the power of your opponent is a weapon to be used against him. In fact, the word *judo* means "the gentle way," which is somewhat antithetical to the football word *power*. According to our *sensei* Tze Lang Chen, the founder of judo, Jigoro Kano, was quoted as saying that "resisting a more powerful opponent will result in your defeat, while adjusting to and evading your opponent's attack will cause him to lose his balance, his power will be reduced, and you will defeat him. This can apply whatever the relative values of power, thus making it possible for weaker opponents to beat significantly stronger ones." I believe a paraphrase of the profound statement might well be "the bigger they are, the harder they fall."

We quickly learned that the more we resisted the force of our sensei, the sooner we would find ourselves flat on our backs looking up at this rather small man hovering over us. Such is the nature of power versus influence. Power can be used to force movement while influence may be hardly felt at all.

*R. B. Cialdini, *Influence: Science and Practice*, 5th ed. (Boston: Pearson Education, 2009).

Gender Differences in Managing Upward: How Male and Female Managers Get Their Way

HIGHLIGHT 4.5

Both male and female managers in a *Fortune* 100 company were interviewed and completed surveys about how they influence upward—that is, how they influence their own bosses. The results generally supported the idea that female managers' influence attempts showed greater concern for others, whereas male managers' influence attempts showed greater concern for self. Female managers were more likely to act with the organization's broad interests in mind, consider how others felt about the influence attempt, involve others in planning, and focus on both the task and interpersonal aspects of the situation. Male managers, on the other hand, were more likely to act out of self-interest, show less consideration for how others might feel about the influence attempt, work alone in developing their strategy, and focus primarily on the task.

One of the most surprising findings of the study was that, contrary to prediction, female managers were less likely than male managers to compromise or negotiate during their influence attempts. The female managers were actually more likely to persist in trying to persuade their superiors, even to the point of open opposition. At first this may seem inconsistent with the idea that the female managers' influence style involved greater concern for their relatedness to others. However, it seems consistent with the higher value placed by the women managers on involvement. Perhaps female managers demonstrate more commitment to their issues, and greater self-confidence that they are doing the "right thing," precisely because they have already interacted more with others in the organization and know they have others' support.

While male and female managers emphasized different influence techniques, it is important to note that neither group overall was more effective than the other. Nonetheless, there may be significant implications of the various techniques for a manager's career advancement. At increasingly higher management levels in an organization, effectiveness may be defined primarily by its fit with the organization's own norms and values. Managers whose style most closely matches that of their superior may have an advantage in evaluations and promotion decisions. This may be a significant factor for women, given the highly skewed representation of males in the most senior executive ranks.

Source: K. E. Lauterbach and B. J. Weiner, "Dynamics of Upward Influence: How Male and Female Managers Get Their Way," *Leadership Quarterly 7*, no. 1 (1996), pp. 87–107.

power relative to the target person. Although it may not be surprising that people select influence tactics as a function of their power relationship with another person, it is striking that this relationship holds true so universally across different social domains—for business executives, for parents and children, and for spouses. There is a strong tendency for people to resort to hard tactics whenever they have an advantage in clout if other tactics fail to get results.[58] As the bank robber Willie Sutton once said, "You can get more with a kind word and a gun than you can get with just a kind word." This sentiment is apparently familiar to bank managers, too. The latter reported greater satisfaction in handling subordinates' poor performance when they were relatively more punishing.[59] Highlight 4.5 offers thoughts on how men and women managers sometimes use different influence techniques.

It is not power that corrupts, but fear. Fear of losing power corrupts those who wield it and fear of the scourge of power corrupts those who are subject to it.
Aung San Suu Kyi

All forms of tampering with human beings, getting at them, shaping them against their will to your own pattern, all thought control and conditioning, is, therefore, a denial of that in men which makes them men and their values ultimate.
A. A. Berle Jr., writer about corporations

Although hard tactics can be effective, relying on them can change the way we see others. This was demonstrated in an experiment wherein leaders' perceptions and evaluations of subordinates were assessed after they exercised different sorts of authority over the subordinates.[60] Several hundred business students acted as managers of small work groups assembling model cars. Some of the students were told to act in an authoritarian manner, exercising complete control over the group's work; others were told to act as democratic leaders, letting group members participate fully in decisions about the work. As expected, authoritarian leaders used more hard tactics, whereas democratic leaders influenced subordinates more through rational methods. More interesting was the finding that subordinates were evaluated by the two types of leaders in dramatically different ways even though the subordinates of both types did equally good work. Authoritarian leaders judged their subordinates as less motivated, less skilled, and less suited for promotion. Apparently, bosses who use hard tactics to control others' behavior tend not to attribute any resultant good performance to the subordinates themselves. Ironically, the act of using hard tactics leads to negative attributions about others, which, in turn, tend to corroborate the use of hard tactics in the first place.

Finally, we should remember that using influence tactics can be thought of as a social skill. Choosing the right tactic may not always be enough to ensure good results; the behavior must be *skillfully executed*. We are not encouraging deviousness or a manipulative attitude toward others (although that has certainly been done by some as illustrated in Highlight 4.6, and will be discussed more in the next chapter on ethics), merely recognizing the obvious fact that clumsy influence attempts often come across as phony and may be counterproductive. See Highlight 4.7 for a perspective of a political leader who used power appropriately but was arguably the quintessential master of using influence effectively.

A Concluding Thought about Influence Tactics

In our discussion here, an implicit lesson for leaders is the value of being conscious of what influence tactics one uses and what effects are typically associated with each tactic. Knowledge of such effects can help a leader make better decisions about her or his manner of influencing others. It might also be helpful for leaders to think carefully about why they believe a particular influence tactic will be effective. Research indicates that some reasons for selecting among various possible influence tactics lead to successful outcomes more frequently than others. Specifically, thinking an act would improve an employee's self-esteem or morale was frequently associated with successful influence attempts. On the other hand, choosing an influence tactic because it followed company policy and choosing one because it was a way to put a subordinate in his place were frequently

The Clout of Influence and the Big Con

HIGHLIGHT 4.6

The confidence game, or "con game" is certainly nothing new, although some might argue it has been taken to new heights by the likes of Bernie Madoff. The term *confidence man* was first used by the New York press during the trial of William Thompson in 1849. What remains unchanged over the years is that the con game is not about violence or power but much more about the illicit use of influence. It is about the nefarious manipulation of trust.

Amy Reading has written a detailed history of "The Big Con" while wrapping it around a fascinating story of one of the largest swindles in America. Reading describes the preparations and staging necessary to win over the "mark" as if it were a form of theater. The mark in her historical account is one J. Frank Norfleet, a man who by his own description is as straight as they come. "I don't drink, chew tobacco, smoke, cuss, or tell lies," he would say. And he trusted others, which led to his involvement in the Big Con. Here is how Reading sets the stage.

> When Norfleet stepped into the St. George Hotel, he entered a tightly scripted drama with nine acts, each with its own distinct function in conveying the mark toward the climax when his money will be whisked away. Even the mark has his lines, and just because he doesn't know them does not mean he won't say them at exactly the right moment. He will, because the dialogue is designed so that his responses are the most predictable things he *would* say in such a situation. The play hinges on three psychological moments, when the mark must make a decision that will propel him further inside. Any objections he might muster have already been taken into account and rejoinders to them devised. Norfleet's role called for him to play himself, a part at which he excelled, but in a context designed so that his own earnest words would betray him. Confidence men took inordinate pride in the structured nature of their profession. Instead of the violence and mayhem of other kinds of theft, they

relied solely on a perfectly constructed piece of theater . . . The big con works because it makes use of a time-honored technique from stage magic, the one-ahead, in which the trick begins before the performer formally introduces it to the audience.

While not intending to glamorize the swindlers, or "grifters" as they are often called, their use of psychological influence is quite remarkable and instructive. Perhaps most telling are psychological traps one and two in the series of three.

In the prelude to the first psychological moment, Norfleet has graciously refused a $100 reward for returning a wallet he found in the hotel lobby—a wallet planted, of course, by the grifters. The swindlers then announced they had to go conclude a business deal involving the use of what we would today refer to as "insider trading." Since Norfleet had refused the reward, would he mind if they took that same money and "invest it along with their own." Twenty minutes later, the swindlers return and proudly offer Norfleet the $800 return on his declined $100 reward money. As Reading then notes:

> Who could resist *the convincer*? [The swindler] was standing before Norfleet, holding out money with absolutely no strings attached, money that Norfleet had no reason to refuse because in no way did it violate his code of honor. The mark had reached the fifth act and the first psychological moment. Would he reach out and take the money? . . . It is a con man's truism that no mark in history has ever walked away from the big con once *the convincer* has had its effect.

And speaking of convincing, perhaps no aspect of the big con is more so than the second psychological moment. This is also the most telling difference between street crime, where the engine is power, and the confidence game, where the engine is influence. Again, we turn to Reading's description:

> Norfleet stood poised at the second psychological moment of the big con, the moment that has

continued

continued

received the greatest amount of attention in the literature of confidence artistry: the moment when the mark is invited into a shady deal. To the swindlers themselves, the analysis of this moment couldn't be simpler. You may not be able to cheat an honest man, but a dishonest man has it coming to him. The big con works because so many legitimate businessmen will so readily discard legality and morality if the money is easy enough . . .The key is to structure the secret so that it is worthless unless the grifter can share it with someone trustworthy. The con man alone cannot realize the profit just beyond his reach, but he will let the mark in on the deal and split the pot if the mark contributes his own particular value. And so the con man extends generosity to the mark, but not in the way that you might expect. He grants the mark the opportunity to give the con man something he needs. The swindler has created a gratifying paradox, a situation in which the mark can act in the highest fulfillment of his own self-interest only by helping someone else.

The big con succeeds not because it *forces* the mark to hand over his valuables. It succeeds because it *influences* the mark to believe that he is not only acting in his own self-interest but is also helping others, even if it is acknowledged to be with a wink and a smile. Those interested in how this plays out, both in a theatrical sense and in the big con, would find Reading's book informative.

Sources: A. Reading, *The Mark Inside: A Perfect Swindle, a Cunning Revenge, and a Small History of the Big Con* (New York: Alfred A. Knopf, 2012).

Nelson Mandela: The Master of Political Influence

HIGHLIGHT 4.7

Invictus is both the title of the cited poem that provided inspiration to Nelson Mandela during his 27-year imprisonment for fighting apartheid and also became the title of the 2009 Clint Eastwood movie. This film takes us from Mandela's 1994 election through South Africa's World Cup journey the following year. The poem becomes the central inspirational gift from Mandela (played by Morgan Freeman) to Springbok rugby team captain François Pienaar (played by Matt Damon).

Invictus
William Ernest Henley

Out of the night that covers me,
Black as the pit from pole to pole,
I thank whatever gods may be
For my unconquerable soul.

In the fell clutch of circumstance
I have not winced nor cried aloud.
Under the bludgeonings of chance
My head is bloody, but unbowed.

Beyond this place of wrath and tears
Looms but the Horror of the shade,
And yet the menace of the years
Finds and shall find me unafraid

It matters not how strait the gate,
How charged with punishments the scroll,
I am the master of my fate:
I am the captain of my soul.

Rugby was more than just a game in South Africa; it was a preoccupation. Mandela had won the election as the African National Congress's (ANC) first black president. With that position came power, but Mandela knew that his political victory was tenuous. Even though the ANC dominated Parliament, whites still controlled the economy. And it was the country's history of white-dominated apartheid that had resulted in the national rugby team's exclusion from international sports competitions.

Against the advice of his supporters among the ANC, Mandela fought to retain the Springbok name and their beloved green and gold jerseys.

continued

142 Part Two *Focus on the Leader*

continued

Mandela recognized that this was a reminder of decades of oppression to the now black majority, but he also knew that white extremist Afrikaners posed a continuing threat. Their ongoing resistance to a black-dominated government could plunge the fragile government into anarchy and insurrection. Power would not work—but influence might.

The movie, based upon John Carlin's book *Playing the Enemy: Nelson Mandela and the Game That Made a Nation*, takes us through a moving scene where Mandela exhibits his dramatic ability to influence the struggling rugby team. Taking the team to visit Robben Island where he had been imprisoned for 17 years, Mandela recites *Invictus* as Pienaar and the team imagines the struggles of Mandela and his fellow prisoners. The underdog Springboks rallied to win the Rugby World Cup, hosted by South Africa in 1995. But, as noted by Arlene Getz, "[I]t was South Africa's good fortune that Mandela opted for reconciliation over retribution." It was also South Africa's good fortune that Nelson Mandela was a master of influence.

Sources: J. Carlin, *Playing the Enemy: Nelson Mandela and the Game that Made a Nation,* (New York: Penguin Press, 2008); http://www.newsweek.com/2009/12/09/sports-politics-and-mandela.html

mentioned as reasons for unsuccessful influence attempts.[61] In a nutshell, these results suggest that leaders should pay attention not only to the actual influence tactics they use—to *how* they are influencing others—but also to *why* they believe such methods are called for. It is perhaps obvious that influence efforts intended to build others up more frequently lead to positive outcomes than influence efforts intended to put others down.

Summary

This chapter has defined *power* as the capacity or potential to exert influence, *influence tactics* as the behaviors used by one person to modify the attitudes and behaviors of another, and *influence* as the degree of change in a person's attitudes, values, or behaviors as the result of another's influence tactic. Because power, influence, and influence tactics play such important roles in the leadership process, this chapter provided ideas to help leaders improve their effectiveness. By reflecting on their different bases of power, leaders may better understand how they can affect followers and even expand their power. The five bases of power also offer clues to why subordinates can influence leaders and successfully resist leaders' influence attempts.

Leaders also may gain insight into why they may not enjoy certain aspects of their responsibilities by reflecting on their own need for power or motivation to manage; they may also better understand why some leaders exercise power selfishly by considering McClelland's concepts of personalized power and activity inhibition. Leaders can improve their effectiveness by finding ways to enhance their idiosyncratic credit and not permitting in-group and out-group rivalries to develop in the work unit.

Although power is an extremely important concept, having power is relatively meaningless unless a leader is willing to exercise it. The exercise of power occurs primarily through the influence tactics leaders and followers use to modify each other's attitudes and behaviors. The types of influence tactics used seem to depend on the amount of different types of power possessed, the degree of resistance expected, and the rationale behind the different influence tactics. Because influence tactics designed to build up others are generally more successful than those that tear others down, leadership practitioners should always consider why they are using a particular influence attempt before they actually use it. By carefully considering the rationale behind the tactic, leaders may be able to avoid using pressure and legitimizing tactics and find better ways to influence followers. Being able to use influence tactics that modify followers' attitudes and behaviors in the desired direction while they build up followers' self-esteem and self-confidence is a skill all leaders should strive to master.

Key Terms

power, *116*
influence, *117*
influence tactics, *117*
pecking order, *119*
expert power, *123*
referent power, *124*
legitimate power, *126*
reward power, *127*
coercive power, *128*
need for power, *132*

personalized
 power, *132*
socialized power, *132*
projective personality
 test, *132*
motivation to
 manage, *133*
rational
 persuasion, *135*

inspirational
 appeals, *135*
consultation, *135*
ingratiation, *135*
personal appeals, *135*
exchange, *135*
coalition tactics, *135*
pressure tactics, *135*
legitimizing tactics, *136*

Questions

1. The following questions pertain to the Milgram studies (Highlight 4.2):
   a. What bases of power were available to the experimenter, and what bases of power were available to the subjects?
   b. Do you think subjects with a low need for power would act differently from subjects with a high need for power? What about subjects with differing levels of the motivation to manage?
   c. What situational factors contributed to the experimenter's power?
   d. What influence tactics did the experimenter use to change the behavior of the subjects, and how were these tactics related to the experimenter's power base?
   e. What actually was influenced? In other words, if influence is the change in another's attitudes, values, or behaviors as the result of an influence tactic, then what changes occurred in the subjects as the result of the experimenter's influence tactics?

f. Many people have criticized the Milgram study on ethical grounds. Assuming that some socially useful information was gained from the studies, do you believe this experiment could or should be replicated today?

2. Some definitions of leadership exclude reliance on formal authority or coercion (that is, certain actions by a person in authority may work but should not be considered leadership). What are the pros and cons of such a view?

3. Does power, as Lord Acton suggested, tend to corrupt the power holder? If so, what are some of the ways it happens? Is it also possible subordinates are corrupted by a superior's power? How? Is it possible that superiors can be corrupted by a subordinate's power?

4. Some people say it dilutes a leader's authority if subordinates are allowed to give feedback to the leader concerning their perceptions of the leader's performance. Do you agree?

5. Is *leadership* just another word for *influence*? Can you think of some examples of influence that you would *not* consider leadership?

Activity

This activity will demonstrate how the five bases of power are manifest in behavior. Write the five bases of power on the board or put them on an overhead. Break students into five groups, and give each group a 3 × 5 card that lists one of the five bases of power. Give the group 10 minutes to plan and practice a 1-minute skit that will be presented to the rest of the class. The skit should demonstrate the base of power listed on the 3 × 5 card. After the skit is presented, the remaining groups should guess which base of power is being used in the skit. As an alternative, you might choose a project for out-of-class work. Another variation is to assign the groups the task of finding a 3- to 4-minute segment from a movie or video representing a base of power and bring that in to the class.

Minicase

The Prime Minister's Powerful Better Half

Ho Ching's power has been recognized by many. As chief executive officer of Temasek Holdings, she ranked number 18 on a list of Asia's most powerful businesspeople and number 24 on the *Forbes* list of the world's most powerful women. How did a shy, Stanford-educated electrical engineer end up with this kind of power? Ho was a government scholar who started off in civil service and ended up working for the Defense Ministry in Singapore. There she met and married Lee Hsien Loong, Singapore's current prime minister and the son of Lee Kwan Yew—one of modern Singapore's founding fathers. Ho's experience, education, and connections led to her appointment as chief executive of Temasek, where she oversees a portfolio worth over $50 billion and influences many of Singapore's leading companies.

Temasek Holdings was established in 1974 in an attempt by the Singapore government to drive industrialization. Through Temasek Holdings the Singapore government took stakes in a wide range of companies, including the city-state's best-known companies: Singapore Airlines, Singapore Telecommunications, DBS Bank, Neptune Orient Lines, and Keppel Corp. The company's website describes Temasek's "humble roots during a turbulent and uncertain time" and its commitment "to building a vibrant future [for Singapore] through successful enterprise." Ho's appointment to Temasek in May 2002 caused some controversy; as prime minister her husband has a supervisory role over the firm. Ho denies any conflict of interest:

> The issue of conflict does not arise because there are no vested interests. Our goal is to do what makes sense for Singapore, I don't always agree with him (Mr. Lee) and he doesn't always agree with me. We have a healthy debate on issues.

In her role as CEO, Ho is pushing for a more open policy and an aggressive drive into the Asian market. Under Ho's leadership Temasek has decided to publicly disclose its annual report with details of its performance—details that have formerly remained private and been known only to Temasek executives.

Ho is concentrating on broadening Temasek's focus beyond Singapore, most recently opening an office in India. At a recent conference of top Indian companies, Ho appealed to investors to look to India for opportunities for Asian growth:

> Since the Asian financial crisis in 1997, the word *Asia* had lost a bit of its sparkle. But that sparkle is beginning to return. In the 1960s and 1970s, the Asia economic miracle referred to East Asia, specifically Japan. The 1970s and 1980s saw the emergence of the four Asian Tigers of Korea, Taiwan, Hong Kong, and Singapore.

> Now is India's turn to stir, standing at an inflexion point, after 10 years of market liberalisation and corporate restructuring. Since 1997, Singapore's trade with India grew by 50 percent, or a respectable CAGR of about 7.5 percent. Confidence is brimming in India, and Indian companies began to reach out boldly to the world over the last five years.

> All these waves of development have shown that Asia, with a combined population of 3 billion, has been resilient. If Asia continues to work hard and work smart, honing her competitive strengths and leveraging on her complementary capabilities across borders, the outlook in the next decade or two looks very promising indeed.

1. We have described *power* as the capacity to cause change and *influence* as the degree of actual change in a target's behaviors. Ho Ching's

power as a leader has been recognized by many, but would you describe Ho Ching as an influential leader? Why?

2. Based on the excerpt from Ho Ching's speech, what type of tactics does she use to influence the behavior of others?

3. Ho Ching has been named one of the most powerful leaders in Asia. What are her major sources of power?

Sources: http://www.fastcompany.com/online/13/womenofpr.html;
http://www.forbes.com/finance/lists/11/2004/LIR.jhtml?passListId=11&passYear=2004&
passListType=Person&uniqueId=OO5O&datatype=Person;
http://www.businessweek.com/magazine/content/02_36/b3798161.htm;
http://www.laksamana.net/vnews.cfm?ncat=31&news_id=5292;
http://in.rediff.com/money/2004/apr/03spec.htm;
http://www.theaustralian.news.com.au/ common/story_page/0%2C5744%2C10427548%
255E2703%2C00.html;
http://in.news.yahoo.com/040812/137/2fgoc.html.

End Notes

1. N. Hill, "Self-Esteem: The Key to Effective Leadership," *Administrative Management* 40, no. 9 (1985), pp. 71–76.

2. D. Donno, "Introduction," in *The Prince and Selected Discourses: Machiavelli,* ed. and trans. D. Dunno (New York: Bantam, 1966).

3. J. W. Gardner, *On Leadership* (New York: Free Press, 1990); J. W. Gardener, *The Tasks of Leadership,* Leadership paper no. 2 (Washington, DC: Independent Sector, 1986).

4. T. R. Hinkin and C. A. Schriesheim, "Development and Application of New Scales to Measure the French and Raven (1959) Bases of Social Power," *Journal of Applied Psychology* 74 (1989), pp. 561–67.

5. J. M. Burns, *Leadership* (New York: Harper & Row, 1978).

6. R. J. House, "Power in Organizations: A Social Psychological Perspective," unpublished manuscript, University of Toronto, 1984.

7. B. M. Bass, *Bass and Stogdill's Handbook of Leadership,* 3rd ed. (New York: Free Press, 1990).

8. N. Levina and W. Orlikowski, "Understanding Shifting Power Relations within and across Organizations," *Academy of Management Journal* 52, no. 4 (2009), pp. 672–703.

9. J. Nelson, "Corporate Governance Practices, CEO Characteristics, and Firm Performance," *Journal of Corporate Finance,* 11 (2005), pp. 197–228.

10. D. E. Winkel and B. R. Ragins, "Navigating the Emotional Battlefield: Gender, Power, and Emotion in Entrepreneurial Relationships," *Academy of Management Proceedings* (2008), pp. 1–6.

11. Gardner, *On Leadership;* Gardner, *The Tasks of Leadership.*

12. Gardner, *On Leadership;* Gardner, *The Tasks of Leadership.*

13. C. A. Schriesheim and T. R. Hinkin, "Influence Tactics Used by Subordinates: A Theoretical and Empirical Analysis and Refinement of the Kipnis, Schmidt, and Wilkinson Subscales," *Journal of Applied Psychology* 75 (1990), pp. 246–57.

14. Bass, *Bass and Stogdill's Handbook of Leadership.*

15. J. Ehrlichman, *Witness to Power* (New York: Simon & Schuster, 1982).

16. P. R. Wilson, "The Perceptual Distortion of Height as a Function of Ascribed Academic Status," *Journal of Social Psychology* 74 (1968), pp. 97–102.

17. R. B. Cialdini, *Influence* (New York: William Morrow, 1984).

18. L. Bickman, "The Social Power of a Uniform," *Journal of Applied Social Psychology* 4 (1974), pp. 47–61.

19. M. Mulder, R. D. de Jong, L. Koppelar, and J. Verhage, "Power, Situation, and Leaders' Effectiveness: An Organizational Study," *Journal of Applied Psychology* 71 (1986), pp. 566–70.

20. J. French and B. H. Raven, "The Bases of Social Power," in *Studies of Social Power,* ed. D. Cartwright (Ann Arbor, MI: Institute for Social Research, 1959).

21. French and Raven, "The Bases of Social Power."

22. Associated Press, January 9, 1991.

23. T. J. Peters and R. H. Waterman, *In Search of Excellence* (New York: Harper & Row, 1982).

24. G. Yukl, *Leadership in Organizations,* 2nd ed. (Englewood Cliffs, NJ: Prentice Hall, 1989).

25. E. L. Deci, "Effects of Contingent and Noncontingent Rewards and Controls on Intrinsic Motivation," *Organizational Behavior and Human Performance* 22 (1972), pp. 113–20.

26. E. M. Ryan, V. Mims, and R. Koestner, "Relation of Reward Contingency and Interpersonal Context to Intrinsic Motivation: A Review and Test Using Cognitive Evaluation Theory," *Journal of Personality and Social Psychology* 45 (1983), pp. 736–50.

27. M. M. Wakin, "Ethics of Leadership," in *Military Leadership,* ed. J. H. Buck and L. J. Korb (Beverly Hills, CA: Sage, 1981).

28. S. B. Klein, *Learning,* 2nd ed. (New York: McGraw-Hill, 1991).

29. F. Barnes, "Mistakes New Presidents Make," *Reader's Digest,* January 1989, p. 43.

30. F. Conway and J. Siegelman, *Snapping* (New York: Delta, 1979).

31. G. A. Yukl, *Leadership in Organizations,* 1st ed. (Englewood Cliffs, NJ: Prentice Hall, 1981).

32. Ibid.

33. P. M. Podsakoff and C. A. Schriesheim, "Field Studies of French and Raven's Bases of Power: Critique, Reanalysis, and Suggestions for Future Research," *Psychological Bulletin* 97 (1985), pp. 387–411.

34. T. R. Hinkin and C. A. Schriesheim, "Development and Application of New Scales to Measure the French and Raven (1959) Bases of Social Power," *Journal of Applied Psychology* 74 (1989), pp. 561–67.

35. Yukl, *Leadership in Organizations,* 2nd ed.

36. E. P. Hollander and L. R. Offermann, "Power and Leadership in Organizations," *American Psychologist* 45 (1990), pp. 179–89.

37. J. Pfeffer, "The Ambiguity of Leadership," in *Leadership: Where Else Can We Go?* ed. M. W. McCall Jr. and M. M. Lombardo (Durham, NC: Duke University Press, 1977).

38. D. C. McClelland, *Power: The Inner Experience* (New York: Irvington, 1975).

39. D. C. McClelland and R. E. Boyatzis, "Leadership Motive Pattern and Long-Term Success in Management," *Journal of Applied Psychology* 67 (1982), pp. 737–43.

40. M. J. Stahl, "Achievement, Power, and Managerial Motivation: Selecting Managerial Talent with the Job Choice Exercise," *Personnel Psychology* 36 (1983), pp. 775–89.

41. E. Fodor, "Motive Pattern as an Influence on Leadership in Small Groups," paper presented at the meeting of the American Psychological Association, New York, August 1987.

42. D. C. McClelland and R. E. Boyatzis, "Leadership Motive Pattern and Long-Term Success in Management," *Journal of Applied Psychology* 67 (1982), pp. 737–43.

43. D. C. McClelland, *Human Motivation* (Glenview, IL: Scott Foresman, 1985).

44. J. B. Miner, "Student Attitudes toward Bureaucratic Role Prescriptions and the Prospects for Managerial Shortages," *Personnel Psychology* 27 (1974), pp. 605–13.

45. J. B. Miner, "Twenty Years of Research on Role Motivation Theory of Managerial Effectiveness," *Personnel Psychology* 31 (1978), pp. 739–60.

46. Miner, "Twenty Years of Research."

47. McClelland and Boyatzis, "Leadership Motive Pattern and Long-Term Success in Management."

48. Miner, "Twenty Years of Research."

49. J. C. Magee and A. D. Galinsky, "Social Hierarchy: The Self-Reinforcing Nature of Power and Status," *Academy of Management Annals* 2, no. 1 (2008), pp. 351–98.

50. D. C. Treadway, J. W. Breland, J. Cho, J. Yang, and A. B. Duke, "Performance Is Not Enough: Political Skill in the Longitudinal Performance–Power Relationship," *Academy of Management Proceedings* (2009), pp. 1–6.

51. D. Kipnis and S. M. Schmidt, *Profiles of Organizational Strategies* (San Diego, CA: University Associates, 1982).

52. G. A. Yukl, R. Lepsinger, and T. Lucia, "Preliminary Report on the Development and Validation of the Influence Behavior Questionnaire," in *Impact of Leadership*, ed. K. E. Clark, M. B. Clark, and D. P. Campbell (Greensboro, NC: Center for Creative Leadership, 1992).

53. R. B. Cialdini, *Influence: Science and Practice*, 5th ed. (Boston: Pearson Education, 2009).

54. D. Kipnis and S. M. Schmidt, "The Language of Persuasion," *Psychology Today* 19, no. 4 (1985), pp. 40–46.

55. B. Keys, T. Case, T. Miller, K. E. Curran, and C. Jones, "Lateral Influence Tactics in Organizations," *International Journal of Management* 4 (1987), pp. 425–37.

56. T. Case, L. Dosier, G. Murkison, and B. Keys, "How Managers Influence Superiors: A Study of Upward Influence Tactics," *Leadership and Organization Development Journal* 9, no. 4 (1988), pp. 4, 25–31.

57. Ibid.

58. D. Kipnis and S. M. Schmidt, "The Language of Persuasion," *Psychology Today* 19, no. 4 (1985), pp. 40–46.

59. S. G. Green, G. T. Fairhurst, and B. K. Snavely, "Chains of Poor Performance and Supervisory Control," *Organizational Behavior and Human Decision Processes* 38 (1986), pp. 7–27.

60. D. Kipnis, "Technology, Power, and Control," *Research in the Sociology of Organizations* 3 (1984a), pp. 125–56.

61. L. Dosier, T. Case, and B. Keys, "How Managers Influence Subordinates: An Empirical Study of Downward Influence Tactics," *Leadership and Organization Development Journal* 9, no. 5 (1988), pp. 22–31.

Chapter 5

Values, Ethics, and Character

Introduction

In the previous chapter we examined many facets of power and its use in leadership. Leaders can use power for good or ill, and a leader's personal values and ethical code may be among the most important determinants of how that leader exercises the various sources of power available. That this aspect of leadership needs closer scrutiny seems evident enough in the face of the past decade's wave of scandals involving political, business, and even religious leaders who collectively rocked trust in both our leaders and our institutions. Even in purely economic terms, in 2010 the Association of Certified Fraud Examiners estimated that businesses around the world lose $2.9 billion every year to fraudulent activity.[1] Further, in the 2008 presidential election a serious contender in one of our major parties not only had an ongoing extramarital affair during the campaign, which he lied about at the time (including his possible paternity of a child from that affair, later validated and admitted), but also managed to induce his own staff to cover it up. We might only wonder about what levels of honesty we could have expected from *that* White House had events unfolded differently. In the face of this distressing situation, it is not surprising that scholarly and popular literature have turned greater attention to the question of ethical leadership.[2]

Leadership and "Doing the Right Things"

In Chapter 1 we referred to a distinction between leaders and managers that says leaders do the right things whereas managers do things right. But what are the "right things"? Are they the morally right things? The ethically right things? The right things for the company to be successful? And who says what the right things are?

Leaders face dilemmas that require choices between competing sets of values and priorities, and the best leaders recognize and face them with a commitment to doing what is right, not just what is expedient. Of course the phrase *doing what is right* sounds deceptively simple. Sometimes it takes great moral courage to do what is right, even when the right action seems clear. At other times, though, leaders face complex challenges that lack simple black-and-white answers. Whichever the case, leaders set a moral example to others that becomes the model for an entire group or organization, for good or bad. Leaders who themselves do not honor truth do not inspire it in others. Leaders concerned mostly with their own advancement do not inspire selflessness in others. Leaders should internalize a strong set of **ethics**—principles of right conduct or a system of moral values.

Both Gardner[3] and Burns[4] have stressed the centrality and importance of the moral dimension of leadership. Gardner said leaders ultimately must be judged on the basis of a framework of values, not just in terms of their effectiveness. He put the question of a leader's relations with his or her followers or constituents on the moral plane, arguing (with the philosopher Immanuel Kant) that leaders should always treat others as ends in themselves, not as objects or mere means to the leader's ends (which does not necessarily imply that leaders need to be gentle in interpersonal demeanor or "democratic" in style). Burns took an even more extreme view regarding the moral dimension of leadership, maintaining that leaders who do not behave ethically do not demonstrate true leadership.

Whatever "true leadership" means, most people would agree that at a minimum it is characterized by a high degree of trust between leader and followers. Bennis and Goldsmith[5] described four qualities of leadership that engender trust: vision, empathy, consistency, and integrity. First, we tend to trust leaders who create a compelling *vision:* who pull people together on the basis of shared beliefs and a common sense of organizational purpose and belonging. Second, we tend to trust leaders who demonstrate *empathy* with us—who show they understand the world as we see and experience it. Third, we trust leaders who are *consistent*. This does not mean that we only trust leaders whose positions never change, but that changes are understood as a process of evolution in light of relevant new evidence. Fourth, we tend to trust leaders whose *integrity* is strong, who demonstrate their commitment to higher principles through their actions.

Another important factor affecting the degree of trust between leaders and followers involves fundamental assumptions people make about human nature. Several decades ago Douglas McGregor[6] explained different styles of managerial behavior on the basis of people's implicit attitudes about human nature, and his work remains quite influential today. McGregor identified two contrasting sets of assumptions people make about human nature, calling these **Theory X** and **Theory Y.**

In the simplest sense, Theory X reflects a more pessimistic view of others. Managers with this orientation rely heavily on coercive, external

Leadership cannot just go along to get along . . . Leadership must meet the moral challenge of the day.

Jesse Jackson

control methods to motivate workers, such as pay, disciplinary techniques, punishments, and threats. They assume people are not naturally industrious or motivated to work. Hence it is the manager's job to minimize the harmful effects of workers' natural laziness and irresponsibility by closely overseeing their work and creating external incentives to do well and disincentives to avoid slacking off. Theory Y, on the other hand, reflects a view that most people are intrinsically motivated by their work. Rather than needing to be coaxed or coerced to work productively, such people value a sense of achievement, personal growth, pride in contributing to their organization, and respect for a job well done. Peter Jackson, the director of the *Lord of the Rings* film trilogy, seems to exemplify a Theory Y view of human nature. When asked, "How do you stand up to executives?" Jackson answered, "Well, I just find that most people appreciate honesty. I find that if you try not to have any pretensions and you tell the truth, you talk to them and you treat them as collaborators, I find that studio people are usually very supportive."

But are there practical advantages to holding a Theory X or Theory Y view? Evidently there are. There is evidence that success more frequently comes to leaders who share a positive view of human nature. Hall and Donnell[7] reported findings of five separate studies involving over 12,000 managers that explored the relationship between managerial achievement and attitudes toward subordinates. Overall, they found that managers who strongly subscribed to Theory X beliefs were far more likely to be in their lower-achieving group.

The dilemma, of course, is that for the most part both Theory X and Theory Y leaders would say they have the right beliefs and are doing the right things. This begs the question of what people generally mean by "right," which in turn raises an array of issues involving ethics, moral reasoning, values, and the influence they have on our behavior.

> *There is nothing so fast as the speed of trust.*
> **Stephen Covey**

Values

Values are "constructs representing generalized behaviors or states of affairs that are considered by the individual to be important."[8] When Patrick Henry said, "Give me liberty, or give me death," he was expressing the value he placed on political freedom. The opportunity to constantly study and learn may be the fundamental value or "state of affairs" leading a person to pursue a career in academia. Someone who values personal integrity may be forced to resign from an unethical company. Values are learned through the socialization process, and they become internalized and for most people represent integral components of the self.[9] Thus values play a central role in one's overall psychological makeup and can affect behavior in a variety of situations. In work settings, values can affect decisions about joining an organization, organizational commitment, relationships with co-workers, and decisions about leaving an organization.[10] It is important for leaders to realize that

On the Danger of Making Small Compromises to Your Values

HIGHLIGHT 5.1

What do you think? Is it easier to stick to your values 100 percent of the time or 98 percent of the time? That is a question professor Clay Christensen (an expert in business innovation) posed to his students at Harvard in an end-of-semester lecture requested by them. The students wanted to know whether and how the business principles he taught in class applied to their personal lives.

One of the personal stories Christensen shared in the lecture occurred when he played on the Oxford University basketball team. It was a good team, and it had been a very successful year. They were going to play in the British equivalent of the NCAA tournament, and they made it to the final four. When Christensen saw the tourney schedule, however, he was chagrined: their championship game would be played on a Sunday. Christensen told his students that because of deep religious convictions, he'd made a firm commitment never to play on a Sunday. At the time, his coach and teammates were incredulous; after all, it would be an exception, "just this once." What difference would it really make? Christensen stood by his principles, though, and did not play in the championship game.

The point he was making to his Harvard students was that, as counterintuitive as it might seem, it *is* easier to stick to your values 100 percent of the time than it is to stick to them 98 percent of the time. Tempting as it might be to make an exception "just this once" because of extenuating circumstances, "you've got to define for yourself what you stand for and draw the line in a safe place."

Source: C. M. Christensen, "How Will You Measure Your Life? Don't Reserve Your Best Business Thinking for Your Career," *Harvard Business Review*, July/August (2010), pp. 46–51.

individuals in the same work unit can have considerably different values, especially because we cannot see values directly. We can only make inferences about people's values based on their behavior.

Some of the major values that may be considered important by individuals in an organization are listed in Table 5.1. The instrumental values found in Table 5.1 refer to modes of behavior, and the terminal values refer to desired end states.[11] For example, some individuals value equality, freedom, and a comfortable life above all else; others may believe that family security and salvation are important goals. In terms of instrumental values, such individuals may think it is important always to act in an ambitious, capable, and honest manner, whereas others may think it is

TABLE 5.1

People Vary in the Relative Importance They Place on Values

Source: Adapted from M. Rokeach, *The Nature of Human Values* (New York: Free Press, 1973).

Terminal Values	Instrumental Values
An exciting life	Being courageous
A sense of accomplishment	Being helpful
Family security	Being honest
Inner harmony	Being imaginative
Social recognition	Being logical
Friendship	Being responsible

154   Part Two   *Focus on the Leader*

important only to be ambitious and capable. We should add that the instrumental and terminal values in Table 5.1 are only a few of those Rokeach has identified.

Various researchers have said that the pervasive influence of broad forces like major historical events and trends, technological changes, and economic conditions tends to create common value systems among people growing up at a particular time that distinguish them from people who grow up at different times.[12–14] They attribute much of the misunderstanding that may exist between older leaders and younger followers to the fact that their basic value systems were formulated during different social and cultural conditions, and these analyses offer a helpful perspective for understanding how differences in values can add tension to the interaction between some leaders and followers.

Zemke is another researcher who has looked at differences in values across generations and how those value differences affect their approaches to work and leadership.[15] Following is his delineation of four generations of workers, each molded by distinctive experiences during critical developmental periods:

The Veterans (1922–1943): Veterans came of age during the Great Depression and World War II, and they represent a wealth of lore and wisdom. They've been a stabilizing force in organizations for decades, even if they are prone to digressions about "the good old days."

The Baby Boomers (1942–1960): These were the postwar babies who came of age during violent social protests, experimentation with new lifestyles, and pervasive questioning of establishment values. But they're graying now, and they don't like to think of themselves as "the problem" in the workplace even though they sometimes are. Boomers still have passion about bringing participation, spirit, heart, and humanity to the workplace and office. They're also concerned about creating a level playing field for all, but they hold far too many meetings for the typical Gen Xer. As the Boomers enter their retirement years, they take with them a work ethic characterized by ambition, an achievement orientation, and organizational loyalty.[16]

The Gen Xers (1961–1981): Gen Xers grew up during the era of the Watergate scandal, the energy crisis, higher divorce rates, MTV, and corporate downsizing; many were latchkey kids. As a group they tend to be technologically savvy, independent, and skeptical of institutions and hierarchy. They are entrepreneurial and they embrace change. Having seen so many of their parents work long and loyally for one company only to lose their jobs to downsizing, Xers don't believe much in job security; to an Xer, job security comes from having the kinds of skills that make you attractive to an organization. Hence they tend to be more committed to their vocation than to any specific organization. In fact, the free-agency concept born in professional sports also applies to Xers, who are disposed to stay with an organization until a better offer comes along. Among the challenges they present at work is how to meet their need for feedback despite their dislike of close supervision. Xers also seek balance in their lives more than preceding generations; they work to live rather than live to work.

Millennials (1982–2005): This is *your* generation, so any generalizations we make here are particularly risky! In general, however, Millennials share an optimism born, perhaps, from having been raised by parents devoted to the task of bringing their generation to adulthood; they are the children of soccer moms and Little League dads. They doubt the wisdom of traditional racial and sexual categorizing—perhaps not unexpected from a generation rich with opportunities like having Internet pen pals in Asia with whom they can interact any time of the day or night. As they move into the workplace, Millennials are seeking teamwork, security, and work-life balance.[17] As "digital natives," Millennials bring sharing habits born of extensive experience with social media to the workplace; their comfort level with transparency of action may well have a profound long-term effect on the workplace.[18] Of more concern, many college professors perceive Millennials to lack drive and a sense of accountability yet still expect positive evaluations despite marginal effort.[19]

Some research has looked at how the values of Gen Xers impact the leadership process at work. One clear finding from this research involved the distinctively different view of authority held by Xers than previous generations. "While past generations might have at least acknowledged positional authority, this new generation has little respect for and less interest in leaders who are unable to demonstrate that they can personally produce. In other words, this generation doesn't define leading as sitting in meetings and making profound vision statements, but instead as eliminating obstacles and giving employees what they need to work well and comfortably."[20] Gen Xers expect managers to "earn their stripes" and not be rewarded with leadership responsibilities merely because of seniority. Often that attitude is interpreted as an indication of disrespect toward elders in general and bosses in particular. It may be more accurate, however, to characterize the attitude as one of skepticism rather than disrespect.

Lest we overemphasize the significance of intergenerational differences, however, we should consider the results of a scientific sampling of over 1,000 people living in the United States that found *little* evidence of a generation gap in basic values. Indeed, the director of one of the largest polling organizations in the world called the results some of the most powerful he had seen in 30 years of public opinion research. They showed, he said, that even though young people have different tastes, they do *not* have a different set of values than their elders.[21] Considering the weight of

Question authority, but raise your hand first.
Bob Thaues

Main Events in the Lives of Gen Xers

HIGHLIGHT 5.2

A number of historical events over the past three and a half decades have had significant impacts on the lives and worldviews of today's emerging leaders.

GENERAL

1968 Martin Luther King Jr. assassinated

1969 U.S. lands on the moon

1973 Watergate scandal begins

1975 Vietnam war ends

1976 Energy crisis

1979 Iran hostage crisis

1981 Center for Disease Control's first published report on AIDS

1981 Reagan assassination attempt

1984 Ozone depletion detected

1984 Extensive corporate downsizing begins

1986 Space shuttle disaster

1986 Chernobyl disaster

1989 Berlin Wall falls

1990 Persian Gulf War

1991 USSR dissolves

2001 Terrorist attacks on World Trade Center

2003 Enron and other corporate scandals

2004 Southeast Asia tsunami kills over 200,000

2008 Election of first African-American president in U.S. history

TECHNOLOGICAL

1971 Intel's first chip developed

1972 First e-mail management program

1974 Videocassette recorder introduced on the consumer market

1975 Microsoft founded

1975 Personal computer introduced on the consumer market

1979 First commercial cellular telephone system

1980 CNN begins 24-hour broadcasting

1981 MTV launched

1991 World Wide Web launched

2001 Apple unveils the iPod

2006 YouTube explodes on scene

2010 Facebook has 500,000,000 users

Source: Initially adapted from B. Baldwin and S. Trovas, *Leadership in Action* 21, no. 6 (January/February 2002), p. 17.

scholarly research on value differences across generations, it's been said that the idea of a generational gap in values may be more popular culture than good social science.[22] That is consistent with results from a recent study that found "overwhelming consistency" in the ways managers from different generations evaluated the importance of various leadership practices as well as proficiency in them. The study concluded that Boomers, Xers, and Millennials in the managerial workforce are much more similar in their views of organizational leadership than they are different.[23]

Moral Reasoning and Character-Based Leadership

Until now our discussion has focused primarily on the content of people's values—that is, on *what* people claim to value. Related to this are matters concerning *how people think and act concerning matters of right and wrong*, to matters of moral reasoning and character. We will look first at moral reasoning and then turn our attention to the somewhat broader question of leader character.

Moral reasoning refers to the process leaders use to make decisions about ethical and unethical behaviors. It does not refer to the morality of individuals per se, or their espoused values, but rather to the manner by which they solve moral dilemmas.

Values play a key role in the moral reasoning process because value differences among individuals often result in different judgments regarding ethical and unethical behavior. In addition, fundamental and dramatic changes occur during young adulthood in how people define what is morally right or wrong. Those individuals whose moral judgment develops most are those who "love to learn, seek new challenges, who enjoy intellectually stimulating environments, who are reflective, who make plans and set goals, who take risks, and who take responsibility for themselves in the larger social context of history and institutions, and who take responsibility for themselves and their environs."[24]

Of course, not everyone fully develops their moral judgment. For example, research suggests that whereas most people believe they behave ethically, there is considerable reason to believe that they are considerably more biased than they think and that their actions fall short of their self-perceptions of ethical purity. Several unconscious biases affect our moral judgments, and paradoxically, the more strongly one believes that she is an ethical manager, the more one may fall victim to these biases.[25] That is probably one reason why in business and government many organizations are developing practical programs to develop moral decision-making competence among their leaders.[26]

We take it for granted that the effectiveness of any such programs to develop moral decision making depends a lot upon the quality of our understanding of the process itself, and recent research suggests that the psychological processes involved are more complicated than you might imagine. Perhaps this should not be surprising given that philosophers long have disagreed over the essential nature of moral judgment. Philosophers such as Plato and Kant believed mature moral judgment to be an essentially rational process whereas other philosophers, such as David Hume and Adam Smith, believed that emotions are at the heart of moral judgment (no pun intended!). Joshua Greene, a Harvard psychologist, finds research support for both views. He has proposed a **dual-process theory** of moral judgment wherein moral judgments dealing primarily with "rights" and "duties" are made by automatic emotional responses while moral judgments made on a more utilitarian basis are made more cognitively. Greene's methodology is fascinating and includes brain-imaging studies while people are pondering dilemmas similar to those featured in Highlight 5.3.[27–28]

Although moral dilemmas like the trolley problem are useful for scholarly and heuristic purposes, the scenarios may seem far from our everyday experience. A far more common yet still challenging **ethical dilemma**

Studying Moral Judgment: The Trolley Problem

HIGHLIGHT 5.3

The trolley problem, originally posed by philosopher Philippa Foot, involves two different dilemmas, a "switch" dilemma and a "footbridge" dilemma.

In the *switch* dilemma a runaway trolley is racing toward five people who will be killed if the train does not change course. You can save these five people by diverting the train onto another set of tracks. That alternative set of tracks only has one person on it, but if you divert the train onto those tracks that person will be killed. Is it morally permissible to switch the train onto the other track and thus save five lives at the cost of one? According to Greene's research most people say yes.

In the *footbridge* dilemma the trolley is again heading for five people. You happen to be standing next to a large man on a footbridge spanning the tracks, and if you push the man off the footbridge and into the path of the trolley you can save the other five people. Is it morally permissible to push the man into the path of the trolley? According to Greene, most people say no.

These results pose a challenge for moral philosophers: Why does it seem right to most people to sacrifice one person to save five others in the first situation but not in the second? Greene's answer to that puzzle is his dual-process theory mentioned in the text.

involves choosing between two "rights." Rushworth Kidder has identified four ethical dilemmas that are so common to our experience that they serve as models or paradigms:[29]

- **Truth versus loyalty,** such as honestly answering a question when doing so could compromise a real or implied promise of confidentiality to others.
- **Individual versus community,** such as whether you should protect the confidentiality of someone's medical condition when the condition itself may pose threat to the larger community.
- **Short-term versus long-term,** such as how a parent chooses to balance spending time with children now as compared with investments in a career that may provide greater benefits for the family in the long run.
- **Justice versus mercy,** such as deciding whether to excuse a person's misbehavior because of extenuating circumstances or a conviction that he or she has "learned a lesson."

Kidder offers three principles for resolving ethical dilemmas such as these: ends-based thinking, rule-based thinking, and care-based thinking.

Ends-based thinking is often characterized as "do what's best for the greatest number of people." It is also known as utilitarianism in philosophy, and it's premised on the idea that right and wrong are best determined by considering the consequences or results of an action. Critics of this view argue that it's almost impossible to foresee all the consequences of one's personal behavior, let alone the consequences of collective action like policy decisions affecting society more broadly. Even if outcomes could be known, however, there are other problems with this approach. For example, would this view ethically justify the deaths of dozens of infants in medical research if the result might save thousands of others?

Rule-based thinking is consistent with Kantian philosophy and can be colloquially characterized as "following the highest principle or duty." This is determined not by any projection of what the results of an act may be but rather by determining the kinds of standards everyone should uphold all the time, whatever the situation. In Kant's words, "I ought never to act except in such a way that I can also will that my maxim should become a universal law." Lofty as the principle may sound, though, it could paradoxically *minimize* the role that human judgment plays in ethical decision making by consigning all acts to a rigid and mindless commitment to rules absent consideration of the specific context of a decision ("If I let you do this, then I'd have to let *everyone* do it").

Care-based thinking describes what many think of as the Golden Rule of conduct common in some form to many of the world's religions: "Do what you want others to do to you." In essence, this approach applies the criterion of reversibility in determining the rightness of actions. We are asked to contemplate proposed behavior as if we were the object rather than the agent, and to consult our feelings as a guide to determining the best course.

It's important to emphasize that Kidder does not suggest any one of these principles is always best. Rather, he proposes that it would be a wise practice when considering the rightness of an action to invoke them all and reach a decision only after applying each to the specific circumstances one is facing and weighing the collective analyses. In other words, one principle may provide wise guidance in one situation whereas a different one may seem most helpful in a different one. There can be such critical yet subtle differences across situations that all three principles should be tentatively applied before any final course of action is chosen.

Despite the fact that most of the research and training applications pertaining to ethical behavior has focused on the essentially cognitive process of moral reasoning, it is important to recognize that the ability to make reasoned judgments about ethically laden situations does not guarantee a person will *act* ethically (witness the cases of retired former CIA Director David Petraeus, who resigned when his extramarital affair became public, or athlete Lance Armstrong, who after many years of public lies to the contrary finally admitted he had long taken performance-enhancing drugs to win his many Tour de France races).

Research has identified four particular biases that can have a pervasive and corrosive effect on our moral decision making. One of these is **implicit prejudice.** Although most people purport to judge others by their merits, research shows that implicit prejudice often distorts their judgments. The insidious nature of implicit prejudice lies in the fact that one is by nature unconscious of it. When one is queried, for example, about whether one

What Are Critical Elements of Developing Ethical Leadership?

HIGHLIGHT 5.4

Howard Prince and his associates have developed an impressive and comprehensive proposal for ethical leadership development at the undergraduate level. Here is a summary of what they view as critical elements of such a program:

- Knowledge of leadership and ethics to provide a conceptual framework for understanding the practice of ethical leadership.
- Opportunities to practice leadership roles requiring collective action where the learner has some responsibility for outcomes that matter to others.
- Opportunities to study, observe, and interact with leaders, especially those who have demonstrated moral courage.

- Formal and informal assessment of the efforts of those learning to lead ethically.
- Feedback to the learner, and opportunities for the learner to reflect on that feedback.
- Strengthening the learner's personal ethics and core values.
- Inspiring students to think of themselves as leaders and to accept leadership roles and responsibilities, including students who had not previously thought of themselves as leaders.

Source: H. T. Prince, G .R. Tumlin, and S. L. Connaughton, "An Interdisciplinary Major in Ethical Leadership Studies: Rationale, Challenges, and Template for Building an Adaptable Program," *International Leadership Journal*, 2009, pp. 91–128.

harbors prejudice against, say, Eskimos, one answers based on one's self-awareness of such attitudes. Some people are overtly racist or sexist, but offensive as such prejudice may be, it is at least something known to the person. In the case of implicit prejudice, however, judgments about some group are systematically biased *without their awareness.*

This has been documented in a fascinating series of experimental studies designed to detect unconscious bias.[30] These studies require people to rapidly classify words or images as "good" or "bad." Using a keyboard, individuals make split-second classifications of words like "love," "joy," "pain," and "sorrow." At the same time, they sort images of faces that are black or white, young or old, fat or thin (depending on the type of bias being examined). The critical results indicating implicit prejudice involve subtle shifts in reaction time in associating a particular image (such as a black face) with "good" words. People who consciously believe they have no prejudice or negative feelings about particular groups, say black Americans or the elderly, are nonetheless systematically slower in associating "good" words with those faces than they are in associating white or young faces with them.

Another bias that affects moral decision making is **in-group favoritism.** Most of us can readily point to numerous favors and acts of kindness we've shown toward others, and we understandably regard such acts as indicators of our own generosity and kindly spirit. If the whole pattern of one's generous acts were examined, however, ranging from things like job recommendations to help on a project, there is typically a clear pattern to those whom we've helped: most of the time they're "like us." This may not seem surprising, but one needs to consider who's not being helped: people "not like us." In other words, when we may make an exception favoring an "on the bubble" job applicant who is "like us," and fail to make such an exception for an identical candidate who is "not like us," we have effectively discriminated against the latter.[31]

Overclaiming credit is yet another way we may fool ourselves about the moral virtue of our own decision making. In many kinds of ways we tend to overrate the quality of our own work and our contributions to the groups and teams we belong to.[32] This has been widely documented, but one of the most telling studies was a 2007 poll of 2,000 executives and middle managers conducted by *BusinessWeek* magazine. One question in that poll asked respondents, "Are you one of the top 10 percent performers in your company?" If people were objective in rating themselves, presumably 10 percent would have placed themselves in the top 10 percent. But that's not what the results showed. Overall, 90 percent of the respondents placed themselves in the top 10 percent of performers![33]

Finally, our ethical judgments are adversely impacted by **conflicts of interest.** Sometimes, of course, we may be conscious of a potential conflict of interest, as when you benefit from a recommendation to someone else (such as getting a sales commission for something that may not be in the consumer's best interest). Even then, though, we misjudge our own ability to discount the extent to which the conflict actually biases our perception of the situation in our own favor.[34]

Other research strikes even more fundamentally at the idea that progress in understanding ethical behavior and increasing its likelihood or prevalence can adequately be based on a purely rational or reasoning-based approach.[35] The nature of human information processing at the cognitive and neurological levels inherently involves nonconscious processes of association and judgment. In an earlier paragraph we introduced the term *implicit prejudice,* but the word *implicit* should not itself be deemed undesirable. Some of the most impressive—and distinctly human—aspects of our thinking are inherently tacit or implicit. For example, one line of study suggests that in making moral judgments people often follow something more like scripts than any formal and rational process of ethical reasoning. Behavioral scripts from one's religious tradition (such as the Good Samaritan story) may be subconsciously triggered and lead to ethical behavior without explicit moral reasoning.[36] Some go so far as to say that "moral reasoning is rarely the direct cause of ethical judgment."[37] While that kind of perspective initially may seem to represent a pessimistic outlook on the possibility of truly improving ethical conduct, the reality is not so gloomy. Advocates of this view recognize that constructive things can be done to enhance ethical decision making. They also propose that a more complete answer lies not only in enhancing ethical and moral reasoning but also in approaches that enhance people's awareness of their ways of construing or constructing moral dimensions of any situation.

So near is a falsehood to truth that a wise man would do well not to trust himself on the narrow edge.

Cicero

As noted earlier, just because we profess certain values or moral codes does not ensure we will act that way when confronted with situations that engage them. It should be no surprise that in general when people are confronted with situations they've never faced before, their behavior may be different than they might have predicted. Unexpected natural disasters or threatening engagements with ill-willed people easily come to mind as situations where our own behavior can surprise us. But it's also true that we don't always behave as ethically as we think we would in morally demanding situations.

Social psychologist Ryan Brown has studied how accurately people can forecast their own ethical behavior, and found that while their predictions were generally consistent with their personal values, their actual behavior often was not. The general design of these experiments placed individuals in situations where they could choose to behave rather selflessly or somewhat more selfishly. A typical situation required the individual to choose between one of two sets of anagrams to complete (ostensibly as part of a study having a different purpose): either a short set of anagrams that would take only about 10 minutes to complete, or a longer set that would take about 45 minutes to complete. Whichever set the subject did *not* select presumably would be given to another soon-to-arrive experimental subject. As it turned out, 65 percent of the participants acted selfishly, selecting the easier task for themselves. Maybe you're saying to yourself, "Well, of course . . . you'd be crazy not to choose the easier one for yourself if given the chance to get the same credit for it." Perhaps, but only 35 percent predicted that they would make a selfish choice. It seems that when we are asked to *forecast* our behavior, we take our actual personal values into account. But the results of these studies also make a persuasive case that our personal values represent how we think we ought to act rather than how we often actually do act.[38]

These results should give us some pause when, in the face of unethical behavior by others, we feel confident that we would have acted differently facing the same situation. Such apparent overconfidence seems to be caused by the bias of idealizing our own behavior, and this bias, ironically, may leave us ill-prepared to make the most ethical choices when we actually confront ethically challenging situations. Being aware of this bias is a good first step in avoiding the same trap. Highlight 5.5 offers some suggestions for this kind of self awareness.[39]

A related aspect of ethical conduct involves the mental gymnastics by which people can dissociate their moral thinking from their actions. As noted before, the ability to reason about hypothetical moral issues, after all, does not ensure that one will *act* morally; one's moral actions may not always be consistent with one's espoused values. Bandura, in particular, has pointed out several ways people with firm moral principles nonetheless may behave badly without feeling guilt or remorse over their behavior. We should look at each of these, especially since Bandura's analysis has been further validated in a recent major study of moral disengagement at work—in other words, why employees do bad things.[40–42]

Moral justification involves reinterpreting otherwise immoral behavior in terms of a higher purpose. This is most dramatically revealed in the behavior of combatants in war. Moral reconstruction of killing is dramatically illustrated by the case of Sergeant York, one of the phenomenal fighters in the history of modern warfare. Because of his deep religious convictions, Sergeant York registered as a conscientious objector, but his numerous appeals were denied. At camp, his battalion commander quoted chapter and verse from the Bible to persuade him that under appropriate conditions it was Christian to fight and kill. A marathon mountainside prayer finally convinced him that he could serve both God and country by becoming a dedicated fighter.[43]

Another way to dissociate behavior from one's espoused moral principles is through **euphemistic labeling.** This involves using cosmetic words to defuse or disguise the offensiveness of otherwise morally repugnant or distasteful behavior. Terrorists, for example, may call themselves "freedom fighters," and firing someone may be referred to as "letting him or her go." **Advantageous comparison** lets one avoid self-contempt for one's behavior by comparing it to even more heinous behavior by others. ("If you think *we're* insensitive to subordinates' needs, you should see what it's like working for Acme.")

Through **displacement of responsibility** people may violate personal moral standards by attributing responsibility to others. Nazi concentration camp guards, for example, attempted to avoid moral responsibility for their behavior by claiming they were merely carrying out orders. A related

Ask Yourself These Questions

HIGHLIGHT 5.5

An important foundation of behaving ethically at work is to become more self-conscious of one's own ethical standards and practices. The National Institute of Ethics uses the following questions in its self-evaluation to facilitate that kind of self-reflection:

- How do I decide ethical dilemmas?
- Do I have set ethical beliefs or standards?
- If so, do I live by these beliefs or standards?
- How often have I done something that I am ashamed of?
- How often have I done things that I am proud of?
- Do I admit my mistakes?
- What do I do to correct mistakes that I make?

- Do I often put the well-being of others ahead of mine?
- Do I follow the Golden Rule?
- Am I honest?
- Do people respect my integrity?
- What are the three best things that have ever happened to me?
- What is the most dishonest thing I have ever done?
- Did I ever rectify the situation?
- What is the most honest thing I have ever done?

All leaders should regularly ask themselves questions like these.

Source: From N. Trautman, *Integrity Leadership,* Director, *National Institute of Ethics, www.ethicsinstitute.com.*

mechanism is **diffusion of responsibility,** whereby reprehensible behavior becomes easier to engage in and live with if others are behaving the same way. When everyone is responsible, it seems, no one is responsible. This way of minimizing individual moral responsibility for collective action can be a negative effect of group decision making. Through **disregard** or **distortion of consequences,** people minimize the harm caused by their behavior. This can be a problem in bureaucracies when decision makers are relatively insulated by their position from directly observing the consequences of their decisions. **Dehumanization** is still another way of avoiding the moral consequences of one's behavior. It is easier to treat others badly when they are dehumanized, as evidenced in epithets like "gooks" or "Satan-worshippers." Finally, people sometimes try to justify immoral behavior by claiming it was caused by someone else's actions. This is known as **attribution of blame.**

How widespread are such methods of minimizing personal moral responsibility? When people behave badly, Bandura said, it is *not* typically because of a basic character flaw; rather, it is because they use methods like these to construe their behavior in a self-protective way.[44]

Perhaps, but there is a demonstrable crisis of confidence in leadership,[45] and even if character flaws per se among leaders are not the root cause, it is still telling that scholars have been giving increasing attention to that very concept of character. It's rather remarkable, in fact, that a term that until recently was virtually ignored in the scholarly literature is now described as "an indispensable component of sustainable leadership performance"[46] and "a central and defining feature of ethical leadership."[47] One reason may be belated recognition that the long-standing preoccupation with the narrower concept of moral judgment simply did not square with the fact that it explained only about 80 percent of the variance in ethical behavior. That has led Hannah and Avolio to recommend greater attention be paid to a concept they call **moral potency.**[48] It has three main components:

- **Moral ownership:** A felt sense of responsibility not only for the ethical nature of one's own behavior but also for one's commitment not to allow unethical things to happen within their broader sphere of influence including others and the organization.

- **Moral courage:** The fortitude to face risk and overcome fears associated with taking ethical action.

- **Moral efficacy:** Belief or confidence in one's capability to mobilize various personal, interpersonal, and other external resources to persist despite moral adversity.

Riggio and his associates have taken a complementary approach to studying leader character in their focus on the virtues of prudence, temperance, fortitude, and justice as hallmarks of an ethical leader. And while they freely admit that this approach is in some ways "just" a renewed call to recognize age-old wisdom, their development of an assessment instrument (the *Leadership Virtues Questionnaire*) should generate new ways of studying and deeper ways of understanding these ideas.[49]

Another advance in the challenging task of assessing seemingly hard-to-measure constructs was the analysis of alternative approaches to measuring managerial integrity by Kaiser and Hogan.[50] They suggest that the common method of measuring managerial integrity using co-worker ratings of observed ethical behavior probably seriously underestimates the problem since it is relatively rare for managers to actually get caught in ethical lapses. As an alternative, they recommend assessing managerial integrity using what they call the *dubious reputation* approach. In essence, this approach asks subordinates (presumably the most likely group to see a manager's "dark side") to speculate on the likelihood that the manager *would be likely* to behave unethically, as distinguished from having directly observed such behavior.

Profiles in Leadership 5.1 offers a somewhat different look at the role of character in leadership.

> *Beware of the man who had no regard for his own reputation, since it is not likely he should have any for yours.*
>
> **George Shelley**

The Wit and Wisdom of Winston Churchill

PROFILES IN LEADERSHIP 5.1

Sir Winston Churchill was one of the towering figures of the 20th century. He served as British prime minister two times, most famously and importantly throughout World War II. His leadership of Britain during WWII ranks among the most inspiring in history, as time and time again his bulldog spirit rallied the British people during those early years of WWII he called the country's "darkest hour." In a real sense his character strengthened the national character, and vice versa. Perhaps no one before or since exercised leadership through the written and spoken word so effectively as Churchill.

Churchill's masterful use of words was not limited to debate and speeches. After the war he won the Nobel Prize for Literature for his six-volume memoir, *The Second World War*. He was also notorious for his barbed comments about people he didn't like, including his political adversaries. For example, he said of Clement Attlee, who succeeded Churchill as prime minister after the war, "A modest man, who has much to be modest about."

To follow are a few more examples of the wit and wisdom of Winston Churchill:

We make a living by what we get, but we make a life by what we give.

From now on, ending a sentence with a proposition is something up with which I shall not put.

You have enemies? Good. That means you've stood for something, sometime in your life.

You can always count on Americans to do the right thing—after they've tried everything else.

History will be kind to me for I intend to write it.

The best argument against democracy is a five-minute conversation with the average voter.

Courage is what it takes to stand up and speak; courage is also what it takes to sit down and listen.

Continuous effort—not strength or intelligence—is the key to unlocking our potential.

Men occasionally stumble over the truth, but most of them pick themselves up and hurry off as of nothing had happened.

I am prepared to meet my Maker. Whether my Maker is prepared for the great ordeal of meeting me is another matter.

We are all worms. But I believe that I am a glow-worm.

Kites rise highest against the wind—not with it.

He has all of the virtues I dislike and none of the vices I admire.

Character-Based Approaches to Leadership

Can you be a good leader without being a good person? Does it make any sense to say, for example, that Hitler was an effective leader even if he was an evil person? In that sense, while some might consider the phrase *ethical leadership* to be redundant, Avolio and his associates have defined ethical leadership as having two core components: the **moral person** and the **moral manager**.[51] The moral person is seen as a principled decision maker who cares about people and the broader society.[52] The actions of such people indicate they try to do the right things personally and professionally, and they can be characterized as honest, fair, and open. In addition, ethical leaders have clear ethical standards that they pursue in the face of pressure to do otherwise. More than being just moral people, ethical leaders are moral managers who "make ethics an explicit part of their leadership agenda by communicating an ethics and values message, by visibly and intentionally role modeling ethical behavior."[53] In recent years there has been a rekindling of interest in approaches to leadership that are inherently and explicitly based on the interdependence between effective leadership and certain value systems. This is in bold contrast to decades of tradition in the social sciences of being self-consciously "values-free" in pursuit of objectivity. Two prominent approaches in this movement are described in greater detail here.

Authentic leadership is grounded in the principle found in the familiar adage "to thine own self be true." Authentic leaders exhibit a consistency between their values, their beliefs, and their actions.[54] The roots of authentic leadership are also in various expressions of the humanistic movement in psychology including Maslow's theory of self-actualization (see Chapter 9) and Carl Rogers's concept of the fully functioning person.[55] Central to both Maslow's and Rogers's theories is the idea that individuals can develop modes of understanding and interacting with their social environments so as to become more truly independent of others' expectations of them (individual, group, and cultural) and guided more by the dictates of universal truths and imperatives. Such individuals manifest congruence between how they feel on the inside and how they act, between what they say and what they do. They have realistic self-perceptions, free from the blind spots and misperceptions of self that are common to most people. At the same time, they are accepting of themselves, their nature, and that of others too.

Authentic leaders have strong ethical convictions that guide their behavior not so much to avoid doing "wrong" things as to always try to do the "right" things, including treating others with respect and dignity. They know where they stand on fundamental values and key issues. Authentic leaders behave as they do because of personal conviction rather than to attain status, rewards, or other advantages. As Avolio puts it, authentic leaders both are self-aware and self-consciously align their actions with their inner values.[56] He points out that such authenticity is not just something you either "have or don't have." Authenticity as a leader is something that you must always be striving to enhance. It requires regularly identifying with your best self, checking in with your core values concerning your leadership agendas and operating practices, and verifying that your actions are aligned with the highest ethical and moral principles you hold. In this way, practicing authentic leadership becomes taking actions that serve high moral principles concerning relationships, social responsibilities, and performance standards.[57]

One way to understand authentic leadership is to contrast it with what might be called *inauthentic* leadership. If you think of a leader who "plays a role," or puts on different acts with different audiences to manage their impressions, that is being inauthentic. For example, two detectives playing the roles of "good cop" and "bad cop" when interviewing a suspect are being inauthentic (you may believe that it makes sense for them to do so, but it's inauthentic nonetheless). A boss who exaggerates his anger at an employee's mistake to "teach a lesson" is being inauthentic. A leader who denies that her feelings were affected by critical feedback from her direct reports is being inauthentic.

The study of authentic leadership has gained considerable momentum in the last decade because of beliefs that (1) enhancing self-awareness can help people in organizations find more meaning and connection at work; (2) promoting transparency and openness in relationships—even between leader and followers—builds trust and commitment; and (3) fostering more inclusive structures and practices in organizations can help build more positive ethical climates.[58] In contrast to stereotypical notions of the stoic "hero leader" who shows no weakness and shares no feelings, authentic leaders are willing to be viewed as vulnerable by their followers—a vital component of building a trusting leader–follower relationship. Equally important to building trust is a leader's willingness to be transparent—in essence, to say what she means and mean what she says. A recent major review of the scholarly literature on authentic leadership concluded by noting that the "assumption of authentic leadership theory that people in organizations can effectively lead, and follow, in a way that enables them to express their own unique identity and style, has created a sense of excitement among leadership scholars and practitioners."[59]

Servant leadership has since 1970 described a quite different approach to leadership than that derived from a bureaucratic and mechanistic view

The most important thing in acting is honesty. Once you've learned to fake that, you're in.

Samuel Goldwyn, early film producer

of organizations wherein workers are thought of as mere cogs in a machine. In the latter, the leader's primary role may be understood as doing whatever it takes to ensure that things run smoothly, tasks are performed, and goals are met. This has commonly involved a hierarchical approach to leadership. From the contrasting perspective of servant leadership, the leader's role is literally to serve others.

The modern idea of servant leadership was developed and popularized by Robert Greenleaf after he read a short novel by Herman Hesse called *Journey to the East*.[60-61] This is the mythical story of a group of people on a spiritual quest. Accompanying the party is a servant by the name of Leo, whose nurturing character sustained the group on its journey until one day he disappeared. The group fell apart and abandoned its quest when it realized that it was helpless without its servant. Finally, after many years of continued searching, the story's narrator found the religious order that had sponsored the original quest. It turned out that Leo, whom the narrator had only known as a servant, was actually the order's revered leader. To Greenleaf, this story meant that true leadership emerges when one's primary motivation is to help others.

The idea of servant leadership, of course, has been around for thousands of years. It stems at least in part from the teachings of Jesus, who instructed his disciples that servanthood is the essence of worthy leadership (such as through the example of *him* washing *their* feet). Ten characteristics are often associated with servant leaders. As you'll see, most of them also seem in line with the idea of authentic leadership just described:[62]

- *Listening:* While all leaders need to communicate effectively, the focus is often on communicating *to* others; but servant leadership puts the emphasis on *listening* effectively to others.
- *Empathy:* Servant leaders need to understand others' feelings and perspectives.
- *Healing:* Servant leaders help foster each person's emotional and spiritual health and wholeness.
- *Awareness:* Servant leaders understand their own values, feelings, strengths, and weaknesses.
- *Persuasion:* Rather than relying on positional authority, servant leaders influence others through their persuasiveness.
- *Conceptualization:* Servant leaders need to integrate present realities and future possibilities.
- *Foresight:* Servant leaders need to have a well-developed sense of intuition about how the past, present, and future are connected.
- *Stewardship:* Servant leaders are stewards who hold an organization's resources in trust for the greater good.

- *Commitment to others' growth:* The ultimate test of a servant leader's work is whether those served develop toward being more responsible, caring, and competent individuals.
- *Building community:* Such individual growth and development is most likely to happen when one is part of a supportive community. Unfortunately numerous factors like geographic mobility and the general impersonalism of large organizations have eroded people's sense of community. Thus it is the servant leader's role to help create a sense of community among people.

Not surprisingly, the concept of servant leadership has detractors as well as adherents. The most common criticism is that although the idea of servant leadership has a certain popular appeal in what we might call its "soft" form (for example, leaders should be more concerned about others' well-being and development, should create a more developmental climate in their organizations, and should seek what's good for the whole organization rather than just their own advancement), when taken more literally and extremely the concept seems to suggest that serving others is an end in itself rather than a means to other organizational goals and purposes. That version strikes many as impractical even if laudable.

A recent scholarly review of the theory of servant leadership noted an almost irreconcilable conflict between the ideas of servant leadership and the inherent realities of organizational life: Servant leaders develop people, helping them to strive and flourish. Servant leaders want those they serve to become healthier, wiser, freer, and more autonomous. Servant leaders serve followers. But managers are hired to contribute to organizational goal attainment. It would seem that these goals can be attained only by having subordinates (not followers) solving tasks that lead to productivity and effectiveness.[63] Productivity and effectiveness, however, may not be inherently incompatible with servant leadership. For example, the results of one recent study suggest that servant leadership can impact profits by increasing trust in the organization, reducing customer turnover and increasing employee satisfaction.[64]

The Roles of Ethics and Values in Organizational Leadership

Just as individuals possess a set of personal values, so too do organizations have dominant values. Many times these values are featured prominently in the company's annual report, website, and posters. These values represent the principles by which employees are to get work done and treat other employees, customers, and vendors. Whether these stated

Subordinates cannot be left to speculate as to the values of the organization. Top leadership must give forth clear and explicit signals, lest any confusion or uncertainty exist over what is and is not permissible conduct. To do otherwise allows informal and potentially subversive "codes of conduct" to be transmitted with a wink and a nod, and encourages an inferior ethical system based on "going along to get along" or the notion that "everybody's doing it."

Richard Thornburgh, former U.S. attorney general

values represent true operating principles or so much "spin" for potential investors will depend on the degree of alignment between the organization's stated values and the collective values of top leadership.[65,66] For example, many corporate value statements say little about making money, but this is the key organizational priority for most business leaders, and as such is a major factor in many company decisions. There is often a significant gap between a company's stated values and the way the company truly operates. Knowing the values of top leadership can sometimes tell you more about how an organization actually operates than will the organization's stated values. Two ancient and contrasting sets of values are described in Highlight 5.6.

In any organization, the top leadership's collective values play a significant role in determining the dominant values throughout the organization, just as an individual leader's values play a significant role in determining team climate. Related to the notion of culture and climate is employee "fit." Research has shown that employees with values similar to the organization or team are more satisfied and likely to stay; those with dissimilar values are more likely to leave.[67,68] Thus one reason why leaders fail is not due to a lack of competence but rather is due to a misalignment between personal and organizational values. Although the advantages of alignment between personal and organizational values may seem self-evident, leaders with *dissimilar* values may be exactly what some organizations need to drive change and become more effective.

Finally, values are often a key factor in both intrapersonal and interpersonal conflict. Many of the most difficult decisions made by leaders are choices between opposing values. A leader who valued both financial reward and helping others, for example, would probably struggle mightily when having to make a decision about cutting jobs to improve profitability. A leader who highly valued financial reward and did *not* strongly value helping others (or vice versa) would have much less trouble making the same decision. Likewise, some leaders would have difficulties making decisions if friendships get in the way of making an impact, or when taking risks to gain visibility runs counter to maintaining comfortable levels of stability in a team or organization. Values also play a key role in conflict between groups. The differences between Bill O'Reilly and Al Franken, the Israelis and Palestinians, the Shiite and Sunni Muslims in Iraq, the Muslims and Hindus in Kashmir, and Christians and Muslims in Kosovo are all at least partly based on differences in values. Because values develop early and are difficult to change, it's usually extremely difficult to resolve conflicts between such groups.

In sum, it's vital for a leader to set a personal example of values-based leadership, and it is also important for leaders—especially senior ones—to make sure clear values guide *everyone's* behavior in the organization. That's likely to happen only if the leader sets an example of desired

Ancient Eastern Philosophies and the Boardroom

HIGHLIGHT 5.6

Thirty years ago a best-selling business book called *Theory Z* purported to help Western business leaders apply the art of Japanese management to their own circumstances. Since then other Eastern philosophies have also gained popularity among Western leaders, albeit often in simplified forms. One perspective that has become popular in the West is based on the Chinese philosopher Sun Tzu, whose classic work *The Art of War* was written 2,500 years ago. Another is the *Bhagavad Gita,* a sacred Indian text containing the wisdom of Lord Krishna, believed to have been written nearly as long ago. Different implications for leadership are derived from these classic writings, a few of which are noted here:

	The Art of War	*Bhagavad Gita*
On Material Incentives	People need extrinsic incentives to be motivated. Give your soldiers shares of the booty and conquered territory.	Never act for material rewards only. Focus instead on doing well, and good things will follow.
On Handling Followers	Rule with iron discipline. Maintain your authority over them, knowing that too much kindness toward your followers could make them useless.	Enlightened leaders are selfless and compassionate toward others. Followers who are treated as equals are more motivated to enthusiastically support their leader.
On the Ultimate Goal	Winning requires cleverness and sometimes even deception.	Success means satisfying multiple stakeholders.

It doesn't seem likely that these perspectives, which obviously have stood the test of time, could simply be either right or wrong. How do you reconcile their differences?

Source: Adapted from *BusinessWeek,* October 30, 2006.

behavior. You might think of this as a necessary but not sufficient condition for principled behavior throughout the organization. If there is indifference or hypocrisy toward values at the highest levels, it is fairly unlikely that principled behavior will be considered important by others throughout the organization. Bill O'Brien, the former CEO of a major insurance company, likened an organization's poor ethical climate to a bad odor one gets used to:

> Organizations oriented to power, I realized, also have strong smells, and even if people are too inured to notice, that smell has implications. It affects

performance, productivity, and innovation. The worst aspect of this environment is that it stunts the growth of personality and character of everyone who works there.[69]

Carried to an extreme, this can lead to the kinds of excesses all too frequently evident during the past decade:

> Who knew the swashbuckling economy of the 1990s had produced so many buccaneers? You could laugh about the CEOs in handcuffs and the stock analysts who turned out to be fishier than storefront palm readers, but after a while the laughs became hard. Martha Stewart was dented and scuffed [and subsequently convicted]. Tyco was looted by its own executives. Enron and WorldCom turned out to be the twin towers of false promises. They fell. Their stockholders and employees went down with them. So did a large measure of faith in big corporations.
>
> *Time Magazine,* January 2, 2003

Leading by Example: the Good, the Bad, and the Ugly

One of the most quoted principles of good leadership is "leadership by example." But what does it mean to exemplify ethical leadership and be an ethical role model? In one study, people from a range of organizations were interviewed about a person they knew who had been an ethical role model at work. Not all ethical role models exhibited exactly the same qualities, but four general categories of attitudes and behaviors seemed to characterize the group:[70]

- *Interpersonal behaviors*: They showed care, concern, and compassion for others. They were hardworking and helpful. They valued their relationships with others, working actively to maintain and sustain them. They tended to focus on the positive rather than the negative, and accepted others' failures.
- *Basic fairness*: A specific quality of their interpersonal behaviors was manifested in the fairness shown others. They were not only open to input from others but actively sought it. They tended to offer explanations of decisions. They treated others respectfully, never condescendingly, even amid disagreements.
- *Ethical actions and self-expectations*: They held themselves to high ethical standards and behaved consistently in both their public and private lives. They accepted responsibility for and were open about their own ethical failings. They were perceived as honest, trustworthy, humble, and having high integrity.
- *Articulating ethical standards:* They articulated a consistent ethical vision and were uncompromising toward it and the high ethical standards it implied. They held others ethically accountable and put ethical standards above personal and short-term company interests.

Arguably the most important example for anyone is his or her boss, and it raises difficult and complex challenges when a boss is a *bad* ethical role model. This becomes a challenge far greater than merely the hypocrisy inherent in being told, "Do as I say, not as I do."

It should go without saying that those in responsible positions have a particular responsibility to uphold ethical standards—but what if they *don't*? What should you do when your own boss does not behave ethically?

One approach to addressing these challenges is to reject the notion that organizational leadership is synonymous with formal position or hierarchical power in the organization, and to embrace instead the idea that *all* organizational members have a role in organizational leadership, including responsibility for ethical leadership in the organization. The term **upward ethical leadership** has been used to refer to "leadership behavior enacted by individuals who take action to maintain ethical standards in the face of questionable moral behaviors by higher-ups."[71]

However, there are almost always reasons that may constrain employee behavior in such situations, including fear of retribution by bosses. More generally, do employees feel they have a safe outlet for raising ethical concerns about misbehavior by superiors in the organization?

One variable that moderates an employee's likelihood of raising such concerns is the general quality of ethical climate in the organization. **Ethical climates** refer to those in which ethical standards and norms have been consistently, clearly, and pervasively communicated throughout the organization and embraced and enforced by organizational leaders in both word and example. **Unethical climates** are those in which questionable or outright unethical behavior exists with little action taken to correct such behavior, or (worse) where such misbehavior is even condoned.[72] It's likely that employees experience some degree of moral distress whenever a manager is perceived to behave unethically, but the distress is usually greater in unethical climates.

Even in ethical climates, however, some individuals may be more likely than others to address perceived ethical problems in an active and constructive manner. This inclination is likely to be enhanced among individuals who feel a sense of personal power. Employees tend to feel greater power, for example, if they believe they have attractive opportunities in the broader employment marketplace, if they're respected for their credibility and competence in the organization, and if others within the organization are somewhat dependent on them. Organizations can further enhance the likelihood that employees will address perceived ethical problems in an active and constructive manner by nurturing a culture that is not all "command and control," by fostering a sense of shared leadership more than hierarchy, and by valuing upward leadership.[73] In the end, though, the most powerful way organizations can enhance the likelihood that employees will address ethical problems

A man who wants to lead the orchestra must turn his back on the crowd.

Max Lucado

in a constructive manner is by proactively creating an ethical climate throughout the organization, and that is not just a responsibility of informal ethical leaders throughout the organization but inescapably a responsibility of formal organizational leaders.

In fact, being in a formal leadership role imposes unique ethical responsibilities and challenges. Leaders more than followers (1) possess unique degrees of both legitimate and coercive power; (2) enjoy greater privileges; (3) have access to more information; (4) have greater authority and responsibility; (5) interact with a broader range of stakeholders who expect equitable treatment; and (6) must balance sometimes competing loyalties when making decisions.[74] With conditions like these, which sometimes also may represent seductive temptations to excuse one's own behavior, it is all the more important for leaders to take positive steps to create an ethical climate and hold themselves accountable to it.

It's important that people know what you stand for. It's equally important that they know what you won't stand for.
Mary Waldrop

Creating and Sustaining an Ethical Climate

So how do leaders do this? Several "fronts" of leadership action are needed to establish an ethical organizational climate:[75]

- *Formal ethics policies and procedures:* It's sometimes said that "you can't legislate morality," and the same may be said about legislating an ethical climate. Nonetheless, certain formal policies and procedures are probably necessary if not sufficient conditions for creating an ethical climate. These include formal statements of ethical standards and policies, along with reporting mechanisms, disciplinary procedures, and penalties for suspected ethical violations.

- *Core ideology:* A core ideology is basically an organization's heart and soul. It represents the organization's purpose, guiding principles, basic identity, and most important values. Starbucks is a good example. Starbucks' guiding principles include (1) respect and dignity for partners (employees); (2) embracing diversity; (3) applying the highest standards of excellence to the business; (4) developing "enthusiastically satisfied customers"; (5) contributing positively to local communities and to the environment more generally; and (6) maintaining profitability.[76]

- *Integrity:* The core ideology cannot be a mere set of boardroom plaques or other exhortations to behave well. The core ideology must be part of the fabric of every level and unit in the organization. Just as personal integrity describes an individual whose outward behavior and inward values are congruent and transparent, organizational integrity describes an organization whose pronouncements are congruent with its public and private actions at every level and in every office.

- *Structural reinforcement:* An organization's structure and systems can be designed to encourage higher ethical performance and discourage unethical performance. Performance evaluation systems that provide opportunities for anonymous feedback increase the likelihood that "dark side" behaviors would be reported, and thus discourage their enactment. Reward systems can promote honesty, fair treatment of customers, courtesy, and other desirable behaviors. If poorly designed, however, reward systems can also promote dishonesty. In an effort to increase the speed of repairs in its auto repair facilities, for example, Sears gave its mechanics a sales goal of $147 an hour. What that did, however, was to encourage the mechanics to overcharge for services and "repair" things that didn't need repairing.[77]

- *Process focus:* There also needs to be explicit concern with process, not just the achievement of tangible individual, team, and organizational goals. *How* those goals are achieved needs to be a focus of attention and emphasis too. When senior leaders set exceptionally high goals and show that they expect goals to be achieved whatever it takes, it's a recipe that may tempt and seemingly turn a blind eye to unethical behavior by employees.

Another way to think about the essence of creating an ethical climate in organizations is to recognize that it is not simply the sum of the collective moralities of its members. Covey has developed and popularized an approach called **principle-centered leadership,**[78] which postulates a fundamental interdependence between the personal, the interpersonal, the managerial, and the organizational levels of leadership. The unique role of each level may be thought of like this:

Personal: The first imperative is to be a trustworthy person, and that depends on both one's character *and* competence. Only if one is trustworthy can one have trusting relationships with others.

Interpersonal: Relationships that lack trust are characterized by self-protective efforts to control and verify each other's behavior.

Managerial: Only in the context of trusting relationships will a manager risk empowering others to make full use of their talents and energies. But even with an empowering style, leading a high-performing group depends on skills such as team building, delegation, communication, negotiation, and self-management.

Organizational: An organization will be most creative and productive when its structure, systems (training, communication, reward, and so on), strategy, and vision are aligned and mutually supportive. Put differently, certain organizational alignments are more likely than others to nurture and reinforce ethical behavior.

Interestingly, the interdependence between these levels posited in principle-centered leadership is quite similar to recent conceptualizations of authentic leadership that also view it as a multilevel phenomenon. That is, authentic leadership can be thought of not only as a quality

The Cult of Enron

HIGHLIGHT 5.7

Enron has come to represent the epitome of greed, ethical lapse, and spectacular failure in the business world. Its senior executives CEO Kenneth Lay and Jeffrey Skilling were blamed and prosecuted for the company's collapse and callous indifference to the welfare of its employees. But the problems at Enron ran deeper than just the shoddy ethics and illegal actions of a few people at the top. A large part of the problem was the Enron culture itself that people *throughout* the company perpetuated.

A root of the problem may be that Enron's culture had many characteristics of a cult. Cults are characterized as having these four qualities:

- Charismatic leadership.
- A compelling and totalistic vision.
- A conversion process.
- A common culture.

Here are some of the ways that Enron's corporate culture was like a cult. You can see how corporations as well as religious cults can encourage counterproductive conformity and penalize dissent.

CHARISMATIC LEADERSHIP

Enron's leaders created an aura of charisma around themselves through ever more dramatic forms of self-promotion. Skilling, for example, cultivated his image as the Enron version of Darth Vader, even referring to his traders as "Storm Troopers." The reputations of Skilling and other top executives at Enron were further reinforced by the ways in which they were lionized in respected business publications and by the opulent lifestyles they enjoyed.

COMPELLING AND TOTALISTIC VISION

Hyperbole was rampant at Enron, as in banners proclaiming its vision of being the "world's leading company." Such exalted self-images encourage members to feel a sense of privilege and destiny. Employees were bombarded with messages that they were the best and the brightest. Their commitment to organizational success had an almost evangelistic fervor, and workweeks of even 80 hours were considered normal.

CONVERSION AND INDOCTRINATION

From an employee's recruitment to Enron onward, communication was one-way: top-down. In the early stages this involved intense and emotionally draining rituals over several days wherein the recruit would hear powerful messages from the leaders. Group dynamics research has shown that such initiation rituals incline people to exaggerate the benefits of group membership in their minds. In Enron's case the purpose was to ingrain in employees a single-minded personal commitment to continued high rates of corporate growth.

COMMON CULTURE

Despite all the effort put into selecting new employees and imbuing them with a sense of privilege, a punitive internal culture was also nurtured through which all the psychic and material benefits of being in Enron could be withdrawn on a managerial whim. Enron was quick to fire any of these "best and brightest" who did not conform; they could be branded, almost overnight, as "losers" in others' eyes. This could happen for mere dissent with the corporate line as well as for failing to meet Enron's exceedingly high performance goals.

Source: D. Tourish and N. Vatcha, "Charismatic Leadership and Corporate Cultism at Enron: The Elimination of Dissent, the Promotion of Conformity, and Organizational Collapse," *Leadership* 1, no. 4 (2005), pp. 455–80.

characterizing certain individual leaders but also as a quality of certain leader–follower dyads, groups or teams, and even organizations. Thus it makes just as much sense to talk about authentic organizations as it does to talk about authentic leaders.[79]

In concluding this chapter, we would be remiss not to explicitly address a question that has been implicit throughout it: *why* should a company go to the trouble of creating and sustaining an ethical climate?[80] One answer—perhaps a sufficient one—is because it's the right thing to do. Sometimes, however, it's too easy merely to assume that because something is the right thing to do there must be some costs or disadvantages associated with it. As is apparent from this chapter, it's not easy to create and sustain an ethical environment in an organization; it takes conviction, diligence, and commitment. In some ways, such continuing focus and effort can be thought of as a cost. However, such focus and effort can pay dividends beyond an intrinsic sense of satisfaction.

Johnson has identified a number of tangible positive outcomes for an organization that creates an ethical climate. One of these is greater collaboration within the organization: an ethical climate produces greater trust within an organization, and trust is a key element underlying collaboration. Another positive outcome can be improved social standing and improved market share for the organization. Eighty-four percent of Americans said that if price and quality were similar, they would switch allegiance to companies associated with worthy causes. Over $2 trillion is now invested in mutual funds focusing on companies demonstrating commitment to the environment, ethics, and social responsibility.[81,82] There also is evidence that ethical companies often outperform their competitors.[83]

Similar tangible advantages were identified by Harvard professors John Kotter and James Heskett among companies that aligned espoused values with organizational practices. Such companies increased revenues by an average of 682 percent versus 166 percent for companies that didn't.[84] Paying attention to ethics and values *can* be good business.

Summary

This chapter has reviewed evidence regarding the relationships among ethics, values, and leadership. Ethics is a branch of philosophy that deals with right conduct. Values are constructs that represent general sets of behaviors or states of affairs that individuals consider important, and they are a central part of a leader's psychological makeup. Values affect leadership through a cultural context within which various attributes and behaviors are regarded differentially—positively or negatively.

It's not just the content of one's beliefs about right and wrong that matters, though. *How* one makes moral or ethical judgments, or the manner by which one solves moral problems, is also important and is referred to as moral reasoning.

Only mediocrities rise to the top in a system that won't tolerate wave making.

Lawrence J. Peter, author of *The Peter Principle*

I do believe in the spiritual nature of human beings. To some it's a strange or outdated idea, but I believe there is such a thing as a human spirit. There is a spiritual dimension to man which should be nurtured.

Aung San Suu Kyi

Ethical action, of course, involves more than just the cognitive process of moral reasoning. That's why people's behavior does not always conform to how they predict they'll act, or with their espoused values. Furthermore, the thorniest ethical dilemmas people face tend not to involve choices between what is right or wrong but between two different "rights." In such cases it is useful to apply several different principles for resolving moral dilemmas.

Recently many approaches to leadership have explicitly addressed the interdependencies between effective leadership and particular value systems. The concepts of authentic leadership and servant leadership are among these. There also has been increased interest in recent years in the kinds of practices that can be instituted within organizations to enhance the likelihood that they will have ethical climates.

Key Terms

ethics, *151*
Theory X, *151*
Theory Y, *151*
values, *152*
moral reasoning, *157*
dual-process
  theory, *157*
ethical dilemmas, *157*
truth versus
  loyalty, *158*
individual versus
  community, *158*
short-term versus
  long-term, *158*
justice versus
  mercy, *158*
ends-based
  thinking, *158*
rule-based
  thinking, *159*

care-based
  thinking, *159*
implicit prejudice, *159*
in-group
  favoritism, *160*
overclaiming
  credit, *161*
conflicts of
  interest, *161*
moral justification, *163*
euphemistic
  labeling, *163*
advantageous
  comparison, *163*
displacement of
  responsibility, *163*
diffusion of
  responsibility, *164*
distortion of
  consequences, *164*

disregard, *164*
dehumanization, *164*
attribution of
  blame, *164*
moral potency, *164*
moral ownership, *164*
moral courage, *164*
moral efficacy, *164*
moral person, *166*
moral manager, *166*
authentic
  leadership, *166*
servant
  leadership, *167*
upward ethical
  leadership, *173*
ethical climate, *173*
unethical climate, *173*
principle-centered
  leadership, *175*

Questions

1. Do you think it always must be "lonely at the top" (or that if it is not, you are doing something wrong)?

2. How do you believe one's basic philosophy of human nature affects one's approach to leadership?

3. Identify several values you think might be the basis of conflict or misunderstanding between leaders and followers.

4. Can a leader's public and private morality be distinguished? Should they be?

5. Can a bad person be a good leader?
6. Are there any leadership roles men and women should not have equal opportunity to compete for?
7. What is the relationship between an individual's responsibility for ethical behavior and the idea of organizational ethical climate? Does focus on the latter diminish the importance of the former or reduce the importance of individual accountability?
8. Could two different groups have quite different ethical climates if the same people were members of both?

Activities

1. Each person should select his or her own 10 most important values from the following list, and then rank-order those 10 from most important (1) to least important (10). Then have an open discussion about how a person's approach to leadership might be influenced by having different value priorities. The values are achievement, activity (keeping busy), advancement, adventure, aesthetics (appreciation of beauty), affiliation, affluence, authority, autonomy, balance, challenge, change/variety, collaboration, community, competence, competition, courage, creativity, economic security, enjoyment, fame, family, friendship, happiness, helping others, humor, influence, integrity, justice, knowledge, location, love, loyalty, order, personal development, physical fitness, recognition, reflection, responsibility, self-respect, spirituality, status, and wisdom.

2. Explore how the experiences of different generations might have influenced the development of their values. Divide into several groups and assign each group the task of selecting representative popular music from a specific era. One group, for example, might have the 1950s, another the Vietnam War era, and another the 1990s. Using representative music from that era, highlight what seem to be dominant concerns, values, or views of life during that period.

Minicase

Balancing Priorities at Clif Bar

Gary Erickson is a man of integrity. In the spring of 2000 Erickson had an offer of more than $100 million from a major food corporation for his company Clif Bar Inc. He had founded Clif Bar Inc. in 1990 after a long bike ride. Erickson, an avid cyclist, had finished the 175-mile ride longing for an alternative to the tasteless energy bars he had brought along. "I couldn't make the last one go down, and that's when I had an epiphany—make a product that actually tasted good." He looked at the list of ingredients on the package and decided he could do better. He called on his experience in his family's bakery, and after a year in the kitchen, the Clif Bar—named for Erickson's father—was launched in 1992. Within five years sales had skyrocketed to $20 million. He considered the $100 million offer on the table and what it meant for his company and decided against the deal. He realized that the vision he had for the company would be compromised once he lost control, so he walked away from the $100 million deal.

He has stuck to his vision and values ever since. His commitment to environmental and social issues are evident in everything he does. On the environmental front, his company has a staff ecologist who is charged with reducing Clif Bar's ecological footprint on the planet. More than 70 percent of the ingredients in Clif Bars are organic. A change in packaging has saved the company (and the planet) 90,000 pounds of shrink-wrap a year. And the company funds a Sioux wind farm to offset the carbon dioxide emissions from its factories. On the social side, Erickson launched a project called the 2,080 program (2,080 is the total number of hours a full-time employee works in one year). Through the 2,080 program employees are encouraged to do volunteer work on company time. Recently Erickson agreed to support (with salaries and travel expenses) employees who wanted to volunteer in Third World countries.

Erickson is also committed to his team. He thinks about things like, "What should our company be like for the people who come to work each day?" He sees work as a living situation and strives to make Clif Bar Inc.'s offices a fun place to be—there are plenty of bikes around; a gym and dance floor; personal trainers; massage and hair salon; a game room; an auditorium for meetings, movies, and music; dog days every day; and great parties.

As the company grows, however, maintaining such values may not be easy. Clif Bar already has 130 employees, and revenue has been rising by more than 30 percent a year since 1998, according to Erickson. "We're at a point where we have to find a way to maintain this open culture while we may be getting bigger," says Shelley Martin, director of operations. "It's a balancing act."

1. Without knowing Gary Erickson's age, where would you guess he falls in the four generations of workers as delineated by Zemke?

2. Consider the key work values in Table 5.1. Recalling that leaders are motivated to act consistently with their values, what values appear to be most important to Gary Erickson?

3. Clif Bar Inc. possesses a definite set of organizational values. If you visit the company website (www.clifbar.com), you will see evidence of these values: "Fight Global Warming" and "Register to Vote" are just as prominent as information about the product. Knowing some of the values of Gary Erickson, how closely aligned do you think the organizational values are to the way the company actually operates?

Sources: http://www.fortune.com/fortune/smallbusiness/managing/articles/ 0,15114,487527,00.html; http://www.clifbar.com; *The Costco Connection,* "Marathon Man," July 2004, p. 19.

End Notes

1. C. Moore, J. R. Detert, L. K. Trevino, V. L. Baker and D. M. Mayer, "Why Employees Do Bad Things: Moral Disengagement and Unethical Behavior," *Personnel Psychology* 65 (2012), pp 1–48.

2. M. E. Brown and L. K. Trevino, "Ethical Leadership: A Review and Future Directions," *The Leadership Quarterly* 17 (2006), pp. 595–616.

3. J. W. Gardner, *On Leadership* (New York: Free Press, 1990).

4. J. M. Burns, *Leadership* (New York: Harper & Row, 1978).

5. W. Bennis and J. Goldsmith, *Learning to Lead* (Reading, MA: Perseus Books, 1997).

6. D. McGregor, *Leadership and Motivation* (Cambridge, MA: MIT Press, 1966).

7. J. Hall and S. M. Donnell, "Managerial Achievement: The Personal Side of Behavioral Theory," *Human Relations* 32 (1979), pp. 77–101.

8. L. V. Gordon, *Measurement of Interpersonal Values* (Chicago: Science Research Associates, 1975), p. 2.

9. W. L. Gardner, B. Avolio, F. Luthans, D. May, and F. Walumbwa, "'Can You See the Real Me?' A Self-Based Model of Authentic Leader and Follower Development," *Leadership Quarterly* 16 (2005), pp. 343–72.

10. R. E. Boyatzis and F. R. Skelly, "The Impact of Changing Values on Organizational Life," in *Organizational Behavior Readings*, 5th ed., eds. D. A. Kolb, I. M. Rubin, and J. Osland (Englewood Cliffs, NJ: Prentice Hall, 1991), pp. 1–16.

11. M. Rokeach, *The Nature of Human Values* (New York: Free Press, 1973).

12. Boyatzis and Skelly, "The Impact of Changing Values on Organizational Life."

13. M. Maccoby, "Management: Leadership and the Work Ethic," *Modern Office Procedures* 28, no. 5 (1983), pp. 14, 16, 18.

14. M. Massey, *The People Puzzle: Understanding Yourself and Others* (Reston, VA: Reston, 1979).

15. R. Zemke, C. Raines, and B. Filipczak, *Generations at Work: Managing the Class of Veterans, Boomers, Xers, and Nexters in Your Workplace* (New York: AMA Publications, 2000).

16. C. S. Alkexander and J. M. Sysko, "A Study of the Cognitive Determinants of Generation Y's Entitlement Mentality," *Academy of Educational Leadership Journal* 16 (2012), pp. 63–68.

17. N. Howe and W. Strauss, "The Next 20 Years: How Customer and Workforce Attitudes Will Evolve," *Harvard Business Review*, July/August (2007), pp. 41–51.

18. A. McAfee, "How Millennials' Sharing Habits Can Benefit Organizations," *Harvard Business Review*, November (2010), p. 24.

19. Alkexander and Sysko, "A Study of the Cognitive Determinants of Generation Y's Entitlement Mentality."

20. J. J. Deal, K. Peterson, and H. Gailor-Loflin, *Emerging Leaders: An Annotated Bibliography* (Greensboro, NC: Center for Creative Leadership, 2001).

21. E. C. Ladd, "Generation Gap? What Generation Gap?" *The New York Times*, December 9, 1994, p. A16.

22. F. Giancola, "The Generation Gap: More Myth Than Reality," endnote 22, *Resource Planning* 29, no. 4 (2006), pp. 32–37.

23. W. A. Gentry, T. L. Griggs, J. J. Deal, S. P. Mondore, and B. D. Cox, "A Comparison of Generational Differences in Endorsement of Leadership Practices with Actual Leadership Skill Level," *Consulting Psychology Journal: Practice and Research*, 63 (2011), pp. 39–49.

24. J. Rest, "Research on Moral Judgment in College Students," in *Approaches to Moral Development: New Research and Emerging Themes*, ed. A. Garrod (New York: Teachers College Press, Columbia University, 1993), pp. 201–13.

25. M. R. Banaji, M. H. Bazerman, and D. Chugh, "How (Un)ethical Are You?" *Harvard Business Review* 81, no. 12 (2003), pp. 56–64.

26. S. Seiler, A. Fischer, and S. A. Voegtli, "Developing Moral Decision-Making Competence: A Quasi-Experimental Intervention Study for the Swiss Armed Forces," *Ethics & Behavior*, in press.

27. J. Greene, "From Neural 'Is' to Moral 'Ought': What Are the Moral Implications of Neuroscientific Moral Psychology?" *Nature Reviews/Neuroscience* 4 (2003), pp. 847–50.

28. J. Greene, "The Cognitive Neuroscience of Moral Judgment," in *The Cognitive Neurosciences*, 4th ed., ed. M. S. Gazzaniga (Cambridge, MA: MIT Press, 2009).

29. R. Kidder, *How Good People Make Tough Choices: Resolving the Dilemmas of Ethical Living* (New York: Harper Collins, 1995).

30. A. G. Greenwald, D. E. McGhee, and J. L. K. Schwartz, "Measuring Individual Differences in Implicit Cognition: The Implicit Association Test," *Journal of Personality and Social Psychology* 74 (1998), pp. 1464–80.

31. Banaji, Bazerman, and Chugh, "How (Un)ethical Are You?"

32. Ibid.

33. P. Coy, "Ten Years from Now," *BusinessWeek*, August 20 and 27, 2007, pp. 42–44.

34. Banaji, Bazerman, and Chugh, "How (Un)ethical Are You?"

35. S. Sohenshein, "The Role of Construction, Intuition, and Justification in Responding to Ethical Issues at Work: The Sensemaking–Intuition Model," *Academy of Management Review* 32, no. 4 (2007), pp. 1022–40.

36. Ibid.

37. J. Haidt, "The Emotional Dog and Its Rational Tail: A Social Intuitionist Approach to Moral Judgment," *Psychological Review* 108, pp. 814–34.

38. C. D. Barnes and R. P. Brown, "A Value-Congruent Bias in the Forgiveness Forecasts of Religious People," *Psychology of Religion and Spirituality* 2 (2010), pp. 17–29.

39. R. T. Marcy, W. Gentry, and R. McKinnon, "Thinking Straight: New Strategies Are Needed for Ethical Leadership," *Leadership in Action* 28, no. 3 (2008), pp. 3–7.

40. A. Bandura, *Social Foundations of Thought and Action* (Englewood Cliffs, NJ: Prentice Hall, 1986).

41. A. Bandura, "Mechanisms of Moral Disengagement," in *Origins of Terrorism: Psychologies, Ideologies, Theologies, States of Mind*, ed. W. Reich (Cambridge: Cambridge University Press., 1990), pp. 161–91.

42. C. Moore, J. R. Detert, L. K. Trevino, V. L. Baker, and D. M. Mayer, "Why Employees Do Bad Things: Moral Disengagement and Unethical Behavior," *Personnel Psychology* 65 (2012), pp. 1–48.

Chapter 5 *Values, Ethics, and Character* **183**

43. Bandura, "Mechanisms of Moral Disengagement."

44. A. Bandura, "Self-Efficacy: Toward a Unifying Theory of Behavioral Change," *Psychological Review* 84 (1977), pp. 191–215.

45. S. T. Hannah and B. J. Avolio, "Moral Potency: Building the Capacity for Character-Based Leadership," *Consulting Psychology Journal: Practice and Research* 62 (2010), pp. 291–310

46. S. T. Hannah and B. J. Avolio, "The Locus of Leader Character," *The Leadership Quarterly* 22 (2011), pp. 979–83.

47. T. A. Wright and J. C. Quick, "The Role of Character in Ethical Leadership Research," *The Leadership Quarterly* 22 (2011), pp. 975–78.

48. S. T. Hannah and B. J. Avolio, "Moral Potency: Building the Capacity for Character-Based Leadership," *Consulting Psychology Journal: Practice and Research* 62 (2010), pp. 291–310.

49. R. E. Riggio, W. Zhu, C. Rheina, and J. A. Maroosis, "Virtue-Based Measurement of Ethical Leadership: The Leadership Virtues Questionnaire," *Consulting Psychology Journal: Practice and Research* 62 (2010), pp. 235–50.

50. R. B. Kaiser and R. Hogan, "How To (and How Not To) Assess the Integrity of Managers," *Consulting Psychology Journal: Practice and Research* 62 (2010), pp. 216–34.

51. F. O. Walumbwa, B. Avolio, W. Gardner, T. Wernsing, and S. Peterson, "Authentic Leadership: Development of a Theory-Based Measure," *Journal of Management* 34, no. 1 (2008), pp. 89–126.

52. M. E. Brown and L. Trevino, "Ethical Leadership: A Review and Future Directions," *Leadership Quarterly* 17 (2006), pp. 595–616.

53. Ibid., p. 597.

54. Walumbwa et al. "Authentic Leadership."

55. C. Rogers, *On Becoming a Person: A Therapist's View of Psychotherapy* (London: Constable, 1961).

56. B. J. Avolio and T. S. Wernsing, "Practicing Authentic Leadership," in *Positive Psychology: Exploring the Best in People (Vol. 4: Exploring Human Flourishing)*, ed. Shane Lopez (Santa Barbara: Praeger, 2008).

57. Ibid., p. 161.

58. B. J. Avolio and W. L. Gardner, "Authentic Leadership Development: Getting to the Root of Positive Forms of Leadership," *The Leadership Quarterly* 16 (2005), pp. 315–38.

59. B. J. Avolio and R. Reichard, "The Rise of Authentic Followership," in *The Art of Followership: How Great Followers Create Great Leaders and Organizations*, eds. R. E. Riggio, I. Chaleff, and J. Lipman-Bluman (San Francisco: Jossey-Bass, 2008), pp. 325–37.

60. L. Spears, "Practicing Servant-Leadership," *Leader to Leader* 34 (Fall 2004), pp. 7–11.

61. R. K. Greenleaf, *Servant Leadership* (New York: Paulist Press, 1977).

62. Spears, "Practicing Servant-Leadership."

63. J. A. Andersen, "When a Servant-Leader Comes Knocking . . ." *Leadership & Organization Development Journal* 30, no. 1 (2009), pp. 4–15.

184   Part Two   *Focus on the Leader*

64. D. Jones, "Does Servant Leadership Lead to Greater Customer Focus and Employee Satisfaction?" *Business Studies Journal* 4 (2012), pp. 21–23.

65. R. T. Hogan, J. Hogan, and B. W. Roberts, "Personality Measurement and Employment Decisions: Questions and Answers," *American Psychologist* 51, no. 5 (1996), pp. 469–77.

66. R. T. Hogan and G. J. Curphy, "Leadership Matters: Values and Dysfunctional Dispositions," working paper, 2004.

67. Hogan, Hogan, and Roberts, "Personality Measurement and Employment Decisions."

68. Hogan and Curphy, "Leadership Matters."

69. B. O'Brien, "Designing an Organization's Governing Ideas," in *The Fifth Discipline Fieldbook*, eds. P. Senge et al. (New York: Doubleday, 1994), p. 306.

70. G. Weaver, L. Trevfino, and B. Agle, "Somebody I Look Up To: Ethical Role Models in Organizations," *Organizational Dynamics* 34, no. 4 (2005), pp. 313–30.

71. M. Uhl-Bien and M. Carsten, "Being Ethical When the Boss Is Not," *Organizational Dynamics* 36, no. 2 (2007), pp. 187–201.

72. Ibid.

73. Ibid.

74. C. E. Johnson, *Meeting the Ethical Challenges of Leadership: Casting Light or Shadow,* 2nd ed. (Thousand Oaks, CA: Sage, 2005).

75. C. E. Johnson, "Best Practices in Ethical Leadership, 2007," in *The Practice of Leadership: Developing the Next Generation of Leaders,* eds. J. Conger and R. Riggio (San Francisco: Jossey-Bass, 2006), pp. 150–71.

76. Ibid.

77. M. H. Bazerman and A. E. Tenbrunsel, "Ethical Breakdowns," *Harvard Business Review* 89, no. 4 (2011), pp. 58–65.

78. S. R. Covey, *Principle-Centered Leadership* (New York: Simon & Schuster, 1990).

79. F. J. Yammarino, S. D. Dionne, C. A. Schriesheim, and F. Dansereau, "Authentic Leadership and Positive Organizational Behavior: A Meso, Multi-Level Perspective," *The Leadership Quarterly* 19 (2008), pp. 693–707.

80. Johnson, "Best Practices in Ethical Leadership, 2007."

81. Ibid.

82. P. Kottler and N. Lee, *Corporate Social Responsibility: Doing the Most Good for Your Company and Your Cause* (New York: Wiley, 2005).

83. S. A. Waddock and S. B. Graves, "The Corporate Social Performance–Financial Performance Link," *Strategic Management Journal* 18 (1997), pp. 303–19.

84. J. P. Kotter and J. L. Heskett, *Corporate Culture & Performance* (New York: Free Press, 1992).

Chapter 6

Leadership Attributes

Introduction

*Watch your thoughts,
for they become words.
Watch your words, for
they become actions.
Watch your actions, for
they become habits.
Watch your habits, for
they become character.
Watch your character,
for it becomes your
destiny.*

Anonymous

In Chapter 1 leadership was defined as "the process of influencing an organized group toward accomplishing its goals." Given this definition, one question that leadership researchers have tried to answer over the past century is whether certain personal attributes or characteristics help or hinder the leadership process. In other words, does athletic ability, height, personality, intelligence, or creativity help a leader to build a team, get results, or influence a group? Put in the context of national U.S. presidential elections, are candidates who win the primaries and eventually go on to become president smarter, more creative, more ambitious, or more outgoing than their less successful counterparts? Do these leaders act in fundamentally different ways than their followers, and are these differences in behavior owing to differences in their innate intelligence, certain personality traits, or creative ability? If so, could these same characteristics be used to differentiate successful from unsuccessful leaders, executives from first-line supervisors, or leaders from individual contributors? Questions such as these led to what was perhaps the earliest theory of leadership, the **Great Man theory.**[1]

The roots of the Great Man theory can be traced back to the early 1900s, when many leadership researchers and the popular press maintained that leaders and followers were fundamentally different. This led to hundreds of research studies that looked at whether certain personality traits, physical attributes, intelligence, or personal values differentiated leaders from followers. Ralph Stogdill was the first leadership researcher to summarize the results of these studies, and he came to two major conclusions. First, leaders were not qualitatively different from followers; many followers were just as tall, smart, outgoing, and ambitious as the people who were leading them. Second, some characteristics, such as intelligence, initiative, stress tolerance, responsibility, friendliness, and dominance, were modestly related to leadership success. In other words, people who were smart, hardworking, conscientious, friendly, or willing to take charge were often more successful at building teams and influencing a group to accomplish its goals than people who were less smart, lazy, impulsive, grumpy, or not fond of giving orders.[2] Having "the right stuff" did not guarantee leadership success, but it improved the odds of successfully influencing a group toward the accomplishment of its goals.

Subsequent reviews involving hundreds of more sophisticated studies came to the same two conclusions.[3] Although these reviews provided ample evidence that people with the right stuff were more likely to be successful as leaders, many leadership researchers focused solely on the point that leaders were not fundamentally different from followers. However, given that most people in leadership positions also play follower roles (supervisors report to managers, managers report to directors, and so forth), this finding is hardly surprising. This erroneous interpretation of the findings, along with the rising popularity of behaviorism in the 1960s and 1970s, caused many leadership researchers to believe that personal characteristics could not be used to predict future leadership success and resulted in a shift in focus toward other leadership phenomena. Not until the publication of seminal articles published in the 1980s and 1990s did intelligence and personality regain popularity with leadership researchers.[4–6] Because of these articles and subsequent leadership research, we now know a lot about how intelligence and various personality traits help or hinder leaders in their efforts to build teams and get results.[7–10] This research also provided insight on the role that various situational and follower characteristics have in affecting how a leader's intelligence and personality play out in the workplace. The purpose of this chapter is to summarize what we currently know about personality, intelligence, and leadership. In other words, what does the research say about the leadership effectiveness of people who are smart, outgoing, innovative, and calm versus those who are dumb, shy, practical, and excitable? Do smarter people always make better leaders? Are there situations where tense and moody leaders are more effective than calm leaders? This chapter answers many common questions regarding the roles of personality, intelligence, creativity, and emotional intelligence in leadership effectiveness. As an overview, the chapter defines these four key attributes, reviews some key research findings for these attributes, and discusses the implications of this research for leadership practitioners.

Personality Traits and Leadership

What Is Personality?

Despite its common usage, Robert Hogan noted that the term **personality** is fairly ambiguous and has at least two quite different meanings.[6] One meaning refers to the impression a person makes on others. This view of personality emphasizes a person's *public reputation* and reflects

There is an optical illusion about every person we ever meet. In truth, they are all creatures of a given temperament, which will appear in a given character, whose boundaries they will never pass: but we look at them, they seem alive, and we presume there is impulse in them. In the moment, it seems like an impulse; in the year, in the lifetime, it turns out to be a certain uniform tune, which the revolving barrel of the music box must play.

Ralph Waldo Emerson

not only a description but also an evaluation of the person in the eyes of others. From the standpoint of leadership, this view of personality addresses two distinct issues: "What kind of leader or person is this?" and "Is this somebody I would like to work for or be associated with?" In a practical sense, this view of personality comes into play whenever you describe the person you work for to a roommate or friend. For example, you might describe him or her as pushy, honest, outgoing, impulsive, decisive, friendly, and independent. Furthermore, whatever impression this leader made on you, chances are others would use many of the same terms of description. In that vein, many people would probably say that U.S. President Barack Obama is smart, self-confident, poised, articulate, ambitious, and level-headed. (See Profiles in Leadership 6.1.)

The second meaning of personality emphasizes the underlying, unseen structures and processes inside a person that explain why we behave the way we do—why each person's behavior tends to be relatively *similar across different situations*, yet also *different from another person's behavior*. Over the years psychologists have developed many theories to explain how such unseen structures may cause individuals to act in their characteristic manner. For example, Sigmund Freud believed that the intrapsychic tensions among the id, ego, and superego caused one to behave in characteristic ways even if the real motives behind the behaviors were unknown to the person (that is, unconscious).[11] Although useful insights about personality have come from many different theories, most of the research addressing the relationship between personality and leadership success has been based on the **trait approach,** and that emphasis is most appropriate here.

Traits refer to recurring regularities or trends in a person's behavior, and the trait approach to personality maintains that people behave as they do because of the strengths of the traits they possess.[6] Although traits cannot be seen, they can be inferred from consistent patterns of behavior and reliably measured by personality inventories. For example, the personality trait of conscientiousness differentiates leaders who tend to be hardworking and rule abiding from those who tend to be lazy and are more prone to break rules. Leaders getting higher scores on the trait of conscientiousness on personality inventories would be more likely to come to work on time, do a thorough job in completing work assignments, and rarely leave work early. We would also infer that leaders getting lower scores on the trait of conscientiousness would be more likely to be late to appointments, make impulsive decisions, or fail to follow through with commitments and achieve results.

Men acquire a particular quality by constantly acting a particular way. You become a just man by performing just actions, temperate by performing temperate actions, and brave by performing brave actions.

Aristotle

Personality traits are useful concepts for explaining why people act fairly consistently from one situation to the next. This cross-situational consistency in behavior may be thought of as analogous to the seasonal weather patterns in different cities.[12,13] We know that it is extremely cold and dry in Minneapolis in January and hot and humid in Hong Kong in

Angela Merkel

PROFILES IN LEADERSHIP 6.1

Angela Merkel is commonly acknowledged as the most powerful female in the world. Assuming office in November 2005, she is the first female to have been elected as the chancellor of Germany, the first person from the former German Democratic Republic to lead a unified Germany, and is also only the third female to serve on the G8 council.

Merkel grew up in a rural community in Eastern Germany and showed an aptitude for math and science at an early age. A member of the communist youth movement in Eastern Germany, she went on to earn both undergraduate and doctoral degrees in physics, specializing in quantum chemistry. She spent much of the 1970s and 1980s in academic positions doing cutting-edge chemical research and publishing her work in such periodicals as *Molecular Physics* and *International Journal of Quantum Chemistry*. Chancellor Merkel did not get involved in politics until the fall of the Berlin Wall in 1989.

In the 1990s she was appointed to several ministerial positions in the Helmut Kohl government and was a young protégé of Chancellor Kohl's. A quick study, she learned the intricacies of national politics and international diplomacy under Kohl's mentorship and used this knowledge to run for and win national elections in Germany in 2005. Merkel currently is party chair of the Christian Democratic Union and leads a coalition of parties representing both the left and right wings of German politics. She is leading efforts to liberalize Germany's economy by allowing employers to increase the workweek from 35 to 40 hours and lay off employees during economic downturns. She also plans to shut down Germany's nuclear power plants after 2020 and is opposed to Turkey becoming a full member of the European Union. Despite strong public outcry, Merkel supported the U.S. invasion of Iraq, has sent German soldiers to Afghanistan, endorsed global climate change legislation, and provided funds to support Greece, Portugal, and other European Union countries to prevent these countries from defaulting on their loans. When it comes to economic policy she is known as "the decider" and seen as the de facto leader of the 27-member European Union.

Given her background, what can you discern about Chancellor Merkel's public reputation, personality traits, values, and intelligence?

Sources: http://www.fullissue.com/index.php/angela-merkel-biography-1964-.html; http://www.imdb.com/name/nm1361767/bio; http://www.biography.com/articles/Angela-Merkel-9406424; http://www.economist.com/world/europe/displaystory.cfm?story_id=16116811; http://www.forbes.com/profile/angela-merkel/

August. Therefore, we can do a pretty good job of predicting what the weather will generally be like in Minneapolis in January, even though our predictions for any particular day will not be perfect. Although the average January temperature in Minneapolis hovers around 20°F, the temperature ranges from –30°F to 30°F on any single day in January. Similarly, knowing how two people differ on a particular personality trait can help us predict more accurately how they will tend to act in a variety of situations. (See Highlight 6.1.)

Just as various climate factors can affect the temperature on any single day, so can external factors affect a leader's behavior in any given situation. The trait approach maintains that a leader's behavior reflects an interaction between his or her personality traits and various situational factors (see, for example, Highlight 6.1). Traits play a particularly

Personality and the Presidency

HIGHLIGHT 6.1

Traits are unseen dispositions that can affect the way people act. Their existence can be inferred by a leader's consistent pattern of behaviors. For example, one way of examining a leader's standing on the trait of achievement orientation is to examine her or his achievements and accomplishments over a life span. Leaders with higher levels of achievement orientation tend to set high personal goals and are persistent in the pursuit of these goals. When considering the following leader's achievements and accomplishments, think about this person's standing on this personality trait, and try to guess who this person might be:

Age 23: lost a job.

Age 23: was defeated in a bid for state legislature.

Age 24: failed in a business venture.

Age 25: was elected to state legislature.

Age 26: sweetheart died.

Age 27: experienced several emotional problems.

Age 27: was defeated in a bid to be speaker of the house.

Age 34: was defeated for nomination to Congress.

Age 37: was elected to Congress.

Age 39: lost renomination to Congress.

Age 40: was defeated in a bid for land office.

Age 45: was defeated in a bid for U.S. Senate.

Age 47: was defeated for nomination to be vice president.

Age 49: was defeated in a second bid for U.S. Senate.

Age 51: was elected president of the United States.

The person was Abraham Lincoln.

important role in determining how people behave in unfamiliar, ambiguous, or what we might call **weak situations.** On the other hand, situations that are governed by clearly specified rules, demands, or organizational policies—**strong situations**—often minimize the effects traits have on behavior.[14–18]

The strength of the relationship between personality traits and leadership effectiveness is often inversely related to the relative strength of the situation; that is, personality traits are more closely related to leadership effectiveness in weak or ambiguous situations. Given the accelerated pace of change in most organizations today, it is likely that leaders will face even more unfamiliar and ambiguous situations in the future. Therefore, personality traits may play an increasingly important role in a leader's behavior. If organizations can accurately identify the personality traits of leadership and the individuals who possess them, they should be able to do a better job of promoting the right people into leadership positions. And if the right people are in leadership positions, the odds of achieving organizational success should be dramatically improved. The next section describes some research efforts to identify those personality traits that help leaders build teams and get results through others.

The Five Factor or OCEAN Model of Personality

Although personality traits provide a useful approach to describing distinctive, cross-situational behavioral patterns, one potential problem is the sheer number of traitlike terms available to describe another's stereotypical behaviors. As early as 1936 researchers identified over 18,000 trait-related adjectives in a standard English dictionary.[19] Despite this large number of adjectives, research has shown that most of the traitlike terms people use to describe others' behavioral patterns can be reliably categorized into five broad personality dimensions. Historically this five-dimension model was first identified as early as 1915 and independently verified in 1934, but over the years a number of researchers using diverse samples and assessment instruments have noted similar results.[5,20,21] Given the robustness of these findings, a compelling body of evidence appears to support these five dimensions of personality. These dimensions are referred to in personality literature as the **Five Factor Model (FFM) or OCEAN model of personality,** and most modern personality researchers endorse some version of this model.[5,22–28]

At its core, the Five Factor or OCEAN model of personality is a categorization scheme. Most, if not all, of the personality traits that you would use to describe someone else could be reliably categorized into one of the five OCEAN personality dimensions. A description of the model can be found in Table 6.1. The five major dimensions include openness to experience, conscientiousness, extraversion, agreeableness, and neuroticism. The first of these dimensions, openness to experience, is concerned with curiosity, innovative thinking, assimilating new information, and being open to new experiences. Leaders higher in **openness to experience** tend to be imaginative, broad-minded, and curious and are more strategic, big-picture thinkers; they seek new experiences through travel, the arts, movies, sports, reading, going to new restaurants, or learning about new cultures. Individuals lower in openness to experience tend to be more practical, tactical, and have narrower interests; they like doing things

A great leader's courage to fulfill his vision comes from passion, not position.

John Maxwell,
author

TABLE 6.1
The Five Factor or OCEAN Model of Personality

Factor	Behaviors/Items
Openness to experience	I like traveling to foreign countries.
	I enjoy going to school.
Conscientiousness	I enjoy putting together detailed plans.
	I rarely get into trouble.
Extraversion	I like having responsibility for others.
	I have a large group of friends.
Agreeableness	I am a sympathetic person.
	I get along well with others.
Neuroticism	I remain calm in pressure situations.
	I take personal criticism well.

using tried-and-true ways rather than experimenting with new ways. Note that openness to experience is not the same thing as intelligence—smart people are not necessarily intellectually curious.

A key research question is whether people who are curious and big-picture thinkers are more effective leaders than those who are more pragmatic. Research has shown that openness to experience is an important component of leadership effectiveness and seems particularly important at higher organizational levels or for success in overseas assignments.[5,29–33] People with higher openness to experience scores take a more strategic approach to solving problems, and this can help CEOs and other senior leaders keep abreast of market trends, competitive threats, new products, and regulatory changes. And because people with higher openness to experience scores also like new and novel experiences, they often enjoy the challenges associated with living and leading in foreign countries. Nonetheless, there are many leadership positions where curiosity, innovation, and big-picture thinking are relatively unimportant. For example, production foremen on assembly lines, store managers at McDonald's, or platoon leaders for the U.S. Army do not need to be particularly strategic. These jobs put a premium on pragmatic decision making rather than on developing elegant solutions, so being higher in openness to experience in these roles can harm leadership effectiveness.

Conscientiousness concerns those behaviors related to people's approach to work. Leaders who are higher in conscientiousness tend to be planful, organized, and earnest, take commitments seriously, and rarely get into trouble. Those who are lower in conscientiousness tend to be more spontaneous, creative, impulsive, rule bending, and less concerned with following through with commitments. The characters Bart and Lisa Simpson from the television show *The Simpsons* provide a nice illustration of low and high conscientiousness trait scores. Lisa is organized, hardworking, and reliable and never gets into trouble; Bart is disorganized, mischievous, and lazy and rarely keeps promises. Research shows that individuals with higher conscientiousness scores are more likely to be effective leaders than those with lower scores.[5,25–33]

In many ways conscientiousness may be more concerned with management than leadership. That is because people with higher scores are planful, organized, goal oriented, and prefer structure; but they are also risk averse, uncreative, somewhat boring, and dislike change. Although the situation will determine how important these tendencies are for building teams and getting results, research has shown that conscientiousness is a good predictor of leadership potential. Along these lines, conscientiousness seems to be a particularly good predictor of leadership success in jobs that put a premium on following procedures, managing budgets, coordinating work schedules, monitoring projects, and paying attention to details. People having higher scores on conscientiousness would probably do well in the production foreman, store manager, and platoon leader jobs

Persistence. Nothing in the world can take the place of persistence. Talent will not; nothing is more common than unsuccessful men with talent. Genius will not; unrewarded genius is almost a proverb. Education will not; the world is full of educated derelicts. Persistence and determination alone are omnipotent. "Press on" has solved and always will solve the problems of the human race.

Calvin Coolidge, U.S. President

We are given to the cult of personality; when things go badly we look for some messiah to save us. If by chance we think we have found one, it will not be long before we destroy him.

Constantine Karamanlis

described earlier but may not be as effective if leading sales or consulting teams, college professors, or musicians.

Extraversion involves behaviors that are more likely to be exhibited in group settings and are generally concerned with getting ahead in life.[5,32] Such behavioral patterns often appear when someone is trying to influence or control others, and individuals higher in extraversion come across to others as outgoing, competitive, decisive, outspoken, opinionated, and self-confident. Individuals lower in extraversion generally prefer to work by themselves and have relatively little interest in influencing or competing with others. Because leaders' decisiveness, competitiveness, and self-confidence can affect their ability to successfully influence a group, build a team, and get results, it is not surprising that leaders often have higher extraversion scores than nonleaders.[5,27,28,32,34,35] You can see differences in people's standing on extraversion every time a group of people gets together. Some people in a group are going to be outgoing and will try to get the group to do certain things; others are more comfortable going along with rather than arguing over group activities.

This strong need to assume leadership positions in groups is often associated with taking risks, making decisions, and upward mobility. A key question is whether these extraverted behaviors are exhibited to facilitate team performance or for self-aggrandizement. There is a subset of leaders who demonstrate self-confidence, decisiveness, and risk taking for the sole purpose of getting promoted. These ambitious, upwardly mobile individuals could care less about team or group results and are able convince team members to complete high visibility (but often low impact) projects that enable them to move up the corporate ladder. There is another subset of leaders who demonstrate extraverted behaviors in order to help their groups to perform at higher levels. Because both subsets of leaders make strong first impressions, it will take time before people are able to differentiate between these two subsets of leaders. Too much extraversion can also be problematic, as these leaders do not take others' inputs into consideration, think they are the only ones capable of making decisions, and make overly risky decisions. Many times those with the highest extraversion scores make poor decisions about their projects or fail to get the people on their projects to work together effectively. Although possessing too much extraversion can be problematic, in general people who are more decisive, self-confident, and outgoing seem to be more effective leaders, and thus extraversion is an important measure of leadership potential.

Another OCEAN personality dimension is **agreeableness,** which concerns how one gets along with, as opposed to gets ahead of, others. [5,30,32] Individuals high in agreeableness come across to others as charming, diplomatic, warm, empathetic, approachable, and optimistic; those lower in agreeableness are more apt to appear as insensitive, socially clueless, grumpy, cold, and pessimistic. Agreeableness essentially concerns one's

Ascending to the top of any organization is a political game. Building a winning organization is a leadership game.

R. T. Hogan and Tim Judge, leadership researchers

Thermonuclear coaching sessions can be very effective techniques for getting the attention of pilots.

Anthony Burke, F-16 pilot

need for approval. Some people work hard to be liked by others, are known as being "a good guy," and are quite popular. Others would rather stick to the facts, no matter how uncomfortable, and do not care whether they are liked or not. The latter is often associated with jobs requiring the evaluation of others, such as judges, referees, police officers, or quality assurance representatives. Differences in agreeableness can easily be observed in the movie *Shrek*. Donkey is friendly, inclusive, and does all he can to be liked whereas Shrek initially comes across as gruff, mean, and does all he can to be left alone.

Although people with high agreeableness trait scores are well liked and tend to be better at building teams than those with lower scores, they can struggle with getting results through others. This is because persons with higher scores believe relationships trump performance and often have trouble making unpopular decisions or dealing with conflict and performance issues, which can negatively erode the effectiveness of their teams. Because of these difficulties, research has shown that agreeableness has had mixed results in predicting leadership effectiveness.[5,27,28,30,32]

Neuroticism is concerned with how people react to stress, change, failure, or personal criticism. Leaders lower in neuroticism tend to be thick-skinned, calm, and optimistic, tend not to take mistakes or failures personally, and hide their emotions; those higher in neuroticism are passionate, intense, thin-skinned, moody, and anxious and lose their tempers when stressed or criticized. Followers often mimic a leader's emotions or behaviors under periods of high stress, so leaders who are calm under pressure and thick-skinned can often help a group stay on task and work through difficult issues. Unfortunately the opposite is also true.

Differences in neuroticism can be difficult to observe in predictable, routine situations but become readily apparent during times of uncertainty or crises. Under stress, those lower in neuroticism stay cool, calm, and collected, whereas those higher on this trait become nervous, tense, and emotional. Emotional volatility certainly can affect a person's ability to build teams and get results, and research has shown that neuroticism is another good predictor of leadership potential.[5,27–35] Although lower neuroticism scores are generally associated with leadership effectiveness, people with low scores can struggle to rally the troops when extra effort is needed to achieve results or drive change. This is because these individuals are so flat emotionally that they have a hard time exhibiting any passion or enthusiasm. Charismatic leaders, on the other hand, often have higher neuroticism scores.[26]

> *On far too many occasions I have had to remind people that leadership is a verb, not a noun.*
>
> **James Michael, organizational consultant**

Implications of the Five Factor or OCEAN Model

The trait approach and the Five Factor or OCEAN model of personality give leadership researchers and practitioners several useful tools and insights. Personality traits help researchers and practitioners explain leaders' and

Leadership Success, Career Success, and Public Reputation

HIGHLIGHT 6.2

It turns out that people spend a lot of time discussing the **public reputations** of others. Many of our conversations about roommates, friends, classmates, co-workers, bosses, significant others, sports figures, and celebrities involve judgments or evaluations of how curious, outgoing, planful, humorous, impulsive, tense, trustworthy, easygoing, hardworking, law-abiding, or creative they may be. Knowing a person's public reputation can help predict their future behavior as a roommate, boss, or spouse, so getting this right is critically important. So how can one evaluate another's public reputation? One of the most common ways to do this is by talking to mutual friends, as there is usually a lot more agreement than disagreement when it comes to their judgments of another's public reputation. Another way to do this is by looking at social media; Facebook and Google+ pages and LinkedIn profiles typically say a lot about public reputations. OCEAN personality inventories are a third way to evaluate public reputations, as they describe how an individual is likely to be perceived by others.

Leadership and career success are two very different outcomes that are related to public reputation. The fundamental question for leadership success is whether the team is winning. Does the team have a good win–loss record and consistently outperform the competition? The key question for career success is whether a leader gets promoted. Does the leader have a track record of rising rapidly through the ranks? One might think that leadership and career success go hand-in-hand, but the public reputation needed to get to the top of organizations can look quite different than that needed to build winning teams. Many of those who make it to the top, particularly in large bureaucratic organizations, cultivate public reputations of being loyal soldiers, doing whatever is asked, not making mistakes, and carefully cultivating relationships with organizational power players. Those more focused on building winning teams often don't care about these matters and have public reputations for surrounding themselves with the right people, painting a vision of the future, motivating others, overcoming obstacles, and getting things done. Perhaps the clearest example of leadership versus career success can be seen in the U.S. military. According to Ricks, many lieutenants, captains, majors, and lieutenant colonels are good at building loyal teams that get things done, but many of those who make it to general are more likely to be politicians than leaders. Which of these is more important at your school or in your organization?

Sources: T. E. Ricks, *The Generals* (New York: The Penguin Press, 2012); I. S. Oh, G. Wang, and M. K. Mount, "Validity of Observer Ratings of the Five Factor Model of Personality Traits: A Meta-Analysis," *Journal of Applied Psychology,* 96, no. 4, (2011), pp. 762–73; R. T. Hogan and T. Chamorro-Premuzic, "Personality and Career Success," in *APA Handbook of Personality and Social Psychology* (Vol. 3), eds. L. Cooper and R. Larsen (Washington, D.C.: American Psychological Association, 2012); Hogan Press, *Sticks & Stones: Gossip, Reputation and How Whispered Words Kill Careers* (Tulsa, OK, 2012); M. Barney, "A Victor in the Science Wars," http://www.forbes.com/sites/infosys/2011/12/16/business-leadership-bte-2/

followers' tendencies to act in consistent ways over time. They tell us why some leaders appear to be dominant versus deferent, outspoken versus quiet, planful versus spontaneous, warm versus cold, and so forth. Note that the behavioral manifestations of personality traits are often exhibited automatically and without much conscious thought. People high in extraversion, for example, will often maneuver to influence or lead whatever groups or teams they are a part of without even thinking about it. Although personality traits predispose us to act in certain ways, we can nonetheless learn to modify our behaviors through experience, feedback, and reflection. (See Highlight 6.2.)

FIGURE 6.1
The Building
Blocks of Skills

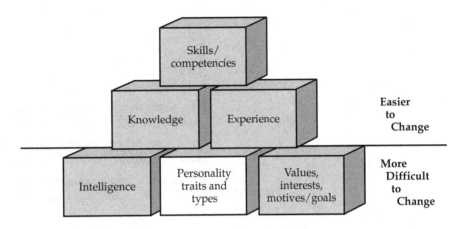

As shown in Figure 6.1, personality traits are a key component of behavior and are relatively difficult to change. Moreover, because personality traits tend to be stable over the years and the behavioral manifestations of traits occur somewhat automatically, it is important for leaders and leaders-to-be to have insight into their personalities. For example, consider a leader who is relatively high in the trait of neuroticism and is deciding whether to accept a high-stress/high-visibility job. On the basis of his personality trait scores, we might predict that this leader could be especially sensitive to criticism and could be moody and prone to emotional outbursts. If the leader understood that he may have issues dealing with stress and criticism, he could choose not to take the position, modify the situation to reduce the level of stress, or learn techniques for effectively dealing with these issues. A leader who lacked this self-insight would probably make poorer choices and have more difficulties coping with the demands of this position.[6]

The OCEAN model has proven useful in several other ways. Most personality researchers currently embrace some form of this model because it has provided a useful scheme for categorizing the findings of the personality–leadership performance research.[6,27–29,32] Because research has shown personality to be an effective measure of leadership potential, organizations now use the results of OCEAN personality assessments for hiring new leaders, for giving leaders developmental feedback about various personality traits, and as a key component when promoting leaders.[34]

One advantage of the OCEAN model is that it is a useful method for profiling leaders. An example of a school principal's results on an OCEAN personality assessment can be found in Figure 6.2. According to this profile, this leader will generally come across to others as self-confident, goal-oriented, competitive, outgoing, eager to be the center

FIGURE 6.2
Example OCEAN
Profile

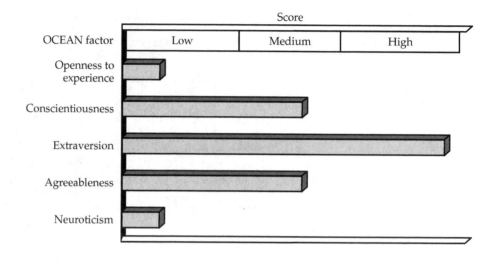

of attention, but also distractible and a poor listener (high extraversion); optimistic, resilient, and calm under pressure (low neuroticism); reasonably warm and approachable (medium agreeableness); moderately planful, rule abiding, and earnest (medium conscientiousness); and a pragmatic, tactical thinker (low openness to experience). Other leaders will have different behavioral tendencies, and knowing this type of information *before* someone gets hired or promoted into a leadership position can help improve the odds of organizational success. (See Highlight 6.3.)

Another advantage of the OCEAN model is that it appears universally applicable across cultures.[6,29,33,36-37] People from Asian, Western European, Middle Eastern, Eastern European, and South American cultures seem to use the same five personality dimensions to categorize, profile, or describe others. Not only do people from different cultures describe others using the same five-factor framework—these dimensions all seem to predict job and leadership performance across cultures. For example, in a comprehensive review of the research, Salgado reported that all five of the OCEAN dimensions predicted blue-collar, professional, and managerial performance in various European countries.[29] But the strength of the personality–job performance relationship depends on the particular job. Some jobs, such as sales, put a premium on interpersonal skills and goal orientation (extraversion and agreeableness), whereas manufacturing jobs put more of a premium on planning and abiding by safety and productivity rules (conscientiousness). Researchers often get much stronger personality–job performance relationships when the personality traits being measured have some degree of job-relatedness.[6,27,28] (See Profiles in Leadership 6.2.)

People believe what they want to believe and disregard the rest.
Paul Simon and Art Garfunkel, musicians

Personality and Life

HIGHLIGHT 6.3

Many organizations currently use personality testing as part of their process for hiring leaders or in leadership development programs. Despite their prevalence in both the private and public sector, there is still some controversy surrounding the use of personality testing in organizational settings. Some of the arguments against using personality testing are that (1) personality test scores are unrelated to job performance; (2) personality tests are biased or "unethical"; and (3) personality test results can be faked. These are important questions: if personality test scores are biased, are unrelated to job performance, and can be faked, there would be little reason to use them in work settings. However, a comprehensive review of personality research reveals the following:

- Personality traits predict overall managerial effectiveness, promotion rates, and managerial-level attainment.

- Personality traits predict leader emergence and effectiveness.

- Personality traits predict charismatic or transformational leadership.

- Personality traits predict expatriate performance.

- Personality traits predict career success.

- Personality traits predict effort, persistence, creativity, and willingness to help others.

- Personality traits predict overall job performance across virtually all job types.

- Personality traits predict absenteeism and other counterproductive work behaviors.

- Personality traits predict job and career satisfaction.

- Personality traits predict mortality rates, divorce, alcohol and drug use, health behaviors, and occupational attainment.

- Personality test scores predict teamwork and team performance.

- Personality test scores yield similar results for protected groups. In other words, males, females, African Americans, Hispanics, and Asian Americans generally score the same on personality tests.

- Personality tests results can be faked to some extent, but the degree to which test scores are faked depends on the test setting and administration. Faking, however, does not seem to affect the overall relationships between personality test results and work outcomes and can be detected and corrected.

- Personality tests suffer less from adverse impact and faking than traditional selection techniques, such as résumés and job interviews.

These findings show that personality tests can help organizations hire leaders who have the potential to be effective and can help leaders hire followers who are more likely to be successful. The arguments against the use of personality testing simply do not stand up to the facts, and because of these findings there has been a renewed interest in personality among leadership researchers.

Sources: L. M. Hough and F. L. Oswald. "Personality Testing and Industrial–Organizational Psychology: Reflections, Progress, and Prospects," *Industrial and Organizational Psychology: Perspectives on Science and Practice* 1, no. 3 (2008), pp. 272–90; G. J. Curphy, *Hogan Assessment Systems Certification Workshop Training Manual* (Tulsa, OK: Hogan Assessment Systems, 2003); G. J. Curphy, "Comments on the State of Leadership Prediction," in *Predicting Leadership: The Good, the Bad, the Indifferent, and the Unnecessary,* J. P. Campbell and M. J. Benson (chairs), symposium conducted at the 22nd Annual Conference for the Society of Industrial and Organizational Psychology, New York, April 2007; R.T. Hogan and T. Chamorro-Premuzic, "Personality and Career Success," in *APA Handbook of Personality and Social Psychology* (Vol. 3), eds. L. Cooper and R. Larsen (Washington, D.C.: American Psychological Association, 2012); D. S. Chiaburu, I. S. Oh, C. M. Berry, N. Li, and R. G. Gardner, "The Five Factor Model of Personality Traits and Organizational Citizenship Behaviors: A Meta-Analysis," *Journal of Applied Psychology* 96, no. 6 (2011), pp. 1140–65; J. Antonakis, D. V. Day, and B. Schuns, "Leadership and Individual Differences: At the Cusp of a Renaissance," *Leadership Quarterly* 23, no. 4, (2012), pp. 643–50; A. E. Colbert, T. A. Judge, D. Choi, and G. Wang, "Assessing the Trait Theory of Leadership Using Self and Observer Ratings of Personality: The Mediating Role of Contributions to Group Success," *Leadership Quarterly* 23, no. 4, (2012), pp. 670–85.

Robert "RT" Hogan

PROFILES IN LEADERSHIP 6.2

Robert Hogan has arguably been one of the most prominent and influential leadership researchers for the past 30 years. His papers and books are among the most widely cited in the behavioral sciences, and he is constantly asked to give keynote presentations to government, business, and academic audiences. His personality inventories are widely recognized as "best in class" and are used around the world to hire and develop everyone from truck drivers to CEOs. At this point well over 3 million individuals have taken one or more Hogan assessments, and the popularity of these instruments continues to grow.

Hogan grew up in East Los Angeles and was the first in his family to attend college. He attended UCLA and obtained an engineering degree on a Navy ROTC scholarship before spending the next seven years working on a destroyer in the U.S. Navy. It was in the Navy that Hogan became interested in leadership and psychology; he read all he could about Freud, Jung, and other prominent psychologists while at sea. After leaving the Navy Hogan became a parole officer for the Los Angeles police department. As a parole officer Hogan realized that the process used to determine a juvenile's fate was based completely on the whim of his or her parole officer and that there was no standardized system or process for keeping these individuals out of trouble. Thinking there had to be a better way to do this, Hogan decided to attend UC Berkeley to obtain a PhD in personality psychology. While working on his graduate degree, Hogan conducted personality testing on police officers and devised selection systems to combat unfair hiring and promotion practices. After graduation he spent some time as a professor at Johns Hopkins University before becoming a professor at the University of Tulsa. Hogan eventually became chair of the psychology department at the University of Tulsa while starting his own company.

A true entrepreneur, RT and his wife, Joyce (another well-known PhD psychologist), started Hogan Assessment Systems; the company now has 70 full-time employees and distributor partnerships around the globe. Hogan Assessment Systems has been a great way for RT to mentor and develop graduate students and to help junior faculty get published. He has also been able to leverage the data they have collected through their instruments to publish hundreds of articles and books about personality and leadership, many of which can be found in the most prestigious psychology journals. One of the authors of this textbook, Gordy Curphy, credits the Hogans with having a bigger impact on his thinking about leadership and success as a leadership consultant than anyone else with whom he has worked.

Personality Types and Leadership

The Differences between Traits and Types

Traits are not the only way to describe stereotypical behaviors. An alternative framework to describe the differences in people's day-to-day behavioral patterns is through **types,** or in terms of a **personality typology.** Superficially there may appear to be little difference between traits and types; even some of the same words are used to name them. Extraversion, for example, is the name of a factor in the OCEAN model, but another framework may talk about extraverted *types*. And these differences are more than skin deep. We emphasize only one aspect of these differences—

the one we believe is most fundamental conceptually. Each personality factor in the OCEAN model (such as neuroticism) is conceptualized as a continuum along which people can vary, typically in a bell-curve distribution. A person may be relatively lower or higher on that trait, and the differences in behavioral patterns between any two people may be thought of as roughly proportional to how close or far apart they are on the scale. Types, on the other hand, are usually thought of as relatively *discrete categories*.

This distinction may become clearer with an example. Let us take the trait of dominance and compare it with a hypothetical construct we will call a "dominant type." Psychological typologies are often expressed in terms of polar opposites, so let us further suppose that our typology also refers to the bipolar opposite of dominant types, which we'll call submissive types. Importantly, people are considered to *be one or the other*, just as everyone is either male or female. If you are a dominant type, you are considered to be more like all the other dominant types than you are like any submissive type; if you are a submissive type, you are considered to be more like every submissive type than you are like any dominant type. In other words, typologies tend to put people into discrete psychological categories and emphasize the *similarities* among all people in the same category regardless of actual score (as long as it is in the "right" direction). Furthermore, typologies tend to emphasize *differences* between people of different types (such as between dominant and submissive types) regardless of actual score.

Figure 6.3 illustrates this point. The upper line refers to the continuum of the trait defined at one end by submissiveness and at the other end by dominance. The trait scores of four different individuals—Jim, John, Joe, and Jack—are indicated on the scale. You can infer from their relative positions on the scale that John is more like Joe than he is like either Jim or Jack. Now look at the lower line. This refers to the typology of submissive and dominant types. The theory behind personality types suggests that John is more like Jim than Joe, and Joe is more like Jack than John.

FIGURE 6.3
Traits and Types

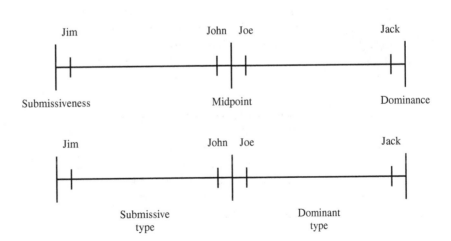

Psychological Preferences as a Personality Typology

One popular personality typology involves psychological preferences, or what we might call "mental habits." Like traits, our preferences play a role in the characteristic and unique ways we behave from day to day.

According to Jung,[38] preferences influence our choice of careers, ways of thinking, relationships, and work habits. Over 2 million people take the **Myers-Briggs Type Indicator (MBTI)** test every year,[39] which not only is the most popular measure of preferences but also makes it one of the most popular psychological tests. The MBTI is often used in college-level leadership and adult education courses, formal leadership training programs, and various team-building interventions. Moreover, numerous books and articles have been published about how the MBTI can be used to better understand oneself, co-workers, partners in intimate relationships, children, and educational and occupational choices. Because of the overall popularity of preferences and the MBTI, we believe it is worthwhile to review this framework and its most popular assessment instrument in some detail.

Somewhat paradoxically, one reason knowledge about our psychological preferences is important is precisely because it is so easy to forget about them. It is easy to forget how subjective and idiosyncratic preferences really are; we easily confuse our *preferences* with *the way things are or ought to be*. For example, those who value being organized may prefer *everyone* to be organized. They may get annoyed when working with others who are less organized than they are. In other words, it is easy to let preferences affect judgments about others (people "should" be organized, and therefore not being organized is a deficiency). Many people are unaware of the extent to which their preferences shape their perceptions of reality.

According to Myers and Myers,[40] there are four basic preference dimensions in which people can differ. These four dimensions include extraversion–introversion, sensing–intuition, thinking–feeling, and judging–perceiving. These four dimensions are bipolar, meaning that individuals generally prefer being either, say, extraverted or introverted. A more in-depth description of the day-to-day behavioral patterns of these four dimensions follows.

The **extraversion–introversion** dimension is fundamentally concerned with where people get their energy. Some leaders are naturally gregarious and outgoing. Their spontaneous sociability makes it easy for them to strike up conversations with anyone about almost anything. Not surprisingly, extraverts have a breadth of interests and a large circle of acquaintances. They are energized by being around others, but their tendency to "think out loud" and speak whatever is on their mind can sometimes get them into trouble. Other leaders are more comfortable being alone or with just a few others. Introverts can interact effectively with others, but they are fundamentally more reserved and deliberate than extraverts.

Question: How do you tell an extraverted engineer from an introverted engineer?
Answer: Extraverted engineers look at your shoes when they are talking to you.

Anonymous

Introverted leaders prefer to think things through and announce only final decisions, and followers may have a difficult time understanding the process such a leader used to reach his or her conclusions. Because introverts find being around others to be draining, they may come across as less approachable than extraverts. This preference dimension can be easily seen at parties and social settings. Extraverts work the crowd and are often the last to leave; introverts keep to themselves or talk to a small group of friends and leave early. Of course everyone needs to act in both introverted and extraverted ways at various times; however, some of us are more comfortable with one than the other.

The **sensing–intuition** dimension is concerned with how people look at data. Leaders who prefer the sensing mode like facts and details; the focus of information gathering concerns the real, the actual, the literal, the specific, and the present. Hence sensing leaders tend to be practical, orderly, and down-to-earth decision makers. By contrast, leaders who rely on their intuition look for the big picture beyond particular facts and details; information is most meaningful for its pattern, trend, figurative meaning, and future possibilities. Intuitive leaders tend to be innovative and conceptual (though sometimes impractical) and are more comfortable with their hunches and inspirations. This preference dimension can often be seen in presentations. A sensing leader will use a relatively large number of slides to explain all the facts leading up to a practical decision. An intuitive leader will use a few slides to summarize key trends and describe the possible implications of these trends. Intuitive leaders sitting through a sensor's presentation might get bored with the details and think, "They just don't get it." Sensing leaders sitting through an intuitive's presentation will wonder, "Where are the data?" and ask questions about the assumptions and facts underlying the trends and conclusions.

Whereas the sensing–intuition dimension is concerned with how leaders and followers look at data, the **thinking–feeling** dimension is concerned with the considerations leaders prefer when making decisions. Thinking leaders like to analyze, criticize, and approach decisions impersonally and objectively. They use their heads to adopt a relatively detached stance toward decisions and pay more attention to operational, bottom-line considerations. Feeling leaders naturally empathize and appreciate, and they prefer to approach decisions personally and subjectively. They value humaneness and social harmony and use their hearts to weigh the impact of any decision on people. As an example, say a thinking leader was the head of a customer service support center, and his feeling follower just got a call that her child was sick at school and she needed to go pick her up. The leader's first thought might be "How will I be able to field customer calls during my follower's absence?" whereas the follower's first thought might be "I hope my child is okay." Similarly, the

You psychologists focus on what is wrong with people; I want to focus on what is right and what could be right.

Isabel Myers, MBTI coauthor

CEO of a large home improvement retail organization was a strong thinker, and one of his division presidents was a strong feeler. The CEO would look at monthly financial reports and make decisions that would improve shareholder value. The division president would look at these decisions and immediately think about how they would affect his 26,000 employees. Both the CEO and division president looked at the same reports; they just approached their decisions differently based on their preferences.

The **judging–perceiving** dimension describes the amount of information a leader needs before feeling comfortable making a decision. Judging leaders strive for closure; they like things settled and come across as decisive, methodical, and organized. Judgers get nervous *before* decisions get made and want to see only the minimal amount of information needed to make decisions. Although they make up their minds quickly, they may not have all the relevant facts and as a result can make poor decisions. Perceiving leaders like to keep their options open; they are curious, spontaneous, and flexible. Perceivers prefer to collect as much data as possible before making decisions and get nervous *after* they are made because they may not feel all the information was collected or analyzed correctly. Although perceivers are good at gathering and analyzing data, they sometimes are accused of suffering from "analysis paralysis." This personality preference can readily be seen in meetings. Judging leaders prefer to have an agenda, stick to it, and make as many decisions as possible in the meeting. Perceivers dislike agendas, do not mind going off on tangents, and may or may not make any decisions at meetings. They also have no problem revisiting decisions made in earlier meetings if new information comes to light. Judging followers can get frustrated working for perceiving leaders and vice versa over these meeting and decision-making issues.

As with personality traits, many leaders and followers exhibit the behaviors associated with their preference dimensions almost automatically, particularly in weak or stressful situations. However, it is important to note that people are not locked into exhibiting only those behaviors associated with their preferences. Leaders can and do exhibit behaviors associated with the opposite side of any preference dimension, but it takes personal insight and conscious energy and effort to do so. Moreover, the more extreme a preference score, the more likely the associated behaviors will be exhibited and the more effort it will take to exhibit nonpreference behaviors. One advantage of this framework is that the predominant preferences can be used to create 16 psychological types. For example, someone with high preferences for introversion, sensing, thinking, and judging would be categorized as an ISTJ type. A listing of the 16 types can be found in Table 6.2, and preference researchers believe that individuals within any particular type are more similar to each other than they are to individuals in any of the other 15 types.[39–41]

TABLE 6.2   The 16 Psychological Types

Characteristics and Careers Frequently Associated with Each Myers-Briggs Type	
ISTJ (14%)[a] Responsible, organized, perfectionistic, detail oriented, private, punctual, dutiful, cautious, would rather be friendless than jobless, insensitive to hardships of others *Favored Careers:* Scientist, Engineer *Disfavored Careers:* Entertainer, Musician	**ESFP (1%)** Outgoing, social, talkative, modest, emotional, happy, disorganized, spontaneous, touchy feely, suggestible, prone to crying, likes being the center of attention, likes teamwork *Favored Careers:* Hair Stylist, DJ, Nurse *Disfavored Careers:* Researcher, Programmer
ISFJ (2%) Polite, rule abiding, dutiful, dislikes competition, frightens easily, timid, socially uncomfortable, not spontaneous, apprehensive, guarded, suspicious, dislikes change *Favored Careers:* Homemaker, Librarian *Disfavored Careers:* Performer, CEO	**ESTJ (23%)** Organized, group oriented, focused, conventional, planful, realistic, hard working, stiff, content, regular, strict, disciplined, meticulous, strong sense of purpose *Favored Careers:* Executive, Banker, Lawyer *Disfavored Careers:* Poet, Artist, Musician
ISTP (2%) Hidden, private, loner, insensitive to others, dislikes sharing feelings, lower energy, messy, avoidant, submissive, dislikes being in charge, prefers intellectual pursuits over relationships *Favored Careers:* Engineer, Programmer *Disfavored Careers:* Artist, Florist, Teacher	**ESFJ (2%)** Outgoing, does not like being alone, open, easy to read, considerate, complimentary, loving, follows the rules, clean, altruistic, values organized religion *Favored Careers:* Wedding Planner, Nurse *Disfavored Careers:* Scientist, Astronaut
ISFP (1%) Disorganized, easily distracted and disturbed, self-doubting and not self-confident, indecisive, prone to discouragement, does not like leading, private, modest, prone to laziness *Favored Careers:* Teacher, Singer, Carpenter *Disfavored Careers:* Marketer, Judge, Lawyer	**INFJ (1%)** Anxious, cautious, creative, smart, private, values solitude, does not like to be looked at, easily offended, moody, prone to feelings of sadness and loneliness, fears rejection *Favored Careers:* Therapist, Editor, Painter *Disfavored Careers:* Pilot, Business Owner
ESTP (2%) Emotionally stable, content, thick skinned, decisive, adjusts easily, likes crowds, outgoing, disorganized, messy, risk taker, fearless, enjoys sports, likes to lead, good presenter *Favored Careers:* CEO, Pilot, Spy, Bar Owner *Disfavored Careers:* Novelist, Librarian, Florist	**INTJ (9%)** Loner, detached, values solitude, socially uncomfortable, unhappy, analytical, critical, suspicious, orderly, prepared, clean, punctual, perfectionistic, rarely shows anger *Favored Careers:* Engineer, Neurosurgeon *Disfavored Careers:* Performer, Ad Executive

(Continued)

INFP (1%)

Idealist, daydreamer, smart, creative, impulsive, moody, disorganized, prone to lateness, private, attracted to sad things, prone to regret, submissive, easily discouraged

Favored Careers: Cartoonist, Writer, Activist

Disfavored Careers: Executive, Administrator

INTP (5%)

Likes the esoteric, likes science fiction, skeptical, rule breaker, unemotional, loner, detached, does not think they are weird but others do, fantasy prone, disorganized

Favored Careers: Philosopher, Mortician

Disfavored Careers: Social Worker, Supervisor

ENFP (2%)

Outgoing, social, disorganized, easily talked into doing silly things, pleasure seeking, irresponsible, thrill seeker, unconventional, impulsive, prone to losing things

Favored Careers: Actor, Artist, Filmmaker

Disfavored Careers: Analyst, Banker, Engineer

ENTP (9%)

Thrill seeker, rule breaker, risk taker, adventurous, life of a party, outgoing, adaptable, not easily offended, emotional stable, dominant, improviser, carefree

Favored Careers: Homemaker, Librarian

Disfavored Careers: Performer, CEO

ENFJ (4%)

Emotional, loving, social, positive, affectionate, image conscious, considerate, easily hurt, religious, neat, perfectionistic, ambitious, hard working, touchy, seductive

Favored Careers: Critic, News Anchor, Dancer

Disfavored Careers: Scientist, Truck Driver

ENTJ (22%)

Decisive, adventurous, fearless, engaged, self centered, image conscious, opinionated, ambitious, hates to be bored, narcissistic, arrogant, driven, critical, orderly

Favored Careers: Consultant, Lawyer, Spy

Disfavored Careers: Chef, Singer, Artist

[a]The percentage of managers falling into each of the 16 types.

Source: http://www.similarminds.com

The test is not valid or legal to use for personnel assignments, hiring, or promotion. It does not have predictive validity for such uses. It is a useful guide, and no more. Problem is, people go to a workshop, get excited and treat the Myers-Briggs as a secret window into the minds of their co-workers.

David M. Boje, professor

Implications of Preferences and Types

Preference advocates maintain that no one type is necessarily better than others in terms of leadership effectiveness, and that each type has unique strengths and potential weaknesses.[39–41] There is little published evidence to support this claim, but evidence shows that leaders are disproportionately distributed across a handful of types. As shown in Table 6.2, many more leaders are ISTJs, ESTJs, and ENTJs than other types. More research is needed concerning how preferences affect leadership, but it seems reasonable that awareness and appreciation of them can enhance any leader's effectiveness. (See Highlight 6.4.)

Although the MBTI is an extremely popular and potentially useful instrument, leadership practitioners need to be aware of its limitations and possible misuses. The four preference dimensions can provide useful insights about oneself and others, but the fundamental concept of type is problematic. First, types are not stable over time. Some research indicates that at least one letter in the four-letter type may change in half the people

Positive Psychology and Strengths-Based Leadership

HIGHLIGHT 6.4

Much of traditional psychology has focused on the diagnosis and treatment of mental disorders. Positive psychology looks at the other end of the mental health continuum and asks what people can do to promote genius, talent, competence, and happiness. Rather than worrying about what is going wrong, what would happen if people thought only about what is going right? Would this approach result in more career success, higher incomes, and greater satisfaction with life? Some people, such as Norman Vincent Peale, Joel Osteen, and Tony Robbins, have developed loyal followings and made millions of dollars by emphasizing the positive. This approach has proved so popular that it has spilled over to the leadership arena, and one way it has done so is known as **strengths-based leadership**.

The strengths-based leadership approach is predicated on three tenets, which are to (1) get clarity about what a person is good at, (2) find jobs or tasks that leverage each person's strengths, and (3) minimize the time spent improving weaknesses, as this negatively impacts overall effectiveness. The StrengthsFinder 2.0 assessment is a personality-like tool that helps leaders identify their top five strengths (i.e., traits). The authors of this assessment believe the most effective leaders spend the majority of their time doing the activities in which they excel and surrounding themselves with followers whose strengths make up for their shortcomings.

Although this approach is intuitively appealing, as leaders need to do only what they are good at and can ignore or staff around their shortcomings, there are five problems with strengths-based leadership. First, as evidenced by the many who are "leadership legends" in their own minds but are "charismatically challenged" in the eyes of others, what leaders believe to be their own strengths may not match up to their public reputations. A self-rated StrengthsFinder 2.0 assessment may indicate a particular leader is good at five things, but people who know the leader well could think there are five other things the leader is good at. Thus, the leader could spend all his or her time doing the wrong activities. Second, the strengths-based

approach can become a convenient excuse for narcissism; people may think they are really good at X, Y, and Z and as a result believe they only have to do X, Y, and Z. Although the job requires the person to do tasks A, B, and C, he or she may not do these activities because they do not fit with their "strengths". Third, simply ignoring weaknesses will not make them go away. If a leader is not very good at visioning, building teams, or inspiring others, then it can be hard to staff around these shortcomings. Fourth, situations are in a constant state of flux. Leaders get new bosses, are assigned new tasks or responsibilities, are promoted, move to different divisions or companies, and more. At the end of the day, the leaders need to get results, but there may be only a remote chance that all of these changes are going to line up with their strengths or they will be able to staff around them. Finally, there is ample research to show that overleveraging strengths can result in managerial incompetence. Leaders who are naturally charming can become arrogant, and those who are detail-oriented can become micromanagers when leveraging their strengths. Many leaders prescribing to the strengths-based approach tend to overdo the approach and alienate their teams as a result. Leaders should have insight into their strengths, but the best leaders are those who understand the implications of overusing their strengths and who work on improving their weaknesses.

Sources: M. E. P. Seligman and M. Csikszentmihalyi, "Positive Psychology: An Introduction," *American Psychologist* 55, no. 1 (2000), pp. 5–14; T. Rath and B. Conchie, *Strengths Based Leadership: Great Leaders, Teams, and Why People Follow* (New York: Gallup, 2009); J. Asplund, S. J. Lopez, T. Hodges, and J. Harter, *The Clifton StengthsFinder 2.0 Technical Report: Development and Validation* (New York: Gallup, 2009); R. B. Kaiser and D. V. Overfield, "Strengths, Strengths Overused, and Lopsided Leadership," *Consulting Psychology Journal* 63, no. 2 (2011), pp. 89–109; R. B. Kaiser and J. Hogan, "Personality, Leader Behavior, and Overdoing It," *Consulting Psychology Journal* 63, no. 4 (2011), pp. 219–42; H. Le, I. S. Oh, S. B. Robbins, R. Ilies, E. Holland, and P. Westrick, "Too Much of a Good Things: Curvilinear Relationships between Personality Traits and Job Performance," *Journal of Applied Psychology* 96, no. 1 (2011), pp. 113–33.

Michelle Rhee

PROFILES IN LEADERSHIP 6.3

Michelle Rhee was the chancellor of the Washington, D.C., public school system from 2007 to 2011. Her parents were first-generation immigrants from South Korea, and her first educational experiences were with the Korean public school system. Her first classroom had 70 students, everyone in her class was ranked from 1 to 70, and the rankings were posted right outside the classroom. Instead of being a source of humiliation, Rhee believed these public rankings caused parents and students to take academics very seriously.

Rhee spent her formative years attending public schools in Toledo, Ohio, and did well enough to get into Cornell. She managed a sandwich shop during her breaks; one summer she complained to the owner that one of her co-workers refused to take out the trash. The owner told Rhee to "send a message" to the problem employee. Rhee subsequently fired the girl in the middle of the shift and asked the remaining co-workers, "Does anyone else have a problem?" Upon graduation, Rhee began her career with Teach for America, a program that sent promising young teachers to the toughest urban schools. As a teacher in the Baltimore public school system Rhee noticed that students had different reactions to different teachers and incorporated those practices that keep students interested and motivated into her own teaching style.

In 2007 Rhee was asked by the mayor of Washington, D.C., Adrian Fenty, to turn around the city's public school system. The system had some of the lowest achievement test scores and high school graduation rates in the country, yet was spending more money per student than many other cities. On one of her first visits Rhee encountered a sign in a school that said, "Teachers cannot make up for what parents and students will not do"—a sign that Rhee believed summed up everything that was wrong with the D.C. public school system. During her four years as Chancellor, Rhee fired 241 teachers, 36 principals, and 22 assistant principals, and renegotiated the contract with the teachers' union to allow teacher evaluations and merit pay. As a result of these changes Rhee had a very public spat with the head of the American Federation of Teachers. The mayor backed Rhee in her battle with the teachers' union, which drove the federation to campaign against Fenty in the next mayoral campaign; Fenty subsequently failed to get reelected. Rhee resigned the chancellor's position shortly thereafter.

What would Michelle Rhee's public reputation be with Adrian Fenty or fellow school chancellors? What would it be with members of the teachers' union, parents, or students? How do you think she would score on the OCEAN scale of agreeableness? Conscientiousness? Do you think she exhibited any overused strengths?

Sources: N. S. Riley, "Seeing Through the School Daze," *The Wall Street Journal*, February 19, 2013, p. A13; M. Rhee. *Radical: Fighting to Put Students First*. (New York: Harper Collins, 2013).

---

taking the test in as little as five weeks.[42] Data also show major development changes in distribution of types with age.[43] It is difficult to see how one should select individuals for teams or provide career guidance to others based on types if the types (or at least the type scores) change, in some cases quickly. Furthermore, because the behavior of two people in the same type may vary as greatly as that of people of different types, the utility of typing systems remains uncertain. (See Profiles in Leadership 6.3)

But perhaps the most serious problem in using typologies concerns the way they are sometimes misused.[44] Unfortunately some people become so enamored with simple systems for classifying human behavior that they begin to see *everything* through "type" glasses. Some people habitually categorize their friends, significant others, and co-workers into types. Knowledge of type should be a basis for appreciating the richness and diversity of behavior and the capabilities in others and ourselves. It is not meant to be a system of categorization that oversimplifies our own and others' behavior. Believing someone is a particular type can become a perceptual filter that keeps us from actually recognizing when that person is acting in a manner contrary to that type's characteristic style. Another misuse occurs when someone uses "knowledge" of type as an excuse or a rationalization for his own counterproductive behaviors ("I know I'm talking on and on and dominating the conversation, but after all, I'm an extravert"). In this case the misuse of type can become a self-fulfilling prophecy that may make it difficult for a leader to change a follower's behavior. The MBTI is a useful tool for enhancing awareness of oneself and others, but leaders need to understand that, like any tool, it can be misused.

> *Perhaps no concept in the history of psychology has had or continues to have as great an impact on everyday life in the Western world as that of general intelligence.*
>
> **Sandra Scarr, researcher**

Intelligence and Leadership

What Is Intelligence?

The first formal linkage between intelligence and leadership was established around 1115 BC in China, where the dynasties used standardized tests to determine which citizens would play key leadership roles in the institutions they had set up to run the country.[45] Using intelligence tests to identify potential leaders in the United States goes back to World War I, and to a large extent this use of intelligence testing continues today. Over 100 years of very comprehensive and systematic research provides overwhelming evidence to support the notion that general intelligence plays a substantial role in human affairs.[46-54] Still, intelligence and intelligence testing are among the most controversial topics in the social sciences today. There is contentious debate over questions like how heredity and the environment affect intelligence, whether intelligence tests should be used in public schools, and whether ethnic groups differ in average intelligence test scores. For the most part, however, we will bypass such controversies here. Our focus will be on the relationship between intelligence and leadership.

> *Good brains don't necessarily translate into good judgment.*
>
> **Peggy Noonan, writer**

We define **intelligence** as a person's all-around effectiveness in activities directed by thought.[46-55] What does this definition of intelligence have to do with leadership? Research has shown that more intelligent leaders are faster learners; make better assumptions, deductions, and inferences; are better at creating a compelling vision and developing strategies to make their vision a reality; can develop better solutions to problems; can see more of the primary and secondary implications of their decisions; and are quicker on their feet than leaders who are less intelligent.[46-64] To a large extent people get placed into leadership positions to solve problems, whether they are customer, financial, operational, interpersonal,

FIGURE 6.4
**The Building
Blocks of Skills**

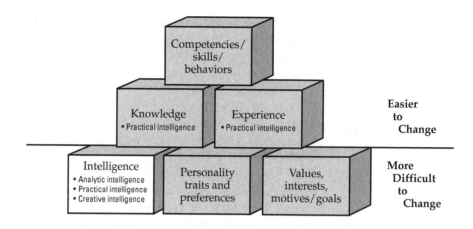

No psychologist has observed intelligence; many have observed intelligent behavior. This observation should be the starting point for any theory of intelligence.

I. Chien, researcher

performance, political, educational, or social in nature. Therefore, given the behaviors associated with higher intelligence, it is easy to see how a more intelligent leader will often be more successful than a less intelligent leader in influencing a group to accomplish its goals. Like personality traits, however, intelligence alone is not enough to guarantee leadership success. Plenty of smart people make poor leaders—just as few intelligent people are great leaders. Nevertheless, many leadership activities seem to involve some degree of decision-making and problem-solving ability, which means a leader's intelligence can affect the odds of leadership success in many situations.

As shown in Figure 6.4, intelligence is relatively difficult to change. Like personality, it is also an unseen quality and can be inferred only by observing behavior. Moreover, intelligence does not affect behavior equally across all situations. Some activities, such as following simple routines, put less of a premium on intelligence than others.[58,65] Finally, our definition of intelligence does not imply that intelligence is a fixed quantity. Although heredity plays a role, intelligence can be modified through education and experience.[46,51,57,65]

The Triarchic Theory of Intelligence

Intelligence and leadership effectiveness are related, but there is still an ongoing debate about the nature of intelligence. Many psychologists have tried to determine the structure of intelligence: is intelligence a unitary ability, or does it involve a collection of related mental abilities?[55,62,66,67] Other psychologists have said that the *process* by which people do complex mental work is much more important than determining the number of mental abilities.[50,51,68] One of the most comprehensive and compelling theories of intelligence developed and tested over the past 30 years is Sternberg's **triarchic theory of intelligence.**[50,51,56,57,68] It also offers some of the most significant implications for leadership. The triarchic theory focuses on what a leader *does* when solving complex mental problems, such

The first method for estimating the intelligence of a ruler is to look at the men he has around him.
Niccolò Machiavelli,
                writer

as how information is combined and synthesized when solving problems, what assumptions and errors are made, and the like. According to this theory, there are three basic types of intelligence. **Analytic intelligence** is general problem-solving ability and can be assessed using standardized mental abilities tests. Analytic intelligence is important because leaders and followers who possess higher levels of this type of intelligence tend to be quick learners, do well in school, see connections between issues, and have the ability to make accurate deductions, assumptions, and inferences with relatively unfamiliar information.

There is still much, however, that analytic intelligence does not explain. Many people do well on standardized tests but not in life.[59,64,65,68] And some people do relatively poorly on standardized intelligence tests but develop ingenious solutions to practical problems. For example, Sternberg and his associates described a situation in which students in a school for the mentally retarded did very poorly on standardized tests yet consistently

Why Athletes Can't Have Regular Jobs

HIGHLIGHT 6.5

The United States seems to put more emphasis on athleticism than intelligence, as least when it comes to the amounts of money allocated to athletic and academic scholarships. The following quotes illustrate the kind of returns the United States is getting from its athletic scholarships:

- Chicago Cubs outfielder Andre Dawson on being a role model: "I want all dem kids to do what I do, to look up to me. I want dem kids to copulate me."

- New Orleans Saints running back George Rogers when asked about the upcoming season: "I want to rush for 1,000 or 1,500 yards, whatever comes first."

- Torrin Polk, University of Houston receiver, on his coach: "He treats us like men. He lets us wear earrings."

- Senior basketball player at the University of Pittsburgh: "I am going to graduate on time, no matter now long it takes."

- Stu Grimson, Chicago Blackhawks wing, explaining why he keeps a color photograph of himself on his locker: "That's so when I forget how to spell my name, I can still find my clothes."

- Chuck Nevitt, North Carolina basketball player, explaining to his coach why he appeared nervous in practice: "My sister's expecting a baby, and I don't know if I am going to be an uncle or an aunt."

- Frank Layden, Utah Jazz President, on a former player: "I told him, 'Son, what is it with you? Is it ignorance or apathy?' He said, 'Coach, I don't know and I don't care.'"

- Football commentator and former player Joe Theisman: "Nobody in football should be called a genius. A genius is a guy like Norman Einstein."

- Shelby Metcalf, basketball coach at Texas A&M, recounting what he told a player who received four Fs and a D: "Son, looks to me like you're spending too much time on one subject."

- In the words of North Carolina State basketball player Charles Shackelford: "I can go to my left or right, I am amphibious."

Source: http://www.vegsource.com/talk/humor/messages/97.html

found ways to defeat the school's elaborate security system. In this situation the students possessed a relatively high level of **practical intelligence,** or "street smarts." People with street smarts know how to adapt to, shape, or select new situations to get their needs met better than people lacking street smarts (e.g., think of a stereotypical computer nerd and an inner-city kid both lost in downtown New York). In other words, practical intelligence involves knowing how things get done and how to do them. For leaders, practical intelligence is important because it involves knowing what to do and how to do it when confronted with a particular leadership situation, such as dealing with a poorly performing subordinate, resolving a problem with a customer, or getting a team to work better together.[64,68]

Because of its potential importance to leadership effectiveness, several other aspects of practical intelligence are worth noting. First, practical intelligence is much more concerned with knowledge and experience than is analytic intelligence (see Figure 6.4). Leaders can build their practical intelligence by building their leadership knowledge and experience. Thus textbooks like this one can help you build your practical intelligence. Getting a variety of leadership experiences, and perhaps more important, reflecting on these experiences, will also help you build practical intelligence. But you should understand that it takes some time before you will become an "expert" at leadership—research shows that it takes 10 years to truly master any particular topic.[69] (See Highlights 6.5 and 6.6.)

Everyone is ignorant, only on different subjects.

Will Rogers, humorist

Why Smart People Can't Learn

HIGHLIGHT 6.6

Being able to learn and adapt is a critical leadership skill, but it turns out that many professionals are not good at it. Leaders get paid to solve problems and are generally good at this, but many are lousy at determining what role *they* played in causing these problems. Leaders are good at **single-loop learning**—reviewing data and facts and identifying the underlying root causes from the information gathered—but are not good at **double-loop learning**—determining what they as leaders need to do differently to avoid problems in the future. The primary reason why many leaders are not good at double-loop learning is because most have not experienced real failure. Many people in positions of authority have enviable track records of success, so when things go badly they erroneously believe that it cannot be their fault because they have always been successful. Something else must be causing the group's substandard performance, such as underachieving followers, market conditions, difficult customers, government regulations, or cutthroat competitors. Thus many leaders react to failure by laying the blame on circumstances or other people. Although external factors can and do affect group performance, a leader's actions or inactions can also be a major cause of team failure. Before leaders point at external factors they need to ask how their actions contributed to the problem. Unfortunately it appears that the more formal education one has, the less likely it is that one will engage in double-loop learning. Intelligence alone will not help people extract the maximum value from their experiences—reflection also plays a key role in learning and adaptation.

Source: Adapted from C. Argyris, "Teaching Smart People How to Learn," *Harvard Business Review*, May–June 1991, Reprint Number 91301.

Practical Intelligence in Action: Al-Qaeda's Tipsheet on Drones

HIGHLIGHT 6.7

Practical intelligence involves knowing how things get done and how to do them. Advice is a form of practical intelligence, as it provides information on how to handle certain situations. A real world example of sharing advice comes from the terrorist group, Al-Qaeda. The United States has used armed drones to take out a number of high level Al-Qaeda leaders across Afghanistan, Pakistan, Iraq, Yemen, and Mali, and the group has countered by developing 22 tips to avoid drone detection. Some of these tips include stretching grass mats or reflective glass on top of cars, hiding under trees, covering cars in mud, and using dolls or statues to imitate public gatherings. These tips have been posted on the Internet for other terrorist groups to use.

Is the Internet a good source of practical intelligence? Why or why not?

Source: www.cbn.com/cbnnews/world/2013/February/Al-Qaeda-tipsheet-on-eluding-drones-found-in-Mali/

There is no better way to get people angry than by making them look dumb in public. Smart people are very good at this.

**Jim Earley,
executive coach**

Second, practical intelligence is *domain specific.* A leader who has a lot of knowledge and experience in leading a pharmaceutical research team may feel like a duck out of water when asked to lead a major fund-raising effort for a charitable institution. As another example, one of the authors worked with a highly successful retail company having over 100,000 employees. All the key leaders had over 20 years of retail operations and merchandising experience, but they also did poorly on standardized intelligence tests. The company had successfully expanded in the United States (which capitalized on their practical intelligence), but their attempt to expand to foreign markets was an abysmal failure. This failure was due in part to the leaders' inability to learn, appreciate, or understand the intricacies of other cultures (analytic intelligence), their lack of knowledge and experience in foreign markets (practical intelligence), and in turn their development of inappropriate strategies for running the business in other countries (a combination of analytic and practical intelligence). Thus practical intelligence is extremely useful for leading in familiar situations, but analytic intelligence may play a more important role when leaders face new or novel situations. (See Highlights 6.7.)

Third, this example points out the importance of having both types of intelligence. Organizations today are looking for leaders and followers who have the necessary knowledge and skills to succeed (practical intelligence) and the ability to learn (analytic intelligence).[50,56,57,68,70] Fourth, high levels of practical intelligence may compensate for lower levels of analytic intelligence. Leaders with lower analytic abilities may still be able to solve complex work problems or make good decisions if they have plenty of job-relevant knowledge or experience. But leaders with more analytic intelligence, all things being equal, may develop their street smarts more quickly than leaders with less analytic intelligence. Analytic intelligence may play a lesser role once a domain of knowledge is mastered, but a more important role in encountering new situations.

The best way to have a good idea is to have a lot of ideas.

Dr. Linus Pauling, scientist

The third component of the triarchic theory of intelligence is **creative intelligence,** which is the ability to produce work that is both novel and useful.[50,51,57,68–73] Using *both* criteria (novel and useful) as components of creative intelligence helps to eliminate outlandish solutions to a potential problem by ensuring that adopted solutions can be realistically implemented or have some type of practical payoff. Several examples might help to clarify the novel and practical components of creative intelligence. The inventor of Velcro got his idea while picking countless thistles out of his socks; he realized that the same principle that produced his frustration might be translated into a useful fastener. The inventor of 3M's Post-it notes was frustrated because bookmarks in his church hymnal were continually sliding out of place, and he saw a solution in a low-tack adhesive discovered by a fellow 3M scientist. The scientists who designed the *Spirit* and *Opportunity* missions to Mars were given a budget that was considerably smaller than those of previous missions to Mars. Yet the scientists were challenged to develop two spacecraft that had more capabilities than the *Pathfinder* and the *Viking Lander.* Their efforts with *Spirit* and *Opportunity* were a resounding success, due in part to some of the novel solutions used both to land the spacecrafts (an inflatable balloon system) and to explore the surrounding area (both were mobile rovers).

Two interesting questions surrounding creativity concern the role of intelligence and the assessment of creative ability. Research shows that analytic intelligence correlates at about the .5 level with creative intelligence.[72] Thus the best research available indicates that analytic intelligence and creativity are related, but the relationship is imperfect. Some level of analytic intelligence seems necessary for creativity, but having a high level of analytic intelligence is no guarantee that a leader will be creative. And like practical intelligence, creativity seems to be specific to certain fields and subfields: Bill Gates cannot write music and Madonna cannot do math.[51,55,70,72–76]

Assessing creativity is no simple matter. Tests of creativity, or **divergent thinking,** differ from tests that assess **convergent thinking.** Tests of convergent thinking usually have a single best answer; good examples here are most intelligence and aptitude tests. Conversely, tests of creativity or divergent thinking have many possible answers.[77] Although Sternberg and his associates showed that it is possible to reliably judge the relative creativity of different responses, judging creativity is more difficult than scoring convergent tests.[70,72,78] For example, there are no set answers or standards for determining whether a movie, a marketing ad, or a new manufacturing process is truly creative. Another difficulty in assessing creativity is that it may wax and wane over time; many of the most creative people seem to have occasional dry spells or writer's block. This is different from analytic intelligence, where performance on mental abilities tests remains fairly constant over time.

The fastest way to succeed is to double the failure rate.

Thomas Watson Sr., IBM

Implications of the Triarchic Theory of Intelligence

Some 200 separate studies have examined the relationship between intelligence test scores and leadership effectiveness or emergence, and these studies have been the topic of major reviews.[1,2,7,46–60,65,70] These reviews provide overwhelming support for the idea that leadership effectiveness or emergence is positively correlated with analytic intelligence. Nonetheless, the correlation between analytic intelligence and leadership success is not as strong as previously assumed. It now appears that personality is more predictive of leadership emergence and effectiveness than analytic intelligence.[5,26–28,32] Leadership situations that are relatively routine or unchanging, or that require specific in-depth product or process knowledge, may place more importance on personality and practical intelligence than analytic intelligence. Having a high level of analytic intelligence seems more important for solving ambiguous, complex problems, such as those encountered by executives at the top levels of an organization. Here leaders must be able to detect themes and patterns in seemingly unrelated information, make accurate assumptions about market conditions, or make wise merger, acquisition, or divestiture decisions. Further evidence that higher levels of analytic intelligence are associated with top leaders can be found in Figure 6.5. (See Highlight 6.8.)

Although a high level of analytic intelligence is usually an asset to a leader, research also suggests that in some situations analytic intelligence may have a *curvilinear* relationship with leadership effectiveness.[1,79] When differences in analytic intelligence between leader and followers are too great, communication can be impaired; a leader's intelligence can become an impediment to being understood by subordinates. An alternative explanation for the curvilinear relationship between analytic intelligence and leadership effectiveness may have to do with how stress affects

FIGURE 6.5
Average Intelligence Test Scores by Management Level

Source: N. Kuncel, "Personality and Cognitive Differences among Management Levels," unpublished manuscript (Minneapolis: Personnel Decisions International, 1996).

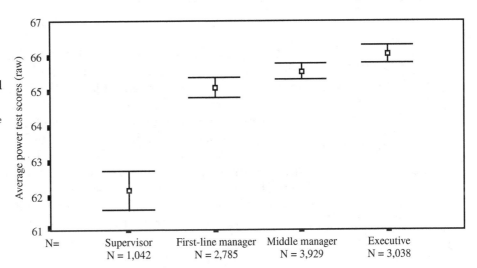

The Competent Hot Potato

HIGHLIGHT 6.8

What should leaders do when a follower is smart, competent, and creative (that is, has a high level of practical, analytic, and creative intelligence) but has difficulties getting along with other team members? Clearly creative followers with high levels of analytic intelligence and domain knowledge can help their teams make better decisions, but the cost of this knowledge is often strained relationships or high levels of turnover among teammates. Research shows that when given a choice, team members would prefer to work with a lovable but incompetent fool than an irritable but competent jerk. On one hand, team performance is likely to suffer if everyone on the team is happy but incompetent. On the other hand, performance is also likely to suffer when a toxic follower is part of a team. It appears that many managers resolve this dilemma by having competent jerks on their teams during the initial phases of projects—when ideas about project direction, possibilities, and solutions are being determined. Once these decisions are made, many managers then arrange to have the competent jerks leave their teams. The good news is that the team gets to capitalize on the competent jerks' expertise during the decision-making phase of the project but doesn't have to suffer their dysfunctional

behavior during the execution phase. The bad news is that a common way to get rid of competent jerks is to promote them. Many managers would rather see a toxic follower become a toxic leader rather than confront difficult performance issues. Subsequent bosses often repeat the "hot potato" process, helping toxic leaders move into roles with ever-increasing responsibilities.

Many times teammates share some of the blame with bosses for these questionable promotions. When teammates complain to their managers about competent jerks and the managers discuss these issues with the problematic individuals, competent jerks usually deny the allegations. And when competent jerks confront their teammates about these allegations, teammates are unwilling to share their complaints. With team members failing to provide feedback, leaders often are accused of harboring ill will toward the competent jerks. Oftentimes the only face-saving way out of this situation is to give a competent jerk a transfer to or promotion in another department.

Sources: J. Sandberg, "Sometimes Colleagues Are Just Too Bad to Not Get Promoted," *The Wall Street Journal*, August 17, 2005, p. A5; J. Casciaro and M. S. Lobo, "Competent Jerks, Lovable Fools, and the Formation of Social Networks," *Harvard Business Review*, June 2006, pp. 92–100.

You'll get hired for your intelligence, but fired for your personality.
Dianne Nilsen,
Business Executive

leader–subordinate interactions. Fiedler and his associates found that smart but inexperienced leaders were less effective in stressful situations than less intelligent, experienced leaders.[80–82] An example of this finding was clearly demonstrated in the movie *Platoon*. In one frantic scene an American platoon is ambushed by the Viet Cong. An inexperienced, college-educated lieutenant calls for artillery support from friendly units. He calls in the wrong coordinates, however, and as a result artillery shells are dropped on his own platoon's position rather than on the enemy's position. The situation comes under control only after an experienced sergeant sizes up the situation and tells the artillery units to cease firing. This example points out the importance of practical intelligence in stressful situations. Leaders revert to well-practiced behaviors under periods of high stress and change, and leaders with high levels of practical intelligence have a relatively broad set of coping and problem-solving behaviors to draw upon in these situations. Because of the levels of stress and change associated with many leadership positions today, systematically improving practical leadership skills through education and experience is important for leaders and leaders-to-be.

With respect to creative intelligence, perhaps the most important point leaders should remember is that their primary role is not so much to be creative themselves as to *build an environment where others can be creative.* This is not to say that leaders should be uncreative, but rather that most innovations have roots in ideas developed by people closest to a problem or opportunity (that is, the workers). Leaders can boost the creativity throughout their groups or organizations in many ways, but particularly through selecting creative employees and providing opportunities for others to develop their creativity, and through broader interventions like making sure the motivation and incentives for others are conducive to creativity and providing at least some guidance or vision about what the creative product or output should look like.[83–95]

Leaders can do several things to improve the group and organizational factors affecting creativity. Leaders should be mindful of the effect various sorts of incentives or rewards can have on creativity; certain types of motivation to work are more conducive to creativity than others. Research has shown that people tend to generate more creative solutions when they are told to focus on their intrinsic motivation for doing so (the pleasure of solving the task itself) rather than focusing on extrinsic motivation (public recognition or pay).[83,96] When they need to foster creativity, leaders may find it more effective to select followers who truly enjoy working on the task at hand rather than relying on rewards to foster creativity.

Creativity can be hindered if people believe their ideas will be evaluated. Experiments by Amabile and Zhou showed that students who were told their projects were to be judged by experts produced less creative projects than students who were not told their projects would be judged.[97–98] A similar phenomenon can occur in groups. When a group knows its work must ultimately be evaluated, there is a pronounced tendency for members to be evaluative and judgmental too early in the solution-generating process. This tends to reduce the number of creative solutions generated, perhaps because of a generally shared belief in the value of critical thinking (and in some groups the norm seems to be the more criticism, the better) and of subjecting ideas to intense scrutiny and evaluation. When members of a group judge ideas as soon as they are offered, two dysfunctional things can happen. People in the group may censor themselves (not share all their ideas with the group) because even mild rejection or criticism has a significant dampening effect, or they may prematurely reject others' ideas through focus on an idea's flaws rather than its possibilities.[99] Given these findings, leaders may want to hold off on evaluating new ideas until they are all on the table, and should encourage their followers to do the same.

Silicon Valley doesn't have better ideas and isn't smarter than the rest of the world, but it has the edge in filtering ideas and executing them.

Sergey Brin, Google

Finally, leaders who need to develop new products and services should try to minimize turnover in their teams and give them clear goals. Teams with unclear goals may successfully develop new or novel products, but these products may have low marketability or usefulness. An example illustrates this point. In the 1980s Texas Instruments (TI) decided to delve into the personal computer business. TI had a reputation for technical excellence, and one of the best managers in the company was asked to head up the project. The manager did not have a clear sense of what customers wanted or what a personal computer should be able to do. This lack of clarity had some dramatic effects. As more and more engineers were added to the project, more innovative hardware ideas were added to the computer design. These additions caused the project to take much longer and cost a lot more than planned, but the TI personal computer ended up winning a number of major engineering awards. Unfortunately it was also a business disaster because the product failed to meet customer needs. The TI project serves as a good example of a concept called **creeping elegance.** Leaders without a clear vision of what a final project should look like may end up with something that fails to meet customer needs. Leaders need to provide enough room for creativity to flourish, but enough direction for effort to be focused.[87,90,91] Table 6.3 shows several factors leaders should keep in mind when trying to foster creativity.

Making the simple complicated is commonplace; making the complicated simple, awesomely simple, that's creativity.

Charles Mingus, jazz bassist and composer

TABLE 6.3
Creativity Killers: How to Squelch the Creativity of Direct Reports

Sources: T. M. Amabile and M. Khaire, "Creativity and the Role of the Leader," *Harvard Business Review*, October 2008, pp. 100–10; T. M. Amabile and J. Zhou, in S. F. Dingfelder, "Creativity on the Clock," *Monitor on Psychology*, November 2003, pp. 56–58.

The following is a list of things leaders can do if they wish to stifle the creativity of their followers:

Take away all discretion and autonomy: People like to have some sense of control over their work. Micromanaging staff will help to either create yea-sayers or cause people to mentally disengage from work.

Create fragmented work schedules: People need large chunks of uninterrupted time to work on novel solutions. Repeated interruptions or scheduling "novel solution generation time" in 15-minute increments around other meetings will disrupt people's ability to be innovative.

Provide insufficient resources: People need proper data, equipment, and money to be creative. Cut these off, and watch creativity go down the tubes.

Focus on short-term goals: Asking a person to be creative at a specific moment is like asking a comedian to be funny the first time you meet him or her. People can be creative and funny if given enough time, but focusing on only short-term outcomes will dampen creativity.

Create tight timelines and rigid processes: The tighter the deadlines and less flexible the processes, the more chance that innovation will be reduced.

Discourage collaboration and coordination: The best ideas often come from teams having members with different work experiences and functional backgrounds. By discouraging cross-functional collaboration, leaders can help guarantee that team members will offer up only tried-and-true solutions to problems.

Keep people happy: If you keep workers happy enough, they will have little motivation to change the status quo.

Innovation in Emerging Economies

HIGHLIGHT 6.9

For the past 100-plus years the Western Hemisphere has been the center of innovation and creativity. Many of the modern conveniences to which we have become accustomed were invented in the United States or Europe. But will the West remain the center of innovation? This is an important question: studies show that future job and economic growth will come from information- or knowledge-based work rather than manufacturing-based work. North America may lead the world in research spending, but globalization and information technology are helping other parts of the world to catch up. The emerging economies of Brazil, Russia, India, and China (BRIC) are graduating millions of scientists and engineers each year, and their economies are becoming robust enough to generate strong domestic bases for new products.

Clever ideas can be found anywhere, and technology is helping to make these ideas into products. The expanding middle class of the BRIC countries is giving more people the income needed to purchase new products. With the number of scientists and engineers graduating from the BRIC countries and their rapidly expanding economies, it may only be a matter of time before the West is no longer the center of innovation. What do you think are the implications of these trends for leaders in the West or the BRIC countries?

Source: "Something New under the Sun," *The Economist*, October 13, 2007, pp. 3–4.

One industry that places a premium on creativity is the motion picture industry. Because creativity is so important to the commercial success of a movie, it is relatively easy for a movie to succumb to creeping elegance. But how do movie directors successfully avoid creeping elegance when dealing with highly creative people having huge egos? Part of the answer may lie in the approach of two of Hollywood's most successful directors. Steven Spielberg and Ron Howard have said that before they shoot a scene they first have a clear picture of it in their own minds. If they don't have a clear picture, they sit down with the relevant parties and work it out. This shows the importance of having a clear vision when managing creativity. (See Highlight 6.9.)

Intelligence and Stress: Cognitive Resources Theory

In the preceding section we noted that intelligence may be a more important quality for leaders in some situations than others. You may be surprised to learn, however, that recent research actually suggests there are times when intelligence may be a disadvantage. A key variable affecting this paradoxical finding seems to be whether the leader is in a stressful situation. Recent research suggests that stress plays a key role in determining how a leader's intelligence affects his or her effectiveness. While it is not surprising that stress affects behavior in various ways, Fiedler and Garcia developed the **cognitive resources theory (CRT)** to explain the interesting relationships between leader intelligence and experience levels, and group performance in stressful versus nonstressful conditions.[100,101]

CRT consists of several key concepts, one of which is intelligence. Fiedler and Garcia defined *intelligence* as we have earlier—it is one's all-around effectiveness in activities directed by thought and is typically measured using standardized intelligence tests (in other words, analytic intelligence). Another key concept is experience, which represents the habitual behavior patterns, overlearned knowledge, and skills acquired for effectively dealing with task-related problems (that is, practical intelligence). Although experience is often gained under stressful and unpleasant conditions, experience also provides a "crash plan" to revert back to when under stress.[80–82,100,101] As Fiedler observed, people often act differently when stressed, and the crash plan describes this change in behavior patterns. For most CRT studies, experience has been defined as time in the job or organization. A third key concept in CRT is stress. *Stress* is often defined as the result of conflicts with superiors or the apprehension associated with performance evaluation.[82,101] This interpersonal stress is believed to be emotionally disturbing and can divert attention from problem-solving activities. In other words, people can get so concerned about how their performance is being evaluated that they may fail to perform at an optimal level. In sum, cognitive resources theory provides a conceptual scheme for explaining how leader behavior changes under stress to impact group performance.

Cognitive resources theory makes two major predictions with respect to intelligence, experience, stress, and group performance. First, because experienced leaders have a greater repertoire of behaviors to fall back on, leaders with greater experience but lower intelligence are hypothesized to have higher-performing groups under conditions of high stress. Experienced leaders have "been there before" and know better what to do and how to get it done when faced with high-stress situations. Leaders' experience levels can interfere with performance under low-stress conditions, however.

That leads to a second hypothesis. Because experience leads to habitual behavior patterns, leaders with high levels of experience tend to misapply old solutions to problems when creative solutions are called for. Experienced leaders rely too much on the tried and true when facing new problems, even under relatively low stress. Thus leaders with higher levels of intelligence but less experience are not constrained by previously acquired behavior patterns and should have higher performing groups under low-stress conditions. In other words, experience is helpful when one is under stress but can hinder performance in the absence of stress.

These two major predictions of CRT can be readily seen in everyday life. For the most part, it is not the most intelligent but the most experienced members of sporting teams, marching bands, acting troupes, or volunteer organizations who are selected to be leaders. These leaders are often chosen because other members recognize their ability to perform well under the high levels of stress associated with sporting events and public performances. In addition, research with combat troops, firefighters, senior executives, and students has provided strong support for the two major tenets of CRT. [80–82,100,101]

Despite this initial empirical support, one problem with CRT concerns the apparent dichotomy between intelligence and experience. Fiedler and Garcia's initial investigations of CRT did not examine the possibility that leaders could be *both* intelligent and experienced. Subsequent research by Gibson showed not only that many leaders were both intelligent and experienced, but also that these leaders would fall back on their experience in stressful situations and use their intelligence to solve group problems in less stressful situations. [82]

Another issue with CRT concerns the leader's ability to tolerate stress. As Schonpflug and Zaccaro correctly pointed out, some leaders are better able than others to tolerate high levels of stress. [102,103] Some leaders have personalities characterized by low neuroticism scores, and they may do well in high-stress situations even when they lack experience because of their inherent ability to handle stress. Further research on this issue seems warranted.

In general, solid evidence appears to support the major tenets of CRT. Because of this research, CRT has several important implications for leaders. First, the best leaders may be smart *and* experienced. Although intelligence tests are good indicators of raw mental horsepower, it is just as important for leaders to broaden their leadership knowledge and experience if they want to succeed in high-stress situations. This latter point may be important today, when the additional stress of globalization, technology, and organizational change may cause the performance of leaders to be scrutinized even more closely than in the past. In fact, this additional scrutiny may cause leaders who were previously successful to perform poorly.

Second, leaders may not be aware of the degree to which they are causing stress in their followers. If followers perceive that their performance is being closely watched, they are likely to revert to their crash plans in order to perform. If a situation calls for new and novel solutions to problems, however, such leader behavior may be counterproductive. A key point here is that leaders may be unaware of their impact on followers. For example, they may want to review their followers' work more closely in order to be helpful, but followers may not perceive it this way.

Third, the level of stress inherent in the position needs to be understood before selecting leaders. Those filling high-stress leadership positions can either look for experienced leaders or reduce the stress in the situation so that more intelligent leaders can succeed. Another alternative could be to hire more intelligent leaders and put them through stress management training or work simulations so the effects of stress are minimized. [81,82] It is also possible that experienced leaders may get bored if placed into low-stress positions. [7] (See Highlight 6.10.)

Reality is the leading cause of stress for those in touch with it.
Jane Wagner, writer

Intelligence and Judgment

HIGHLIGHT 6.10

Robert Hogan argues that the term *intelligent* applies mostly to decisions. Decisions that successfully solve problems or improve organizational performance are deemed "intelligent"; those that do not are usually described as "dumb." Decision making is critically important in business, politics, and warfare where money and people's lives are on the line. According to Hogan, an organization's success can be measured by the collective decisions it makes. Generally speaking, armies that win or companies that outperform their rivals make many more intelligent decisions than those that fail.

Good judgment occurs when leaders choose the right means to solve a problem and change course when information indicates to do so. Bad judgment occurs when people impose the wrong solution onto a problem and then stick with their solutions even when it is obviously not working. Many organizational failures boil down to top leaders picking the wrong solutions to solve problems or not adopting different solutions when presented with information showing that the initial approach is clearly failing. For example, the failure of General Motors in 2008–2009 had much to do with adopting and then sticking with a strategy of selling large trucks and SUVs in the face of climate change legislation, high gasoline prices, and an economic recession.

Given this definition of good versus bad judgment, how would you judge the U.S. war with Iraq? After the terrorist attacks of September 11, 2001, it was clear that the United States was at war, and its enemy was Al-Qaeda. The data linking Al-Qaeda to Iraq, however, was sketchy; the preponderance of evidence showed that Iraq did not have any weapons of mass destruction, and it was unlikely the Iraqi citizens were going to see the coalition forces as "liberators." There is no doubt that Saddam Hussein was an abusive dictator, but at the time many other abusive dictators posed bigger threats to the United States and to world security than Saddam Hussein (consider, for example, Kim Jong-Il in North Korea). Al-Qaeda was well established in Afghanistan, but the United States instead opted to focus on Iraq. The war in Iraq has cost the United States 4,000 lives, 20,000 wounded soldiers, and a trillion dollars. Has this war reduced or eliminated the threat posed by Al-Qaeda? Was the decision to go to war with Iraq an exercise in good or poor judgment? How about the war in Afghanistan? What information would you need to answer these questions?

Sources: R. T. Hogan, Intelligence and Good Judgment, unpublished manuscript (Tulsa, OK: Hogan Assessment Systems, 2009); P. Ingrassa, "How Detroit Drove into a Ditch," *The Wall Street Journal*, October 25–26, 2008, pp. W1–2; T.E. Ricks. *Fiasco: The American Military Adventure in Iraq* (New York: Penguin Press, 2006).

Emotional Intelligence and Leadership

What Is Emotional Intelligence?

So far we have discussed the role personality traits and types play in a leader's day-to-day behavioral patterns. We have also described the role analytic, practical, and creative intelligence play in solving problems and making decisions. And we have discussed how stress can affect a leader's ability to solve problems. An overwhelming body of evidence shows that these enduring patterns of behaviors and mental abilities have a big impact on leadership effectiveness, but we have not discussed the role

There is no single entity called EQ (emotional intelligence quotient) as people have defined it. One sympathetic interpretation of what journalists were saying is that there were a dozen unrelated things, which collectively might predict more than intelligence, things like warmth, optimism, and empathy. But there was nothing new about that. Instead, the story became this fabulous new variable that is going to outpredict intelligence. There is no rational basis for saying that.

John Mayer, EQ researcher

emotions play in leadership success. To put it differently, do moods affect a person's ability to build teams and get results through others? Moods and emotions are constantly at play at work, yet most people are hesitant to discuss moods with anybody other than close friends. It also appears that moods can be contagious, in that the moods of leaders often affect followers in both positive and negative ways. And charismatic or transformational leaders use emotions as the catalyst for achieving better-than-expected results (see Chapter 14). Given the importance and prevalence of emotions in the workplace, there should be a wealth of research regarding mood and leadership effectiveness, but this is not the case. Researchers have begun to seriously examine the role of emotions in leadership only over the past 20 years.

The relationships between leaders' emotions and their effects on teams and outcomes became popularized by researcher Dan Goleman with the publication of the book *Emotional Intelligence*.[104] But what is emotional intelligence (EQ), and how is it the same as or different from personality traits or types or the three types of intelligence described in this chapter? Unfortunately there appear to be at least four major definitions of **emotional intelligence.** The term *emotional intelligence* can be attributed to two psychologists, Peter Salovey and John Mayer, who studied why some bright people fail to be successful. Salovey and Mayer discovered that many of them run into trouble because of their lack of interpersonal sensitivity and skills, and defined emotional intelligence as a group of mental abilities that help people to recognize their own feelings and those of others.[105,106] Reuven Bar-On believed that emotional intelligence was another way of measuring human effectiveness and defined it as a set of 15 abilities necessary to cope with daily situations and get along in the world.[107] Rick Aberman defined emotional intelligence as the degree to which thoughts, feelings, and actions were aligned. According to Aberman, leaders are more effective and "in the zone" when their thoughts, feelings, and actions are perfectly aligned.[108,109] Daniel Goleman, a science writer for *The New York Times*, substantially broadened these definitions and summarized some of this work in his books *Emotional Intelligence* and *Working with Emotional Intelligence*.[104,110] Goleman argued that success in life is based more on one's self-motivation, persistence in the face of frustration, mood management, ability to adapt, and ability to empathize and get along with others than on one's analytic intelligence or IQ. Table 6.4 compares the Salovey and Mayer, Bar-On, and Goleman models of emotional intelligence.

Although these definitions can cause confusion for people interested in learning more about emotional intelligence, it appears that these four definitions of EQ can be broken down into two models: an ability model and a mixed model of emotional intelligence.[106,111] The ability model focuses on how emotions affect how leaders think, decide, plan, and act. This

TABLE 6.4   Ability and Mixed Models of Emotional Intelligence

Ability Model	Mixed Models	
Mayer, Salovey, and Caruso	**Goleman et al.**	**Bar-On**
Perceiving emotions	Self-awareness	Intrapersonal
	Emotional awareness	Self-regard
	Accurate self-assessment	Emotional self-awareness
	Self-confidence	Assertiveness
		Independence
		Self-actualization
Managing emotions	Self-regulation	Adaptability
	Self-control	Reality testing
	Trustworthiness	Flexibility
	Conscientiousness	Problem solving
	Adaptability	
	Innovation	
Using emotions	Motivation	Stress management
	Achievement	Stress tolerance
	Commitment	Impulse control
	Initiative	
	Optimism	
Understanding emotions	Empathy	Interpersonal
	Understanding others	Empathy
	Developing others	Social responsibility
	Service orientation	Interpersonal relationship
	Diversity	
	Political awareness	General mood
		Optimism
	Social skills	Happiness
	Influence	
	Communication	
	Conflict management	
	Leadership	
	Change catalyst	
	Building bonds	
	Collaboration/cooperation	
	Team capabilities	

Sources: R. Bar-On, *Emotional Quotient Inventory* (North Tonawanda, NY: Multi-Health Systems, 2001); D. Goleman, *Working with Emotional Intelligence* (New York: Bantam Doubleday Dell, 1998); D. R. Caruso, J. D. Mayer, and P. Salovey, "Emotional Intelligence and Emotional Leadership," in *Multiple Intelligences and Leadership*, ed. R. E. Riggio, S. E. Murphy, and F. J. Pirozzolo (Mahwah, NJ: Lawrence Erlbaum Associates, 2002), pp. 55–74, http://www. eiconsortium.org

model defines emotional intelligence as four separate but related abilities, which include (1) the ability to accurately perceive one's own and others' emotions; (2) the ability to generate emotions to facilitate thought and action; (3) the ability to accurately understand the causes of emotions and the meanings they convey; and (4) the ability to regulate one's emotions.

According to Caruso, Mayer, and Salovey, some leaders might be good at perceiving emotions and leveraging them to get results through others, but have difficulties regulating their own emotions. Or they could be good at understanding the causes of emotions but not as good at perceiving others' emotions. The ability model is not intended to be an all-encompassing model of leadership, but rather supplements the OCEAN and triarchic models of intelligence.[106,111] Just as leaders differ in neuroticism or practical intelligence, so do they differ in their ability to perceive and regulate emotions. The ability model of EQ is helpful because it allows researchers to determine if EQ is in fact a separate ability and whether it can predict leadership effectiveness apart from the OCEAN personality model and cognitive abilities.

The Goleman and Bar-On definitions of EQ fall into the mixed model category. These researchers believe emotional intelligence includes not only the abilities outlined in the previous paragraph but also a number of other attributes. As such, the mixed model provides a much broader, more comprehensive definition of emotional intelligence. A quick review of Table 6.4 shows that the attributes of emotional intelligence are qualities that most leaders should have, and Goleman, Boyatzis, and McKee maintain that leaders need more or less all of these attributes to be emotionally intelligent.[110,112,113] Moreover, the mixed model of emotional intelligence has been much more popular with human resource professionals and in the corporate world than the ability model. But does the mixed model really tell us anything different from what we already know? More specifically, is the mixed model different from the OCEAN personality model? Research shows that the mixed model assesses the same characteristics as the OCEAN model and is no more predictive of job performance and other important job outcomes than OCEAN personality assessments.[106,111,114–116] Goleman and Bar-On deserve credit for popularizing the notion that noncognitive abilities are important predictors of leadership success. But on the negative side, they also maintain that they have discovered something completely new and do not give enough credit to the 100 years of personality research that underlie many attributes in the mixed model. (See Profiles in Leadership 6.4.)

Can Emotional Intelligence Be Measured and Developed?

The publication of *Emotional Intelligence* has encouraged an industry of books, training programs, and assessments related to measurement and development of emotional intelligence. Mayer, Salovey, and Caruso's Emotional Intelligence Test (MSCEIT) is a measure of the ability model of emotional intelligence; it asks subjects to recognize the emotions depicted in pictures, what moods might be helpful in certain social situations, and so forth.[106,117] Bar-On has self, self–other, youth, and organizational measures of emotional intelligence, such as the Bar-On Emotional Quotient—360 or EQi-S.[118]

Scott Rudin

PROFILES IN LEADERSHIP 6.4

Few people know who Scott Rudin is, but many have seen his work. Rudin has been a Hollywood movie producer for over 25 years and has produced such movies as *The Girl with the Dragon Tattoo, There Will Be Blood, No Country for Old Men, Moonrise Kingdom, The Social Network, The Queen, Team America: World Police, Zoolander, The School of Rock, Notes on a Scandal,* and many others. Rudin also has the reputation of being the most difficult boss to work for in Hollywood; it is estimated that he has fired over 250 assistants over the past five years. His caustic rants, shrieking threats, impulsive firings, and revolving door of assistants are legendary. For example, he allegedly once fired an assistant for bringing in the wrong breakfast muffin. Rudin describes his own leadership style as a cross between Attila the Hun and Miss Jean Brodie, and it is rumored that the role of Miranda Priestly in *The Devil Wears Prada* was loosely modeled after Rudin.

An extreme micromanager, Rudin is involved with every detail of the films he is producing. Because he is producing several films at any one time, it is not unusual for Rudin to make over 400 calls in a single day. Rudin's assistants start their days at 6:00 a.m. with a 30-page annotated list of phone calls that are to be set up that day. During the day assistants will also do anything from picking up dry cleaning to answering phones, scheduling appointments, arranging travel, buying birthday presents, dropping off kids, and so on—you name it, the assistant does it. So why do assistants put up with Rudin? The hours are long but the pay is good—most interns make $70,000 to $150,000 per year. More importantly, aides who survive get a chance to rub shoulders with A-list talent and learn the ins and outs of the movie business. Plus the opportunities for advancement for those who survive are good—many of Rudin's aides have themselves become movie producers.

Given this background, what personality traits help Rudin to produce successful movies? Does he have any overused strengths? How would Rudin stack up on the three types of intelligence? How would you rate Rudin's emotional intelligence?

Source: K. Kelly and M. Marr, "Boss-Zilla!" *The Wall Street Journal,* September 24–25, 2005, p. A1; available at: gawker.com/243908/new-yorks-worst-bosses-scott-rudin

The Emotional Competence Inventory (ECi) was developed by Goleman and consists of 10 questionnaires. These questionnaires are completed by the individual and nine others; the responses are aggregated and given to the participant in a feedback report. Because these researchers have defined emotional intelligence differently and use a different process to assess EQ, it is not surprising that these instruments often provide leaders with conflicting results.[119] Nevertheless, the U.S. Air Force Recruiting Service has used the EQ-i to screen potential recruiters and found that candidates scoring higher on the attributes of assertiveness, empathy, happiness, self-awareness, and problem solving were much less likely to turn over prematurely in the position and had a 90 percent chance of meeting their recruiting quotas.[119]

One issue that most EQ researchers agree on is that emotional intelligence can be developed. Goleman and Aberman have developed one- to five-day training programs to help leaders improve their emotional intelligence; Bar-On has developed 15 e-learning modules that are available at EQ University.com. One big adopter of EQ training has been the sales staff at American Express Financial Advisors (AEFA). Leaders at AEFA discovered that the company had a well-respected set of investment and insurance products for customers, but many sales staff were struggling with how to respond to the emotions exhibited by clients during sales calls. Moreover, the best salespeople seem to be better able to "read" their clients' emotions and respond in a more empathetic manner. Since 1993 more than 5,500 sales staff and 850 sales managers at AEFA have attended a five-day training program to better recognize and respond to the emotions exhibited by clients. AEFA found that sales staff attending this program increased annual sales by an average of 18.1 percent, whereas those who did not attend training achieved only a 16.1 percent increase. However, this sample was small, and the comparison is somewhat unfair because the control group did not receive any kind of sales training in lieu of the EQ training.[119] Therefore, it is uncertain whether the EQ training content actually adds value over and above five days of sales training.

Implications of Emotional Intelligence

Aberman maintained that people can be extremely ineffective when their thoughts, feelings, and actions are misaligned—for example, arguing with someone on a cell phone when driving on a highway.[108,109] It seems likely that leaders who are thinking or feeling one thing and actually doing something else are probably less effective in their ability to influence groups toward the accomplishment of their goals. The EQ literature should also be credited with popularizing the idea that noncognitive abilities, such as stress tolerance, assertiveness, and empathy, can play important roles in leadership success. Today many organizations are using *both* cognitive and noncognitive measures as part of the process of hiring or promoting leaders. Finally, the EQ literature has also helped to bring emotion back to the workplace. Human emotions are important aspects of one-on-one interactions and teamwork,[106,110,113,120–123] but too many leadership practitioners and researchers have chosen to ignore the role they play. When recognized and leveraged properly, emotions can be the motivational fuel that helps individuals and groups to accomplish their goals. When ignored or discounted, emotions can significantly impede a leader's ability to build teams or influence a group. As discussed in the personality section of this chapter, leaders who can empathize and get along with others are often more successful than those who cannot.

Some of the more recent research in emotional intelligence indicates that it moderates employees' reactions to job insecurity and their ability to cope with stress when threatened with job loss. Employees with lower EQ reported more negative emotional reactions and used less effective coping strategies when dealing with downsizing than those with higher EQ.[124] Along these lines, other researchers report relationships between leaders' moods and followers' moods, job performance, job satisfaction, and creativity.[125] And Boyatzis, Stubbs, and Taylor accurately point out that most MBA programs focus more on cognitive abilities and developing financial skills than on those abilities needed to successfully build teams and get results through others.[126]

Given these results, is it possible to develop emotional intelligence? The answer to this question is yes, but the path taken to develop EQ would depend on whether the training program was based on an ability or mixed model of emotional intelligence. An ability-based EQ training program would focus on improving participants' ability to accurately perceive one's own and others' emotions, generate emotions to facilitate thought and action, accurately understand the causes of emotions and the meanings they convey, and regulate one's emotions. These programs make extensive use of videotapes, role plays, and other experiential exercises in order to help people better recognize, exhibit, and regulate emotion. Because the mixed model of EQ encompasses such a wide array of attributes, virtually any leadership development program could be considered an EQ training program.

Despite the positive contributions of emotional intelligence, the concept has several limitations. First, Goleman and his associates and Bar-On have not acknowledged the existence of personality, much less 100 years of personality–leadership effectiveness research. As shown in Table 6.5, Goleman's conceptualization of EQ looks similar to the OCEAN model found in Table 6.1. At least as conceptualized by these two authors, it is difficult to see how EQ is any different from personality. Second, if the EQ attributes are essentially personality traits, it is difficult to see how they will change as a result of a training intervention. Personality traits are difficult to change, and the likelihood of changing 20 to 40 years of day-to-day behavioral patterns as the result of some e-learning modules or a five-day training program seems highly suspect. As described in Chapter 1, people can change their behavior, but it takes considerable effort and coaching over the long term to make it happen. Finally, an important question to ask is whether EQ is really something new or is simply a repackaging of old ideas and findings. If EQ is defined as an ability model, such as the one put forth by Mayer, Salovey, and Caruso, then emotional intelligence probably is a unique ability and worthy of additional research (see Figure 6.6). A leader's skills in accurately perceiving, regulating, and leveraging emotions seem vitally important in building cohesive, goal-oriented teams, and measures like the MSCEIT could be used in conjunction with OCEAN and cognitive abilities measures to hire and develop better leaders. But if EQ is defined as a mixed model, then it is hard to see that Goleman and his associates and Bar-On are really telling us anything new. (See Highlight 6.11.)

What really matters for success, character, happiness and lifelong achievements is a definite set of emotional skills – your EQ – not just purely cognitive abilities that are measured by conventional IQ tests.

Daniel Goleman, EQ researcher

TABLE 6.5
Comparison between the OCEAN Model and Goleman's Model of EQ

Goleman et al.	Likely OCEAN Correlates
Self-awareness	
Emotional awareness	Agreeableness
Accurate self-assessment	Neuroticism
Self-confidence	Extraversion
Self-regulation	
Self-control	Neuroticism, conscientiousness
Trustworthiness	Conscientiousness
Conscientiousness	Conscientiousness
Adaptability	Neuroticism, conscientiousness
Innovation	Openness to experience, conscientiousness
Motivation	
Achievement	Extraversion
Commitment	Extraversion
Initiative	Extraversion
Optimism	Neuroticism
Empathy	
Understanding others	Agreeableness
Developing others	Openness to experience
Service orientation	Agreeableness
Diversity	Agreeableness
Political awareness	Agreeableness
Social skills	
Influence	Extraversion, agreeableness
Communication	Extraversion
Conflict management	Agreeableness
Leadership	Extraversion
Change catalyst	Extraversion
Building bonds	Agreeableness
Collaboration/cooperation	Agreeableness
Team capabilities	Extraversion, agreeableness

FIGURE 6.6
Emotional Intelligence and the Building Blocks of Skills

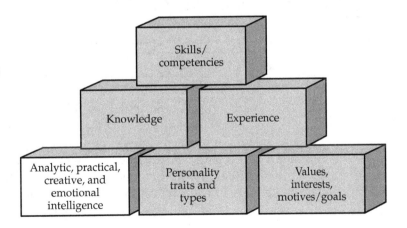

Assessing Leadership Potential

HIGHLIGHT 6.11

As the world of work shifts from manufacturing to information- or knowledge-based work, organizations are beginning to view talent as a strategic resource. Many manufacturing jobs in North America and Europe have shifted to Eastern Europe or Asia, and these jobs have been supplanted by those of software engineers, product designers, marketers, and salespeople at companies like Google, Apple, Microsoft, IBM, Oracle, and Facebook. Even traditional manufacturers, retailers, and consumer products companies such as GE, Dell, Best Buy, Target, Proctor & Gamble, and PepsiCo are putting more emphasis on roles that design new products, brands, and marketing campaigns; manage supply chains; improve information transfer; or improve financial or operational results. And because of the growth potential of emerging markets and the shift in manufacturing, most large companies have sales, operations, and suppliers located around the globe. Because it traditionally takes 20 to 30 years to develop an executive with marketing, sales, operations, finance, and international experience, one of the questions many organizations are asking is whether it is possible to shorten the executive development cycle. In other words, can organizations identify young leaders with the potential to be senior executives and then provide them with the experiences needed to make a successful transition to the C-suite? And can they significantly shorten the time to do this?

Because the companies with the best talent are likely to be the most successful, most *Fortune 500* companies as well as the U.S. military have high-potential leadership programs. These programs identify people early in their professional careers and then put them into rotational programs that provide marketing, sales, human resource, finance, supply chain, and international experience. A key question for leaders-to-be is how to get identified as having high potential. Unfortunately there are as many answers to this question as there are companies with high-potential programs. High-potential talent identification programs range from FOBs (Friends of Bill, the CEO) to sophisticated talent assessments. The more sophisticated approaches typically use some combination of work values instruments, personality type and trait tests, mental abilities tests, EQ assessments, work simulations, and peer and boss feedback to identify candidates with "the right stuff." Many of the tools and techniques described in Chapters 5 to 7 make up these more sophisticated high-potential talent assessment batteries, so understanding these concepts should help leaders to gauge whether organizations take talent management seriously.

Sources: R. Silzer and A. H. Church, "The Pearls and Perils of Identifying Potential," *Industrial and Organizational Psychology* 2 (2009), pp. 377–422; T. Giberson and S. Miklos, "Cognitive Ability Testing in Executive Assessments," *The Industrial and Organizational Psychologist* 50, no. 2 (2012), pp. 130–33; L. Dragoni, I. S. Oh, P. Van Katwyk, and P. E. Tesluk, "Developing Executive Leaders: The Relative Contribution of Cognitive Ability, Personality, and the Accumulation of Experience in Predicting Strategic Thinking Competency," *Personnel Psychology* 64, no. 4 (2011), pp. 829–64.

Summary

This chapter has examined the relationships of personality, intelligence, and emotional intelligence with leadership emergence and effectiveness. In general, all these attributes can help a leader to influence a group toward the accomplishment of its goals, but by themselves they are no guarantee of leadership success. Often the situation will dictate which personality traits or types, components of intelligence, or emotional intelligence attributes will positively affect a leader's ability to build a team or get results through others.

Although the term *personality* has many different meanings, we use the term to describe one's typical or characteristic patterns of behavior. There are several different theories to describe why people act in characteristic ways, but the trait approach to personality has been the most thoroughly researched, and as such plays a key role in the chapter. The adoption of the OCEAN model of personality has helped to clarify the personality–leadership relationships, and researchers have noted that leadership success is positively correlated with the OCEAN personality dimensions of openness to experience, conscientiousness, extraversion, agreeableness, and neuroticism.

Personality types can also be used to categorize stereotypical behavioral patterns. The extraversion–introversion, sensing–intuition, thinking–feeling, and judging–perceiving personality dimensions can be combined to form 16 different types, and the majority of leaders can be found in 4 of these 16 types. Although the relationships between the 16 types and leadership effectiveness are not as strong as those with the OCEAN personality dimensions, the 16 personality types and associated dimensions give leaders valuable insights into human behavior.

A more recent theory for understanding intelligence divides it into three related components: analytic intelligence, practical intelligence, and creative intelligence. All three components are interrelated. Most research shows that leaders possess higher levels of analytic intelligence than the general population, and that more intelligent leaders often make better leaders. Analytic intelligence appears to confer two primary benefits upon leaders. First, leaders who are smarter seem to be better problem solvers. Second, and perhaps more important, smarter leaders seem to profit more from experience.

The roles of practical and creative intelligence in leadership are receiving increasing attention. Practical intelligence, or one's relevant job knowledge or experience, is proving to be extremely important for leaders. Leaders with higher levels of practical intelligence seem to be better at solving problems under stress. Moreover, practical intelligence seems to be the easiest of the three components to change. Creative intelligence involves developing new and useful products and processes, and creativity is extremely important to the success of many businesses today. It is important that leaders learn how to successfully stimulate and manage creativity, even more than being creative themselves.

In some ways emotional intelligence is a relatively new concept; it is generally concerned with accurately understanding and responding to one's own and others' emotions. Leaders who can better align their thoughts and feelings with their actions may be more effective than leaders who think and feel one way about something but then do something different about it. Although emotional intelligence has helped to point out the role emotions and noncognitive abilities play in leadership success, some of it seems to be nothing more than another label for personality. If this is the case, then emotional intelligence may be a leadership fad that will fade over time.

Key Terms

Great Man theory, *185*
personality, *186*
trait approach, *187*
traits, *187*
weak situations, *189*
strong situations, *189*
Five Factor Model
    (FFM) or OCEAN
    model of
    personality, *190*
openness to
    experience, *190*
conscientiousness, *191*
extraversion, *192*
agreeableness, *192*
neuroticism, *193*
public reputation, *194*
types, *198*

personality
    typology, *198*
Myers-Briggs
    Type Indicator
    (MBTI), *200*
extraversion–
    introversion, *200*
sensing–intuition, *201*
thinking–feeling, *201*
judging–perceiving,
    202
strengths-based
    leadership, *205*
intelligence, *207*
triarchic theory of
    intelligence, *208*
analytic
    intelligence, *209*

practical
    intelligence, *210*
single-loop
    learning, *210*
double-loop
    learning, *210*
creative
    intelligence, *212*
divergent
    thinking, *212*
convergent
    thinking, *212*
creeping elegance, *216*
cognitive resources
    theory (CRT), *217*
emotional
    intelligence, *221*

Questions

1. What OCEAN personality traits or EQ components do you think would help professional sports players be more or less successful? Would successful coaches need the same or different personality traits and preferences? Would successful players and coaches need different traits for different sports?

2. How would you rank-order the importance of analytic intelligence, practical intelligence, creative intelligence, or emotional intelligence for politicians? Would this ranking be the same for college professors or store managers at a Walmart or 7-11 store?

3. Think of all the ineffective leaders you have ever worked or played for. What attributes did they have (or perhaps more importantly, lack) that caused them to be ineffective?

4. Individuals may well be attracted to, selected for, or successful in leadership roles early in their lives and careers based on their analytic intelligence. But what happens over time and with experience? Do you think *wisdom*, for example, is just another word for intelligence, or is it something else?

5. What role would downsizing play in an organization's overall level of practical intelligence?

6. We usually think of creativity as a characteristic of individuals, but might some organizations be more creative than others? What factors do you think might affect an organization's level of creativity?

7. Can better leaders more accurately perceive and leverage emotions? How could you determine if this was so?

Activities

1. Your instructor has access to a self-scored personality type assessment as well as to an online OCEAN personality assessment. The online assessment takes about 10 minutes to complete and could be given as homework. Once the assessments are completed, you should review the feedback reports and discuss in class.

2. Your instructor can suspend a 30-foot rope approximately 2 feet off the ground. You and the rest of the class should get on one side of the rope. The rope represents an electrified fence, and your task is to get everyone successfully *over* the rope without touching it. You may not touch, lower, raise, or adjust the rope in any manner. You may not let any part of your skin or clothing touch the rope, nor can you drape anything over the rope to protect you from the "current." There are two rules you must follow to successfully navigate the rope. First, before starting to cross the rope, everyone in the group must form a line parallel to the rope and hold hands with the people on either side. These links with the other people in the group cannot be broken. Second, a quality error is committed if any group member touches the rope. If the group detects their own error, then only the person currently attempting to navigate the rope needs to start over. If the instructor catches the error but the group does not, then the instructor can have the entire group start over. This is analogous to catching a bad product before it is delivered to a customer instead of delivering defective products to customers. You will have about 25 minutes to plan and execute this exercise. After the exercise your group should discuss the role of personality traits as well as analytic, practical, creative, and emotional intelligence in the exercise.

Minicase

Lessons on Leadership from Ann Fudge

How do you rescue one of the largest advertising and media services firms in the world from a downward spiral? That is the question Martin Sorrell faced when his London-based WPP Group acquired Young & Rubicam (Y&R) in 2000. After many years on top, Y&R was starting to lose momentum—and clients. Kentucky Fried Chicken, United Airlines, and Burger King all decided to take their advertising dollars elsewhere. Sorrell needed to stop the exodus, but how? Sorrell decided a fresh face was needed and started a search for a dynamic new CEO to revitalize Y&R. He found such a leader in Ann Fudge.

Ann Fudge was formerly president of Kraft Foods. At Kraft she had been responsible for the success of the $5 billion division that included well-known brands such as Maxwell House, Grape Nuts, Shredded

Wheat, and General Foods International Coffees. Fudge's reputation as a charismatic leader who listens was a major issue for Sorrell when he went looking for a new CEO for Y&R. Among the talents Fudge had to offer was an ability to interact effectively with all constituencies of a consumer business. Mattel chairman and CEO Bob Eckert was Fudge's boss when he was president and CEO of Kraft. Of Fudge, Eckert says, "She is equally comfortable with consumers at the ballpark, factory workers on a production line, and executives in the boardroom. She could engage all three constituents in the same day and be comfortable. She is very comfortable with herself, and she's not pretending to be someone else. That's what makes her such an effective leader."

Fudge's commitment to her work and to the people she works with is evident in the lessons she offers to other leaders:

1. Be yourself; do not feign behavior that you think will make you "successful."

2. Always remember it's the people, not you. A leader cannot be a leader if he or she has no followers. Be honest with people. Give them feedback. Put the right people in the right jobs. Surround yourself with the smartest people you can find—people who will offer differing perspectives and diversity of experience, age, gender, and race.

3. Touch your organization. It's easy to get stuck behind your desk. Fight the burden of paperwork and get out in the field. Don't be a remote leader. You cannot create a dynamic culture if people can't see, hear, and touch you. Let them know you as a person.

4. Steer the wheel with a strategic focus, yet maintain a wide peripheral vision. Know when to stop, speed up, slow down, brake quickly, swerve, or even gun it!

Fudge had a difficult decision to make when she was approached by Sorrell about the position at Y&R. She was in the midst of a two-year break—after 24 years working for corporate America, Fudge had decided to take some time for herself. She had left her position as president of Kraft Foods in 2001 based not on her dissatisfaction with her job, but on a desire to define herself by more than her career. "It was definitely not satisfaction, it was more about life," says Fudge about her sabbatical. During her two-year break she traveled, cycling around Sardinia and Corsica; she took up yoga; and she wrote a book called *The Artist's Way at Work*—a manual for improving creativity and innovation on the job.

Fudge took on the challenge and has not looked back. In her tenure at Y&R she has worked hard to get Y&R back on top. She has traveled the globe to visit Y&R employees. She frequently puts in 15-hour days pushing her strategy to focus on clients, encouraging teamwork, and improving creativity. A major undertaking for Fudge is to bring together the various business entities under the Y&R umbrella to better meet client needs. She's also trying to institute a Six Sigma method for creativity—looking for ways to increase productivity so employees have more time to be creative. Fudge's hard work is paying off. Y&R has recently added Microsoft and Toys R Us to its client list, and if Fudge has her way, the list will continue to grow until Y&R is back on top.

1. Where would Ann Fudge be placed in each of the Five Factor Model (FFM) categories?
2. Consider the components of creative intelligence from Table 6.3. Identify the key components that have affected Ann Fudge's success.
3. Ann Fudge decided to take a sabbatical to focus on her personal life. Based on her experience, what are the benefits of such a break? What might be some drawbacks?

Sources: Diane Brady, "Act Two: Ann Fudge's Two-Year Break from Work Changed Her Life. Will Those Lessons Help Her Fix Young & Rubicam?" *BusinessWeek,* March 29, 2004, p. 72, http://www.internet-marketing-brandin.com/News/african_american.htm; http://www.brandweek.com/brandweek/search/article_display.jsp?vnu_content_id1000506747; http://www.linkageinc.com/conferences/leadership/gild

End Notes

1. R. M. Stogdill, *Handbook of Leadership* (New York: Free Press, 1974).
2. R. M. Stogdill, "Personal Factors Associated with Leadership: A Review of the Literature," *Journal of Psychology* 25 (1948), pp. 35–71.
3. R. D. Mann, "A Review of the Relationships between Personality and Performance in Small Groups," *Psychological Bulletin* 56 (1959), pp. 241–70.
4. R. G. Lord, C. L. DeVader, and G. M. Allinger, "A Meta-analysis of the Relationship between Personality Traits and Leadership Perceptions: An Application of Validity Generalization Procedures," *Journal of Applied Psychology* 71 (1986), pp. 402–10.
5. R. T. Hogan, G. J. Curphy, and J. Hogan, "What Do We Know about Personality: Leadership and Effectiveness?" *American Psychologist* 49 (1994), pp. 493–504.
6. R. T. Hogan, "Personality and Personality Measurement," in *Handbook of Industrial and Organizational Psychology,* Vol. 2, eds. M. D. Dunnette and L. M. Hough (Palo Alto, CA: Consulting Psychologists Press, 1991), pp. 873–919.
7. T. A. Judge, A. E. Colbert, and R. Ilies, "Intelligence and Leadership: A Quantitative Review and Test of Theoretical Propositions," *Journal of Applied Psychology* 89, no. 3 (2004), pp. 542–52.
8. T. A. Judge, J. E. Bono, R. Ilies, and M. W. Gerhardt, "Leadership and Personality: A Qualitative and Quantitative Review," *Journal of Applied Psychology* 87, no. 4 (2002), pp. 765–80.
9. S. J. Zaccaro, "Trait-Based Perspectives on Leadership," *American Psychologist* 62, no. 1 (2007), pp. 6–16.
10. I. S. Oh, G. Wang, and M. K. Mount, "Validity of Observer Ratings of the Five Factor Model of Personality Traits: A Meta-Analysis," *Journal of Applied Psychology* 96, no. 4 (2011), pp. 762–73.

11. S. Freud, *Group Psychology and the Analysis of the Ego,* trans. J. Strachey, 2nd ed. *The Standard Edition of the Complete Works of Psychological Works of Sigmund Freud, Vol. 2* (London: Hogarth Institute for Psycho-Analysis).

12. G. J. Curphy, *The Consequences of Managerial Incompetence,* presentation given at the 3rd Hogan Assessment Systems International Users Conference, Prague, Czech Republic, September 2004.

13. J. Antonakis, D. V. Day, and B. Schyns, "Leadership and Individual Differences: At the Cusp of a Renaissance," *The Leadership Quarterly* 23, no. 4 (2012), pp. 643–50.

14. G. J. Curphy, *Personality, Intelligence, and Leadership,* presentation given to the Pioneer Leadership Program at Denver University, Denver, CO, 1997.

15. G. J. Curphy, "Personality and Work: Some Food for Thought," in *Personality Applications in the Workplace: Thinking Outside the Dots,* R. T. Hogan (chair). Symposium presented at the 12th Annual Conference of the Society of Industrial and Organizational Psychology, St. Louis, MO, 1997.

16. G. J. Curphy, "New Directions in Personality," in *Personality and Organizational Behavior.* R. T. Hogan (chair). Symposium presented at the 104th Annual Meeting of the American Psychological Association, Toronto, Canada, 1996.

17. J. Hogan and B. Holland, "Using Theory to Evaluate Personality and Job-Performance Relations: A Socio-analytic Perspective," *Journal of Applied Psychology* 88, no. 1 (2003), pp. 100–12.

18. R. P. Tett and D. D. Burnett, "A Personality Trait-Based Interactionist Model of Job Performance," *Journal of Applied Psychology* 88, no. 3 (2003), pp. 500–17.

19. G. W. Allport, and H. S. Odbert, "Trait-names: A Psycho-Lexical Study," *Psychological Monographs* 47 (1936), pp. 171–220.

20. J. J. Deary, "A (Latent) Big-Five Personality Model in 1915? A Reanalysis of Webb's Data," *Journal of Applied Psychology* 71, no. 5 (1996), pp. 992–1005.

21. L. L. Thurstone, "The Factors of the Mind," *Psychological Review* 41 (1934), pp. 1–32.

22. M. R. Barrick and M. K. Mount, "The Big Five Personality Dimensions and Job Performance: A Meta-analysis." *Personal Psychology* 44 (1991), pp. 1–26.

23. P. T. Costa Jr. and R. R. McCrae, "Domains and Facets: Hierarchical Personality Assessment Using the Revised NEO Personality Inventory," *Journal of Personality Assessment* 64 (1995), pp. 21–50.

24. M. R. Barrick, "Answers to Lingering Questions about Personality Research," paper presented at the 14th Annual Conference of the Society of Industrial and Organizational Psychology, Atlanta, GA, 1999.

25. C. J. Thoresen, J. C. Bradley, P. D. Bliese, and J. D. Thoresen, "The Big Five Personality Traits and Individual Job Growth Trajectories in Maintenance and Transitional Job Stages," *Journal of Applied Psychology* 89, no. 5 (2004), pp. 835–53.

26. J. E. Bono and T. A. Judge, "Personality and Transformational and Transactional Leadership," *Journal of Applied Psychology* 89, no. 5 (2004), pp. 901–10.

27. L. E. Hough and F. L. Oswald, "Personality Testing and Industrial-Organizational Psychology: Reflections, Progress, and Prospects," *Industrial and Organizational Psychology: Perspectives on Science and Practice* 1, no. 3 (2008), pp. 272–90.

28. D. S. Ones, S. Dilchert, C. Visweswaran, and T. A. Judge, "In Support of Personality Assessment in Organizational Settings," *Personnel Psychology* 60, no. 4 (2007), pp. 995–1028.

29. J. F. Salgado, "Predicting Job Performance Using FFM and non-FFM Personality Measures," *Journal of Occupational and Organizational Psychology* 76, no. 3 (2003), pp. 323–46.

30. R. T. Hogan, "The Role of Big Five Personality Traits in Executive Selection," in *The Role of I/O Psychology in Executive Assessment and Development*, G. J. Curphy (chair). Paper presented at the 15th Annual Conference of the Society of Industrial and Organizational Psychology, New Orleans, LA, 2000.

31. G. J. Curphy and K. D. Osten, *Technical Manual for the Leadership Development Survey*, Technical Report No. 93–14 (Colorado Springs, CO: U.S. Air Force Academy, 1993).

32. R. T. Hogan, *Personality and the Fate of Organizations* (Mahwah, NJ: Lawrence Erlbaum, 2007).

33. F. Lievens, M. H. Harris, E. Van Keer, and C. Bisqueret, "Predicting Cross-Cultural Training Performance: The Validity of Personality, Cognitive Ability, and Dimensions Measures by an Assessment Center and a Behavior Description Interview," *Journal of Applied Psychology* 88, no. 3 (2003), pp. 476–89.

34. T.A. Judge and J.D. Kanmeyer-Mueller, "On the Value of Aiming High: The Causes and Consequences of Ambition," *Journal of Applied Psychology* 97, no. 4 (2012), pp. 758–75.

35. T. A. Judge and A. Erez, "Interaction and Intersection: The Constellation of Emotional Stability and Extraversion in Predicting Performance," *Personnel Psychology* 60 (2007), pp. 573–96.

36. G. J. Curphy, "Comments on the State of Leadership Prediction," in *Predicting Leadership: The Good, The Bad, the Indifferent, and the Unnecessary*, J. P. Campbell and M. J. Benson (chairs). Symposium conducted at the 22nd Annual Conference for the Society of Industrial and Organizational Psychology, New York, April 2007.

37. R. T. Hogan and J. Hogan, *The Leadership Potential Report* (Tulsa, OK: Hogan Assessment Systems, 2002).

38. C. G. Jung, *Psychological Types*, trans. R. F. C. Hall (Princeton, NJ: Princeton University Press, 1971).

39. N. L. Quenk, *In the Grip*, 2nd ed. (Mountain View, CA: CPP, 2000).

40. P. B. Myers and K. D. Myers, *The Myers-Briggs Type Indicator Step II (Form Q) Profile* (Palo Alto, CA: Consulting Psychologists Press, 2003).

41. N. L. Quenk and J. M. Kummerow, *The Myers-Briggs Type Indicator Step II (Form B) Profile* (Palo Alto, CA: Consulting Psychologists Press, 2001).

42. I. B. Myers and B. H. McCaulley, *Manual: A Guide to the Development and Use of the Myers-Briggs Type Indicator* (Palo Alto, CA: Consulting Psychologists Press, 1985).

43. W. H. Cummings, "Age Group Differences and Estimated Frequencies of the MBTI Types: Proposed Changes," *Proceedings of the Psychology in the Department of Defense Thirteenth Symposium* (Colorado Springs, CO: United States Air Force Academy, April 1992).

44. F. W. Gibson and G. J. Curphy, "The MBTI: Skewering a Sacred Cow," presentation given to the Colorado Organizational Development Network, Denver, CO, 1996.

45. P. H. Dubois, "A Test Dominated Society: China 1115 B.C.–1905," in *Testing Problems in Perspective,* ed. A. Anastasi. (American Council on Education, 1964).

46. R. D. Arvey et al., "Mainstream Science on Intelligence," *The Wall Street Journal,* December 13, 1994.

47. R. E. Riggio, "Multiple Intelligences and Leadership: An Overview," in *Multiple Intelligences and Leadership,* ed. R. E. Riggio, S. E. Murphy, and F. J. Pirozzolo (Mahwah, NJ: Lawrence Erlbaum Associates, 2002), pp. 1–7.

48. F. L. Schmidt and J. E. Hunter, "Development of a Causal Model of Job Performance," *Current Directions in Psychological Science* 1, no. 3 (1992), pp. 89–92.

49. S. Scarr, "Protecting General Intelligence: Constructs and Consequences for Interventions," in *Intelligence: Measurement, Theory, and Public Policy,* ed. R. L. Linn (Chicago: University of Illinois Press, 1989).

50. R. J. Sternberg, "The Concept of Intelligence: Its Role in Lifelong Learning and Success," *American Psychologist* 52, no. 10 (1997), pp. 1030–37.

51. R. J. Sternberg, "Creativity as a Decision," *American Psychologist,* May 2002, p. 376.

52. F. Schmidt, H. Le, I. Oh, and J. Schaffer, "General Mental Ability, Job Performance, and Red Herrings: Responses to Osterman, Hauser, and Schmitt," *The Academy of Management Perspectives* 21, no. 4 (2007), pp. 64–76.

53. T. A. Judge, R. Ilies, and N. Dimotakis, "Are Health and Happiness the Product of Wisdom? The Relationship of General Mental Ability to Education and Occupational Attainment, Health, and Well-Being," *Journal of Applied Psychology* 95, no. 3, pp. 454–68.

54. T. A. Judge, R. L. Klinger, and L. S. Simon, "Time Is on My Side: Time General Mental Ability, Human Capital, and Extrinsic Career Success," *Journal of Applied Psychology* 95, no. 1, pp. 92–107.

55. L. J. Cronbach, *Essentials of Psychological Testing,* 4th ed. (San Francisco: Harper & Row, 1984).

56. R. J. Sternberg, "WICS: A Model of Leadership in Organizations," *Academy of Management: Learning and Education* 2, no. 4 (2003), pp. 386–401.

57. R. J. Sternberg, "A Model of Leadership: WICS," *American Psychologist* 62, no. 1 (2007), pp. 34–42.

58. J. F. Salgado, N. Anderson, S. Moscoso, C. Bertua, F. de Fruyt, and J. P. Rolland, "A Meta-analytic Study of General Mental Ability Validity for Different Occupations in the European Community," *Journal of Applied Psychology* 88, no. 6 (2003), pp. 1068–81.

59. C. A. Scherbaum, H. W. Goldsmith, K. P. Yusko, R. Ryan, and P. J. Hanges, "Intelligence 2.0: Reestablishing a Research Program on G in I-O Psychology," *Industrial and Organizational Psychology* 5, no. 2 (2012), pp. 128–48.

60. R. J. Herrnstein and C. Murray, *The Bell Curve: Intelligence and Class Structure in American Life* (New York: Free Press, 1994).

61. G. J. Curphy, "Concluding Remarks on Executive Assessment and Development," in *The Role of I/O Psychology in Executive Assessment and Development*, G. J. Curphy (chair). Symposium presented at the 15th Annual Conference of the Society for Industrial and Organizational Psychology, New Orleans, LA, 2000.

62. G. J. Curphy, "Early Leadership Talent Identification and Development," paper presented at the Conference for Executives of Saudi Aramco, Dhahran, Saudi Arabia, October 2001.

63. G. J. Curphy, "What Role Should I/O Psychologists Play in Executive Education?" in *Models of Executive Education*, R. T. Hogan (chair). Presentation given at the 17th Annual Society for Industrial and Organizational Psychology, Toronto, Canada, April 2002.

64. G. J. Curphy, "Leadership Transitions and Succession Planning," in *Developing and Implementing Succession Planning Programs*, J. Lock (chair). Symposium conducted at the 19th Annual Conference for the Society of Industrial and Organizational Psychology, Chicago, April 2004.

65. R. T. Hogan and J. Hogan, *The Hogan Business Reasoning Inventory* (Tulsa, OK: Hogan Assessment Systems, 2007).

66. B. Azar, "Searching for Intelligence Beyond G," *APA Monitor* 26, no. 1 (1995), p. 1.

67. H. Gardner, *Frames of Mind: The Theory of Multiple Intelligences* (New York: Basic Books, 1983).

68. R. J. Sternberg, *Beyond IQ: A Triarchic Theory of Human Intelligence* (New York: Cambridge University Press, 1985).

69. R. J. Sternberg, *Handbook of Creativity* (New York: Cambridge University Press, 1999).

70. R. J. Sternberg, "A Broad View of Intelligence: The Theory of Successful Intelligence," *Journal of Consulting Psychology* 55, no. 3 (2003), pp. 139–54.

71. L. M. Kersting, "What Exactly Is Creativity?" *Monitor on Psychology*, November 2003, pp. 40–41.

72. R. J. Sternberg and T. I. Lubart, "Investing in Creativity," *American Psychologist* 52, no. 10 (1997), pp. 1046–50.

73. R. J. Sternberg, E. L. Grigorenko, and J. L. Singer, *Creativity: From Potential to Realization* (Washington DC: American Psychological Association Press, 2004).

74. J. C. Kaufman and J. Baer, "Hawking's Haiku, Madonna's Math: Why It Is Hard to Be Creative in Every Room," in *Creativity: From Potential to Realization*, eds. R. J. Sternberg, E. L. Grigorenko, and J. L. Singer (Washington DC: American Psychological Association Press, 2004).

75. T. Lubart and J. H. Guigard, "The Generality-Specificity of Creativity: A Multivariate Approach," in *Creativity: From Potential to Realization*, eds. R. J. Sternberg, E. L. Grigorenko, and J. L. Singer (Washington DC: American Psychological Association Press, 2004).

76. G. J. Feist., "The Evolved Fluid Specificity of Human Creative Talent," in *Creativity: From Potential to Realization*, ed. R. J. Sternberg, E. L. Grigorenko, and J. L. Singer (Washington DC: American Psychological Association Press, 2004).

77. J. P. Guilford, *The Nature of Human Intelligence* (New York: McGraw-Hill, 1967).

78. R. J. Sternberg, "What Is the Common Thread of Creativity? Its Dialectical Relationship to Intelligence and Wisdom," *American Psychologist* 56, no. 4 (2001), pp. 360–62.

79. E. E. Ghiselli, "Intelligence and Managerial Success," *Psychological Reports* 12 (1963), p. 89.

80. F. E. Fiedler, "The Effect and Meaning of Leadership Experience: A Review of Research and a Preliminary Model," in *Impact of Leadership*, ed. K. E. Clark, M. B. Clark, and D. P. Campbell (Greensboro, NC: Center for Creative Leadership, 1992).

81. F. E. Fiedler, "The Curious Role of Cognitive Resources in Leadership," in *Multiple Intelligences and Leadership*, eds. R. E. Riggio, S. E. Murphy, and F. J. Pirozzolo (Mahwah, NJ: Lawrence Erlbaum Associates, 2002), pp. 91–104.

82. F. W. Gibson, "A Taxonomy of Leader Abilities and Their Influence on Group Performance as a Function of Interpersonal Stress," in *Impact of Leadership*, eds. K. E. Clark, M. B. Clark, and D. P. Campbell (Greensboro, NC: Center for Creative Leadership, 1992).

83. M. A. Collins and T. M. Amabile, "Motivation and Creativity," in *Handbook of Creativity*, ed. R. J. Sterberg (New York: Cambridge University Press, 1999).

84. T. M. Amabile, E. A. Schatzel, G. B. Moneta, and S. J. Kramer, "Leader Behaviors and the Work Environment for Creativity: Perceived Leader Support," *The Leadership Quarterly* 15, no. 1 (2004), pp. 5–32.

85. R. Reiter-Palmon and R. Ilies, "Leadership and Creativity: Understanding Leadership from a Creative Problem Solving Perspective," *The Leadership Quarterly* 15, no. 1 (2004), pp. 55–77.

86. J. Zhou, "When the Presence of Creative Co-Workers Is Related to Creativity: Role of Supervisor Close Monitoring, Developmental Feedback, and Creative Personality," *Journal of Applied Psychology* 88, no. 3 (2003), pp. 413–22.

87. C. E. Shalley and L. L. Gilson, "What Leaders Need to Know: A Review of the Social and Contextual Factors That Can Foster or Hinder Creativity," *The Leadership Quarterly* 15, no. 1 (2004), pp. 33–53.

88. S. F. Dingfelder, "Creativity on the Clock," *Monitor on Psychology*, November 2003, p. 58.

89. M. Basadur, "Leading Others to Think Innovatively Together: Creative Leadership," *The Leadership Quarterly* 15, no. 1 (2004), pp. 103–21.

90. R. Florida and J. Goodnight, "Managing for Creativity," *Harvard Business Review*, July–August 2005, pp. 125–31.

91. R. Florida, R. Cushing, and G. Gates, "When Social Capital Stifles Innovation," *Harvard Business Review*, August 2002, p. 20.

92. M. D. Mumford, G. M. Scott, B. Gaddis, and J. M. Strange, "Leading Creative People: Orchestrating Expertise and Relationships," *The Leadership Quarterly* 13, no. 6 (2002), pp. 705–50.

93. R. J. Sternberg, "WICS: A Model of Leadership in Organizations," *Academy of Management: Learning and Education* 2, no. 4 (2003), pp. 386–401.

94. X. Zhang and K. M. Bartol, "Linking Empowering Leadership and Employee Creativity: The Influence of Psychological Empowerment, Intrinsic Motivation, and Creative Process Engagement," *Academy of Management Journal* 53, no. 1 (2010), pp. 107–28.

95. T. M. Amabile and M. Khaire, "Creativity and the Role of the Leader," *Harvard Business Review,* October 2008, pp. 100–10.

96. T. M. Amabile, "Beyond Talent: John Irving and the Passionate Craft of Creativity," *American Psychologist* 56, no. 4 (2001), pp. 333–36.

97. T. M. Amabile, "The Motivation to Be Creative," in *Frontiers in Creativity: Beyond the Basics,* ed. S. Isaksen (Buffalo, NY: Bearly, 1987).

98. J. Zhou, "Feedback Valence, Feedback Style, Task Autonomy, and Achievement Orientation: Interactive Effects on Creative Performance," *Journal of Applied Psychology* 83, no. 2 (1998), pp. 261–76.

99. G. M. Prince, "Creative Meetings through Power Sharing," *Harvard Business Review* 50, no. 4 (1972), pp. 47–54.

100. F. E. Fiedler and J. E. Garcia, *New Approaches to Leadership: Cognitive Resources and Organizational Performance* (New York: John Wiley, 1987).

101. F. E. Fiedler, "Cognitive Resources and Leadership Performance," *Applied Psychology: An International Review* 44, no. 1 (1995), pp. 5–28.

102. W. Schonpflug, "The Noncharismatic Leader-Vulnerable," *Applied Psychology: An International Review* 44, no. 1 (1995), pp. 39–42.

103. S. J. Zaccaro, "Leader Resources and the Nature of Organizational Problems," *Applied Psychology: An International Review* 44, no. 1 (1995), pp. 32–36.

104. D. Goleman, *Emotional Intelligence* (New York: Bantam Doubleday Dell, 1995).

105. P. Salovey and J. D. Mayer, "Emotional Intelligence," *Imagination, Cognition, and Personality* 9 (1990), pp. 185–211.

106. J. D. Mayer, P. Salovey, and D. R. Caruso, "Emotional Intelligence: New Ability or Eclectic Traits?" *American Psychologist* 63, no. 6 (2008), pp. 503–17.

107. R. Bar-On, *The Emotional Quotient Inventory (EQ-i)* (Toronto, Canada: Multi-Health Systems, 1996).

108. R. Aberman, "Emotional Intelligence," paper presented at the Quarterly Meeting of the Minnesota Human Resource Planning Society, Minneapolis, MN, November 2000.

109. R. Aberman, "Emotional Intelligence and Work," presentation given to the Minnesota Professionals for Psychology Applied to Work, Minneapolis, MN, January, 2007.

110. D. Goleman, *Working with Emotional Intelligence* (New York: Bantam Doubleday Dell, 1998).

111. D. R. Caruso, J. D. Mayer, and P. Salovey, "Emotional Intelligence and Emotional Leadership," in *Multiple Intelligences and Leadership,* eds. R. E. Riggio, S. E. Murphy, and F. J. Pirozzolo (Mahwah, NJ: Lawrence Erlbaum Associates, 2002, pp. 55–74).

112. D. Goleman, R. Boyatzis, and A. McKee, "Primal Leadership: The Hidden Driver of Great Performance," *Harvard Business Review,* December 2001, pp. 42–53.

113. D. Goleman, R. Boyatzis, and A. McKee, *Primal Leadership: Realizing the Power of Emotional Intelligence* (Boston: Harvard Business School Press, 2002).

114. F. Cavazotte, V. Moreno, and M. Hickmann, "Effects of Leader Intelligence, Personality, and Emotional Intelligence on Transformational Leadership and Managerial Performance," *The Leadership Quarterly* 23, no. 3 (2012), pp. 443–55.

115. D. L. Van Rooy and C. Viswesvaran, "Emotional Intelligence: A Meta-Analytic Investigation of Predictive Validity and Nomological Net," *Journal of Vocational Behavior* 65, pp. 71–95.

116. D. L. Joseph and D. A. Newman, "Emotional Intelligence: An Integrative Meta-Analysis and Cascading Model," *Journal of Applied Psychology* 95, no. 1, pp. 54–78.

117. J. D. Mayer, D. R. Caruso, and P. Salovey, " Selecting a Measure of Emotional Intelligence: The Case for Ability Testing," in *Handbook of Emotional Intelligence*, eds. R. Bar-On and J. D. A. Parker (New York: Jossey-Bass, 2000).

118. R. Bar-On, "The Bar-On Emotional Quotient Inventory (EQ-i): Rational, Description, and Summary of Psychometric Properties," in *Measuring Emotional Intelligence: Common Ground and Controversy*, eds. Glenn Geher (Hauppauge, NY: Nova Science Publishers, 2004), pp. 111–42.

119. T. Schwartz, "How Do You Feel?" *Fast Company,* June 2000, pp. 297–312.

120. V. U. Druskat, and S. B. Wolff, "Building the Emotional Intelligence of Groups," *Harvard Business Review,* March 2001, pp. 80–91.

121. T. Sy, S. Cote, and R. Saavedra, "The Contagious Leader: Impact of the Leader's Mood on the Mood of Group Members, Group Affective Tone, and Group Processes," *Journal of Applied Psychology* 90, no. 2 (2005), pp. 295–305.

122. C. Ting Fong, "The Effects of Emotional Ambivalence on Creativity," *Academy of Management Journal* 49, no. 5 (2006), pp. 1016–30.

123. F. Walter, M. S. Cole, and R. H. Humphrey, "Emotional Intelligence: Sine Qua Non of Leadership or Folderol?" *The Academy of Management Perspectives* 25, no. 1 (2011), pp. 45–59.

124. P. J. Jordan, N. M. Ashkanasy, and C. E. J. Hartel, "Emotional Intelligence as a Moderator of Emotional and Behavioral Reactions to Job Security," *Academy of Management Review* 27, no. 3 (2002), pp. 361–72.

125. C. S. Wong, and K. S. Law, "The Effects of Leader and Follower Emotional Intelligence on Performance and Attitude: An Exploratory Study," *The Leadership Quarterly* 13, no. 3 (2002), pp. 243–74.

126. R. E. Boyatzis, E. C. Stubbs, and S. N. Taylor, "Learning Cognitive and Emotional Intelligence Competencies through Graduate Management Education," *Academy of Management Learning and Education* 1, no. 2 (2002), pp. 150–62.

Chapter 7

Leadership Behavior

Introduction

Researcher:	Are all the captains you fly with pretty much the same?
Aircrew Member:	Oh, no. Some guys are the greatest guys in the world to fly with. I mean they may not have the greatest hands in the world, but that doesn't matter. When you fly with them, you feel like you can work together to get the job done. You really want to do a good job for them. Some other captains are just the opposite . . . you just can't stand to work with them. That doesn't mean you'll do anything that's unsafe or dangerous, but you won't go out of your way to keep him or her out of trouble either. So you'll just sit back and do what you have to and just hope he or she screws up.
Researcher:	How can you tell which kind of captain you're working with?
Aircrew Member:	Oh, you can tell.
Researcher:	How?
Aircrew Member:	I don't know how you tell, but it doesn't take very long. Just a couple of minutes and you'll know.

Throughout this book we have been talking about different ways to assess leaders. But when all is said and done, how can we tell good leaders from bad ones? This is a critically important question: if we can specifically identify what leaders actually do that makes them effective, then we can hire or train people to exhibit these behaviors. One way to differentiate leaders is to look at what they do on a day-to-day basis. Some leaders do a good job of making decisions, providing direction, creating plans, giving regular feedback, getting their followers the resources they need to be successful, and building cohesive teams. Other leaders have difficulties

241

The truth of the matter is that you always know the right thing to do. The hard part is doing it.

Norman Schwartzkopf, U.S. Army

making decisions, set vague or unclear goals, and ignore followers' requests for equipment and subsequently cannot build teams. Although a leader's values, personality, and intelligence are important, variables like these have only an indirect relationship with leadership effectiveness. Their effect presumably comes from the impact they have on leader behavior, which appears to have a more direct relationship with a leader's ability to build teams and get results through others. One advantage of looking at leaders in terms of behavior instead of, say, personality is that behavior is often easier to measure; leadership behaviors can be observed, whereas personality traits, values, or intelligence must be inferred from behavior or measured with tests. Another advantage of looking at leader behavior is that many people are less defensive about—and feel in more control of—specific behaviors than they are about their personalities or intelligence.

Nonetheless, leaders with certain traits, values, or attitudes may find it easier to effectively perform some leadership behaviors than others. For example, leaders with higher agreeableness scores (as defined in Chapter 6) may find it relatively easy to show concern and support for followers but may also find it difficult to discipline followers. Likewise, leaders with a low friendship value (Chapter 5) and who score low on the personality trait of extraversion (Chapter 6) will prefer working by themselves versus with others. Because behavior is under conscious control, we can always choose to change our behavior as leaders if we want to. However, the ease with which we exhibit or can change behavior will partly be a function of how we are hardwired, that is, our values, personality, and intelligence.

Followers and the situation are the two other major factors to keep in mind when evaluating leadership behavior. As described in Chapter 6, strong situational norms can play pervasive roles in leaders' behavior. Similarly, follower and situational factors can help determine whether a particular leadership behavior is "bad" or "good." Say a leader gave a group of followers extremely detailed instructions on how to get a task accomplished. If the followers were new to the organization or had never done the task before, this level of detail would probably help the leader get better results through others. But if the followers were experienced, this same leader behavior would likely have detrimental effects. The same would be true if the company were in a financial crisis versus having a successful year.

This chapter begins with a discussion of why it is important to study leadership behavior. We then review some of the early research on leader behavior and discuss several ways to categorize different leadership behaviors. The next section describes a model of community leadership, and we conclude the chapter by summarizing what is currently known about a common leadership behavior assessment technique: the 360-degree, or multirater, feedback questionnaire.

Studies of Leadership Behavior

Why Study Leadership Behavior?

Thus far we have reviewed research on a number of key variables affecting leadership behavior, but we have not directly examined what leaders actually do to successfully build a team or get results through others. For example, what behaviors did Ratan Tata exhibit as a student at Cornell, as a front-line worker at Tata Steel, or as Chairman of the Board for Tata Sons (see Profiles in Leadership 7.2)? What did President Barack Obama specifically do to rescue the financial services and automotive industries, pass comprehensive health care legislation, deal with the oil spill in the Gulf of Mexico, and end the wars in Iraq and Afghanistan? What do Mark Zuckerberg, CEO of Facebook, and Meg Whitman, the CEO of Hewlett-Packard, do to keep their companies profitable? What exactly has Aung San Suu Kyi done to lead the opposition in Myamar or Craig Venter done to lead a laboratory that created the first artificial life? To answer questions such as these, it is appropriate to turn our attention to leader behavior itself; if we could identify how successful leaders act compared with unsuccessful leaders, we could design leadership talent management systems allowing organizations to hire, develop, and promote the skills necessary for future success. Unfortunately, as we can see in the *Dilbert* comic strip, *The Office* television series, and the explosive growth of management consulting firms, many people in positions of authority either do not know how to build teams or get results through others or do not realize how their behavior negatively affects the people who work for them.[1–10]

Before we describe the different ways to categorize what leaders do to build teams or influence a group, let's review what we know about leadership skills and behaviors. As shown in Figure 7.1, leadership behaviors (which include skills and competencies) are a function of intelligence, personality traits, emotional intelligence, values, attitudes, interests, knowledge, and experience. The factors in the bottom layer of blocks are relatively difficult to change, and they predispose a leader to act in distinctive ways. As described in Chapter 6, one's personality traits are pervasive and almost automatic, typically occurring without much conscious attention. The same could be said about how values, attitudes, and intelligence affect behaviors. Over time, however, leaders can learn and discern which behaviors are more appropriate and effective than others. It is always useful to remember the pivotal roles individual differences, followers, and situational variables can play in a leader's actions[2,6,7] (see Profiles in Leadership 7.1 and 7.2).

The Early Studies

If you were asked to study and identify the behaviors that best differentiated effective from ineffective leaders, how would you do it? You could

244   Part Two   *Focus on the Leader*

FIGURE 7.1
The Building Blocks of Skills

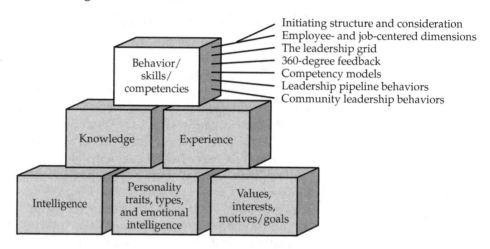

Initiating structure and consideration
Employee- and job-centered dimensions
The leadership grid
360-degree feedback
Competency models
Leadership pipeline behaviors
Community leadership behaviors

Captains Thomas Musgrave and George Dalgarno

PROFILES IN LEADERSHIP 7.1

Three hundred miles south of New Zealand are the Auckland islands. They are isolated and forbidding, and 150 years ago they brought almost certain death to ships that got too close. The howling sub-Antarctic winds drove ships onto the shallow reefs and most sailors quickly drowned. Those who made it to shore died of exposure and starvation. The few who survived did so in dreadful conditions. In *Island of the Lost,* Joan Druett (2007) recounts the story of two parties who were shipwrecked in 1864 on opposite sides of the island; this is a story of leadership and teamwork.

The first, a party of five led by Captain Thomas Musgrave of England, behaved like Shackleton's crew stranded in the Weddell Sea. Encouraged by Musgrave, the men banded together in a common quest for survival. Over a period of 20 months, using material salvaged from their ship, they built a cabin, found food, rotated cooking duties, nursed one another, made tools, tanned seal hides for shoes, built a bellows and a furnace, made bolts and nails, and then built a boat that they used to sail to safety.

Meanwhile, 20 miles away, a Scottish ship led by Captain George Dalgarno went aground, and

19 men made it safely to shore. Delgarno became depressed and went "mad," and the rest of the crew fell into despair, anarchy, and then cannibalism. A sailor named Robert Holding tried to encourage the others to act together to build shelter and find food, but other members of the crew threatened to kill and eat him. After three months, only three men were alive and subsequently rescued.

Although these events happened almost 150 years ago, the story has strong parallels to modern leadership. How did the leadership behaviors exhibited by Captains Musgrave and Dalgarno differ, and what impact did these behaviors have on their crews? Are there any parallels between these two captains and leaders in government, industry, or philanthropic organizations?

Sources: R. T. Hogan, *The Pragmatics of Leadership* (Tulsa, OK: Hogan Assessment Systems, 2007); G. J. Curphy and R. T. Hogan, *A Guide to Building High Performing Teams* (North Oaks, MN: Curphy Consulting Corporation, 2009); G. J. Curphy and R. T. Hogan, *The Rocket Model: Practical Advice for Building High Performing Teams* (Tulsa, OK: Hogan Press, 2012); Druett, *Island of the Lost: Shipwrecked on the Edge of the World* (Chapel Hills, NC: Algonquin Books, 2007)

Ratan Tata

PROFILES IN LEADERSHIP 7.2

Ratan Tata recently retired after 20 years as the Chairman and CEO of Tata Group, an Indian-based holding company made up of more than 100 different firms in seven different business sectors. As India's largest privately held business, this portfolio of companies generated over $100 billion in revenues in 2012 and represents 7 percent of the Indian Stock Market. The companies in the portfolio are quite diverse and include Tata Steel, Tata Motors, Tata Consultancy Services, Tata Global Beverages, Tata Power, Tata Hotels, and Tata Communications, which together employ more than 450,000 people and operate in 80 different countries.

Ratan Tata grew up in Mumbai and went to college at Cornell to get an undergraduate degree in architecture. Tata returned to India after college and started his career at Tata Group, as a fifth-generation family member, shoveling limestone and handling blast furnaces at one of the Tata Steel facilities. He quickly rose through the ranks and in 1991 became Chairman and CEO of the Tata Group. With a love for mechanics and a streak of perfectionism, Ratan Tata engineered several major acquisitions, including Jaguar and Land Rover car companies and Tetley Teas. Under his reign Tata Group has been able to develop a reputation for honesty, has stood up to crony capitalism and corporate corruption, and has kept its distance from politics.

Ratan Tata was the king of the Indian corporate scene and the company grew considerably under his leadership. Like many other portfolios, however, whereas some subsidiaries consistently reported strong business results, others have not been very good. When asked by shareholders to take a more Western approach to the portfolio by "killing, curing, or selling" underperforming companies to improve stock prices, Tata Group dismissed these criticisms as comically machismo and shortsighted. According to Ratan, the purpose of Tata Group was to foster nation-building, employment, and acquiring technical skills rather than achieving quarterly financial goals.

What behaviors did Ratan Tata exhibit that made him an effective or ineffective leader?

Sources: "Ratan Tata's Legacy," *The Economist*, December 1, 2012, p. 12; "From Pupil to Master: A New Bass at Tata," *The Economist*, December 1, 2012, pp. 69–70; www.tata.com/aboutus/sub_index.ampx?sectid=8hOk5Qq3EFQ.

> *We know what a person thinks not when he tells us what he thinks, but by his actions.*
>
> **Isaac Bashevis Singer, writer**

ask leaders what they do, follow the leaders around to see how they actually behave, or administer questionnaires to ask them and those they work with how often the leaders exhibited certain behaviors. These three approaches have been used extensively in past and present leadership research.

Much of the initial leader behavior research was conducted at Ohio State University and the University of Michigan. Collectively, the Ohio State University studies developed a series of questionnaires to measure different leader behaviors in work settings. These researchers began by collecting over 1,800 questionnaire items that described different types of leadership behaviors. These items were collapsed into 150 statements, and these statements were then used to develop a questionnaire called the **Leader Behavior Description Questionnaire (LBDQ).**[11,12] To obtain information about a particular leader's behavior, subordinates were asked to rate the extent to which their leader performed behaviors like the following:

He lets subordinates know when they've done a good job.

He sets clear expectations about performance.

He shows concern for subordinates as individuals.

He makes subordinates feel at ease.

In analyzing the questionnaires from thousands of subordinates, the statistical pattern of responses to all the different items indicated that leaders could be described in terms of two independent dimensions of behavior called consideration and initiating structure.[13,14] **Consideration** refers to how friendly and supportive a leader is toward subordinates. Leaders high in consideration engage in many different behaviors that show supportiveness and concern, such as speaking up for subordinates' interests, caring about their personal situations, and showing appreciation for their work. **Initiating structure** refers to how much a leader emphasizes meeting work goals and accomplishing tasks. Leaders high in initiating structure engage in many different task-related behaviors, such as assigning deadlines, establishing performance standards, and monitoring performance levels.

The LBDQ was not the only leadership questionnaire developed by the Ohio State researchers. They also developed, for example, the Supervisory Descriptive Behavior Questionnaire (SBDQ), which measured the extent to which leaders in industrial settings exhibited consideration and initiating structure behaviors.[15] The Leadership Opinion Questionnaire (LOQ) asked leaders to indicate the extent to which they believed different consideration and initiating behaviors were important to leadership success.[16] The LBDQ-XII was developed to assess 10 other categories of leadership behaviors in addition to consideration and initiating structure.[17] Some of the additional leadership behaviors assessed by the LBDQ-XII included acting as a representative for the group, being able to tolerate uncertainty, emphasizing production, and reconciling conflicting organizational demands.

Rather than trying to describe the variety of behaviors leaders exhibit in work settings, the researchers at the University of Michigan sought to identify leader behaviors that contributed to effective group performance.[18] They concluded that four categories of leadership behaviors are related to effective group performance: leader support, interaction facilitation, goal emphasis, and work facilitation.[19]

Both goal emphasis and work facilitation are **job-centered dimensions** of behavior similar to the initiating structure behaviors described earlier. **Goal emphasis** behaviors are concerned with motivating subordinates to accomplish the task at hand, and **work facilitation** behaviors are concerned with clarifying roles, acquiring and allocating resources, and

TABLE 7.1
Early Leadership
Behavior
Dimensions

Ohio State Dimensions	University of Michigan Dimensions
Initiating structure	Goal emphasis and work facilitation
Consideration	Leader support and interaction facilitation

reconciling organizational conflicts. Leader support and interaction facilitation are **employee-centered dimensions** of behavior similar to the consideration dimension of the various Ohio State questionnaires (see Table 7.1). **Leader support** includes behaviors where the leader shows concern for subordinates; **interaction facilitation** includes those behaviors where leaders act to smooth over and minimize conflicts among followers. Like the researchers at Ohio State, those at the University of Michigan also developed a questionnaire, the Survey of Organizations, to assess the degree to which leaders exhibit these four dimensions of leadership behaviors.[19]

Although the behaviors composing the task-oriented and people-oriented leadership dimensions were similar across the two research programs, there was a fundamental difference in assumptions underlying the work at the University of Michigan and that at Ohio State. Researchers at the University of Michigan considered job-centered and employee-centered behaviors to be at *opposite ends of a single continuum of leadership behavior.* Leaders could theoretically manifest either strong employee- *or* job-centered behaviors, but not both. On the other hand, researchers at Ohio State believed that consideration and initiating structure were *independent continuums.* Thus leaders could be high in both initiating structure and consideration, low in both dimensions, or high in one and low in the other.

The key assumption underlying both research programs was that certain behaviors could be identified that are universally associated with a leader's ability to successfully influence a group toward the accomplishment of its goals. Here are the kinds of questions researchers were interested in:

- From the University of Michigan perspective, who tends to be more effective in helping a group to accomplish its goals—job- or employee-centered leaders?
- From the Ohio State perspective, are leaders who exhibit high levels of *both* task- and people-oriented behaviors more effective than those who exhibit *only* task or people behaviors?
- What role do situational factors play in leadership effectiveness? Are employee-centered leadership behaviors more important in nonprofit organizations or downsizing situations, whereas job-centered behaviors are more important in manufacturing organizations or start-up situations?

The answers to these questions have several practical implications. If leaders need to exhibit only job- or employee-centered behaviors, selection and training systems need to focus on only these behaviors. But if situational factors play a role, researchers need to identify which variables are the most important and train leaders in how to modify their behavior accordingly. As you might suspect, the answer to all these questions is "It depends." In general, researchers have reported that leaders exhibiting a high level of consideration or employee-centered behaviors have more satisfied subordinates. Leaders who set clear goals, explain what followers are to do and how to get tasks accomplished, and monitor results (that is, initiating structure or job-centered) often have higher-performing work units if the group faces relatively ambiguous or ill-defined tasks.[20–22] At the same time, however, leaders whose behavior is highly autocratic (an aspect of initiating structure) are more likely to have relatively dissatisfied subordinates.[20] Findings like these suggest that *no universal set of leader behaviors is always associated with leadership success.* Often the degree to which leaders need to exhibit task- or people-oriented behaviors depends on the situation, and this finding prompted the research underlying the contingency theories of leadership described in Chapter 13. If you review these theories, you will see strong links to the job- and employee-centered behaviors identified 50 years ago.

The Leadership Grid

The Ohio State and University of Michigan studies were good first steps in describing what leaders actually do. Other researchers have extended these findings into more user-friendly formats or developed different schemes for categorizing leadership behaviors. Like the earlier research, these alternative conceptualizations are generally concerned with identifying key leadership behaviors, determining whether these behaviors have positive relationships with leadership success, and helping people develop behaviors related to leadership success. One popular conceptualization of leadership is really an extension of the findings reported by the University of Michigan and Ohio State leadership researchers. The **Leadership Grid**® profiles leader behavior on two dimensions: **concern for people** and **concern for production.**[23,24] The word "concern" reflects how a leader's underlying assumptions about people at work and the importance of the bottom line affect leadership style. In that sense, then, the Leadership Grid deals with more than just behavior. Nonetheless, it is included in this chapter because it is such a direct descendant of earlier behavioral studies.

As Figure 7.2 shows, leaders can get scores ranging from 1 to 9 on both concern for people and concern for production depending on their responses to a leadership questionnaire. These two scores are then plotted on the Leadership Grid, and the two score combinations represent different leadership orientations. Each orientation reflects a unique set of

FIGURE 7.2
The Leadership Grid

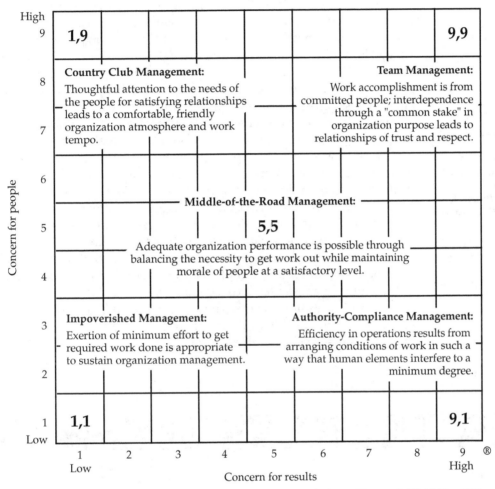

Source: Robert R. Blake and Anne Adams McCanse, *Leadership Dilemmas—Grid Solutions* (Houston: Gulf Publishing, 1991), p. 29. Copyright 1991. Reprinted with permission of Grid International.

assumptions for using power and authority to link people to production.[23] Amid the different leadership styles, the most effective leaders are claimed to have both high concern for people and high concern for production, and Leadership Grid training programs are designed to move leaders to a 9,9 leadership style. Whereas this objective seems intuitively appealing, where do you think the Supreme Leader of North Korea, Kim Jong-Un, or the Secretary-General of the United Nations, Ban Ki-Moon, score on these two dimensions? Do both of them show a high concern for production and people? Are there differences between the two leaders, or are both 9,9 leaders?

Although the Leadership Grid can be useful for describing or categorizing different leaders, we should note that the evidence to support the assertion that 9,9 leaders are the most effective comes primarily from Blake, Mouton, and their associates. However, other research might shed some light on whether 9,9 leaders are really the most effective. Robie, Kanter, Nilsen, and Hazucha studied 1,400 managers in the United States, Germany, Denmark, the United Kingdom, Italy, Spain, France, and Belgium to determine whether the same leadership behaviors were related to effectiveness across countries. They reported that leadership behaviors associated with problem solving and driving for results (initiating structure or 9,1 leadership) were consistently related to successfully building teams, influencing a group to accomplish its goals, and getting results, regardless of country.[25] Similar results about initiating structure and job performance were reported by Judge, Piccolo, and Ilies.[21] Using 800 managers in a U.S. high-tech firm, Goff reported that managers who spent more time building relationships (consideration or 1,9 leadership) also had more satisfied followers who were less likely to leave the organization.[26] Likewise, other researchers reported strong support for the notion that higher consideration behavior can reduce employee turnover.[21,22] These results seem to indicate that the most effective leadership style might depend on the criteria used to judge effectiveness. The context and style of leaders' behavior are also factors that affect their ability to build teams and get results through others (see Highlights 7.1 and 7.2).

> *No institution can possibly survive if it needs geniuses or supermen to manage it. It must be organized in such a way as to be able to get along under a leadership composed of average human beings.*
>
> **Peter Drucker, management expert**

Behaviors versus Skills

HIGHLIGHT 7.1

Leadership behaviors differ somewhat from leadership skills. A **leadership behavior** concerns a specific action, such as "setting specific performance goals for team members." A **leadership skill** consists of three components, which include a well-defined body of knowledge, a set of related behaviors, and clear criteria of competent performance. Perhaps leadership skills may be better understood by using a basketball analogy. People differ considerably in their basketball skills; good basketball players know when to pass and when to shoot and are adept at making layups, shots from the field, and free throws. Knowing when to pass and when to shoot is an example of the knowledge component, and layups and free throws are examples of the behavioral component of skills. In addition, shooting percentages can be used as one criterion for evaluating basketball skills. Leadership skills, such as delegating, can be seen much the same way. Good leaders know when and to whom a particular task should be delegated (knowledge); they effectively communicate their expectations concerning a delegated task (behavior); and they check to see whether the task was accomplished in a satisfactory manner (criteria). Thus a leadership skill is knowing when to act, acting in a manner appropriate to the situation, and acting in such a way that it helps the leader accomplish team goals.

Do You Need to Be Thin to Win?

HIGHLIGHT 7.2

Do personal appearance and fitness levels play a role in getting promoted and being an effective leader? Research conducted at the Center for Creative Leadership (CCL) can shed some light on this question. The Center regularly conducts weeklong leadership development programs for senior executives, and includes personality, mental ability, and physiological testing; public speaking assessments; and the results of leadership behavior feedback surveys from bosses, peers, and direct reports (i.e., 360-degree feedback, which is described later in this chapter). This research looked at the relationship between body mass index (BMI), a measure of body fat, and leadership behavior feedback results for 757 executives between 2006 and 2010 and found that overweight executives tended to get lower leadership behavior ratings from others. In other words, fatter leaders tended to be seen as less effective in the eyes of their co-workers.

Workplace obesity is a taboo subject in most organizations, yet this research shows that personal appearance matters when it comes to hiring and promotion decisions. Very few Fortune 500 CEOs are overweight, and the CCL researchers attribute this to the fact that people at the top need to be in good shape to handle the high workloads and travel schedules associated with these jobs. But is this really true, or does bias play a role in determining who gets to the top? Do thin people have an inherent advantage when it comes to getting results and building cohesive, goal-oriented teams? Or is being thin more important to managing one's career and getting promoted than it is to building winning teams?

What do you think?

Source: L. Kwoh, "Want to Be CEO? What's Your BMI?" *The Wall Street Journal,* January 16, 2013, pp. B1, B6.

Competency Models

So far in this section we have described several ways to categorize leaders or leadership behaviors, but what are the implications of this research for leadership practitioners? Believe it or not, you can see the practical application of this leadership behavior research in just about every Global 1,000 company. **Competency models** describe the behaviors and skills managers need to exhibit if an organization is to be successful.[2,27–34] Just as leaders in different countries may need to exhibit behaviors uniquely appropriate to each setting to be successful, different businesses and industries within any country often emphasize different leadership behaviors. Therefore, it is not unusual to see different organizations having distinct competency models depending on the nature and size of each business, its business model, its level of globalization, and the role of technology or teams in the business.[2,27,28,30,35,36] An example of a typical competency model for middle managers can be found in Figure 7.3.

Many of the best organizations now have competency models for different levels of management. For example, the behaviors and skills needed by department supervisors, store managers, district managers, regional vice presidents, and division presidents at The Home Depot vary considerably, and these differences are reflected in the competency models for

FIGURE 7.3
An Example of a Leadership Competency Model

Rank	Competency
	Analyzing problems and making decisions: Effectively analyzes issues and makes sound, logical business decisions in a timely manner.
	Thinking strategically: Brings a broad perspective to bear on issues and problems (e.g., considers information from different industries, markets, competitors); deliberately evaluates strategic "fit" of possible decisions and actions.
	Financial and technical savvy: Demonstrates strong technical and financial knowledge when resolving customer, operational, and/or financial problems. Makes sound customer, operational, and financial trade-offs.
	Planning and organizing: Establishes clear goals and action plans, and organizes resources to achieve business outcomes.
	Managing execution: Directs and monitors performance, and intervenes as appropriate to ensure successful achievement of business objectives.
	Inspiring aligned purpose: Successfully engages people in the mission, vision, values, and direction of the organization; fosters a high level of motivation.
	Driving change: Challenges the status quo and looks for ways to improve team or organizational performance. Champions new initiatives and stimulates others to make changes.
	Building the talent base: Understands the talent needed to support business objectives (e.g., qualifications, capabilities); identifies, deploys, and develops highly talented team members.
	Fostering teamwork: Creates an environment where employees work together effectively to achieve goals.
	Creating open communications: Communicates clearly and creates an environment in which important issues are shared.
	Building relationships: Develops and sustains effective working relationships with direct reports, peers, managers, and others; demonstrates that maintaining effective working relationships is a priority.
	Customer focus: Maintains a clear focus on customer needs; demonstrates a strong desire to provide exemplary customer service; actively seeks ways to increase customer satisfaction.
	Credibility: Earns others' trust and confidence; builds credibility with others through consistency between words and actions and follow-through on commitments.
	Personal drive: Demonstrates urgency in meeting objectives and achieving results; pursues aggressive goals and persists to achieve them.
	Adaptability: Confidently adapts and adjusts to changes and challenges; maintains a positive outlook and works constructively under pressure.
	Learning approach: Proactively identifies opportunities and resources for improvement.

Source: G. J. Curphy, K. Louiselle, and S. Bridges, *Talent Assessment Overview: 360-Degree Feedback Report* (Eagan, MN: Advantis Research & Consulting, 2003).

each management group. These models help to clarify expectations of performance for people in different leadership positions and describe the skills necessary for promotion. They also help human resource professionals design selection, development, performance management, and succession planning programs so organizations have a steady supply of leadership talent.[2,4,5,7,28,30,37–40]

According to Hogan and Warrenfelz, the skills and behaviors found in virtually every organizational competency model fall into one of four major categories. **Intrapersonal skills** are leadership competencies and behaviors having to do with adapting to stress, goal orientation, and adhering to rules. These skills and behaviors do not involve interacting with others, and they are among the most difficult to change. **Interpersonal skills** are those that involve direct interaction, such as communicating and building relationships with others. These skills are somewhat easier to develop. **Leadership skills** are skills and behaviors concerned with building teams and getting results through others, and these are more easily developed than the skills and behaviors associated with the first two categories. Finally, competencies concerned with analyzing issues, making decisions, financial savvy, and strategic thinking fall into the **business skills** category. These skills and competencies are often the focus of MBA programs and are among the easiest to learn of the four categories. The Hogan and Warrenfelz domain model of leadership competencies is important because it allows people to see connections between seemingly different organizational competency models and makes predictions about how easy or difficult it will be to change various leadership behaviors and skills.[39] (See Highlight 7.3.)

The Hogan and Warrenfelz model is also important because it points out what behaviors leaders need to exhibit to build teams and get results through others. Because organizational competency models are more alike than different, the behaviors needed to build teams and get results are fairly universal across organizations. Leaders wanting to build high-performing teams need to hire the right people, effectively cope with stress, set high goals, play by the rules, and hold people accountable. They also need to communicate and build relationships with others. Effective leaders also get followers involved in decisions, fairly distribute workloads, develop talent, keep abreast of events that could affect the team, and make sound financial and operational decisions. Thus competency models provide a sort of recipe for leaders wanting to build teams and get results in different organizations. Many of these leadership behaviors may be fairly universal across industries, but there may also be some important differences by company and leadership level. Ancona, Malone, Orlikowski, and Senge aptly point out that most leaders don't possess all the skills listed in many competency models, but effective leaders are those who understand their strengths and have learned how to staff around the areas in which they are less skilled.[41] And longitudinal research

A sense of humor is part of the art of leadership, of getting along with people, of getting things done.

Dwight D. Eisenhower, U.S. President

Does Humor Matter?

HIGHLIGHT 7.3

Leaders exhibit many kinds of behavior. Some are focused on task accomplishment, whereas others are more related to supporting followers. Some leaders are naturally funny, and others seem stern and humorless. Does a leader's sense of humor affect his or her ability to build teams, influence others, or get results? Researchers have examined this question and discovered the answer is not a simple yes or no. The effectiveness of humor seems to depend on the context, the outcomes leaders are trying to achieve, and the leadership style used. Laissez-faire leaders (1,1) who used humor reported having more satisfied followers but did not have higher-performing work groups. Task-focused leaders (9,1) who used humor actually had less satisfied and lower-performing work units. Apparently their use of humor seemed out of sync with their constant focus on goal setting, productivity, and cost-cutting initiatives. Transformational leaders (9,9) and leaders with high levels of emotional intelligence who used humor seemed to have higher-performing work groups. The key lesson from this research appears to be that the impact of a leader's humor depends on the leader's style and the context in which it is delivered. Leaders need to be aware that mean spirited humor can cause employee disengagement and addictive behaviors and even well intended humor can have the opposite effect when organizations are facing economic downturns or difficult organizational dilemmas.

Sources: B. J. Avolio, J. M. Howell, and J. J. Sosik, "A Funny Thing Happened on the Way to the Bottom Line: Humor as a Moderator of Leadership Style Effects," *Academy of Management Journal* 42, no. 2 (1999), pp. 219–27; F. Sala, "Laughing All the Way to the Bank," *Harvard Business Review*, September 2003, pp. 16–17; E. J. Romero and K. W. Cruthirds, "The Use of Humor in the Workplace," *Academy of Management Perspectives* 20, no. 2 (2006), pp. 58–69; Y. Huo, W. Lam, and Z. Chen, "Am I the Only One the Supervisor Is Laughing At? Effects of Aggressive Behavior on Employee Strain and Addictive Behaviors," *Personnel Psychology* 65, no. 4 (2012), pp. 859–86.

has shown that the relative importance of certain competencies has changed over time. For example, building relationships, administrative/organizational skills, and time management skills have grown considerably more important over the past 20 to 25 years.[42] These results are not surprising when one considers the impact on managerial work of technology, globalization, and organizational restructuring.

The Leadership Pipeline

We started this chapter by exploring the notion that there was a universal set of behaviors associated with leadership effectiveness. Yet research shows that initiating structure, interactional facilitation, and 9,9 leadership can be important in some situations and relatively unimportant in others. Situational and follower factors play important roles in determining the relative effectiveness of different leadership behaviors, and researchers and human resource professionals have created competency models to describe the behaviors needed by leaders in particular jobs and companies. Leaders heading up virtual teams of people located around the globe or working in sales versus manufacturing organizations may need to exhibit different types of behaviors to be effective, and competency models are useful in capturing these differences. Although globalization, the industry, and the functional area affect the type of leadership behaviors needed, another factor that impacts leadership behavior is **organizational level**. For example, the behaviors first-line supervisors need to manifest to keep a group of call center employees motivated and on task differ from those a chief executive officer needs to exhibit when meeting a group of investors or running company business strategy sessions. Although both types of leaders need to build teams and get results through others, the types of teams they lead and the results they need to obtain are so dramatically different that they exhibit very different types of behaviors.

The **Leadership Pipeline** is a useful model for explaining where leaders need to spend their time, what they should be focusing on and what they should be letting go, and the types of behaviors they need to exhibit as they move from first-line supervisor to functional manager to chief executive officer.[43–45] The pipeline also describes the lessons people should learn as they occupy a particular organizational level and the challenges they will likely face as they transition to the next level. As such, this model provides a type of road map for people wanting to occupy the top leadership positions in any organization. And because people at different organizational levels need to exhibit different behaviors, many companies have created competency models to describe the behaviors needed to be successful at different organizational levels. According to the Leadership Pipeline model, the most effective leaders are those who can accurately diagnose the organizational level of their job and then exhibit behaviors commensurate with this level. The pipeline also provides potential explanations for why some people fail to advance: these individuals may not be focusing on the right things or may be exhibiting leadership behaviors associated with lower organizational levels.

A depiction of the seven organizational levels and their competency requirements, time application, and work values can be found in Table 7.2. The items listed in Table 7.2 correspond to a large for-profit organization; smaller for-profit or nonprofit organizations may not have all these levels. Nonetheless, the Leadership Pipeline provides a useful framework for thinking about how leadership competencies change as people are promoted through organizations (as illustrated in Profiles in Leadership 7.3).

According to the model, many people who fail to demonstrate the competencies, work values, and time applications commensurate with their positions will struggle with building teams and getting results through others. For example, functional leaders who have not given up acting like first-line supervisors and spend a lot of time coaching and monitoring the performance of the individual contributors not only have no time to build a vision and manage the function; they also disempower the first-line supervisors and midlevel managers in their function. So one key to having a successful

TABLE 7.2
The Leadership Pipeline

Organizational Level	Competency Requirements	Time Applications	Work Values
Individual contributor	Technicaly proficient. Use company tools. Build relationships with team members.	Meet personal due dates. Arrive/depart on time.	Get results through personal proficiency. High-quality work. Accept company values.
First-line supervisor	Plan projects. Delegate work. Coach and provide feedback. Monitor performance.	Annual budget plan. Make time available for followers. Set priorities for team.	Get results through others. Success of followers. Success of the team.
Midlevel manager	Select, train, and manage first-line supervisors. Manage boundaries and deploy resources to teams.	Monitor performance of each team. Make time to coach first-line supervisors.	Appreciate managerial versus technical work. Develop first-line supervisors.
Functional leader	Manage the whole function. Communicate with and listen to everyone in the function. Make subfunction trade-offs. Interact with other functions.	Determine three-year vision for the function. Interact with business unit leader's team.	Clarify how the function supports the business. Value all subfunctions.
Business unit leader	Build cross-functional leadership team. Financial acumen. Balance future goals with short-term business needs.	Develop three-year vision for the business unit. Monitor financial results. Effectively manage time.	Value all staff functions. Value organizational culture and employee engagement.
Group manager	Manage business portfolio. Allocate capital to maximize business success. Develop business unit leaders.	Develop strategies for multiple business units. Monitor financial results for multiple businesses. Interact with CEO's team.	Value the success of all the business units. Interact with internal and external stakeholders.
CEO or enterprise leader	Analyze and critique strategy. Manage the entire company and multiple constituencies. Deliver predictable business results. Set company direction. Create company culture. Manage the board of directors.	Manage external stakeholders. Spend significant time reviewing financial results. Spend significant time doing strategic planning.	Value a limited set of key long-term objectives. Value advice from board of directors. Value inputs from a wide variety of stakeholders.

Source: R. Charan, S. Drotter, and J. Noel, *The Leadership Pipeline: How to Build the Leadership-Powered Company* (San Francisco: Jossey-Bass, 2001).

Indra Nooyi

PROFILES IN LEADERSHIP 7.3

PepsiCo is commonly acknowledged as having one of the best leadership talent management systems in the world. Pepsi's talent management systems make extensive use of competency models, 360-degree feedback tools, personality and intelligence assessments, in-basket simulations, and unit performance indexes. One of the people who has benefited from this in-depth assessment and development is Indra Nooyi. Nooyi is currently the chief executive officer of PepsiCo and is ranked by *Forbes* as the twelfth most powerful woman in the world and the second most powerful businesswoman in the world. Nooyi grew up in India and received an undergraduate degree from Madras Christian College and a postgraduate diploma in management from the Indian Institute in Management. She also has a degree from the Yale School of Management. While in college Nooyi fronted an all-female rock band, and she is refreshingly funny and candid when speaking in public. In May 2005 Nooyi started a controversy when she spoke to Columbia Business School graduates and said the United States "must be careful that when we extend our arm in either a business or a political sense, we take pains to ensure we are giving a hand ... not the finger."

Before emigrating to the United States in 1978, Nooyi was a product manager for Johnson and Johnson and the textile firm Mettur Beardsell in India. Her first job after graduating from Yale was to work as a consultant with The Boston Consulting Group. She then took senior leadership positions at Motorola and Asea Brown Boveri before moving to PepsiCo in 1994. While at Pepsi Nooyi played a vital role in the spin-off of Tricon, which is now known as Yum! Brands Inc. (Taco Bell and Kentucky

Fried Chicken are some of the franchises in Yum! Brands Inc.) She also took the lead in Pepsi's acquisition of Tropicana and Quaker Oats in the late 1990s. Nooyi was promoted to chief financial officer in 2001 and to the CEO position in 2006. As the head of PepsiCo, Nooyi heads up a company of 300,000 employees that generate $66 billion in annual revenues through the worldwide sales of products such as Pepsi, Mountain Dew, Tropicana, Gatorade, Aquafina, Dole, Lipton, Doritos, Ruffles, Lays, Quaker Oats, Life cereal, and Rice-A-Roni. Under Nooyi, Pepsi has developed new products and marketing programs through the liberal use of cross-cultural advisory teams and now manages 22 brands that each generate over $1 billion in annual revenues.

Given Pepsi's global reach and emphasis on brand management, Nooyi's background seems well-suited for a recent leadership challenge. In 2006 a group of individuals in India claimed that both Coke and Pepsi products were tainted with pesticides. Later investigations disproved these allegations, but the surrounding publicity damaged Pepsi's brand in a large, developing market. Nooyi worked hard to restore the Indian public's confidence in the safety of PepsiCo's products and has more recently spent time developing healthier beverages and snacks.

How do you think Indra Nooyi's career matches up to the Leadership Pipeline? What lessons do you think she learned as she traveled through the Leadership Pipeline that help her be a more effective CEO for PepsiCo?

Sources: http://www.forbes.com/lists/2006/11/06/women_Indra-Nooyi; http://www.Pepsico.com/PEP; http://www.businessweek.com/investor/content/aug2006/pi20060814; http://www.hoovers.com/pepsico.

career is exhibiting competencies appropriate for your current organizational level and then letting go of these competencies and learning new ones when moving up the organizational ladder. Charan, Drotter, and Noel maintain that transitioning from individual contributor to first-line supervisor and from functional to business unit leader are the two hardest

258 Part Two *Focus on the Leader*

transitions for people.[45] It is difficult for people who have spent all their time selling to customers or writing code to transition to managing the people who do this work and for people whose entire career has been in sales or IT to manage, value, and leverage the work done by other functions.

Another career implication of this model is worth mentioning: people who skip organizational levels often turn out to be ineffective leaders. For example, it is not unusual for organizations to offer jobs to consultants. A consultant may have been called in to fix a particularly difficult problem, such as implementing a new sales initiative or IT program, and because the solution was so successful he or she is asked to join the company. The problem is that many of these job offers are for functional or business unit leader types of roles, and to a large extent consultants have spent their entire careers doing nothing but individual contributor–level work. Because consultants may have never formally led a team or managed multiple teams or functions, they continue to exhibit those behaviors they got rewarded for in the first place, which is individual contributor–level work. No matter how good these former consultants are at doing individual contributor work, these jobs they are put in are much too big for them to do all the sales calls, write all the computer code, or the like. If they do not adjust their leadership behaviors to fit the demands of the position, they quickly burn out and will be asked to pursue other options. So if your career aspirations include leading a function, business unit, or company, you need to think through the sequence of positions that will give you the right experiences and teach you the right competencies needed to prepare you for your ultimate career goal.

> *Fifty percent of organizations with annual revenues over $500 million report having "no meaningful succession plans."*
> **Personnel Decisions International**

Community Leadership

Although organizational competency models have played a pervasive role in selecting, developing, and promoting government and business leaders, they have not been used much in community leadership. **Community leadership** is the process of building a team of volunteers to accomplish some important community outcome and represents an alternative conceptualization of leadership behavior.[46–48] Examples of community leadership might include forming a group to raise funds for a new library, gathering volunteers for a blood drive, or organizing a campaign to stop the construction of a Walmart. Thus community leadership takes place whenever a group of volunteers gets together to make something happen (or not happen) in their local community.

But leading a group of volunteers is very different from being a leader in a publicly traded company, the military, or a nongovernment agency. For one thing, community leaders do not have any position power; they cannot discipline followers who do not adhere to organizational norms, get tasks accomplished, or show up to meetings. They also tend to have

> *Never doubt that a group of thoughtful, committed citizens can change the world. Indeed, it is the only thing that ever has.*
> **Margaret Mead, anthropologist**

FIGURE 7.4
The Components of Community Leadership

Source: J. Krile, G. Curphy, and D. Lund, *The Community Leadership Handbook: Framing Ideas, Building Relationships, and Mobilizing Resources* (St. Paul, MN: Fieldstone Alliance, 2006).

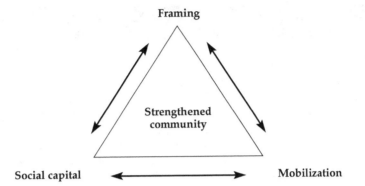

fewer resources and rewards than most other leaders. And because there is no formal selection or promotion process, anyone can be a community leader. But whether such leaders succeed in their community change efforts depends on three highly interrelated competencies (see Figure 7.4). Just as you need the three ingredients of oxygen, fuel, and an igniter to start a fire, so do you need the three competencies of framing, building social capital, and mobilization to successfully drive community change efforts.

Framing is the leadership competency of helping a group or community recognize and define its opportunities and issues in ways that result in effective action. Framing helps the group or community decide *what* needs to be done, *why* it is important that it be done, and *how* it is to be done, and communicate that in clear and compelling ways. Any community could take on myriad potential projects, but many of these projects never get off the ground because the person "in charge" never framed the project in such a way that others could understand the outcome, how they would benefit by the outcome, and what they must do to achieve the outcome. (See Profiles in Leadership 7.4.)

Building social capital is the leadership competency of developing and maintaining relationships that allow people to work together in the community across their differences. Just as financial capital allows individuals to make choices about what they can purchase, such as buying a new television, car, or house, social capital allows a community leader to make choices about which community change initiatives or projects are likely to be successful. If you have little money, your options are severely limited. Likewise, leaders lacking social capital will have a difficult time getting anything done in their communities because they will not be able to mobilize the resources necessary to turn their vision into reality. Social capital is the power of relationships shared between individuals, between an individual and a group, or between groups.

Engaging a critical mass to take action to achieve a specific outcome or set of outcomes is the leadership competency of **mobilization.** Community leaders will have achieved a critical mass when they have enough

Father Greg Boyle

PROFILES IN LEADERSHIP 7.4

Father Greg Boyle grew up in a family of eight children in the Los Angeles area. Working on his father's dairy farm while growing up, Father Greg opted to become a Jesuit after graduating from high school and was ordained as a minister in 1984. After graduating with degrees from Gonzaga University, Loyola Marymount University, and Wheaton College, he spent several years teaching high school, running a mission in Los Angeles, and serving as a chaplain for Folsom Prison and Islas Marias Penal Colony in Mexico. It was while Father Greg was a pastor at the Dolores Mission in Los Angeles that he started Jobs for the Future (JFF), a program designed to keep gang-involved youths out of trouble. JFF involved developing positive alternatives, establishing an elementary school and day care centers, and providing jobs for disadvantaged youth.

Partly as a result of the civil unrest in Los Angeles in 1992, Father Greg started the first of several Homeboy businesses. Homeboy Bakery was created to teach gang-involved youths life and work skills and how to work side-by-side with rival gang members. Other businesses started by Father Greg include Homeboy Silkscreen and Embroidery, Homeboy Maintenance, Homeboy Farmers Markets, Homeboy Diner, Homeboy Grocery, Homeboy/Homegirl Merchandise, and Homegirl Café and Catering. All of these businesses teach needed business, conflict resolution, and teamwork skills to gang members who are eager to leave the streets.

With Los Angeles County home to 34 percent of California's poor, a poverty rate of 16 percent, and a high school dropout rate between 35 and 45 percent for Latinos and African Americans, the county is an epicenter for gang activity. Homeboy Industries is known as the largest gang intervention, rehabilitation, and reentry program in the United States. Having run as a nonprofit company since 2001, it has expanded several times to keep up with the increasing demand for its services. Some of these services include tattoo removal; employment, education, legal, substance abuse, and mental health services; and solar panel installation certification training. The organization currently serves well over 1,000 people as either employees or participants in its many outreach programs. Although Homeboy Industries generates revenues, it does not generate enough cash to fund all of its programs and uses donations and speaking fees to cover any financial shortfalls.

Where do the concepts of framing, social capital, and mobilization come into play with the start-up of Homeboy Industries? What skills does Father Greg possess that help him build teams and achieve results? Do you think public money is better spent getting gang members to join Homeboy Industries or putting them in prison?

Sources: G. Boyle, *Tattoos on the Heart: The Power of Boundless Compassion.* (New York: Free Press, 2010; http://www.homeboyindustries.org; T. Gross, "Interview with Greg Boyle," *Fresh Air*, May 21, 2010; www.homeboyindustries.org.

human and other resources to get what they want done. People, money, equipment, and facilities are often needed to pass bond issues or attract new businesses to a community. Mobilization is strategic, planned purposeful activity to achieve clearly defined outcomes. Almost anyone can get resources moving, but it takes leadership to get enough of the right resources moving toward the same target.

How would the community leadership model come into play if you wanted to have a new student union built on your campus? First, you would need to frame the issue in such a way that other students understood what was in it for them and what they would need to do to make a new student union become reality. Second, you would need to reach out and build relationships with all of the current and potential users of the new student union. You would need to identify the formal and informal leaders of the different user groups and meet with them to gain and maintain their trust. Third, you would need these different user groups to take action to get the new student union built. Some of these actions might include raising funds, making phone calls, canvassing students to sign petitions, mounting a publicity campaign, and meeting with university and state officials who are the key decision makers about the issue.

It is worth noting that you need to do all three of the community leadership components well if you are to build teams of volunteers and successfully accomplish community outcomes. You might be able to succinctly frame the issue, but if you lack social capital or can not get a critical mass mobilized, you will probably not get far in building the new student union. The same would be true if you had a broad and well-established network of students but did not frame the issue in such a way that followers could take action. It is likely that as many community change efforts fail as succeed, and the reasons for failure often have to do with inadequate framing, social capital, or mobilization. These three components are critical when it comes to building teams of volunteers and achieving community goals.

> *Pity the leader caught between unloving critics and uncritical lovers.*
>
> **John Gardner,**
> **writer**

Assessing Leadership Behaviors: Multirater Feedback Instruments

One way to improve leader effectiveness is to give leaders feedback regarding the frequency and skill with which they perform various types of leadership behaviors. A $200 million industry has developed over the past three decades to meet this need. This is the **360-degree,** or **multirater, feedback** instrument industry, and it is difficult to overestimate its importance in management development both in the United States and overseas. Jack Welch, the former CEO of General Electric, has stated that these tools have been critical to GE's success.[49] Practically all of the Global 1,000 companies are using some type of multirater feedback instrument for managers and key individual contributors.[1,2,7,8,50–58] Multirater feedback instruments have been translated into 16 different languages, and well over 5 million managers have now received feedback on their leadership skills and behaviors from these instruments.[50] Because of the pervasiveness of multirater feedback in both the public and private sectors, it will be useful to examine some issues surrounding these instruments.

Many managers and human resource professionals have erroneously assumed that a manager's self-appraisal is the most accurate source of information regarding leadership strengths and weaknesses. This view has changed, however, with the introduction of multirater feedback instruments. These tools show that direct reports, peers, and superiors can

FIGURE 7.5
Sources for
360-Degree
Feedback

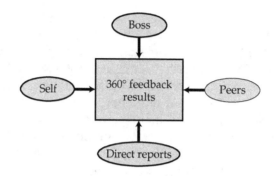

have very different perceptions of a leader's behavior, and these perspectives can paint a more accurate picture of the leader's strengths and development needs than self-appraisals alone (see Figures 7.5 and 7.6). A manager may think he or she gets along well with others, but if 360-degree feedback ratings from peers and direct reports indicate that the manager is difficult to work with, the manager should gain new insights on what to do to improve his or her leadership effectiveness. Prior to the introduction of 360-degree instruments, it was difficult for managers to get accurate information about how others perceived their on-the-job behaviors because the feedback they received from others in face-to-face meetings tended to be adulterated or watered down.[1,5,7,50–60] Moreover, the higher one goes in an organization, the less likely one is to ask for feedback, which results in bigger discrepancies between self and other perceptions.[2,60–62] And, as described in Chapter 6, many of the most frequent behaviors exhibited by leaders are rooted in personality traits and occur almost automatically; as a result many leaders do not understand or appreciate their impact on others. It was difficult for managers to accurately determine their leadership strengths and development needs until the advent of 360-degree feedback instruments. Today most organizations use 360-degree tools as an integral part of the training, coaching, succession planning, and performance management components of a comprehensive leadership talent management system.[1,50,52,53,56,58]

Given the pervasive role 360-degree feedback plays in many organizations today, it is not surprising that there has been an extensive amount of research on the construction, use, and impact of these tools. Much of this research has explored how to use competency models to build effective 360-degree questionnaires, whether 360-degree feedback matters, whether self–observer perceptual gaps matter, whether leaders' ratings can improve over time, and whether there are meaningful culture/gender/race issues with 360-degree feedback ratings. With respect to the first issue, researchers have reported that the construction of 360-degree feedback questionnaires is very important. Poorly conceived competency models and ill-designed questionnaire items can lead to

FIGURE 7.6
Example of 360-Degree Feedback

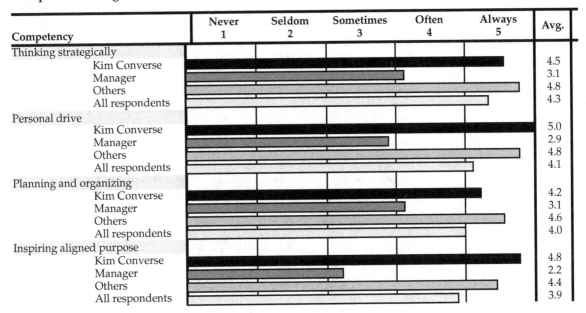

Competency	Never 1	Seldom 2	Sometimes 3	Often 4	Always 5	Avg.
Thinking strategically						
Kim Converse						4.5
Manager						3.1
Others						4.8
All respondents						4.3
Personal drive						
Kim Converse						5.0
Manager						2.9
Others						4.8
All respondents						4.1
Planning and organizing						
Kim Converse						4.2
Manager						3.1
Others						4.6
All respondents						4.0
Inspiring aligned purpose						
Kim Converse						4.8
Manager						2.2
Others						4.4
All respondents						3.9

Inspiring Aligned Purpose

Successfully engages people in the mission, vision, values, and direction of the organization; fosters a high level of motivation.

Average Ratings for Each Item and Respondent Type

Items	Self	Manager	Others	All Respondents
1. Communicates a compelling vision of the future.	5.0	1.0	4.5	3.8
2. Provides a clear sense of purpose and direction for the team.	5.0	3.0	4.3	4.0
3. Sets challenging goals and expectations.	5.0	4.0	4.5	4.4
4. Fosters enthusiasm and buy-in for the direction of the team/organization.	5.0	1.0	4.8	4.0
5. Supports initiatives of upper management through words and actions.	4.0	2.0	4.0	3.2

Source: K. Louiselle, G. J. Curphy, and S. Bridges, *C3 360-Degree Feedback Report* (Eagan, MN: Advantis Research and Consulting, 2003). Reprinted with permission of Advantis Research and Consulting.

spurious feedback results, thus depriving managers of the information they need to perform at a higher level.[1,5,34,53,54,61–63] In terms of whether 360-degree feedback matters, a number of researchers have held that leaders who received 360-degree feedback had higher-performing work units than leaders who did not receive this type of feedback. These results indicate that 360-degree feedback ratings do matter.[1,64–73] But a study of 750 firms by Watson-Wyatt, a human resource consulting firm, reported that companies that used 360-degree feedback systems had a 10.6 percent decrease in shareholder value.[74] Although this research provides strong evidence that 360-degree feedback may not "work," it is important to note how these systems were being used in these firms. For the most part, Pfau and Kay examined firms using 360-degree feedback for performance appraisal, not development purposes. This distinction is important because most 360-degree feedback systems are not designed to make comparisons *between* people. Instead these systems are designed to tell leaders about their own relative strengths and development needs. But because 360-degree feedback tools are data based and provide good development feedback, many organizations have decided to modify the process for performance appraisal purposes. This can be a mistake: many 360-degree feedback tools used in performance appraisals are often poorly constructed and result in such inflated ratings that the resulting feedback no longer differentiates between high, average, and low-level performers. The end result is a costly, time-intensive performance appraisal system that has little if any benefit to the individual or the boss and yields organizational results similar to those reported by Watson-Wyatt. The bottom line is that 360-degree feedback systems can add tremendous value, but only if they are well-conceived and constructed.[1,50,53,54,56–58,64,73,74,75]

> *In many cases the only person who is surprised by his or her 360-degree feedback results is the feedback recipient.*
>
> **Dianne Nilsen,**
> **business executive**

As stated earlier, one advantage of 360-degree feedback is that it provides insight into self-perceptions and others' perceptions of leadership skills. But do self–observer gaps matter? Are leaders more effective if they have a high level of insight—that is, if they rate their strengths and weaknesses as a leader the same as others do? As depicted in Figure 7.6, some level of disagreement is to be expected because bosses, peers, and direct reports may have different expectations for a leader. Nevertheless, insight does not seem to matter for leadership effectiveness. Even leaders with large self–observer gaps were effective as long as they had high observer ratings. On the other hand, the least effective leaders were those with high self and low others' ratings. The important lesson here is that leadership is in the eyes of others. And the key to high observer ratings is to develop a broad set of leadership skills that will help groups to accomplish their goals.[1,76–80] (See Highlight 7.4.)

Another line of research has looked at whether 360-degree feedback ratings improve over time. In other words, is it possible to change others' perceptions of a leader's skills? One would hope that this would be the

Facebook, LinkedIn, and Online Personae

HIGHLIGHT 7.4

Social networking sites such as Facebook, MySpace, Google+, and LinkedIn have made it much easier for people to connect with others. In an effort to attract attention, many entries on these sites contain highly personal information about sexual practices, drug and alcohol use, philosophies toward life and work, and so on. Some of this information may be true and some just hyperbole, but all of it is in the public domain. The bad news is that companies are now searching these same sites and eliminating applicants based on their online personae. An interesting exercise is to identify a critical leadership position and define the organizational level, key competencies, time application, and work values needed to do this position. Then pick out four or five random online personae from LinkedIn and determine whether you would hire any of these individuals if they had applied for the position. Now look at your own online persona (if you have one). Would you get hired if an organization were looking for a competent manager to fill this position? What should carry more weight in determining a person's leadership potential—work experiences and education or online persona?

Source: Adapted from Alan Finder, "For Some, Online Persona Undermines Résumé," *The New York Times,* June 11, 2006.

case, given the relationship between others' ratings and leadership effectiveness. Walker and Smither reported that managers who shared their 360-degree feedback results with their followers and worked on an action plan to improve their ratings had a dramatic improvement in others' ratings over a five-year period.[81] Johnson and Johnson looked at 360-degree ratings over a two-year period and reported leadership productivity improvements of 9.5 percent for 515 managers in a manufacturing company.[82] A more recent article reviewed the findings from 24 different studies and concluded that 360-degree feedback ratings do change over time, but the amount of change tends to be small.[55] Other researchers aptly point out that 360-degree feedback alone is not a panacea to improve leadership skills. In addition to gaining insight from 360-degree feedback, leaders must also create a set of development goals and commit to a development plan if they want to see improvement in others' ratings (and, in turn, leadership effectiveness) over time.[1,50,81-85]

The last line of research has explored whether there are important cultural, racial, or gender issues with 360-degree feedback. In terms of cultural issues, some countries, such as Japan, do not believe peers or followers should give leaders feedback.[85,86] Other countries, such as Saudi Arabia, tend more to avoid conflict and provide only positive feedback to leaders. The latter phenomenon also appears in the United States, where researchers working in small organizations or in rural communities often report similar findings. People seem more hesitant to give leaders constructive feedback if they have to deal with the consequences of this feedback both at and away from work. These findings further support the notion that 360-degree feedback is not a management panacea; societal or organizational culture plays a key role in the accuracy and utility of the 360-degree feedback process.[1,4,32,33,50,52,60,74,86]

With respect to racial differences, a comprehensive study by Mount, Sytsma, Hazucha, and Holt looked at the pattern of responses from bosses, peers, and subordinates for over 20,000 managers from a variety of U.S. companies. In general, these researchers reported that blacks tended to give higher ratings to other blacks, irrespective of whether they were asked to provide peer, subordinate, or boss ratings. However, the overall size of this effect was small. White peers and subordinates generally gave about the same level of ratings to both black and white peers and bosses. This was not the case for white bosses, however, who tended to give significantly higher ratings to whites who reported directly to them. These findings imply that black leaders are likely to advance at a slower pace than their white counterparts because 80 to 90 percent of salary, bonus, and promotion decisions are made solely by bosses.[87,88]

With respect to gender issues, research indicates that there are some slight gender differences. Female managers tend to get higher ratings on the majority of skills, yet their male counterparts are generally perceived as having higher advancement potential. There does not appear to be any same-sex bias in 360-degree feedback ratings, and female managers tend to be lower self-raters. Male managers tend to have less accurate self-insight and more blind spots when compared to their female counterparts. In summary, male and female 360-degree feedback ratings are similar, and any differences are of little practical significance.

What should a leadership practitioner take away from this 360-degree feedback research? First, given the popularity of the technique, it is likely that you will receive 360-degree feedback sometime in your career. Second, 360-degree feedback should be built around a competency model, which will describe the leadership behaviors needed to achieve organizational goals. Third, the organization may have different competency models to reflect the different leadership behaviors needed to succeed at different organizational levels. Fourth, 360-degree feedback may be one of the best sources of "how" feedback for leadership practitioners. Leaders tend to get plenty of "what" feedback—what progress they are making toward group goals, what level of customer service is being achieved, win–loss records, and so on; but they get little feedback on how they should act to get better results. Multirater instruments provide feedback on the kinds of things leaders need to do to build cohesive, goal-oriented teams and get better results through others. Fifth, effective leaders seem to have a broad set of well-developed leadership skills—they do not do just one or two things well and do everything else poorly. Instead they seem to possess a broad array of leadership strengths. Sixth, leaders need to create specific goals and development plans in order to improve leadership skills—360-degree feedback results give leaders ideas on what to

Leadership Behavior: What We Know and What Remains to Be Answered

HIGHLIGHT 7.5

An important objective for leadership researchers has been to identify the behaviors that help or hinder a person's ability to get results through others or build cohesive, goal-oriented teams. The thousands of studies involving millions of leaders that have been conducted over the past 50 years show that the effective leadership behavior findings are fragmented and offer only a few general truths. About all we know at this point is that leaders who demonstrate more monitoring, problem solving, planning, supporting, developing, empowering, facilitating, and networking behaviors are seen as more effective than those leaders who exhibit less of these behaviors. Because good marketing always trumps good science, many authors have used these findings as justification for writing books that advocate that the best leaders are those who adopt these five behaviors, seven habits, and more.

There are several reasons why the findings concerning leadership behaviors are so limited and the advice offered by the books advocating certain behaviors is wrong. First, leadership researchers tend to use different competency models and behavioral definitions, which makes it difficult to aggregate results. Second, situational and follower variables often dictate which leadership behaviors will be effective. Empowering someone to take the controls may not lead to good results if a person does not know how to fly and the plane is on fire. Third, the quality and timeliness of leadership behavior can have just as much impact as the frequency in which it is exhibited—just doing more coaching

may not be as helpful as doing high quality coaching at the right time. Fourth, leadership is a team sport, and getting groups of people to work effectively to solve problems or create action plans is much more complicated and requires a different set of behaviors than doing so on a one-on-one basis. Many leadership researchers and authors confuse the individual versus team distinction. Finally, many leadership researchers define leadership as those occupying positions of authority. For example, researchers may define leaders as all the store managers for a grocery chain. But what if the majority of the store managers were not very good at building teams or getting results through others? The results obtained may say more about the types of behaviors needed to get promoted than get results through others or build teams. As you will see in Chapter 15, somewhere between 50 to 65 percent of the people in positions of authority are perceived to be incompetent, and if this group is included in a research study then it will obscure the results obtained. The upshot of all of this behavioral research is that we know more about what not to do than what to do to be effective leaders.

Sources: G. Yukl, " Effective Leadership Behavior: What We Know and What Questions Need More Attention," *Academy of Management Perspectives* 26, no. 4 (2012), pp. 66–85; G. Curphy, "Investing in the Wrong Vehicle: The Neglect of Team Leadership," in *Why Is the Leadership Development Industry Failing?* R. B. Kaiser (chair). Symposium conducted at the 28th Annual Conference for the Society of Industrial and Organizational Psychology, Houston, May 2013.

improve but may not be enough in and of themselves to affect behavioral change. Seventh, leadership behavior can change over time, but it may take a year or two to acquire new skills and for the changes to be reflected in 360-degree feedback ratings. Finally, some cultural, racial, and gender issues are associated with 360-degree feedback, and practitioners should be aware of these issues before implementing any 360-degree feedback process.[56,73,88,89] (See Highlight 7.5.)

Summary

People in leadership positions exhibit a wide variety of behaviors, and researchers have explored whether there is a universal set of behaviors that differentiates effective from ineffective leaders or if there are situational or follower factors that impact the types of behavior needed to build teams or get results through others. To answer the first question, there does not appear to be a universal set of leadership behaviors that guarantees success across many or all situations. Although some types of task and relationship-oriented leadership behaviors will likely improve the odds of success, the nature of the work to be performed, the situation, and the number and types of followers affect the specific kinds of task and relationship behaviors leaders need to demonstrate to be effective. Chapter 12 describes a much more comprehensive list of the situational factors affecting leadership behavior, but some of the key situational factors reviewed in this chapter include the setting (community or organization) and organizational level. Competency models and 360-degree feedback can be used to describe how well someone is performing the behaviors needed to succeed in a particular position.

Leadership practitioners need to realize that they will ultimately be judged by the results they obtain and the behaviors they exhibit. Yet prior experience, values, and attributes play critical roles in how leaders go about building teams and achieving results through others. For example, leaders who move into roles that involve solving complex business problems but lack relevant experience, analytic intelligence, and strong commercial values will struggle to be successful, and those with the opposite characteristics are much more likely to succeed. Having the right attributes, values, and experience does not guarantee that leaders will exhibit the right behaviors, but this improves the odds considerably.

This chapter offers some vital yet subtle suggestions on how to be effective as a leader. First, people moving into leadership roles need to understand the performance expectations for their positions. These expectations not only include the results to be achieved; they also include the behaviors that need to be exhibited. Organizational levels and competency models can help leaders determine the specific types of behaviors required to build teams and get results through others for the position in question. These frameworks also describe the behavioral changes leaders will need to make as they transition into new roles.

Second, understanding the behavioral requirements of various leadership positions and exhibiting needed behaviors can be two quite different things. That being the case, 360-degree feedback can give leaders insight into whether they need to do anything differently to build stronger teams or get better results through others. Although getting feedback from others can be an uncomfortable experience, this information is vital if people want to succeed as leaders. 360-degree feedback makes the process of getting feedback from others more systematic and actionable, and as such it is an important tool in the development of leaders.

Third, getting feedback from others in and of itself may not result in behavioral change. For example, many people know they need to lose weight, yet they may not do anything about it. But if they build a plan that includes a modified diet and regular exercise and get regular feedback and encouragement from others, they are much more likely to lose weight. The same holds true for changing leadership behaviors. Building development plans and getting coaching from others will improve the odds of changing targeted behaviors or acquiring needed skills, so leaders who want to be more effective should have written development plans.

Key Terms

Leader Behavior
 Description
 Questionnaire
 (LBDQ), *245*
consideration, *246*
initiating
 structure, *246*
job-centered
 dimensions, *246*
goal emphasis, *246*
work facilitation, *246*
employee-centered
 dimensions, *247*
leader support, *247*
interaction
 facilitation, *247*

Leadership Grid, *248*
concern for
 people, *248*
concern for
 production, *248*
leadership
 behavior, *250*
leadership skill, *250*
competency
 models, *251*
intrapersonal
 skills, *253*
interpersonal
 skills, *253*
leadership skills, *253*

business skills, *253*
organizational
 levels, *255*
Leadership
 Pipeline, *255*
community
 leadership, *258*
framing, *259*
building social
 capital, *259*
mobilization, *259*
360-degree, or
 multirater,
 feedback, *261*

Questions

1. Could you create a competency model for college professors? For college students? If you used these competency models to create 360-degree feedback tools, who would be in the best position to give professors and students feedback?

2. What competencies would be needed by a U.S.-born leader being assigned to build power plants in China? What competencies would be needed by a Chinese-born leader being assigned to run a copper mine in Kenya?

3. What are the competencies needed to be an effective U.S. senator? A famous musician or actor? How are these competencies similar or different?

4. Is the U.S.-based Tea Party movement an example of community leadership? Why or why not?

Activities

1. Identify two leadership positions and then determine the relative importance of the 16 competencies shown in Figure 7.3. You can do this by ranking each competency in order of importance, with the most important competency being assigned a 1, the second most important a 2, and so on. If you do this exercise with several partners ranking the same positions, does everyone give the 16 competencies about the same ranking? Why or why not?

2. Collect competency models from two organizations and assign them to the intrapersonal, interpersonal, leadership, and business categories described by Hogan and Warrenfelz. Do the competencies fit easily into the four categories? Which categories seem to be underrepresented or overrepresented by the competency models?

3. Identify two leadership positions at your school and determine their organizational levels using the Leadership Pipeline.

4. Given the model of community leadership described earlier in this chapter, analyze an ongoing community change initiative. Has the leader framed the issue in a way that makes it easy for others to take action? Do the group members have strong bonds with other groups? Have they created a plan and mobilized a critical mass of people and resources to make the change become reality?

Minicase

Paying Attention Pays Off for Andra Rush

Paying attention has been a key for Andra Rush. As a nursing school graduate she was paying attention when other nurses complained about unfair treatment and decided she wanted to do something about it—so she enrolled in the University of Michigan's MBA program so she could do something about how employees were treated. As she completed her business courses and continued to work as a nurse, she was paying attention when a patient described his experience in the transport business. The business sounded intriguing, and so, with minimal experience and minimal resources, Rush took a risk and started her own trucking business. She scraped together the funds to buy three trucks by borrowing money from family and using her credit cards. She specialized in emergency shipping and accepted every job that came her way, even if it meant driving the trucks herself. She answered phones, balanced her books, and even repaired the trucks. She paid attention to her customers and made a point of exceeding their expectations regardless of the circumstances. When the terrorist attacks of September 11, 2001, shut down local bridges, Rush rented a barge to make sure a crucial shipment for DaimlerChrysler made it to its destination on time.

Rush continues to pay attention and credits her listening skills as a major reason for her success. Rush is distinct in the traditionally white male–dominated trucking industry—a woman and a minority (Rush is Native American) who credits her heritage and the "enormous strength" of her Mohawk grandmother for helping her prevail:

> It is entirely possible that my Native spirit, communicated to me by my grandmother and my immediate family, have enabled me to overcome the isolation, historical prejudice, and business environment viewed as a barrier to Native- and woman-owned businesses. The willingness to listen, to understand first, and act directly and honestly with integrity is a lesson and code of conduct my elders have bequeathed to me. Being an entrepreneur has reinforced those lessons again and again.

Her Mohawk heritage is pervasive. Rush's company logo is a war staff with six feathers representing the Six Nations of the Iroquois: Mohawk, Onondaga, Oneida, Cayuga, Tuscarora, and Seneca. She believes in the power of a diverse workforce; as a result more than half of the 390 employees at Rush Trucking are women, and half are minorities.

Rush keeps close tabs on her company and its employees. Though the company has grown from its humble three-truck beginning to a fleet of 1,700 trucks, Rush still takes time to ride along with drivers. She has provided educational programs like "The Readers' Edge," a literacy program, to improve the skills and lives of her employees. Rush is actively involved in several organizations that work to improve the position of minorities—she's on the boards of directors of the Michigan Minority Business Development Council, the Minority Enterprise Development/Minority Business Development Agency, and the Minority Business Roundtable, and she has served as president of the Native American Business Alliance.

1. As we have discussed, competency models describe the behaviors and skills managers need to exhibit if an organization is to be successful. Consider the general competencies found in Figure 7.3 and apply these to Andra Rush, providing examples of how these competencies apply.

2. How does the Leadership Pipeline apply to Andra Rush?

3. Andra Rush belongs to several volunteer organizations. Would her leadership style need to change as the president of the Native American Business Alliance versus the CEO of Rush Trucking? How would the Community Leadership Model apply to Andra Rush?

Sources: http://www.inc.com/magazine/20040401/25rush.html; http://www.crains detroit.com/cgi-bin/page.pl?pageId=400; http://www.readfaster.com/pr20030912.pdf; http://www.turtle-tracks.org/issue41/i41_3.html; http://www.indiancountry.com/?2224.

End Notes

1. G. Curphy, "Investing in the Wrong Vehicle: The Neglect of Team Leadership," in *Why Is the Leadership Development Industry Failing?* R.B. Kaiser (chair). Symposium conducted at the 28th Annual Conference for the Society of Industrial and Organizational Psychology, Houston, May 2013.

2. R. B. Kaiser, J. Lindberg McGinnis, and D. V. Overfield, "The How and What of Leadership," *Consulting Psychology Journal: Practice and Research* 64, no. 2 (2012), pp. 119–35.

3. G. J. Curphy, "Leadership Transitions and Teams," presentation given at the Hogan Assessment Systems International Users Conference, Istanbul, September 2003.

4. G. J. Curphy, "The Consequences of Managerial Incompetence," presentation given at the 3rd Hogan Assessment Systems International Users Conference, Prague, Czech Republic, September 2004.

5. G. J. Curphy, "Comments on the State of Leadership Prediction," in *Predicting Leadership: The Good, The Bad, the Indifferent, and the Unnecessary*, J. P. Campbell and M. J. Benson (chairs). Symposium conducted at the 22nd Annual Conference for the Society of Industrial and Organizational Psychology, New York, April 2007.

6. R. B. Kaiser and D. V. Overfield, "The Leadership Value Chain," *The Psychologist-Manager Journal* 13, no. 3 (2010), pp. 164–83.

7. D. S. Derue, J. D. Nahrgang, N. Wellman, and S. E. Humphrey, "Trait and Behavioral Theories of Leadership: An Integration and Meta-Analytic Test of their Relative Validity," *Personnel Psychology* 64, no. 1 (2011), pp. 7–52.

8. R. T. Hogan and G. J. Curphy, *Leadership Effectiveness and Managerial Incompetence*, unpublished manuscript, 2007.

9. R. Charan and G. Colvin, "Why CEOs Fail," *Fortune*, June 21, 1999, pp. 69–82.

10. M. Goldsmith and M. Reiter, *What Got You Here Won't Get You There* (New York: Hyperion, 2007).

11. J. K. Hemphill, "The Leader and His Group," *Journal of Educational Research* 28 (1949), pp. 225–29, 245–46.

12. J. K. Hemphill and A. E. Coons, "Development of the Leader Behavior Description Questionnaire," in *Leader Behavior: Its Description and Measurement*, eds. R. M. Stogdill and A. E. Coons (Columbus: Ohio State University, Bureau of Business Research, 1957).

13. E. A. Fleishman, "Twenty Years of Consideration and Structure," in *Current Developments in the Study of Leadership*, eds. E. A. Fleishman and J. G. Hunt (Carbondale: Southern Illinois University Press, 1973).

14. A. W. Halpin and B. J. Winer, "A Factorial Study of the Leader Behavior Descriptions," in *Leader Behavior: Its Descriptions and Measurement*, eds. R. M. Stogdill and A. E. Coons (Columbus: Ohio State University, Bureau of Business Research, 1957).

15. E. A. Fleishman, *Examiner's Manual for the Supervisory Behavior Description Questionnaire* (Washington, DC: Management Research Institute, 1972).

16. E. A. Fleishman, *Examiner's Manual for the Leadership Opinion Questionnaire*, rev. ed. (Chicago: Science Research Associates, 1989).

17. R. M. Stogdill, *Individual Behavior and Group Achievement* (New York: Oxford University Press, 1959).

18. R. Likert, *New Patterns of Management* (New York: McGraw-Hill, 1961).

19. D. G. Bowers and S. E. Seashore, "Predicting Organizational Effectiveness with a Four Factor Theory of Leadership," *Administrative Science Quarterly* 11 (1966), pp. 238–63.

20. B. M. Bass, *Bass and Stogdill's Handbook of Leadership*, 3rd ed. (New York: Free Press, 1990).

21. T. A. Judge, R. F. Piccolo, and R. Ilies, "The Forgotten Ones? The Validity of Consideration and Initiating Structure in Leadership Research," *Journal of Applied Psychology* 89, no. 1 (2004), pp. 36–51.

22. R. Eisenberger, F. Stinglhamber, C. Vandenberghe, I. L. Sucharski, and L. Rhoades, "Perceived Supervisor Support: Contributions to Perceived Organizational Support and Employee Retention," *Journal of Applied Psychology* 87, no. 3 (2002), pp. 565–73.

23. R. R. Blake and A. A. McCanse, *Leadership Dilemmas—Grid Solutions* (Houston, TX: Gulf, 1991).

24. R. R. Blake and J. S. Mouton, *The Managerial Grid* (Houston, TX: Gulf, 1964).

25. C. Robie, K. Kanter, D. L. Nilsen, and J. Hazucha, *The Right Stuff: Understanding Cultural Differences in Leadership Performance* (Minneapolis, MN: Personnel Decisions International, 2001).

26. M. Goff, *Critical Leadership Skills Valued by Every Organization* (Minneapolis, MN: Personnel Decisions International, 2001).

27. S. Davis, J. Volker, R. C. Barnett, P. H. Batz, and P. Germann, *Leadership Matters: 13 Roles of High Performing Leaders* (Minneapolis, MN: MDA Leadership Consulting, 2006).

28. G. P. Hollenbeck, M. W. McCall, and R. F. Silzer, "Leadership Competency Models," *The Leadership Quarterly* 17 (2006), pp. 398–413.

29. L. Tischler, "IBM's Management Makeover," *Fast Company*, November 2004, pp. 112–16.

30. P. Lievens, J. I. Sanchez, and W. DeCorte, "Easing the Inferential Leap in Competency Modeling: The Effects of Task-Related Information and Subject Matter Expertise," *Personnel Psychology* 57 (2004), pp. 881–904.

31. A. W. King, S. W. Fowler, and C. P. Zeithaml, "Managing Organizational Competencies for Competitive Advantage: The Middle-Management Edge," *Academy of Management Executive* 15, no. 2 (2001), pp. 95–106.

32. G. J. Curphy, *The Blandin Education Leadership Program* (Grand Rapids, MN: The Blandin Foundation, 2004).

33. G.J. Curphy, *Why is the Leadership Development Industry Failing?* Presentation given at the Metro Industrial/Organizational Psychology Association, New York City, NY, 2013.

34. G. J. Curphy and R. T. Hogan, "Managerial Incompetence: Is There a Dead Skunk on the Table?" Working paper, 2004.

35. D. Ulrich, J. Zenger, and N. Smallwood, *Results-Based Leadership* (Boston: Harvard Business School Press, 1999).

36. D. B. Peterson, "Making the Break from Middle Manager to a Seat at the Top," *The Wall Street Journal*, July 7, 1998.

37. R. B. Kaiser and S. B. Craig, *Testing the Leadership Pipeline: Do the Behaviors Related to Managerial Effectiveness Change with Organizational Level?* Presentation given at the 1st Annual Leading Edge Consortium, St Louis, MO, 2008.

38. J. S. Shippmann, R. A. Ash, M. Battista, L. Carr, L. D. Eyde, B. Hesketh, J. Kehoe, K. Pearlman, E. P. Prien, and J. I. Sanchez, "The Practice of Competency Modeling," *Personnel Psychology* 53, no. 3 (2000), pp. 703–40.

39. R. T. Hogan and R. Warrenfelz, "Educating the Modern Manager," *Academy of Management Learning and Education* 2, no. 1 (2003), pp. 74–84.

40. A. H. Church, "Talent Management," *The Industrial-Organizational Psychologist* 44, no. 1 (2006), pp. 33–36.

41. D. Ancona, T. W. Malone, W. J. Orlikowski, and P. M. Senge, "In Praise of the Incomplete Leader," *Harvard Business Review,* February 2007, pp. 92–103.

42. W. A. Gentry, L. S. Harris, B. A. Becker, and J. B. Leslie, "Managerial Skills: What Has Changed since the Late 1980s," *Leadership & Organizational Development Journal* 29, no. 2 (2008), pp. 167–81.

43. R. Charan, S. Drotter, and J. Noel, *The Leadership Pipeline: How to Build the Leadership-Powered Company* (San Francisco: Jossey-Bass, 2001).

44. R. B. Kaiser, S. B. Craig, D. V. Overfield, and P. Yarborough, "Differences in Managerial Jobs at the Bottom, Middle, and Top: A Review of Empirical Research," *The Psychologist-Manager Journal* 14, no. 2 (2011), pp. 76–91.

45. R. B. Kaiser, and S. B. Craig, "Do the Behaviors Related to Managerial Effectiveness Really Change with Organizational Level? An Empirical Test," *The Psychologist-Manager Journal* 14, no. 2 (2011), pp. 92–119.

46. J. Krile, G. J. Curphy, and D. Lund, *The Community Leadership Handbook: Framing Ideas, Building Relationships and Mobilizing Resources* (St Paul, MN: Fieldstone Alliance, 2005).

47. B. C. Crosby and J. M. Bryson, "Integrative Leadership and the Creation and Maintenance of Cross-Sector Collaborations," *The Leadership Quarterly* 21 (2010), pp. 211–30.

48. J. E. Bono, W. Shen, and M. Snyder, "Fostering Integrative Community Leadership," *The Leadership Quarterly* 21 (2010), pp. 324–35.

49. N. M. Tichy and E. Cohen, *The Leadership Engine: How Winning Companies Build Leaders at Every Level* (New York: HarperCollins, 1997).

50. D. P. Campbell, G. J. Curphy, and T. Tuggle, *360-Degree Feedback Instruments: Beyond Theory.* Workshop presented at the 10th Annual Conference of the Society for Industrial and Organizational Psychology, Orlando, FL, May 1995.

51. G. J. Curphy, "Executive Integrity and 360-Degree Feedback," in *Assessing Executive Failure: The Underside of Performance,* R. T. Hogan (chair). Symposium presented at the 18th Annual Conference of the Society of Industrial and Organizational Psychology, Orlando, FL, 2003.

52. G. Toegel and J. A. Conger, "360-Degree Assessment: Time for Reinvention," *Academy of Management Learning and Education* 2, no. 3, pp. 297–311.

53. R. B. Kaiser and S. B. Craig, "Building a Better Mousetrap: Item Characteristics Associated with Rating Discrepancies in 360-Degree Feedback," *Consulting Psychology Journal* 57, no. 4 (2005), pp. 235–45.

54. F. Morgeson, T. V. Mumsford, and M. A. Campion, "Coming Full Circle: Research and Practice to Address 27 Questions about 360-Degree Feedback Programs," *Consulting Psychology Journal* 57, no. 3 (2005), pp. 196–209.

55. J. W. Smither, M. London, and R. R. Reilly, "Does Performance Improve Following Multisource Feedback? A Theoretical Model, Meta-analysis, and Review of Empirical Findings," *Personnel Psychology* 58 (2005), pp. 33–66.

56. K. M. Nowack, "Leveraging Multirater Feedback to Facilitate Successful Behavioral Change," *Consulting Psychology Journal: Practice and Research* 61, no. 4 (2009), pp. 280–97.

57. J. E. Bono and A. E. Colbert, "Understanding Responses to Multi-Source Feedback: The Core of Self-Evaluations," *Personnel Psychology* 58 (2005), pp. 171–203.

58. D. W. Bracken, C. W. Timmreck, and A. H. Church, *The Handbook of Multisource Feedback* (San Francisco: Jossey-Bass, 2000).

59. P. W. B. Atkins and R. E. Wood, "Self-Versus Others' Ratings as Predictors of Assessment Center Ratings: Validation Evidence for 360-Degree Feedback Programs," *Personnel Psychology* 55 (2002), pp. 871–84.

60. K.M. Nowack and S. Mashihi, "Evidence-Based Answers to 15 Questions About Leveraging 360-Degree Feedback," *Consulting Psychologist Journal: Practice and Research* 64, no. 3 (2012), pp. 157–82.

61. J. M. Jackman and M. H. Strober, "Fear of Feedback," *Harvard Business Review*, April 2003, pp. 101–8.

62. M. A. Peiperl, "Getting 360-Degree Feedback Right," *Harvard Business Review*, January 2001, pp. 142–48.

63. F. Sala, "Executive Blind Spots: Discrepancies between Self- and Other-Ratings," *Consulting Psychology Journal* 55, no. 4 (2003), pp. 222–29.

64. A. Kinicki, K. J. L. Jacobson, S. J. Peterson, and G. E. Prussia, "Development and Validation of the Performance Management Behavior Questionnaire," *Personnel Psychology* 66, no. 1 (2013), pp. 1–46.

65. D. Antonioni, "360-Degree Feedback for a Competitive Edge," *Industrial Management* 42 (2000), pp. 6–10.

66. F. Sala and S. A. Dwight, "Predicting Executive Performance with Multirater Surveys: Whom You Ask Makes a Difference," *Consulting Psychology Journal* 55, no. 3 (2003), pp. 166–72.

67. G. J. Curphy, "An Empirical Investigation of Bass' (1985) Theory of Transformational and Transactional Leadership," PhD dissertation, University of Minnesota, 1991.

68. G. J. Curphy, "The Effects of Transformational and Transactional Leadership on Organizational Climate, Attrition, and Performance," in *Impact of Leadership*, eds. K. E. Clark, M. B. Clark, and D. P. Campbell (Greensboro, NC: Center for Creative Leadership, 1992).

69. A. H. Church, "Managerial Self-Awareness in High-Performing Individuals in Organizations," *Journal of Applied Psychology* 82, no. 2 (1997), pp. 281–92.

70. A. H. Church, "Do Higher Performing Managers Actually Receive Better Ratings?" *Consulting Psychology Journal* 52, no. 2 (2000), pp. 99–116.

71. J. Ghorpade, "Managing Six Paradoxes of 360-Degree Feedback," *Academy of Management Executive* 14, no. 1 (2000), pp. 140–50.

72. G. J. Greguras, C. Robie, D. J. Schleicher, and M. Goff III, "A Field Study of the Effects of Rating Purpose on the Quality of Multisource Ratings," *Personnel Psychology* 56, no. 1 (2003), pp. 1–22.

73. A. H. Church and J. Waclawski, "A Five-Phase Framework for Designing a Successful Multisource Feedback System," *Consulting Psychology Journal* 53, no. 2 (2001), pp. 82–95.

74. K. Pfau, "Does 360-Degree Feedback Negatively Affect Company Performance?" *HR Magazine,* June 2002, pp. 55–59.

75. G. J. Curphy, *Afterburner 360 Training Manual* (North Oaks, MN: Curphy Consulting Corporation, 2003).

76. G. J. Greguras and C. Robie, "A New Look at Within-Source Interrater Reliability of 360-Degree Feedback Ratings," *Journal of Applied Psychology* 83, no. 6 (1998), pp. 960–68.

77. M. K. Mount, T. A. Judge, S. E. Scullen, M. R. Sytsma, and S. A. Hezlett, "Trait, Rater, and Level Effects in 360-Degree Performance Ratings," *Personnel Psychology* 51, no. 3 (1998), pp. 557–77.

78. C. Ostroff, L. E. Atwater, and B. J. Feinberg, "Understanding Self-Other Agreement: A Look at Rater and Ratee Characteristics, Context, and Outcomes," *Personnel Psychology* 57, no. 2 (2004), pp. 333–76.

79. L. E. Atwater, C. Ostroff, F. J. Yammarino, and J. W. Fleenor, "Self–Other Agreement: Does It Really Matter?" *Personnel Psychology* 51, no. 3 (1998), pp. 577–98.

80. J. W. Fleenor, C. D. McCauley, and S. Brutus, "Self-Other Rating Agreement and Leader Effectiveness," *Leadership Quarterly* 7, no. 4 (1996), pp. 487–506.

81. A. Walker and J. W. Smither, "A Five-Year Study of Upward Feedback: What Managers Do with Their Results Matters," *Personnel Psychology* 52, no. 2 (1999), pp. 395–423.

82. K. Johnson and J. Johnson, *Economic Value of Performance Change after 360-Degree Feedback* (Minneapolis, MN: Personnel Decisions International, 2001).

83. C. F. Seifert and G. Yukl, "Effects of Repeated Multi-Source Feedback on the Influence Behavior and Effectiveness of Managers: A Field Experiment," *The Leadership Quarterly* 21, no. 5 (2010), pp. 856–66.

84. J. W. Smither, M. London, R. Flautt, Y. Vargas, and I. Kucine, "Can Working with an Executive Coach Improve Multisource Feedback Ratings over Time? A Quasi-Experimental Field Study," *Personnel Psychology* 56, no. 1 (2003), pp. 23–44.

85. W. W. Tornow and M. London, *Maximizing the Value of 360-Degree Feedback* (San Francisco: Jossey-Bass, 1998).

86. J. S. Chhokar, F. C. Brodbeck, and R. J. House, *Culture and Leadership across the World: The Globe Book of In-Depth Studies of 25 Societies* (Mahwah, NJ: Lawrence Erlbaum Associates, 2007).

87. M. K. Mount, M. R. Sytsma, J. F. Hazucha, and K. E. Holt, "Rater–Ratee Effects in Development Performance Ratings of Managers," *Personnel Psychology* 50, no. 1 (1997), pp. 51–70.

88. H. J. Bernardin and R. W. Beatty, *Performance Appraisal: Assessing Human Behavior at Work* (Boston: Kent, 1984).

89. Personnel Decisions International, *PROFILOR® Certification Workshop Manual* (Minneapolis, MN: Author, 2007).

Chapter 9

Motivation, Satisfaction, and Performance

Introduction

Polls estimate that if companies could get 3.7 percent more work out of each employee, the equivalent of 18 more minutes of work for each eight-hour shift, the gross domestic product in the U.S. would swell by $355 billion, twice the total GDP of Greece.
The Gallup Organization

Hardly a competent workman can be found in a large establishment who does not devote a considerable amount of his time to studying just how slow he can work and still convince his employer that he is going at a good pace.
Frederick W. Taylor, industrial engineer

Why do followers join some teams but not others? How do you get followers to exhibit enough of the critical behaviors needed for the team to succeed? And why are some leaders capable of getting followers to go above and beyond the call of duty? The ability to motivate others is a fundamental leadership skill and has strong connections to building cohesive, goal-oriented teams and getting results through others. The importance of follower motivation is suggested in findings that most people believe they could give as much as 15 percent or 20 percent more effort at work than they now do with no one, including their own bosses, recognizing any difference. Perhaps even more startling, these workers also believed they could give 15 percent or 20 percent *less* effort with no one noticing any difference. Moreover, variation in work output varies significantly across leaders and followers. The top 15 percent of workers in any particular job may produce 20 to 50 percent more output than the average worker, depending on the complexity of the job. Put another way, the best computer programmers or salesclerks might write up to 50 percent more programs or process 50 percent more customer orders.[1,2] Might better methods of motivating workers lead to higher productivity from *all* workers? Is motivating an individual follower different than motivating a group of followers? Are more motivated workers happier or more satisfied workers? Does money increase productivity and satisfaction, or can leaders do other things to increase the motivation and satisfaction levels of their followers? For example, the U.S. Army pays over $1 billion in retention bonuses each year.[3] Is this money well spent?

Creating highly motivated and satisfied followers depends mostly on understanding others. Therefore, whereas motivation is an essential part

331

of leadership, it is appropriate to include it in this part of the book, which focuses on followers. As an overview, this chapter will address three key areas. First, we will examine the links among leadership, motivation, satisfaction, and performance—four closely related concepts. Second, we will review some major theories and research about motivation and satisfaction. Last, and perhaps most important, we will discuss what leaders can do to enhance the motivation and satisfaction of their followers if they implement these different theories.

Defining Motivation, Satisfaction, and Performance

Motivation, satisfaction, and performance seem clearly related. For example, Colin Powell was the U.S. Army Chief of Staff during the first Gulf War and Secretary of State during the second Gulf War. Powell probably could have pursued a number of different vocations but was *motivated* to complete ROTC as an undergraduate and join the U.S. Army. He was also motivated to put in extra time, energy, and effort in his various positions while in the U.S. Army and was judged or rated by his superiors as being an exceptional performer. His outstanding *performance* as an officer was crucial to his promotion as the head of the Joint Chiefs of Staff during the Reagan and George H. W. Bush administrations and his later appointment as Secretary of State. We could also infer that he was happy or *satisfied* with military life because he was a career officer in the U.S. Army. Figure 9.1 provides an overview of the general relationships among leadership, motivation, satisfaction, and performance. As we can see, some leadership behaviors, such as building relationships or consideration (Chapter 7), result in more satisfied followers. Satisfied followers are more likely to remain with the company and engage in activities that help others at work (organizational citizenship behaviors). Other leadership behaviors, such as setting goals, planning, providing feedback, and rewarding good performance (initiating structure from Chapter 7), appear to more directly influence followers to exert higher levels of effort toward the accomplishment of group goals. Research has shown that these follower behaviors result in higher levels of customer satisfaction and loyalty, which in turn lead to better team performance in retail, sales, or restaurant settings.[4-18] And individuals and teams with higher performance levels often achieve more rewards, which further increase follower satisfaction and performance.[19,20] Thus the leader's ability to motivate followers is vitally important to both the morale and performance of the work group. However, the leader's use of motivational techniques is not the only factor affecting group performance. Selecting the right people for the team, correctly using power and influence tactics, being seen as ethical and credible, possessing the right personality traits and high levels of intelligence, acquiring the necessary resources, and developing follower

FIGURE 9.1
Relationships among Leadership, Job Satisfaction, and Performance

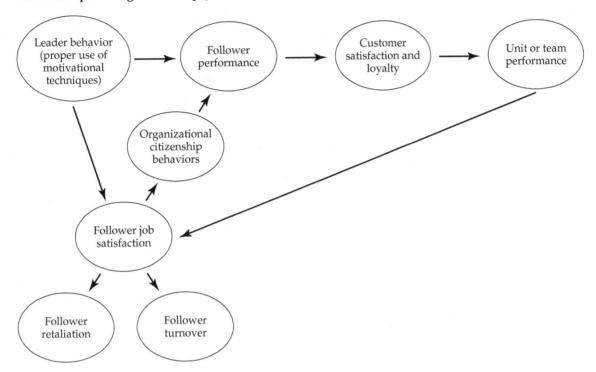

Sources: M. A. Huselid, "The Impact of Human Resource Management Practices on Turnover, Productivity, and Corporate Financial Performance," *Academy of Management Journal* 38, no. 4 (1995), pp. 635–72; T. Butorac, *Recruitment and Retention: The Keys to Profitability at Carlson Companies*, presentation given at Personnel Decisions International, Minneapolis, MN, June 11, 2001; D. J. Koys, "The Effects of Employee Satisfaction, Organizational Citizenship Behavior, and Turnover on Organizational Effectiveness: A Unit-Level, Longitudinal Study," *Personnel Psychology* 54, no. 1 (2001), pp. 101–14; J. Husserl, "Allied's Organizational Life Cycle," *Management Education & Development* 24, no. 3 (1998), p. 8; Sirota Consulting, *Establishing the Linkages between Employee Attitudes, Customer Attitudes, and Bottom-Line Results* (Chicago, IL: Author, 1998); D. S. Pugh, J. Dietz, J. W. Wiley, and S. M. Brooks, "Driving Service Effectiveness through Employee–Customer Linkages," *Academy of Management Executive* 16, no. 4 (2002), pp. 73–84; B. Schneider, P. J. Hanges, D. B. Smith, and A. N. Salvaggio, "Which Comes First: Employee Attitudes or Organizational, Financial and Market Performance?" *Journal of Applied Psychology* 88, no. 5 (2003), pp. 836–51.

skills are other leadership factors affecting a group's ability to accomplish its goals.

Most people probably think of motivation as dealing with choices about what we do and how much effort we put into doing it. Most researchers define **motivation** as anything that provides *direction, intensity,* and *persistence* to behavior.[21–23] Thus motivation comes into play whenever someone chooses an activity or task to engage in, puts forth a certain level of effort toward this activity, and persists with this effort for some time. Like personality traits and types, motivation is not directly observable; it must be inferred from behavior. We would infer that one person is highly motivated to do well in school if she spent a lot of time studying for exams. She could choose to spend her time and energy on socializing, intramurals, or volunteer work, but because she is spending time outlining readings and

You have brains in your head. You have feet in your shoes. You can steer yourself in any direction you choose.

Dr. Seuss

reviewing class notes, we say she is motivated to do well in school. At work, if one person regularly assembles twice as many iPads as any other person in his work group—assuming all have the same abilities, skills, and resources—then we likely would say this first person is more motivated than the others. We use the concept of motivation to explain differences we see among people in the energy and direction of their behavior. Thus the energy and effort Ang Lee expended creating *Life of Pi* or the governments of Iran and North Korea spend developing their nuclear capabilities would be examples of the direction, intensity, and persistence components of motivation.

Performance, on the other hand, concerns behaviors directed toward the organization's mission or goals or the products and services resulting from those behaviors. At work or school we can choose to perform a wide variety of behaviors, but performance would include only those behaviors related to the production of goods or services or obtaining good grades. Performance differs from **effectiveness,** which generally involves making judgments about the adequacy of behavior with respect to certain criteria such as work group or organizational goals. Ang Lee spent several years creating the movie *Life of Pi*. The behaviors he exhibited in getting the film made constitute performance; the revenues generated and Academy Awards won by the movie indicate his effectiveness as a movie director. However, performance is affected by a variety of factors. Intelligence, skill, and the availability of key resources can affect a follower's behavior in accomplishing organizational goals (that is, performance) independently of that person's level of motivation. *Thus an adequate level of motivation may be a necessary but insufficient condition of effective performance.*

Job satisfaction is not how *hard* one works or how *well* one works, but rather how much one *likes* a specific kind of job or work activity. Job satisfaction deals with one's attitudes or feelings about the job itself, pay, promotion or educational opportunities, supervision, co-workers, workload, and so on.[11,24,25] Various polls over the past half-century have consistently shown that a majority of men and women report liking their jobs.[26-30] Research has also shown that people who are more satisfied with their jobs are more likely to engage in **organizational citizenship behaviors**— behaviors not directly related to one's job but helpful to others at work. Organizational citizenship behaviors create a more supportive workplace. Examples might include volunteering to help another employee with a task or project or filling in for another employee when asked. Happier workers tend to be more helpful workers.[31-37]

Although people generally like the work they do, several events have caused a downturn in job satisfaction levels among employees in the United States over the past decade. From roughly 2002 to 2007 the United States enjoyed strong economic growth, and companies rapidly expanded the products and services they provided. Because it took time to hire and train employees to meet increased demand, those already employed

A company is always perfectly designed to produce what it is producing. If it has quality problems, cost problems, or productivity problems, then the behaviors associated with these outcomes are being reinforced. This is not conjecture. This is the cold, hard reality of human behavior.

Anonymous

There is one virtue to the 35-hour workweek. It is one of the few French ideals that we don't need to worry about copyrighting. Nobody else wants it.

Nicolas Sarkozy, former prime minister of France

had to cope with larger workloads. This period also saw a tremendous amount of consolidation (companies buying one another) and reorganization (restructuring functions, processes, and personnel) to better meet increased demand. Change was an overarching theme from 2002 to 2007, and leaders and followers were constantly devising new ways to deliver products and services to customers. This continuing cycle of consolidation, reorganization, and change made it difficult for employees to develop any loyalty for their organizations—they never knew if their work unit was going to be sold or merged with another work unit. This period, perhaps more than most, broke the implicit contract between employers and employees. Before 2002 many employees felt if they worked hard they could spend their entire careers at a single company. But after all the acquisitions, downsizings, and restructurings many employees developed more of a mercenary attitude toward employers. If they worked for a company that did not treat them well, had a bad boss, or did not get the pay or promotions they felt they deserved, they would find a position with another employer. And with the economy enjoying strong growth, there were plenty of opportunities for people to find other employment.

Although people were working longer hours and coping with more change than ever before, most people found 2002 to 2007 to be a cakewalk compared to what they experienced during the economic recession of 2008 to 2010. The global recession caused companies to freeze hiring and training programs and lay off record numbers of employees. The unemployment rate in the United States increased from 5 to over 10 percent, and many people went months or even years without finding meaningful work. Those lucky enough to remain employed wound up doing more than they did before with fewer resources and lower pay. Employees generally felt lucky to have a job and were not apt to complain (for fear of losing their jobs), but many were frustrated with their employers. This increased workload and sense of frustration cut job satisfaction to record lows, and a big question was whether the best and brightest employees were leaving for other opportunities once the economy started picking up.[38] Companies can ill afford to lose their best people just when their fortunes are improving, so many have implemented programs to retain their high-potential talent.[39,40]

Today many leaders face the dual challenges of having to achieve increasingly difficult team goals while having fewer followers available to do the work. The best leaders and organizations understand that one way to meet these challenges is to recruit, develop, and retain top leadership and technical talent. Savvy companies that spend considerably more time and effort attracting, developing, and retaining the best people often report superior financial results.[9,11,39–46] For example, many of the organizations appearing in *Fortune* magazine's "The 100 Best Companies to Work For" also do well when compared to the S&P 500 Index. *The best leaders may be those who can motivate workers to perform at a high level while maintaining an equally high level of job satisfaction.* See Highlight 9.1 for a discussion of productivity and job satisfaction.

People who have jobs, rather than careers, worry about work–life balance because they are unable to have fun at work.

Tomas Chamorro-Premuzic, consultant

Productivity and Satisfaction across the Globe

HIGHLIGHT 9.1

The global recession has caused American and European businesses to downsize considerably, but many have been able to maintain customer satisfaction and revenue levels with fewer employees. In terms of the number of hours worked, the average U.S. employee works 137 hours per year more than the typical Japanese employee, 260 hours more per year compared to the average British employee, and 499 hours more than the average French employee. In other words, over a 40-year work career, U.S. employees will work the equivalent of 10 more years than the average French employee. The work ethic of the French has been mocked by outsiders for years and is seen as a significant barrier to the country's ability to compete in the global marketplace. American companies are noted for having some of the highest productivity in the world, but might there also be a downside to these high productivity levels? Research has shown that some of the risks associated with longer workweeks include job dissatisfaction, poorer physical and mental health, and distressed family and social relationships. But other research by Chamorro-Premuzic shows that workaholics have higher social status, high achievers live longer, and the ten most workaholic nations produce most of the world's gross domestic product. Chamorro-Premuzic argues that many employees have become self-indulgent, pampered, and so enthralled with the pursuit of well-being that they have forgotten the value of hard work and achievement. He believes the pursuit of work–life balance is a myth perpetrated by positive psychologists and self-help gurus trying to make people feel good about their failures and inability to achieve things. People who put in long hours and hate their jobs are likely to suffer all the negative effects identified earlier. Those who are engaged, have fun at work, and view their current positions as part of a career path versus a job do not suffer these ill effects and end up being much more successful.

Do you think that workers today are not as motivated or achievement oriented as those in the past? Is there such a thing as work–life balance? Is working longer hours a good or bad thing?

Sources: J. M. Brett and L. K. Stroh, "Working 61 Plus Hours a Week: Why Do Managers Do It?" *Journal of Applied Psychology* 88, no. 1 (2003), pp. 67–78; "Schumpeter: Overstretched" *The Economist*, May 22, 2010, p. 72; "Schumpeter: The French Way of Work" *The Economist*, November 19, 2011, p. 71; H. Schachter, "Get Over It: There Is No Work–Life Balance, Just Work," *The Globe and Mail*, February 28, 2013; http://blogs.hbr.org/cs/2013/02/embrace_work-life_imbalan.html; http://news.yahoo.com/s/ap/20100105/ap_on_bi_ge/us_unhappy_workers.

Having now defined motivation, performance, and job satisfaction, we can explore their relationships a bit further. We have already noted how motivation does not always ensure good performance. If followers lack the necessary skills or resources to accomplish a group task, then trying to motivate them more could be unproductive and even frustrating.[47,48] For example, no high school basketball team is likely to defeat the Los Angeles Lakers, however motivated the players may be. The players on the high school team simply lack the abilities and skills of the Lakers players. Higher motivation will usually affect performance only if followers already have the abilities, skills, and resources to get the job done. Motivating others is an important part of leadership, but not all of it; pep talks and rewards are not always enough.

Ping Fu

PROFILES IN LEADERSHIP 9.1

Ping Fu is the Chinese-born cofounder and CEO of Geomagic, a company that provides 3D imaging used in engineering, art, archeology, metrology, and biomechanical product design. Started in 1997, Geomagic's technology is used in the creation of customized prosthetic limbs, and if you wore braces growing up they may have been designed with the help of Geomagic technology.

Ping Fu's journey to becoming a corporate CEO is far from typical. She grew up in Shanghai in the home of two well-educated parents. At the age of eight she was listed as a "black" citizen—someone who had to atone for the greed and corruption committed by her parents and ancestors when Mao's cultural revolution swept the country. She spent the next years separated from her parents, working 14 hour days in a factory, foraging for scraps, and tending to her little sister between shifts. When the Cultural Revolution ended she enrolled in school and eventually wrote her dissertation on China's one-child policy, where she found that the government's use of brutal enforcement techniques was causing shockingly high rates of infanticide. Her dissertation was leaked to the press, and its wide publication was a major embarrassment to the Chinese government. In 1984 China quietly deported Ping Fu to the United States.

Ping Fu learned English and computer programming while working as a babysitter, maid, and waitress. She eventually landed a job with the National Center for Supercomputing Applications (NCSA) where she worked on earthquake prediction modeling and 3D imaging. In 1997 she made a New Year's resolution to "create something of value" and left the NCSA to start up Geomagic. In early 2013 she sold the company to 3D Systems, a 3D printing company, for $55 million.

What theory or theories of motivation best explain Ping Fu's journey to CEO?

Sources: P. Fu. *Bend, Not Break* (New York: Penguin Group, 2012); "An Executive Memoir: The World Is 3D," *The Economist,* January 12, 2013, p. 72; M. Kirkpatrick, "The Art of Resilience," *The Wall Street Journal,* January 9, 2013, p. A11.

> *Always bear in mind that your resolution to succeed is more important than any other one thing.*
>
> **Abraham Lincoln, U.S. president**

The relationships between motivation and job satisfaction are more straightforward; in fact many theories of motivation are also theories of job satisfaction. The implicit link between satisfaction and motivation is that satisfaction increases when people accomplish a task, particularly when the task requires a lot of effort. It might also seem logical that *performance* must be higher among more satisfied workers, but this is not always so.[12,17,24,49,50] Although satisfaction and performance are correlated, happy workers are not always the most productive ones; nor are unhappy or dissatisfied workers always the poorest performers. It is possible, for example, for poorly performing workers to be fairly satisfied with their jobs (maybe because they are paid well but do not have to work hard). It is also possible for dissatisfied workers to be relatively high performers (they may have a strong work ethic, have no other employment options, or be trying to improve the chances of getting out of their current job). Despite the intuitive appeal of believing that satisfied workers usually perform better, satisfaction has only an indirect effect on performance. Nevertheless, having both satisfied *and* high-performing followers is a goal leaders should usually strive to achieve. One example of a high performer is featured in Profiles in Leadership 9.1.

Understanding and Influencing Follower Motivation

What do leaders do to motivate followers to accomplish group goals? Are all leaders and followers motivated the same way? Is there a universal theory of motivation? In other words, did Osama bin Laden and General David Petraeus, one time commander of U.S. forces in Afghanistan, use the same or different techniques to motivate their followers? As described in Highlight 9.2, organizations spend billions on motivating employees; but do these interventions actually improve job satisfaction, retention, and performance? Research can answer these questions, and few topics of human behavior have been the subject of so much attention as that of motivation. So much has been written about motivation that a comprehensive review of the subject is beyond the scope of this book. We will, however, survey several major approaches to understanding follower motivation, as well as

Organizations Spend Billions on Motivational Programs for Employees, and All They Get Are Burned Feet

HIGHLIGHT 9.2

Organizations are constantly looking for quick fixes for their performance and effectiveness problems. The barriers to team or organizational performance often include a lack of resources and skills, unclear goals, poor performance or accountability standards, or incompetent leadership. But rather than adopting methods to directly address these issues, many organizations instead have employees listen to motivational speakers or engage in whitewater rafting, bungee jumping, or firewalking events. The motivational speaking circuit includes former professional athletes, astronauts, fighter pilots, and military generals, successful and failed business leaders, politicians, psychologists, and consultants. Motivational speaking engagements can be lucrative—one of the authors worked with a speaker who gave one speech in Las Vegas at lunch and the same speech that evening in Minneapolis and made $150,000 for the day. The author also has worked with a group of ex-fighter pilots who do half-day "Business Is Combat" seminars for $30,000 to $75,000.

Companies think nothing of spending like this to motivate employees. For example, the software consulting firm EMC has spent $625,000 to have 5,000 employees walk over burning coals. But do

expensive speakers and extreme activities actually improve organizational performance? Unfortunately exhaustive research has shown virtually no link between motivational spending and company revenues, profitability, or market share. Perhaps the biggest problem is that employees may find it difficult to see the link between walking over a bed of hot coals or participating in a Business Is Combat mission planning event and making another 20 sales calls every week. The problem is that these events do not address the root cause of many organizational woes but instead covertly shift the burden to "underperforming" employees. Other than bankrolling the motivation industry, these programs have another effect: nine U.S. Air Force recruiters had to go to the emergency room after they received second- and third-degree burns on their feet after one of these motivational programs.

Sources: D. Jones, "Firms Spend Billions to Fire Up Workers—With Little Luck," *USA Today,* May 10, 2001, pp. 1–2A; P. G. Chronis, "9 Burn Feet in National Guard Recruiters' Fire Walk," *Denver Post,* December 28, 1998, pp. 1A, 17A; G. J. Curphy and R. T. Hogan, "Managerial Incompetence: Is There a Dead Skunk on the Table?" working paper, 2004; G. J. Curphy, M. J. Benson, A. Baldrica, and R. T. Hogan, *Managerial Incompetence,* unpublished manuscript, 2007.

address the implications of these approaches for follower satisfaction and performance. These motivational theories and approaches give leaders a number of suggestions to get followers to engage in and persist with different behaviors. However, some motivational theories are particularly useful in certain situations but not as applicable in others. Just as a carpenter can build better wooden structures or furniture by having a larger set of tools, so can leaders solve a greater number of motivational problems among followers by becoming familiar with different motivational theories and approaches. People who have only hammers in their toolkits are likely to see every problem as a nail needing hammering, and it is not unusual for less effective leaders to call on a limited number of approaches to any motivational problem. *Leaders who know about different motivational theories are more likely to choose the right theory for a particular follower and situation, and often have higher-performing and more satisfied employees as a result.*

Most performance problems can be attributed to unclear expectations, skill deficits, resource/equipment shortages, or a lack of motivation. Of these underlying causes, leaders seem to have the most difficulty in recognizing and rectifying motivation problems. An example might help to illustrate this point. A major airline was having serious problems with the customer service of its flight attendants. Passenger complaints were on the rise, and airplane loading (the average number of people per flight) was decreasing. The perceived lack of customer service was beginning to cost the airline market share and revenues; to fix the problem it decided to have all 10,000 flight attendants go through a two-day customer service training program. Unfortunately passenger complaints only got worse after the training. A thorough investigation of the underlying cause of the problem revealed that flight attendants knew what they were supposed to do, had all the skills necessary to perform the behaviors, and usually had the resources and equipment necessary to serve customers. The root cause was a lack of motivation to go the extra mile for customers. When asked what they found to be the most motivating aspect of being a flight attendant, most stated "time off." In other words, the flight attendants were most motivated when they were *not* at work. (Because of work schedules, flight attendants typically get two weeks off per month.) Given that a strong union represented the flight attendants, how would you go about solving this dilemma? The next section will give you some ideas on how to resolve this and other motivation problems that you may face as a leader.

As stated earlier, leaders can use many different theories and approaches to motivate followers. In this section we will discuss the key aspects of five popular and useful approaches to understanding motivation in work or leadership contexts. Some may wonder why these motivational approaches were included and others excluded from this section, and sound arguments could be made for changing the motivational approaches described. Our intention is to provide a broad view of different

The truth of the matter is that you always know the right thing to do. The hard part is doing it.
Norman Schwarzkopf, U.S. Army

TABLE 9.1
Five Motivational Approaches

Theory or Approach	Major Themes of Characteristics
Maslow's hierarchy of needs	Satisfy needs to change behavior
Achievement orientation	Possess certain personality traits
Goal setting	Set goals to change behavior
Operant approach	Change rewards and punishments to change behavior
Empowerment	Give people autonomy and latitude to increase their motivation for work

Your job is to figure out what you have to do in order to do what you want to do.

**Jim Earley,
consultant**

motivational approaches and not be so comprehensive as to overwhelm readers. The five theories and approaches are listed in Table 9.1. For illustrative purposes we will also discuss how leadership practitioners could apply these approaches to motivate two fictitious followers, Julie and Ling Ling. Julie is a 21-year-old ski lift operator in Banff, Alberta, Canada. Her primary job is to ensure that people get on and off her ski lift safely. She also does periodic equipment safety checks and maintains the lift lines and associated areas. Julie works from 8:30 a.m. to 5:00 p.m. five days a week, is paid a salary, and has a pass that allows her to ski for free whenever she is off work. Ling Ling is a 35-year-old real estate agent in Hong Kong. She works for an agency that locates and rents apartments for people on one- to three-year business assignments for various multinational companies. She works many evenings and weekends showing apartments, and she is paid a salary plus a commission for every apartment she rents. How the five approaches could be used to motivate Julie and Ling Ling will be discussed periodically throughout this section.

Maslow's Hierarchy of Needs: How Does Context Affect Motivation?

One way to get followers to engage in and persist with the behaviors needed to accomplish group goals is to appeal to their needs. **Needs** refer to internal states of tension or arousal, or uncomfortable states of deficiency people are motivated to change. Hunger would be a good example of a need: people are motivated to eat when they get hungry. Other needs might include the need to live in a safe and secure place, to belong to a group with common interests or social ties, or to do interesting and challenging work. If these needs were not being met, people would choose to engage in and persist with certain behaviors until they were satisfied. According to this motivational approach, leadership practitioners can get followers to engage in and persist with certain behaviors by correctly identifying and appeasing their needs.

According to Maslow, people are motivated by five basic types of needs.[51] These include the need to survive physiologically, the need for security, the need for affiliation with other people (that is, belongingness),

FIGURE 9.2
Maslow's Hierarchy
of Needs

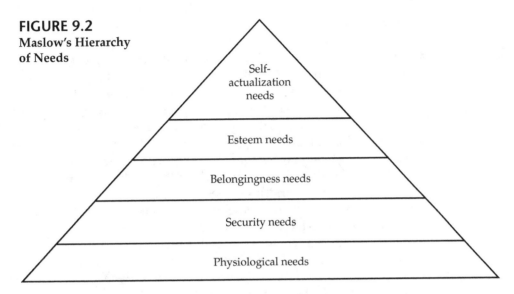

Self-
actualization
needs

Esteem needs

Belongingness needs

Security needs

Physiological needs

the need for self-esteem, and the need for self-actualization. Maslow's conceptualization of needs is usually represented by a triangle with the five levels of needs arranged in a **hierarchy of needs** (see Figure 9.2). According to Maslow, any person's behavior can be understood primarily as the effort directed to satisfy a particular level of need in the hierarchy. Which level happens to be motivating a person's behavior at any time depends on whether lower needs in the hierarchy have been satisfied. According to Maslow, lower-level needs must be satisfied before the next-higher level becomes salient in motivating behavior.

Maslow believed higher-level needs like those for self-esteem or self-actualization would not become salient (even when unfulfilled) until lower needs were satisfied. Thus a practical implication of his theory is that leaders can motivate follower behavior only by taking account of a follower's or team's position on the needs hierarchy. Applying Maslow's hierarchy to Julie, it might be inefficient to try to motivate our ski lift operator by appealing to how much pride she could take in a job well done (that is, to her self-esteem) if she was underdressed for weather conditions. If her boss wanted Julie to do more, she should first make sure that Julie's physiological needs were met, that she worked and lived in a secure place, and that she had ample opportunities to socialize with other employees. Only after these lower needs had been met should the boss try to increase Julie's self-esteem. Thus if leadership practitioners want to use Maslow's hierarchy of needs to motivate employees to work harder, they need to determine where their followers are on the needs hierarchy and ensure that all lower-order needs are satisfied before appealing to their followers' self-esteem or self-actualization needs. Leadership practitioners should watch for mismatches between their motivational efforts and followers' *lowest* (on the hierarchy) unsatisfied needs.

How could you determine the needs of flight attendants, and what kind of program would you implement to improve customer service? Although Maslow's theory provides some useful ideas on how to improve customer service, it has several limitations. For one thing, the theory does not make specific predictions about what an individual will do to satisfy a particular need.[21,52] For example, if Ling Ling was trying to get her belongingness needs met, she might exert considerable effort to establish new friendships at work, try to make friends outside work, or join several professional or business associations. This lack of specificity and predictive power limits the practical applicability of Maslow's theory in real-life settings. On the other hand, awareness of the general nature of the various sorts of basic human needs described in this theory seems fundamentally useful to leaders. Leaders will have a difficult time getting followers to maintain various work behaviors by emphasizing good relationships with co-workers or appealing to their sense of pride if the job pays only minimum wage and followers are having a difficult time making ends meet. A person may be reluctant to volunteer for a self-actualizing opportunity in support of a political campaign if such participation may risk that person's financial security. Perhaps the greatest insight provided by this theory is that leadership practitioners may need to address some basic, fundamental areas before their attempts to get followers and teams to expend more effort on work-related behaviors will be successful.

Along these lines, it may be interesting to look at how Maslow's hierarchy of needs could be applied to U.S. and European workers over the past 10 years. One could argue that during the economic growth years many workers were putting in long hours but operating at the esteem and self-actualization levels. However, during the U.S. and European recessions those who remained employed switched their focus to meeting their security needs. These individuals were working longer hours than ever before, but this was to ensure they had a job versus making a meaningful contribution or being fulfilled. And many of those who were not gainfully employed may have spent much of their time just trying to get food on the table (physiological needs). As the economy in these two regions recovers, it will be interesting to see if leaders will be able to convince followers that their lower-level needs will be met and get them to shift their focus to self-esteem and self-actualization needs.

> *Some players you pat their butts, other players you kick their butts, and some players you leave alone.*
>
> **Pete Rose**

> *The best job goes to the person who can get it done without passing the buck or coming back with excuses.*
>
> **Napoleon Hill, author**

Achievement Orientation: How Does Personality Affect Motivation?

Is it possible that some people are naturally more motivated or have "more fire in the belly" than others? Do some people automatically put forth a higher level of effort toward group goals simply because they are hardwired this way? Unlike Maslow's theory, which claims all people share some fundamental needs, this approach to motivation is simple. To improve group performance, leaders should select only followers who

Employability: Finding and Keeping a Job

HIGHLIGHT 9.3

Employability can be defined as the ability to gain and keep a job, and with high unemployment rates in the United States and Europe this has become an important political topic. Youth unemployment rates in some European countries exceed 25 percent, and 40 percent of the unemployed in the United States have not had jobs in over two years. Situational, follower, and leader factors all play a role in who gets hired, can keep a job, or get fired, and it is worth describing these factors in more detail.

Clearly situational factors play a pervasive role in employability. When the economy is booming jobs are plentiful, but they are few and far between during recessions. Even during growing economies some may lose their jobs because of mergers, restructurings, or bankruptcies. Although economic conditions determine how many jobs are available, follower and leader factors play important roles in who fills these positions. Research shows that leaders are looking for followers who can get the job done (they have relevant experience, often gained through internships, or enough IQ to get up to speed quickly on the position) and possess good interpersonal skills. Intelligence alone is not enough, as height and personal appearance have been found to have just as much bearing on hiring decisions as GPA. Primping and preening apparently have as much impact as studying hard when it comes to many leaders' hiring decisions.

Leader biases also come into play when evaluating the performance of followers after they get hired. It turns out that office politics can play a bigger role in performance evaluations than objective performance results. Research has shown that performance review ratings for salespeople can be more highly correlated with completing paperwork and other administrative tasks than the dollar amounts actually sold. With many jobs lacking more objective performance measures, leader bias may play a pervasive role in performance review ratings. Those who get along with others, do not make any enemies, and flatter their bosses may rise higher in organizations than those who produce actual results.

What role do you think leader biases play in determining who gets hired or promoted into state or federal government, military, human resources, or IT positions? Has bias or favoritism played a role in your being selected for an activity or athletic team? Did this bias work for or against you? What is more important for career success: intelligence, experience, personality, motivation, or appearance?

Sources: R. Hogan, T. Chamorro-Premuzic, and R. B. Kaiser, "Employability and Career Success: Bridging the Gap between Theory and Reality," *Industrial and Organizational Psychology: Perspectives on Science and Practice* 1, no. 6 (2013), pp. 3–16; R. Hogan, "High Potentials Who Fail," in *Who Can Get and Keep a Job? Understanding Employability*, R. Hogan (chair). Symposium presented at the 26th Annual Conference of the Society of Industrial and Organizational Psychology, Chicago, IL, 2011. T. Chamorro-Premuzic, "Hidden Genius, Wasted Talent: Intelligence, Entrepreneurship, and Unemployability," in *Who Can Get and Keep a Job? Understanding Employability*, R. Hogan (chair). Symposium presented at the 26th Annual Conference of the Society of Industrial and Organizational Psychology, Chicago, IL, 2011. G. Curphy, "What We Know about Employability, "in *Who Can Get and Keep a Job? Understanding Employability*, R. Hogan (chair). Symposium presented at the 26th Annual Conference of the Society of Industrial and Organizational Psychology, Chicago, IL, 2011. L. Kwoh, "'Rank and Yank' Retains Loyal Fans," *The Wall Street Journal*, January 31, 2012, p. B6.

both possess the right skills and have a higher level of a personality trait called achievement orientation. (See Highlight 9.3.)

Atkinson has proposed that an individual's tendency to exert effort toward task accomplishment depends partly on the strength of his or her motivation to achieve success, or as Atkinson called it, **achievement orientation**.[21,53] McClelland further developed Atkinson's ideas and said that individuals with a strong achievement orientation (or in McClelland's terms, a strong *need for achievement*) strive to accomplish socially acceptable endeavors and activities. These individuals also prefer tasks that provide immediate and ample feedback and are moderately difficult (that is, tasks that require a considerable amount of effort but are accomplishable). Additionally, individuals with a strong need to achieve feel satisfied when they successfully solve work problems or accomplish job tasks. Individuals with a relatively low need to achieve generally prefer easier tasks and do not feel satisfied by solving problems or accomplishing assigned tasks. McClelland maintained that differences in achievement orientation are a primary reason why people differ in the levels of effort they exert to accomplish assignments, objectives, or goals. Thus achievement orientation is a bit like "fire in the belly"; people with more achievement orientation are likely to set higher personal and work goals and are more likely to expend the effort needed to accomplish them. People with low levels of achievement motivation tend to set lower personal and work goals and are less likely to accomplish them.[54]

Achievement orientation is also a component of the Five Factor Model or OCEAN model of personality dimension of conscientiousness (see Chapter 6). Conscientiousness has been found to be positively related to performance across virtually all jobs as well as predict success in school, in the military, in blue-collar and retail workers, and in management positions. All things being equal, people with higher levels of achievement orientation are likely to do better in school, pursue postgraduate degrees, get promoted more quickly, and get paid higher salaries and bonuses than their lower-scoring counterparts.[46,55-64]

Given that individuals with higher achievement orientation scores set high personal goals and put in the time and effort necessary to achieve them, it is hardly surprising that achievement orientation is often a key success factor for people who advance to the highest levels of the organization. For example, achievement orientation appears to be a common success factor underlying the careers of Ping Fu, Mark Roellig, James Mwangi, and Richard Branson (Profiles in Leadership 9.1 to 9.4, respectively). Although achievement orientation is often associated with higher performance, high achievers can become demoralized when facing unclear or impossible tasks. Working with elite Army Ranger units, Britt found that these units almost always performed at high levels and were often successful. But when given unclear missions with few resources and impossible timelines, these same units could self-destruct quickly. In these situations the units felt they were being set up to fail, and fail they did. This phenomenon is clearly depicted in the movie *Black Hawk Down*, where Army Ranger units were sent to Mogadishu, Somalia, to capture a Somalian warlord. The important lesson here is that leaders need to give high achievers clear goals and the resources they need to succeed.[65] (See Highlight 9.4.)

What Really Motivates Workers?

HIGHLIGHT 9.4

Which of the following items do you think best motivates workers?

A. Recognition

B. Incentives

C. Interpersonal support

D. Support for making progress

E. Clear goals

If you are like 600 managers who were asked this question in 2010, you would choose A. Recognition for good work. However, if we look over daily diaries of hundreds of employees over a multiyear period, the answer seems to be D. Support for making progress. Employees reported striving to do their best and having the strongest positive emotions on days when they felt they were making headway in their work assignments or got support to overcome obstacles. Emotions and drive were lowest on those days when they felt they were spinning their wheels

or encountered roadblocks. These research results indicate that leaders can best motivate followers and teams by providing meaningful goals, resources, and encouragement; being decisive; and minimizing irrelevant demands. Leaders can also help motivate followers by rolling up their sleeves and pitching in and not exerting time pressure so intense that even minor glitches are perceived as major crises.

The good news is that many of the things leaders can to do motivate followers are under their direct control. It is also worth noting that this research reported that recognition helps to improve motivation, but only if people feel they are making progress toward individual or team goals. How does making progress toward goals relate to Maslow's hierarchy of needs or to people with low or high levels of achievement orientation?

Source: T. M. Amabile and S. J. Kramer, "What Really Motivates Workers?" *Harvard Business Review*, January–February 2010, pp. 44–45.

How could a leader apply this knowledge of achievement orientation to improve the performance of Julie, Ling Ling, and the flight attendants? Perhaps the first step would be to ensure that the hiring process selected individuals with higher levels of achievement orientation. Assuming they had higher scores, we would expect Ling Ling to work with her boss to set aggressive goals for renting apartments and then work as many nights and weekends as were needed to achieve them. We might also expect Ling Ling to obtain her MBA from Hong Kong University over the next few years. Julie could also be expected to set high personal and work goals, but she may find that her job limits her ability to pursue these goals. Unlike Ling Ling, who can control the number of nights and weekends she works, Julie has no control over the number of people who ride on her lift. The job itself may limit Julie's ability to fulfill her high level of achievement orientation. As a result, she may pursue other activities, such as becoming an expert skier, joining the ski patrol, doing ski racing, looking for additional responsibilities or opportunities for advancement, or finding another job where she has the opportunity to achieve and get rewarded for her efforts. Because Julie would set and work toward high personal goals, a good boss would work closely with Julie to find work-related ways to capitalize on her achievement orientation. Thus achievement

Capacity is its own motivation.

David Campbell, Center for Creative Leadership

A good goal is like strenuous exercise—it makes you stretch.

Mary Kay Ashe, CEO

orientation may be a dual-edged sword. Leadership practitioners may be able to hire a group of highly motivated followers, but they also need to set clear expectations, provide opportunities for followers to set and achieve work-related goals, and provide feedback on progress toward goals. Otherwise followers may find different ways to fulfill their high levels of achievement orientation.

Applying the achievement orientation approach to the flight attendant situation or to U.S. workers from 2002 to 2009 leads to some interesting thoughts. Perhaps the airline did not screen for conscientiousness when hiring flight attendants and does not have enough people with high scores to deliver good customer service. Or the company could have hired only people with high conscientiousness scores but not set any measurable goals, repeatedly ignored requests for better equipment, failed to back up staff when they were challenged by "bad" travelers, or not given any recognition for jobs well done. In this case the flight attendants could feel that they have been set up for failure. With respect to people working in the United States from 2002 to 2009, those with the highest levels of achievement orientation were most likely to get promoted during the economic boom and stay with their companies during the recession. However, because many companies went under or eliminated entire work units or functions, some achievement-oriented types found themselves out of jobs. Because work is so important to people with high levels of achievement orientation, some of these individuals probably found work elsewhere. Others may have been devastated by their job loss and remain bitter about being set up for failure.

Goal Setting: How Do Clear Performance Targets Affect Motivation?

One of the most familiar and easiest formal systems of motivation to use with followers is **goal setting.** From the leader's perspective, this involves setting clear performance targets and then helping followers create systematic plans to achieve them. According to Locke and Latham, goals are the most powerful determinants of task behaviors. Goals direct attention, mobilize effort, help people develop strategies for achievement, and help people continue exerting effort until the goals are reached. This leads, in turn, to even higher goals.[66–69]

Goal-setting theory has been rated #1 in importance among 73 management theories by organizational behavior scholars.

Ed Locke, University of Maryland

Locke and Latham reported that nearly 400 studies involving hundreds of tasks across 40,000 individuals, groups, and organizations in eight different countries have provided consistent support for several aspects of goal setting. First, this research showed goals that were both *specific* and *difficult* resulted in consistently higher effort and performance when contrasted to "do your best" goals. Second, *goal commitment* is critical. Merely having goals is not enough. Although follower participation in setting goals is one way to increase commitment, goals set either by leaders unilaterally or through participation with followers can lead to necessary levels of commitment. Commitment to assigned goals was often as high

Mark Roellig

PROFILES IN LEADERSHIP 9.2

Mark Roellig is currently the executive vice president and general counsel of MassMutual Financial Group. Growing up in Michigan, Mark attended the University of Michigan to obtain an undergraduate degree in mathematics in three years. He went on to earn his law degree at George Washington University and an MBA degree from the University of Washington. Mark started his professional career as an attorney practicing civil litigation at two law firms in Seattle before joining Pacific Northwestern Bell Telephone Company in 1983. He spent the next 17 years working in the law division of the company as it transformed from Pacific Northwestern Bell to US West to Qwest Communications. During this time Mark rapidly moved through the ranks and eventually became the executive vice president of public policy, human resources, and law for US West. In this role Mark managed a group of over 1,000 employees and an annual budget of $250,000,000.

After US West was acquired by Qwest, Mark spent some time as the general counsel for Storage Technology Corporation and Fisher Scientific International before moving into his current role in 2005. MassMutual Financial Group is a financial services company that has over $450,000,000,000 in assets under management and is ranked as a *Fortune* 100 firm. Mark is currently responsible for the law, public policy, and corporate services divisions and manages a team of 500 employees and a $160,000,000 annual budget. Having been the top lawyer and board secretary for four *Fortune* 500 companies, Mark has learned a number of valuable lessons about leadership and management over the years. Some of these key lessons include developing strategic plans that support and advance the

business objectives, surrounding oneself with top talent, setting clear goals to support plans, using metrics to track progress, rewarding top performers, building teams, and creating performance-based cultures. Some of Mark's accomplishments since joining MassMutual include the following:

- A 57 percent reduction in outside counsel costs.
- A 27 percent reduction in total legal costs.
- An 18 percent reduction in dispute resolution costs.
- A 15 percent increase in customer satisfaction ratings.
- Consistently receiving some of the best employee satisfaction scores across the company.

Mark obsesses over talent and spends a considerable amount of time hiring top lawyers and then putting them in various training programs and rotational assignments to help them develop needed legal and leadership skills. Over the years a number of his direct reports have gone on to be general counsels or top lawyers in a number of other firms, and because of his unique combination of skills Mark is constantly asked to lead projects and functions outside the legal area, as well as provide advice on complex business, public policy, board of director, and personnel issues.

How would you use Maslow's hierarchy of needs, achievement orientation, goal setting, and the operant approach to describe Mark Roellig's career? Which motivational approaches best describe his leadership philosophy?

Sources: http://boston.citybizlist.com/lstg/lstgDetail .aspx?id-4030; M. Roellig, *Summary of 2009 Law Division Activities*, presentation given to the MassMutual Audit Committee on April 13, 2010, in Springfield, MA.

as commitment to goals followers helped to set, provided the leader was perceived to have legitimate authority, expressed confidence in followers, and provided clear standards for performance. Third, followers exerted the greatest effort when goals were accompanied by *feedback*; followers getting goals or feedback alone generally exerted less effort. (See Highlight 9.5 for a practical application of goal-setting theory.)

The Balanced Scorecard

HIGHLIGHT 9.5

A practical method for implementing goal setting in organizations involves the creation of balanced scorecards. Kaplan and Norton argue that most of the measures typically used to assess organizational performance are too limited in scope. For example, many organizations set goals and periodically review their financial performance, but these indicators suffer from time lags (it may take a month or longer before the financial results of specific organizational activities are available) and say little about other key organizational performance indicators, such as customer satisfaction, employee turnover, and operational performance. To get around these problems, Kaplan and Norton advocate creating a set of goals and metrics for customers, employees, internal operations, and finance. Customer and employee goals and metrics make up leading indicators because problems with customer satisfaction and employee turnover often result in subpar operational and financial performance.

Curphy has developed balanced scorecards for rural Minnesota hospitals and school districts. For example, hospitals begin this process with a comprehensive review of their market demographics, customer trends, financial performance, internal operations (pharmacy, surgical use, infection rates, radiology and lab use, and so on), and staffing and facility data. Key community and health care leaders then create a new five-year vision for the hospital and set strategic priorities in the customer, financial, internal operations, and workforce and facilities categories. These priorities are refined further to create clear, measurable goals with readily available metrics to track monthly progress. These balanced scorecard goals are used to drive specific department goals and track hospital performance and have been very effective in helping all hospital employees understand how their efforts contribute to the hospital's overall performance. In several cases hospital performance has dramatically improved as a result of these balanced scorecard efforts. A partial example of a typical balanced scorecard for one of these rural hospitals is as follows:

- **Customer:** Improve patient satisfaction ratings from 74 to 86 percent by 1 January 2015.
- **Customer:** Increase the number of live births from 12 to 20 per month by 1 January 2015.
- **Financial:** Reduce average accounts payable from 84 to 53 days by 1 January 2015.
- **Financial:** Increase operating margins from 2 to 6 percent by 1 January 2015.
- **Internal operations:** Increase orthopedic surgeries from 4 to 8 per day by 1 March 2015.
- **Internal operations:** Reduce patient infection rates from 1 to .5 percent by 1 March 2015.
- **Workforce:** Reduce days needed to hire nurses from 62 to 22 days by 1 March 2015.
- **Workforce:** Reduce employee turnover rates from 27 to 12 percent by 1 March 2015.

A monthly balanced scorecard report is included in all employee pay statements and is a key topic of discussion in hospital and department staff meetings. Staff members review goal progress and regularly devise strategies for achieving department and hospital goals. A nice thing about the balanced scorecard is that it helps employees be proactive and gives them permission to win. In too many organizations employees work hard but never see how their results contribute to team or organizational performance. Adopting balanced scorecards is a way to get around these problems.

Sources: G. J. Curphy, *The Blandin Education Leadership Program* (Grand Rapids, MN: The Blandin Foundation, 2004); R. S. Kaplan and D. P. Norton, "The Balanced Scorecard: Measures That Drive Performance," *Harvard Business Review,* January–February 1992, pp. 71–79; R. S. Kaplan and D. P. Norton, *The Balanced Scorecard* (Boston, MA: Harvard Business School Press, 1996); R. S. Kaplan and D. P. Norton, *The Strategy Focused Organization* (Boston, MA: Harvard Business School Press, 2001); G. Curphy and R Hogan, *The Rocket Model: Practical Advice for Building High Performing Teams* (Tulsa, OK: Hogan Press, 2012).

Several other aspects of goal setting are also worth noting. First, goals can be set for any aspect of performance, be it reducing costs, improving the quality of services and products, increasing voter registration, or winning a league championship. Nevertheless, leaders need to ensure that they do not set conflicting goals because followers can exert only so much effort over a given time.[70] Second, determining just how challenging to make goals creates a bit of a dilemma for leaders. Successfully completed goals give followers a sense of job satisfaction, and easy goals are more likely to be completed than difficult goals. However, easily attainable goals result in lower levels of effort (and performance) than do more difficult goals. Research suggests that leaders might motivate followers most effectively by setting moderately difficult goals, recognizing partial goal accomplishment, and making use of a continuous improvement philosophy by making goals incrementally more difficult.[71–76]

A leader's implicit and explicit expectations about goal accomplishment can also affect the performance of followers and teams. Research by Dov Eden and his associates in Israel has provided consistent support for the Pygmalion and Golem effects.[77,78] The **Pygmalion effect** occurs when leaders articulate high expectations for followers; in many cases these expectations alone will lead to higher-performing followers and teams. Unfortunately the **Golem effect** is also true—leaders who have little faith in their followers' ability to accomplish a goal are rarely disappointed. Thus a leader's expectations for a follower or team have a good chance of becoming a self-fulfilling prophecy (Chapter 2). These results indicate that leaders wanting to improve individual or team performance should set high but achievable goals and express confidence and support that the followers can get the job done.[79,80]

How could leadership practitioners apply goal setting to Julie and Ling Ling to increase their motivation levels? Given the research findings just described, Julie and Ling Ling's bosses should work with these two followers to set specific and moderately difficult goals, express confidence that they can achieve their goals, and provide regular feedback on goal progress. Julie and her boss could look at Julie's past performance or other lift operators' performance as a baseline, and then set specific and measurable goals for the number of hours worked, the number of people who fall off the lift during a shift, customer satisfaction survey ratings from skiers, the length of lift lines, or the number of complaints from customers. Similarly, Ling Ling and her boss could look at some real estate baseline measures and set goals for the number of apartments rented for the year, the total monetary value of these rentals, the time it takes to close a lease and complete the necessary paperwork, customer complaints, and sales expenses. Note that both Ling Ling and Julie's bosses would need to take care that they do not set conflicting goals. For example, if Julie had a goal only for the number of people who fell off the lift, she might be likely to run the lift slowly, resulting in long lift lines and numerous customer

Well-defined goals help organizations avoid the "crisis du jour" mode of operating and give them permission to celebrate success.

**Bill Mease,
consultant**

In the absence of clearly defined goals we become strangely loyal to performing daily trivia until we ultimately become enslaved by it.

**Robert Heinlein,
author**

350   Part Three   *Focus on the Followers*

*If you can't measure it,
then you can't manage
it.*

**Peter Drucker,
leadership
researcher**

*You get what you
reinforce, but you do not
necessarily get what you
pay for.*

**Fred Luthans,
University of
Nebraska, and
Alexander
Stajkovic,
University of
California, Irvine**

complaints. In a similar vein, bosses need to ensure that individual goals do not conflict with team or organizational goals. Ling Ling's boss would need to make sure that Ling Ling's goals did not interfere with those of the other real estate agents in the firm. If Ling Ling's goals did not specify territorial limits, she might rent properties in other agents' territories, which might cause a high level of interoffice conflict. Both bosses should also take care to set measurable goals; that way they could give Julie and Ling Ling the feedback they need to stay on track.

Goal setting could also help the airline company motivate flight attendants to provide better service to customers. Airline executives may believe customer satisfaction is critically important for keeping planes full, but they may not have set a specific goal for or devised a good way to measure customer satisfaction on individual flights. Customer service may improve only when the airline sets a clear customer satisfaction goal, makes feedback against the goal readily available, and holds flight attendants accountable for improved customer satisfaction results. Likewise, goal setting was also very prevalent for U.S. workers from 2002 to 2010. The first five years of this period saw a steady increase in market share, revenues, new product, profitability, and similar goals set each year, but the economic recession resulted in most if not all corporate goals being scaled back to where they were five years earlier. For example, a company with a $500,000,000 revenue goal in 2003 and steady growth may have had a $700,000,000 revenue goal by 2007. With the recession this revenue goal may have been scaled back to $500,000,000 in 2008. Although many key organizational goals were scaled back during the 2008 to 2010 recession, most leaders had significantly fewer people to get the goals accomplished. In many cases those who remained found that they needed to get much more work done with many fewer people. Those who were laid off often set goals for finding new jobs and the activities they would engage in to make this happen. Because goal setting is such a widely used and powerful motivational technique, more about this topic can be found in Chapter 11.

The Operant Approach: How Do Rewards and Punishment Affect Motivation?

One popular way to change the direction, intensity, or persistence of behavior is through rewards and punishments. It will help at the outset of this discussion of the **operant approach** to define several terms. A **reward** is any consequence that *increases* the likelihood that a particular behavior will be repeated. For example, if Julie gets a cash award for a suggestion to improve customer service at the ski resort, she will be more likely to forward additional suggestions. **Punishment** is the administration of an aversive stimulus or the withdrawal of something desirable, each of which *decreases* the likelihood that a particular behavior will be repeated.[81] Thus if Ling Ling loses her bonus for not getting her paperwork in on time, she will be less likely to do so again in the future. Both rewards and punishments

James Mwangi

PROFILES IN LEADERSHIP 9.3

One of the factors limiting economic growth in Africa is poor infrastructure. Much of Africa lacks the roads, train lines, electrical grids, and Internet access needed to move goods and services from place to place. One of these infrastructure limitations is banking. Many African nations operate on a cash basis and do not have the financial service systems needed to make deposits, transfer money, or take out loans.

In 1994 the Equity Building Society, a bank in rural Kenya that provided financial services to the poor, was on the verge of bankruptcy. Bad management, an economic downturn, and a number of bad loans had brought the bank to the brink of failure. The Board of Directors turned to James Mwangi for help, and he started the bank's transformation by converting loan owners to shareholders. This gave those holding loans an equity stake in the bank's future, and the number of bad loans eventually shrank to less than 1.5 percent of the total shillings loaned. Mwangi also changed the focus of the bank from providing home mortgages to issuing microloans to poor farmers and shopkeepers. Farmers could take out loans as small as 500 shillings (about $9.00) and use this money for seed, fertilizer, tools, and cell phones. Under Mwangi's leadership the Equity Building Society returned to solvency and expanded across Kenya. In 2000 the bank reported a net profit of 33.6 million shillings that had grown to over 12 billion shillings by the end of 2012.

Do you think Maslow's hierarchy of needs, achievement orientation, goal setting, the operant approach, or empowerment best explain the success of the Equity Building Society?

Source: "Kenya's Biggest Bank: The Cult of Equity," *The Economist*, December 8, 2012, p. 76.

can be administered in a contingent or noncontingent manner. **Contingent** rewards or punishments are administered as *consequences of a particular behavior*. Examples might include giving Julie a medal immediately after she wins a skiing race or giving Ling Ling a bonus check for exceeding her sales quota. **Noncontingent** rewards and punishments are not associated with particular behaviors. Monthly paychecks might be examples if both Julie and Ling Ling receive the same amount of base pay every month whatever their actual effort or output. Finally, behaviors that are not rewarded may eventually be eliminated through the process of **extinction.**

When properly implemented, there is ample evidence to show that the operant approach can be an effective way to improve follower motivation and performance.[82–90] Some of this research has also shown that rewards work better than punishments, particularly if administered in a contingent manner.[83,85,88,91–94] When comparing the relative impact of different types of rewards, Stajkovic and Luthans reported that incentive pay targeted at specific follower behaviors was the most effective, followed by social recognition and performance feedback, for improving follower performance in credit card processing centers.[85] Although some may argue otherwise, the research clearly shows that leaders who properly design and implement contingent reward systems do indeed increase follower productivity and performance. See Highlight 9.6 for more information about incentive systems.

Professional Athlete and Executive Salary Demands

HIGHLIGHT 9.6

General managers are responsible for the overall performance of their professional sports teams. They help select players and coaches; negotiate media, player, coach, and stadium contracts; keep team morale at a high level; and take action to ensure the team wins the championship and makes money. One of the most difficult issues general managers deal with is negotiating contracts with players. Players look at their own pay and performance and compare them to those of other athletes in the league. If they feel their compensation is not consistent with that of other players, they usually ask to be traded or for a new contract to be negotiated. These comparisons have led to the $100 million–plus salaries now commanded by star players in basketball, football, and baseball. But what happens to team morale, the win–loss record, and financial performance when one or two players make substantially more money than the rest of the team? Research on professional baseball teams over an eight-year period indicated that teams with high pay dispersion levels (large gaps between the highest- and lowest-paid starting players) did less well financially and were less likely to win division championships. Researchers surmised that this drop in team performance was due to the high levels of pay dispersion, which eroded team performance and increased inequity for other players on the team. The trick for general managers seems to be to find enough financial rewards to induce higher levels of performance but not create inequity situations for the rest of the team.

The effects of pay inequity that are readily apparent with professional athletes' pay also hold true for top executives. Many boards of directors worry that if they do not pay their CEOs and top executives at least on par with those in other companies, they run the risk of executive turnover. But executives who negotiate large signing bonuses and big annual pay packages don't necessarily achieve better results than their lower-paid counterparts. Far too many executives tout the benefits of pay for performance but appear much more concerned with their own pay than their company's performance. For example, the compensation for the average United States worker rose at a 0.3 percent annual rate from 1980 to 2004, yet the average CEO's compensation grew at a rate of 8.5 percent annually. CEOs promised an average of 11.5 percent annual earnings growth over this period but actually only achieved 6 percent growth, which was slightly less than the annual percentage growth rate for the overall economy from 1980 to 2004. Despite the fact that the average CEO performed no better than the overall economy, in 1980 the average CEO made 42 times as much as the average worker, and by 2004 this had increased to 280 times the average worker's salary. The top executives in Japanese companies currently make 20 to 30 times more than the average employee, and one has to wonder if companies with high pay dispersions achieve the same suboptimal results as do professional athletic teams with high pay dispersions. With workers putting in longer hours for less pay and the people on top getting fat paychecks and bonuses irrespective of results, is it any wonder that workers are less satisfied and engaged?

Sources: M. Bloom, "The Performance Effects of Pay Dispersions on Individuals and Organizations," *Academy of Management Journal* 42, no. 1 (1999), pp. 25–40; J. Lublin, "Boards Tie CEO Pay More Tightly to Performance," *The Wall Street Journal,* February 21, 2006, pp. A1 and A14; L. A. Bebchuk and J. M. Fried, "Pay without Performance: Overview of the Issues," *The Academy of Management Perspectives* 20, no. 1 (2006), pp. 5–24; J. Bogle, "Reflections on CEO Compensation," *The Academy of Management Perspectives* 22, no. 2 (2008), pp. 21–25.

How can a leader design and implement an operant system for improving followers' motivation and performance levels? Using operant principles properly to improve followers' motivation and performance requires several steps. First, *leadership practitioners need to clearly specify what behaviors are important.* This means that Julie's and Ling Ling's leaders will need to specify what they want them to do, how often they should do it, and the level of performance required. Second, *leadership practitioners need to determine if those behaviors are currently being punished, rewarded, or ignored.* Believe it or not, sometimes followers are actually rewarded for behaviors that leaders are trying to extinguish, and punished for behaviors that leaders want to increase. For example, Julie may get considerable positive attention from peers by talking back to her leader or for violating the ski resort dress code. Similarly, Ling Ling may be overly competitive and get promoted ahead of her peers (such as by renting apartments in her peers' territories), even when her boss extols the need for cooperation and teamwork. And leaders sometimes just ignore the behaviors they would like to see strengthened. An example here would be if Julie's boss consistently failed to provide rewards when Julie worked hard to achieve impressive safety and customer service ratings (see Highlight 9.7).

Third, *leadership practitioners need to find out what followers actually find rewarding and punishing.* Leaders should *not* make the mistake of assuming that all followers will find the same things to be rewarding or punishing. One follower's punishment may be another follower's reward. For example, Ling Ling may dislike public attention and actually exert less effort after being publicly recognized, yet some of her peers may find public attention rewarding. Fourth, *leadership practitioners need to be wary of creating perceptions of inequity when administering individually tailored rewards.* A peer may feel that she got the same results as Ling Ling, yet she received a smaller bonus check for the quarter. Leaders can minimize inequities by being clear and consistent with rewards and punishments. Fifth, *leadership practitioners should not limit themselves to administering organizationally sanctioned rewards and punishments.* Often leaders are limited in the amount of money they can give followers for good performance. However, research has shown that social recognition and performance feedback significantly improved productivity in followers, and these rewards do not cost any money.[84,85] Using ingenuity, leaders can often come up with an array of potential rewards and punishments that are effective and inexpensive and do not violate organizational norms or policies. Julie might find driving the snow cat to be enjoyable, and her boss could use this reward to maintain or increase Julie's motivation levels for operating the ski lift. Finally, because the administration of noncontingent consequences has relatively little impact, *leadership practitioners should administer rewards and punishments in a contingent manner whenever possible.* Highlight 9.7 provides examples of the unintended consequences of implementing an operant approach to boost organizational performance.

How am I supposed to feed my family on only $14 million a year?

Latrell Sprewell, professional basketball player

The Folly of Rewarding A While Hoping for B

HIGHLIGHT 9.7

Steven Kerr has written a compelling article detailing how many of the reward systems found in government, sports, universities, businesses, medicine, and politics often compel people to act in a manner contrary to that intended. For example, voters want politicians to provide the specifics of their programs or platform, yet politicians often get punished for doing so. Some constituency is bound to be hurt or offended whenever the specifics of a program are revealed, which in turn will cost the politician votes. If a politician keeps overall goals vague, more voters are likely to agree with the politician and vote for him or her in the next election. Businesses, like universities and politicians, often use inappropriate reward systems. According to Kerr, the following are some of the more common management reward follies:

We hope for . . .	But we often reward . . .
Long-term growth	Quarterly earnings
Teamwork	Individual effort
Commitment to total quality	Shipping on schedule, even with defects
Reporting honest news	Reporting good news, whether it is true or not

Kerr states that managers who complain about unmotivated workers should consider the possibility that their current reward system is incongruent with the performance they desire. And nowhere is this lack of congruence between what companies want and what they reward more visible than with executive compensation. Boards often have to front millions of dollars to new CEOs to get them to join the company, and then often must provide stock options and other forms of compensation to retain these individuals even though they consistently fail to hit their numbers. Many corporations talk a good game when it comes to pay for performance, but their actions indicate they are more likely to reward tenure while hoping for improved performance.

Sources: S. Kerr, "On the Folly of Rewarding A, While Hoping for B," *Academy of Management Executive* 9, no. 1 (1995), pp. 7–14; S. Kerr, "Establishing Organizational Goals and Rewards," *Academy of Management Executive* 18, no. 4 (2004), pp. 122–23; S. D. Levitt and S. J. Dubner, *Freakonomics* (New York: HarperCollins Publishers, 2005); L. Bebchuck and J. Fried, *Pay without Performance* (Boston, MA: Harvard University Press, 2004); L. Bebchuck and J. Fried, "Pay without Performance: Overview of the Issues," *The Academy of Management Perspectives* 20, no. 1 (2006), pp. 5–24; P. Dvorak, "Limits on Executive Pay: Easy to Set, Hard to Keep," *The Wall Street Journal*, April 9, 2007, pp. B1 and B5; J. S. Lublin, "Boards Tie CEO Pay More Tightly to Performance," *The Wall Street Journal*, February 21, 2006, pp. A1 and A4.

The operant approach can also be used to improve customer service for flight attendants. Using the tenets described earlier, the airline would need to specify which customer satisfaction behaviors were important, determine if those behaviors were being reinforced or punished, determine what attendants found to be rewarding, and administer valued rewards whenever attendants demonstrated good customer service behaviors.

The operant approach to motivation was alive and well in the United States from 2002 to 2012 and continues to be a popular motivational technique in many companies today. Most organizations tout a "pay for performance" culture and pay bonuses or commissions for results obtained. This can most clearly be seen in sales positions, where salespeople are paid a percentage of the total dollars they sell. Needless to say, salespeople experienced a large drop in compensation when customers stopped buying products and services during the 2008 to 2010 recession, despite exhibiting all the behaviors needed to retain customers or get new business in the door. This example points out a shortcoming of the operant technique, which is that situational factors can overwhelm the effectiveness of a reward program. Sometimes people can get big bonuses or commissions without working hard because they are selling a hot product or the economy is experiencing a boom. Other times they may do all the right things but nobody wants to buy their products because of factors beyond their control (such as selling pickup trucks when gasoline is $4.00 per gallon). (See Highlight 9.8.)

The Culture of Praise

HIGHLIGHT 9.8

There is no doubt that the generation of people entering the workforce these days has had more positive reinforcement while growing up than any previous generation. As children these individuals got positive strokes in the form of rewards, ribbons, plaques, and certificates for just showing up to athletic events or school activities. For example, one of this book's authors went to a school assembly for one of his children and watched teachers pass out awards to all 300 students in the elementary school. Some of the awards were for student achievement or citizenship, but many were for "completing your homework for three days in a row" and "having a nice smile." Thirty years ago it was difficult to earn an athletic letter in one or two sports, but some of today's athletic jackets have 20 to 30 awards and letters. This culture of praise was intended to boost self-esteem and better prepare students for life after high school, but as described in Highlight 9.7, the use of unconditional praise has had some unintended implications that organizations must deal with.

One implication is that people now entering the workforce are much more likely to be self-centered, "narcissistic praise junkies" than the people they are working for. Because of the constant positive reinforcement they received when growing up, a much higher percentage of people

in this generation think they are special and should get rewarded for anything and everything they do. Organizations, recognizing this need in their youngest employees, are taking some extraordinary steps to boost the self-esteem of (and retain) these individuals. For example, Lands' End and Bank of America teach managers how to compliment employees using e-mail, prize packages, and public displays of appreciation. The Scooter Store has a "celebration assistant" whose job is to throw 25 pounds of confetti and pass out 100 to 500 helium balloons to employees each week. The Container Store estimates that one of its 4,000 employees is rewarded every 20 seconds.

But what is the impact of these praise and recognition programs? Company officials argue they would see high levels of turnover without these programs. But if this younger generation gets constant recognition just for meeting minimum standards, what happens when they get promoted into supervisory positions? The short-term consequence may be improved retention of young employees, but the long-term consequence may be leaders who are unable to deal with difficult business or personnel issues.

Source: J. Zaslow, "The Most Praised Generation Goes to Work," *The Wall Street Journal,* April 20, 2007, pp. W1 and W7.

Empowerment: How Does Decision-Making Latitude Affect Motivation?

Empowerment is the final approach to motivation that will be discussed in this chapter. In general, people seem to fall into one of two camps with respect to empowerment. Some people believe empowerment is about delegation and accountability; it is a top-down process in which senior leaders articulate a vision and specific goals and hold followers responsible for achieving them. Others believe empowerment is more of a bottom-up approach that focuses on intelligent risk taking, growth, change, trust, and ownership; followers act as entrepreneurs and owners who question rules and make intelligent decisions. Leaders tolerate mistakes and encourage cooperative behavior in this approach to empowerment.[95–99] Needless to say, these two conceptualizations of empowerment have very different implications for leaders and followers. And it is precisely this conceptual confusion that has caused empowerment programs to fail in many organizations.[95] Because of the conceptual confusion surrounding empowerment, companies such as Motorola will not use this term to describe programs that push decision making to lower organizational levels. These companies would rather coin their own terms to describe these programs, thus avoiding the confusion surrounding empowerment.

We define empowerment as having two key components. For leaders to truly empower employees, they must delegate leadership and decision making down to the lowest level possible. Employees are often the closest to the problem and have the most information, and as such can often make the best decisions. A classic example was the UPS employee who ordered an extra 737 aircraft to haul parcels that had been forgotten in the last-minute Christmas rush. This decision was clearly beyond the employee's level of authority, but UPS praised his initiative for seeing the problem and making the right decision. The second component of empowerment, and the one most often overlooked, is equipping followers with the resources, knowledge, and skills necessary to make good decisions. Often companies adopt an empowerment program and push decision making down to the employee level, but employees have no experience in creating business plans, submitting budgets, dealing with other departments within the company, or directly dealing with customers or vendors. Not surprisingly, ill-equipped employees can make poor, uninformed decisions, and managers in turn are likely to believe that empowerment was not all it was cracked up to be. The same happens with downsizing as employees are asked to take on additional responsibilities but are given little training or support. Such "forced" empowerment may lead to some short-term stock gains but tends to be disastrous in the long run. Thus empowerment has both delegation and developmental components; delegation without development is often perceived as abandonment, and development without delegation can often be

Hemmed in by rules and treated as unimportant, people get even.
Rosabeth Moss Kanter, Harvard University

perceived as micromanagement. Leaders wishing to empower followers must determine what followers are capable of doing, enhance and broaden these capabilities, and give followers commensurate increases in authority and accountability.

The psychological components of empowerment can be examined at both macro and micro levels. Three macro psychological components underlie empowerment: motivation, learning, and stress. As a concept, empowerment has been around since at least the 1920s, and the vast majority of companies that have implemented empowerment programs have done so to increase employee motivation and, in turn, productivity. As a motivational technique empowerment has a mixed record; often empowered workers are more productive than unempowered workers, but at times this may not be the case. When empowerment does not increase productivity, senior leaders may tend to see empowerment through rose-colored glasses. They hear about the benefits an empowerment program is having in another company but do not consider the time, effort, and changes needed to create a truly empowered workforce. Relatedly, many empowerment programs are poorly implemented—the program is announced with great fanfare, but little real guidance, training, or support is provided, and managers are quick to pull the plug on the program as soon as followers start making poor decisions. Adopting an effective empowerment program takes training, trust, and time; but companies most likely to implement an empowerment program (as a panacea for their poor financial situation) often lack these three attributes.[100,101] In addition, worker productivity and job dissatisfaction in the United States and Europe are at an all-time high. Many companies are dealing with high levels of employee burnout, and adding responsibilities to overfilled plates is likely to be counterproductive. As reported by Xie and Johns, some empowerment programs create positions that are just too big for a person to handle effectively, and job burnout is usually the result.[102]

Although the motivational benefits of empowerment are sometimes not realized, the learning and stress reduction benefits of empowerment are more clear-cut. Given that properly designed and implemented empowerment programs include a strong developmental component, a key benefit to these programs is that they help employees learn more about their jobs, company, and industry. These knowledge and skill gains increase the intellectual capital of the company and can be a competitive advantage in moving ahead. In addition to the learning benefits, well-designed empowerment programs can help reduce burnout. People can tolerate high levels of stress when they have a high level of control. Given that many employees are putting in longer hours than ever before and work demands are at an all-time high, empowerment can help followers gain some control over their lives and better cope with stress. Although an empowered worker may have the same high work demands as an unempowered worker, the

Power and Empowerment

HIGHLIGHT 9.9

A famous Lord Acton quote is "Power corrupts," which essentially means that the more power one has the more likely one is to break laws, rules, and societal norms. Leadership researcher Rosabeth Moss Kanter has an interesting variation of this quote that relates to the concept of empowerment. According to Kanter, powerlessness also corrupts. In other words, if workers are given only a small amount of power, they will jealously guard whatever power they have. Employees with little power do not show their unhappiness by voicing their opinions but instead flex their muscles by demanding tribute before responding to requests. They rigidly adhere to the policies governing their position and ensure there are no exceptions to anyone following their rules. Customers are told to submit all required forms, get signed permissions from other entities, and follow bureaucratic procedures to the letter if they want anything done, and it will take requesters months to see tangible results. Because speed is an essential component of execution, powerlessness can paralyze companies needing to quickly build products, process orders, submit invoices, receive payments, service customers, or hire and train new employees.

A good example of how powerlessness can impact a company's public reputation comes from the airline industry. One particular airline had a policy stating three bags could be checked for free but passengers would be charged $200 for each bag over the limit. A group of soldiers were flying home after a one-year deployment in Afghanistan and had checked four bags, which they were authorized to do according to their military orders. The gate agents insisted company policy took precedence over military orders and charged each of the soldiers $200 for the additional bags. Unable to get the issue resolved with the gate agents, two of the solders recorded the incident and posted the videos on YouTube, which soon went viral. The airline endured a major public relations fiasco before quickly apologizing and reimbursing the soldiers.

What motivational approaches would best describe the gate agents? In what ways could the airline industry empower gate agents to better service passengers?

Sources: R. Moss Kanter, "Powerlessness Corrupts," *Harvard Business Review*, July–August 2010, p. 36; http://www.businessweek.com/management/when-scorecards-and-metrics-kill-employee-engagement-07122011.html.

empowered worker will have more choices in how and when to accomplish these demands and as such will suffer from less stress. Giving workers more control over their work demands can reduce turnover and in turn improve the company's bottom line. (See Highlight 9.9.)

There are also four micro components of empowerment. These components can be used to determine whether employees are empowered or unempowered, and include self-determination, meaning, competence, and influence.[95,96,103] Empowered employees have a sense of self-determination; they can make choices about what they do, how they do it, and when they need to get it done. Empowered employees also have a strong sense of meaning; they believe what they do is important to them and to the company's success. Empowered employees have a high level of competence: they know what they are doing and are confident they can get the job done. Finally, empowered employees have an impact on others and believe that they can influence their teams or work units and that

FIGURE 9.3
The Empowerment Continuum

Empowered Employees ← —— → **Unempowered Employees**

- Self-determined.
- Sense of meaning.
- High competence.
- High influence.

- Other-determined.
- Not sure if what they do is important.
- Low competence.
- Low influence.

co-workers and leaders will listen to their ideas. In summary, empowered employees have latitude to make decisions, are comfortable making these decisions, believe what they do is important, and are seen as influential members of their team. Unempowered employees may have little latitude to make decisions, may feel ill equipped and may not want to make decisions, and may have little impact on their work unit, even if they have good ideas. Most employees probably fall somewhere between the two extremes of the empowerment continuum, depicted in Figure 9.3.

Empowerment and the operant approach make an important point that is often overlooked by other theories of motivation: by changing the situation, leaders can enhance followers' motivation, performance, and satisfaction. Unfortunately many leaders naively assume it is easier to change an *individual* than it is to change the *situation*, but this is often not the case. The situation is not always fixed, and followers are not the only variable in the performance equation. Leaders can often see positive changes in followers' motivation levels by restructuring work processes and procedures, which in turn can increase their latitude to make decisions and add more meaning to work. Tying these changes to a well-designed and well-implemented reward system can further increase motivation. However, leaders are likely to encounter some resistance whenever they change the processes, procedures, and rewards for work, even if these changes are for the better. Doing things the old way is relatively easy—followers know the expectations for performance and usually have developed the skills needed to achieve results. Followers often find that doing things a new way can be frustrating because expectations may be unclear and they may not have the requisite skills. Leaders can help followers work through this initial resistance to new processes and procedures by showing support, providing training and coaching on new skills, and capitalizing on opportunities to reward progress. If the processes, procedures, and rewards are properly designed and administered, then in many cases followers will successfully work through their resistance and, over time, wonder how they ever got work done using the old systems. The successful transition to new work processes and procedures will rest squarely on the shoulders of leaders. How could you use empowerment to improve the performance of Julie or Ling-Ling or the customer service levels of flight attendants? What information would you need to gather, how would you implement the program, and what would be the potential pitfalls of your program? And what do you think happened to empowerment as North American and European companies went through the economic recession of 2008 to 2012?

Motivation Summary

Some people believe it is virtually impossible to motivate anyone, and leaders can do little to influence people's decisions regarding the direction, intensity, and persistence of their behavior. Clearly there is a lot followers bring to the motivational equation, but we feel that a leader's actions can and do affect followers' motivation levels. If leaders did not affect followers' motivation levels, it would not matter whom one worked for—any results obtained would be solely due to followers' efforts. But as you will read in Chapter 15, whom one works for matters a lot. We hope that after reading this chapter you will have a better understanding of how follower characteristics (needs and achievement orientation), leader actions (goal setting), and situational factors (contingent rewards and empowerment) affect how you and your followers are motivated (and demotivated). Moreover, you should be able to start recognizing situations where some theories provide better insights about problems in motivation levels than others. For example, if we go back to the survival situation described in Chapter 1, we can see that Maslow's hierarchy of needs provides better explanations for the behavior of the survivors than empowerment or the operant approach. On the other hand, if we think about the reasons we might not be doing well in a particular class, we may see that we have not set specific goals for our grades or that the rewards for doing well are not clear. Or if we are working in a bureaucratic organization, we may see few consequences for either substandard or superior performance; thus there is little reason to exert extra effort. Perhaps the best strategy for leaders is to be flexible in the types of interventions they consider to affect follower motivation. That will require, of course, familiarity with the strengths and weaknesses of the different theories and approaches presented here.

Similarly, we need to consider how the five motivational approaches can be used with both individuals and teams. Much of this section focused on applying the five approaches to individuals, but the techniques can also be used to motivate teams of followers. For example, leaders can set team goals and provide team rewards for achieving them. Leaders can also hire team members who have high levels of achievement orientation and then provide everyone on the team with the decision-making latitude and skills needed to adequately perform their jobs. Leaders can also assess where their teams are currently at on the hierarchy of needs and take actions to ensure that lower-order needs are satisfied. Again, having a good understanding of the five motivational approaches will help leaders determine which ones will be most effective in getting teams to change behavior and exert extra energy and effort.

One of the most important tools for motivating followers has not been fully addressed in this chapter. As described in Chapter 14, charismatic or transformational leadership is often associated with extraordinarily high levels of follower motivation, yet none of the theories described in this chapter can adequately explain how these leaders get their followers to do more than they thought possible. Perhaps this is due to the fact that the theories in this chapter take a rational or logical approach to motivation, yet transformational leadership uses emotion as the fuel to drive followers' heightened motivational levels. Just as our needs, thoughts, personality traits, and rewards can motivate us to do something different, so can our emotions drive us to engage in and persist with particular activities. A good example here may be political campaigns. Do people volunteer to work for these campaigns because of some underlying need or personal goals, or because they feel they will be rewarded by helping out? Although these are potential reasons for some followers, the emotions generated by political campaigns, particularly where the two leading candidates represent different value systems, often seem to provide a better explanation for the large amount of time and effort people contribute. Leadership practitioners should not overlook the interplay between emotions and motivation, and the better able they are to address and capitalize on emotions when introducing change, the more successful they are likely to be.

A final point concerns the relationship between motivation and performance. Many leadership practitioners equate the two, but as we pointed out earlier in this chapter, they are not the same concepts. Getting followers to put in more time, energy, and effort on certain behaviors will not help the team to be more successful if they are the wrong behaviors to begin with. Similarly, followers may not know how and when to exhibit behaviors associated with performance. Leadership practitioners must clearly identify the behaviors related to performance, coach and train their followers in how and when to exhibit these behaviors, and then use one or more of the theories described in this chapter to get followers to exhibit and persist with the behaviors associated with higher performance levels.

Understanding and Influencing Follower Satisfaction

As stated earlier, job satisfaction concerns one's attitudes about work, and there are several practical reasons why job satisfaction is an important concept for leaders to think about. Research has shown that satisfied workers are more likely to continue working for an organization.[22,104–109] Satisfied workers are also more likely to engage in organizational citizenship behaviors that go beyond job descriptions and role requirements and help reduce the workload or stress of others in the organization. Dissatisfied workers are more likely to be adversarial in their relations with

TABLE 9.2   Why People Leave or Stay with Organizations

Why Do People Leave Organizations?	Why Do People Stay with Organizations?
Limited recognition and praise	Promises of long-term employment
Compensation	Exciting work and challenge
Limited authority	Fair pay
Poor organizational culture	Encourages fun, collegial relationships
Repetitive work	Supportive management

Sources: B. Kaye and S. Jordan-Evans, *Love 'Em or Lose 'Em: Getting Good People to Stay* (4th ed.) (San Francisco: Berrett-Koehler, 2008), www.sigmaassessmentsystems.com; Pace Communication, *Hemispheres Magazine*, November 1994, p. 155; "Keeping Workers Happy," *USA Today*, February 10, 1998, p. 1B.

Seventy to ninety percent of the decisions not to repeat purchases of anything are not about product or price. They are about dimensions of service.

**Barry Gibbons,
Burger King**

Too many highly trained, committed professionals return again and again to the methodology that employee engagement programs are what 'WE might do to make THEM feel invested in US.' They are an HR brand-loyalty marketing program, really.

**Mark Kille, human
resources
consultant**

leadership (filing grievances, for example) and engage in diverse counterproductive behaviors.[110–118] Dissatisfaction is a key reason why people leave organizations, and many of the reasons people are satisfied or dissatisfied with work are within the leader's control (see Table 9.2).[105–107,118]

Although the total costs of dissatisfaction are difficult to measure, the direct costs of replacing a first-line supervisor or an executive can range from $5,000 to $400,000 per hire, depending on recruiting, relocation, and training fees, and these costs do not include those associated with the productivity lost as a result of unfilled positions.[119] Other indirect costs include the loss of customers. A survey of major corporations showed that 49 percent switched to another vendor because of poor customer service.[120] Employees are probably not going to provide world-class service if they are unhappy with their job, boss, or company. The inability to retain customers directly affects revenues and makes investors think twice about buying stock in a company. Relatedly, Schellenbarger reported that 35 percent of investor decisions are driven by nonfinancial factors. Number 5 on a list of 39 factors investors weighed before buying stock was the company's ability to attract and retain talent. These findings imply that a company's stock price is driven not only by market share and profitability, but also by service and bench strength considerations. Thus employee satisfaction (or dissatisfaction) can have a major impact on the organization's bottom line.[121] (See Highlight 9.10.)

Of these outcomes, perhaps employee turnover has the most immediate impact on leadership practitioners. It would be hard for Julie's or Ling Ling's bosses to achieve results if, respectively, ski resort or real estate personnel were constantly having to be replaced and the leader was spending an inordinate amount of time recruiting, hiring, and training replacements. Although some level of **functional turnover** is healthy for an organization (some followers are retiring, did not fit into the organization, or were substandard performers), dysfunctional turnover is not. **Dysfunctional turnover** occurs when the "best and brightest" in an organization become dissatisfied and leave. Dysfunctional turnover is most likely to occur when downsizing is the response to organizational decline

Improving Safety on Offshore Oil Platforms

HIGHLIGHT 9.10

One of the most dangerous jobs in the world is that of an offshore oil rig employee. These employees often work 12- to 16-hour days for two- to four-week shifts operating heavy equipment in confined spaces. Not only is the work long and hard, but many employees face additional dangers from high seas, cold weather, icebergs, hurricanes, and well blowouts. Because of these conditions and the nature of work, many energy companies are concerned with safety. But what can well managers do to create safe oil platforms? It turns out that using a combination of several motivational techniques may be the best way to reduce oil platform accidents.

To reduce accidents, well managers must first set clear goals and performance expectations for safety. If employees believe only production is important to well managers, they will do what they think is right to boost productivity and will pay little attention to safety issues. So managers must set the tone for safety by setting safety goals and constantly reminding employees of safety issues. Second, they must hire employees who are motivated to perform safe work behaviors. Well managers should use personality inventories to hire employees with higher conscientiousness scores because they tend to be risk averse and much more rule abiding than those with lower conscientiousness scores. Third, well managers must ensure that their compensation systems recognize and reward safe behaviors. If the compensation system rewards only productivity, employees will do what they need to in order to maximize their rewards. The same is true if the compensation system rewards both productivity *and* safety. Using this three-pronged approach will not eliminate all oil rig accidents, but it will go a long way toward reducing accident rates.

It appears that BP did not use these proven techniques to improve safety at the Deepwater Horizon oil rig in the Gulf of Mexico. Much of the evidence to date shows that instead BP emphasized productivity and cost cutting. BP used a cheaper (and less safe) well head design, and there were questions whether the equipment used would operate safely at a depth of 5,000 feet. There were ample warnings that the cementing process used to prevent blowouts was not working, and the company did not have good backup plans to deal with blowouts and spills occurring at these depths. The end result was an explosion on the Deepwater Horizon oil rig that killed 11 people and the biggest oil spill in U.S. history. It will take years for the Gulf of Mexico to recover from this environmental disaster, and BP will spend over $23,000,000,000 to cover cleanup and compensation costs.

Unfortunately BP has had a long history of poor safety and environmental performance. In 2005, 15 people were killed and 170 injured in a massive explosion at its Texas City refinery; since then BP refineries have accounted for 760 "egregious, willful" safety violations. These violations are administered when companies demonstrate an intentional disregard of the law or show indifference to employee safety and health. For comparison, other U.S. energy firms had a total of 19 such violations over the same period. What would you do to create an environmentally aware and safety-friendly culture at BP?

Source: R. Gregory, R. T. Hogan, and G. J. Curphy, "Risk-Taking in the Energy Industry," *Well Connected* 5, no. 6 (June 2003), pp. 5–7; http://online.wsj.com/article/SB125991490059781 93.html; http://abcnews.go.com/WN/bps-dismal-safety-record/story?id=10763042; http://www.guardian.co.uk/environment/2010/jul/01/bp-deepwater-horizon-oil-spill.

(increased costs or decreased revenues, market share, or profitability). In these situations, dysfunctional turnover may have several devastating effects. First, those individuals in the best position to turn the company around are no longer there. Second, those who remain are even less capable of successfully dealing with the additional workload associated with the downsizings. Compounding this problem is that training budgets also tend to be slashed during downsizings. Third, organizations that downsize have a difficult time recruiting people with the skills needed to turn the company around. Competent candidates avoid applying for jobs within the organization because of uncertain job security, and the less competent managers remaining with the company may decide not to hire anyone who could potentially replace them. Because leaders can play an important role in followers' satisfaction levels, and because followers' satisfaction levels can have a substantial impact on various organizational outcomes, it is worth going into this topic in greater detail (see Highlight 9.11).[104,105,108,122–124]

Employee Motivation, Satisfaction, and Engagement

HIGHLIGHT 9.11

Engagement has been a hot topic over the past 10 years and many companies have spent millions implementing employee engagement programs. But what is employee engagement, is it different from employee motivation and satisfaction, how is it measured, does it matter, and can it be improved? It can be fairly difficult to answer these questions, as employee engagement is defined, measured, and implemented differently across organizations. Some of the common themes that run through the many definitions of engagement seem to be heightened employee emotional levels and more focused energy directed toward work activities. Engaged employees are believed to be more committed to team and company success, to put forth more effort, and to put in the hours necessary to get the job done; disengaged employees don't care about company success and are more interested in collecting paychecks than in completing assigned tasks. This definition of engagement—choosing to act, increased effort levels, and persistence through task completion—is not much different than the definition of motivation found at the beginning of this chapter.

Surveys are typically used to measure employee engagement levels. These surveys are administered every year or two to all the employees in an organization and the results are analyzed to determine what percentage of people are actively engaged, engaged, disengaged, or actively disengaged. Geographic regions, industry, economic conditions, job types, and engagement definitions all affect the percentage of employees falling into each of these four categories, and companies report that anywhere between 19 to 67 percent of their employees are actively engaged. For example, after 20 years of economic malaise some studies report that Japan has the lowest employee engagement in Asia; others state that engagement in Latin America is among the highest in the world but has dropped precipitously in North America and Europe in 2012. The use of common surveys has allowed companies to benchmark themselves over time, against their competitors, or with companies of similar sizes, in the same geographic regions, and the like.

One of the reasons that the study of employee engagement has become so popular over the last few years is the engagement–shareholder value chain, where it is believed that employee engagement drives higher customer service, customer loyalty, sales, profitability, and share price. Explained another way, companies with higher percentages of actively engaged and engaged employees should ultimately generate higher shareholder returns. Consulting firms that sell employee engagement surveys and improvement programs certainly believe this to be the case and offer statistical data to support the engagement–shareholder value chain, but the facts don't always line up with the marketing hype. It is generally true that companies with higher employee engagement report better business results, but it is uncertain from these findings whether engagement drives performance or performance drives engagement. It could be that employees working for companies with killer apps, great products, or superior business models are made to feel more engaged rather than employee engagement driving improved results. In addition, employee engagement surveys measure feelings and attitudes, whereas organizations are more interested in actions, behaviors, and productivity. The links between emotions and actions may not be direct, as many professional athletes may not have strong loyalties to their teams but perform at high levels, and employees may be emotionally invested in their jobs, but equipment limitations or family circumstances impact their ability to perform.

How people are managed can impact employee engagement levels, so many companies have adopted leadership development and employee engagement programs to improve employee engagement. Some of these programs seem to be based more on the opinions of self-help gurus rather than on solid research. For example, some engagement consultants advocate letting employees work from home, offering regular recognition, or taking employees out to dinner on a regular basis. Although there is nothing inherently wrong with doing any of these things, research shows that these programs can be detrimental to teamwork and employee engagement if employees spend limited time working together or if the leader is boring or incompetent. Best Buy and Yahoo! discontinued their work-at-home programs because managers thought these programs focused employees more on "me" than on "we."

But perhaps the biggest problem with many employee engagement programs is that they seem to be adult versions of the culture of praise described in Highlight 9.8 and they make leaders solely responsible for follower engagement levels. Situational factors are rarely acknowledged, yet the economy, failing businesses, and family circumstances can affect follower engagement. Follower factors also play a role, as employees can choose whether or not to engage. Some may be more motivated to collect paychecks or to make life miserable for others than to engage in work activities. Firing these individuals may be the best thing leaders can do to improve overall engagement levels, but this would be viewed as a setback or a failure of leadership by many engagement advocates.

Do you think employee engagement is important? Is it any different than motivation and satisfaction? What would you do as a leader if you wanted to improve the engagement levels of your followers?

Sources: K. B. Paul and C. L. Johnson, "Engagement at 3M: A Case Study," in *The Executive Guide to Integrated Talent Management,* eds. K. Oakes and P. Galagan (Alexandria, VA: American Society for Training and Development Press, 2011); M. Buckingham and C. Coffman, *First, Break All The Rules* (New York: Simon & Schuster, 1999); J. W. Carlson, "Worker Flexibility Gets a Time-Out," *The Minneapolis Star Tribune,* March 7, 2013, p. A11; Aon Hewitt, *Trends in Global Employee Engagement* (Chicago: Author, 2011); G. Curphy, "Followership: An Overlooked Component in Organizational Success," Presentation given at the ASTD-Lake Superior Chapter Monthly Conference, Duluth, MN, March, 2013; http://www.tlnt .com/2012/11/26/employee-engagement-heres-why-its-a-problem-worldwide/; http://www.forbes.com/sites/ kevinkruse/2012/06/22/employee-engagement-what-and-why/; http://www.bersin.com/blog/post/ TheBusinessOfTalent/; http://www.chartvcourse.com/ enav-172-html/; http://www.ere.net/2012/02/23/what's-wrong-with-employee-engagement-the-top-20-potential-problems/.

Global, Facet, and Life Satisfaction

There are different ways to look at a person's attitudes about work, but researchers usually collect these data using some type of job satisfaction survey.[107,122,123,125,126] Such surveys are usually sent to all employees, the responses are collected and tabulated, and the results are disseminated

TABLE 9.3
Typical Items on a Satisfaction Questionnaire

1. Overall, I am satisfied with my job.
2. I feel the workload is about equal for everyone in the organization.
3. My supervisor handles conflict well.
4. My pay and benefits are comparable to those in other organizations.
5. There is a real future for people in this organization if they apply themselves.
6. Exceptional performance is rewarded in this organization.
7. We have a good health care plan in this organization.
8. In general, I am satisfied with my life and where it is going.

These items are often rated on a scale ranging from *strongly disagree* (1) to *strongly agree* (5).

throughout the organization. Table 9.3 presents examples of three different types of items typically found on a job satisfaction survey. Item 1 is a **global satisfaction** item, which assesses the overall degree to which employees are satisfied with their organization and their job. Items 2 through 7 are **facet satisfaction** items, which assess the degree to which employees are satisfied with different aspects of work, such as pay, benefits, promotion policies, working hours and conditions, and the like. People may be relatively satisfied overall but still dissatisfied with certain aspects of work. For example, from 2001 to 2011 job security was a primary factor driving employee satisfaction, and the economic downturn in 2008 to 2010 only heightened this concern. A recent study by the Society of Human Resources Management indicated that the opportunity to use skills and abilities, compensation, job security, communication, and relationships with immediate supervisors were the biggest drivers of overall job satisfaction.[127] A study of junior officers in the U.S. Army revealed that overall satisfaction had been in decline and a higher percentage of officers were choosing to leave the army. The two primary reasons for this high level of dysfunctional turnover seemed to be dissatisfaction with immediate supervisors and top leadership. Many junior officers reported that they were tired of working for career-obsessed supervisors who had a strong tendency to micromanage and would just as soon throw them under a bus if it would advance their career.[128–130] This decline in global satisfaction is not limited to the U.S. Army: the same phenomenon is happening in many American and European companies today. Much of this decline can be attributed to higher follower expectations, greater follower access to information through technology, economic downturns, organizational downsizings, and incompetent bosses.

Leadership practitioners should be aware of several other important findings regarding global and facet satisfaction. The first finding is that people generally tend to be happy with their vocation or occupation. They may not like the pay, benefits, or their boss, but they seem to be satisfied with what they do for a living. The second finding pertains to the **hierarchy effect:** in general, people with longer tenure or in higher positions tend to have higher global and facet satisfaction ratings than those newer to or lower in the organization.[131] Because people higher in the organization are happier at work, they may not understand or appreciate why people at lower levels are less satisfied. From below, leaders at the top can appear naive and out of touch. From above, the complaints about morale, pay, or resources are often perceived as whining. One of this book's authors once worked with a utilities company that had downsized and was suffering from all the ill effects associated with high levels of dysfunctional turnover. Unfortunately the executive vice president responsible for attracting and retaining talent and making the company "an employer of choice" stated that he had no idea why employees were complaining and that things would be a lot better if they just quit whining. Because the executive did not understand or appreciate the sources of employee complaints, the programs to improve employee morale completely missed the mark, and the high levels of dysfunctional turnover continued. The hierarchy effect also implies that it will take a considerable amount of top leaders' focus and energy to increase the satisfaction levels of nonmanagement employees—lip service alone is never enough. See Highlight 9.12 for examples of companies who do not seem to take employee satisfaction very seriously.

Compensation is another facet of job satisfaction that can have important implications for leadership practitioners. As you might expect, the hierarchy effect can be seen in pay: a survey of 3 million employees reported that 71 percent of senior management, 58 percent of middle management, and only 46 percent of nonmanagers rate their pay as "very good." Of nonmanagers, 33 percent rate their pay as "so-so" and 20 percent rate their pay as "very poor."[132] Given the wage gap between males and females, a disproportionate number of females can probably be found in these less satisfied groups. Many of these females may be the highest performers in their positions; therefore, this wage discrepancy, in combination with relatively small annual pay increases over the past few years, may contribute to disproportionately high levels of dysfunctional turnover among females.

People who are happier with their jobs also tend to have higher life satisfaction ratings. **Life satisfaction** concerns one's attitudes about life in general, and Item 8 in Table 9.3 is an example of a typical life satisfaction question. Because leaders are often some of the most influential people in their followers' lives, they should never underestimate the impact they have on their followers' overall well-being.

Job satisfaction surveys are used extensively in both public and private institutions. Organizations using these instruments typically administer them every one or two years to assess workers' attitudes about different aspects of work, changes in policies or work procedures, or other initiatives. Such survey results are most useful when they can be compared with those from some **reference group.** The organization's past results can be used as one kind of reference group—are people's ratings of pay,

Would life on a slave ship be much better if the galley master first asked the rowers to help write a mission statement? What employers need to come to terms with is the economic, cultural, and societal benefits of being loyal to their employees. If they don't, eventually their abuses will bite them on the ass.

**Daniel Levine,
author**

Leaders are often the only people surprised by employee satisfaction results. In reality, employees have been talking about the issues identified in these surveys for quite some time.

**Dianne Nilsen,
business executive**

The Wall of Shame: The Ten Worst Companies to Work For in America

HIGHLIGHT 9.12

Most people want to work in companies where they feel valued, have good job security, and get paid a fair wage. Many organizations work hard to fulfill these needs and those that do are often seen as some of the best companies to work for in America. But other companies seem to treat employees as widgets in production lines and put little value on employee satisfaction or engagement. In the past it was hard to know how organizations treated their employees, but the advent of satisfaction and engagement surveys, the Internet, and social media has made this much easier. *Forbes* magazine publishes top companies to work for lists based on employee surveys, and the *Indeed*, *Glassdoor*, and *TheJobCrowd* websites allow current and former employees to provide anonymous ratings and comments about employers. There appears to be ample interest in getting unvarnished views of employers, as *Glassdoor* has 14 million registered users and indeed gets over 85 million visits a month.

Although the worst-companies-to-work-for list varies from year to year, it takes a considerable amount of time for a company to move from the bottom of the list. Put another way, the worst companies to work for have been that way for some time and will likely remain that way in the future. Although situational factors can affect employee ratings, more often than not top and middle management get all the credit for creating employee-unfriendly work environments. Some of the worst companies to work for in 2012 were as follows:

10. GameStop. Employees felt this video game company put sales over customer service, and the company made *Consumer Reports* annual "naughty list" in 2011 for poor customer service.

9. Rite Aid. Employees at this drugstore chain believed management did not know what they were doing and forced people to work overtime and on holidays.

8. Hewlett-Packard. Employees were frustrated that this computer giant had seen more upper management turmoil than any other large company in the United States.

7. Robert-Half International. Employers at this temporary staffing agency said the company's focus on "activity metrics" and "growth expectations" over "team morale" created a toxic working environment.

6. Sears. Aging infrastructure, antiquated systems, low pay, and poor benefits got in the way of employees providing good customer service.

5. OfficeMax. Micromanagement and poor pay were the leading reasons why employees chose to leave this office supply company.

4. Hertz. Employees routinely complained about top management being out of touch, low hourly pay, and menial jobs.

3. RadioShack. Reviewers did not like this retail company's complicated commission structure and long hours. Like GameStop, RadioShack also made *Consumer Reports'* list for bad customer service.

2. Dillard's. Dislike for the CEO and the sales incentive program were the biggest frustrations with this retail department store chain.

1. Dish Network. Many reviewers disliked the long hours, mandatory overtime, lack of flexibility, and no holiday work schedules. Caleb Hannan at *Yahoo! Finance* labeled Dish Network as the "meanest company to work for" in 2013.

What theories of motivation or satisfaction would best explain the reasons that people choose to leave the worst companies to work for? What theories would best explain why people choose to remain with these companies? How would these companies stack up to the worst companies to work for in Western Europe or China?

Sources: "Job-Review Sites: Honesty Unvarnished," *The Economist,* December 8, 2012, p. 68; http://finance.yahoo.com/news/dish-network-meanest-company-america-194008712.html?page-1; http://247wallst.com/2012/08/10/americas-worst-companies-to-work-for/2/.

FIGURE 9.4
Results of a Facet Satisfaction Survey

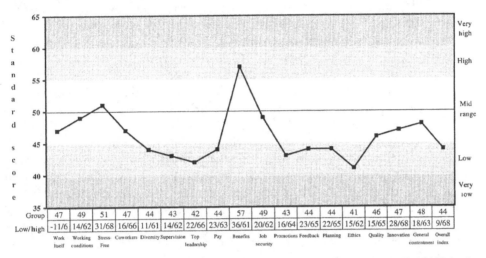

Source: D. P. Campbell and S. Hyne, *Manual for the Revised Campbell Organizational Survey* (Minneapolis, MN: National Computing Systems, 1995).

promotion, or overall satisfaction rising or falling over time? Job satisfaction ratings from similar organizations can be another reference group—are satisfaction ratings of leadership and working conditions higher or lower than those in similar organizations?

Figure 9.4 shows the facet and global satisfaction results for approximately 80 employees working at a medium-sized airport in the western United States. Employees completing the survey included the director of aviation and his supervisory staff ($n = 11$), the operations department ($n = 6$), the airfield maintenance department ($n = 15$), the communications department ($n = 6$), the airport facilities staff ($n = 12$), the administration department ($n = 10$), and the custodial staff ($n = 20$). The airport is owned by the city and has seen tremendous growth since the opening of its new terminal; in fact, less than two years later aircraft loads exceeded the capacity of the new terminal. Unfortunately staffing had remained the same since the opening, and the resulting workload and stress were thought to be adversely affecting morale and job satisfaction. Because of these concerns, the director of aviation decided to use a job satisfaction survey to pinpoint problem areas and develop action plans to resolve them.

Scores above 50 on Figure 9.4 are areas of satisfaction; scores below 50 are areas of dissatisfaction when compared to national norms. Here we see that airport employees are very satisfied with their benefits, are fairly satisfied with the work itself, but are dissatisfied with top leadership, ethics, supervision, feedback, promotion opportunities, and the like. All airport employees got to review these results, and each department discussed the factors underlying the survey results and developed and implemented action plans to address problem areas. Top leadership, in this case the director of aviation, was seen as the biggest source of dissatisfaction by all departments. The director was a genuinely nice person and meant well, but he never articulated his vision for the airport, never explained how employees' actions were related to this mission, failed to set goals for each department, did not provide feedback, never clarified roles or areas of responsibilities for his staff, delegated action items to whomever he happened to see in the hall, often changed his mind about key decisions, and failed to keep his staff informed of airline tenant or city council decisions. When confronted with this information, the director placed the blame on the rapid growth of the airport and the lack of staffing support from the city (the fundamental attribution error from Chapter 2). The city manager then gave the director six months to substantially improve employee satisfaction levels. The director did not take the problem seriously; so, not surprisingly, the survey results six months later were no different for top leadership. The director was subsequently removed from his position because of his failure to improve the morale at the airport.

It is rarely enough to merely administer surveys. Leaders must also be willing to take action on the basis of survey results or risk losing credibility and actually increasing job dissatisfaction. Upon receiving the results of these surveys, leaders with bad results may feel tempted to not share any results with their followers, but this is almost always a mistake. Although the results may not be flattering, the rumors are likely to be much worse than the results themselves. Also, followers will be less willing to fill out subsequent satisfaction surveys if they see denial of the results and little change to the workplace. Furthermore, leaders feeling defensive about such results and tempted to hide them should remember that the bad results may surprise no one but themselves; therefore, what's to hide? On a practical level, leaders should never assess employees' attitudes about work unless they are willing to share the results and take action.

The question: If you had to describe your office environment as a type of television show, what would it be? The responses: "Survivor," 38 percent; soap opera, 27 percent; medical emergency, 18 percent; courtroom drama, 10 percent; science fiction, 7 percent.

**Andrea Nierenberg,
New York
University**

Three Theories of Job Satisfaction

As shown in Table 9.4, all five of the theories of motivation described earlier in this chapter provide insight into followers' levels of job satisfaction too. For example, it would be difficult for Julie to be satisfied with her job if she was consistently underdressed for weather conditions or for Ling Ling to be satisfied if her goals were unclear, she was not given feedback, or she failed to be rewarded for good performance. Nonetheless, several other theories offer even better explanations for job satisfaction, including affectivity, Herzberg's two-factor theory, and organizational justice.

Affectivity: Is the Cup Half Empty or Half Full?

Affectivity refers to one's tendency to react to stimuli in a consistent emotional manner. People with a disposition for **negative affectivity** consistently react to changes, events, or situations in a negative manner. They

TABLE 9.4
Eight Theories of Satisfaction

Theory or Approach	How Leaders Can Improve Job Satisfaction
Maslow's hierarchy of needs	Helping ensure people's needs are satisfied
Achievement orientation	Securing needed resources, clearing obstacles, and allowing people to work on activities that matter to them
Goal setting	Setting high goals and helping people to accomplish them
Operant approach	Administering rewards
Empowerment	Giving people needed training and more decision-making authority
Affectivity	Hiring happier people
Herzberg's two-factor theory	Giving people more meaningful work
Organizational justice	Treating people fairly

tend to be unhappy with themselves and their lives, and are more likely to focus on the downside or disadvantages of a situation. People with a disposition for **positive affectivity** consistently react to changes, events, or situations in a positive manner. They are happy with their lives and tend to take an upbeat, optimistic approach when faced with new situations. People with a positive affective disposition tend to see a cup as half full; people with a negative affective disposition are more likely to describe a glass as half empty. These two groups of individuals are thought to attend to, process, and recall information differently, and these differences affect both job satisfaction and satisfaction with life itself. Researchers have found that negative affectivity is related to job dissatisfaction, and positive affectivity to job satisfaction. Of course such results are not surprising—we all know individuals who never seem happy whatever their circumstances, and others who seem to maintain a positive outlook even in the most adverse circumstances.[133–136] (See Highlight 9.13.)

These findings suggest that leadership initiatives may have little impact on a person's job satisfaction if her affective disposition is either extremely positive or negative. For example, if Ling Ling has a negative affective disposition, she may remain dissatisfied with her pay, working conditions, and so forth *no matter what her leader does*. This is consistent with the findings of a study of identical twins reared apart and together, which discovered that affectivity has a strong genetic component.[134,137] Given that leaders can do little to change followers' genetic makeup, these findings highlight the importance of using good selection procedures when hiring employees. Trying to increase followers' job satisfaction is a reasonable goal, but some followers may be hard to please.

From a leader's perspective, affectivity can have several implications in the workplace. First, a leader's own affectivity can strongly influence followers' morale or satisfaction levels. Say you worked for a leader with

Some people are next to impossible to please.
Anonymous

The Happiest Occupations, States, and Countries

HIGHLIGHT 9.13

Polls show that job and life satisfaction vary considerably by occupation, state, and even the country in which one lives. And although the United States is the richest nation in the world, it ranked only 16th in life satisfaction. Life satisfaction surveys of 130,000+ people reveal the following (listed in order):

Happiest occupations: business owners, professionals, managers/executives, and farming/forestry

Least happy occupations: transportation, services, installation, and construction

Happiest states: Utah, Hawaii, Wyoming, Colorado, and Minnesota

Least happy states: West Virginia, Kentucky, Mississippi, Ohio, and Arkansas

Happiest countries: Denmark, Finland, the Netherlands, and New Zealand

Least happy countries: Zimbabwe, Ukraine, Armenia, and Russia

Sources: http://new.yahoo.com/s/livescience/20100701/sc_livescience/isrichestnationbutnothappiest; http://livescience.com/culture/091110-fifty-happy-states.html; http://finance.yahoo.com/news/Happy-business-owners-changes-apf-1598303505.html?x=0$.v=1; http://abcnews.go.com/Business/Economy/story?id=7585729&page=1; http://thehappinessshow.com/HappiestCountries.htm.

negative affectivity. Chances are he or she would always find fault in your work and constantly complain about organizational policies, resources, and so on. The opposite might be true if you worked for someone with positive affectivity. Second, leading a high percentage of followers having either positive or negative affectivity would likely result in very different leadership experiences. The positive group may be much more tolerant and willing to put up with organizational changes; the negative group would likely find fault in any change the leader made. Increasing job satisfaction through affectivity means hiring those with positive affectivity. However, few, if any, selection systems address this important workplace variable. Because negative affectivity may not be assessed or even apparent until a follower has been on the job for a while, perhaps the best advice for leadership practitioners is that some followers may have a permanent chip on their shoulders, and there may be little you can do to change it.

Herzberg's Two-Factor Theory: Does Meaningful Work Make People Happy?

If you don't want people to have Mickey Mouse attitudes, then don't give them Mickey Mouse work.
Frederick Herzberg,
researcher

Herzberg developed the **two-factor theory** from a series of interviews he conducted with accountants and engineers. Specifically, he asked what satisfied them about their work and found that their answers usually could be sorted into five consistent categories. Furthermore, rather than assuming that what dissatisfied people was always just the opposite of what satisfied them, he also specifically asked what *dissatisfied* people about their jobs. Surprisingly, the list of satisfiers and dissatisfiers represented entirely different aspects of work.

TABLE 9.5
Motivators and
Hygiene Factors of
the Two-Factor
Theory

Source: Adapted from
F. Herzberg, *Work and the
Nature of Men* (Cleveland,
OH: World Publishing, 1966).

Hygiene Factors	Motivators
Supervision	Achievement
Working conditions	Recognition
Co-workers	The work itself
Pay	Responsibility
Policies/procedures	Advancement and growth
Job security	

Herzberg labeled the factors that led to *satisfaction* at work **motivators,** and he labeled the factors that led to *dissatisfaction* at work **hygiene factors.** The most common motivators and hygiene factors are listed in Table 9.5. According to the two-factor theory, efforts directed toward improving hygiene factors will not increase followers' motivation or satisfaction. No matter how much leaders improve working conditions, pay, or sick leave policies, for example, followers *will not* exert additional effort or persist longer at a task. For example, followers will probably be no more satisfied to do a dull and boring job if they are merely given pleasant office furniture. On the other hand, followers may be asked to work in conditions so poor as to create dissatisfaction, which can distract them from constructive work.[138–140] (See Highlight 9.14.)

Given limited resources on the leader's part, the key to increasing followers' satisfaction levels according to this two-factor theory is to just adequately satisfy the hygiene factors while maximizing the motivators for a particular job. It is important for working conditions to be adequate, but it is even more important (for enhancing motivation and satisfaction) to provide plenty of recognition, responsibility, and possibilities for advancement (see Figure 9.5). Although giving followers meaningful work and then recognizing them for their achievement seem straightforward enough, these techniques are underutilized by leaders.[40,45,140] In other words, Herzberg argues that leaders would be better off restructuring work to make it more meaningful and significant than giving out shirts with company logos or decreasing medical copays.

The two-factor theory offers leaders ideas about how to bolster followers' satisfaction, but it has received little empirical support beyond Herzberg's own results. Perhaps it is not an accurate explanation for job satisfaction despite its apparent grounding in data. We present it here partly because it has become such a well-known approach to work motivation and job satisfaction that this chapter would appear incomplete if we ignored it. One problem with two-factor theory, however, seems to lie in the original data on which it was based. Herzberg developed his theory after interviewing only accountants and engineers—two groups who are hardly representative of workers in other lines of work or activity.

Role Ambiguity, Role Conflict, and Job Satisfaction

HIGHLIGHT 9.14

The eight theories of job satisfaction provide useful frameworks for understanding why people may or may not be happy at work. But two other key causes of job dissatisfaction do not fit neatly into one of these frameworks. The first has to do with **role ambiguity,** which occurs whenever leaders or followers are unclear about what they need to do and how they should do it. Many people come to work to succeed, but too many leaders set followers up for failure by not providing them with the direction, training, or resources they need to be successful. In these situations followers may exert a high level of effort, but they often are not working on the right things and as a result get little accomplished. This sense of frustration quickly turns to dissatisfaction and eventually causes people to look for someplace else to work. An example here is an executive vice president of human resources who left a position early in his career after he had been on the job for only two weeks. During those first two weeks he had never seen his boss, did not have a desk, and did not even have a phone. The irony was that he was working for a major Canadian phone company.

Role conflict occurs when leaders and followers are given incompatible goals to accomplish. For example, leaders may be told that their goals are to boost output while reducing headcount. It will be difficult to achieve both goals unless the leader is given some new process, technology, or product that significantly increases worker productivity. When given seemingly incompatible goals, leaders often focus their efforts on accomplishing some goals to the exclusion of others. This may have been the case with BP's Deepwater Horizon oil rig disaster, where managers were told to drill for oil safely and in an environmentally friendly manner while reducing costs and boosting production. The managers on the rig seemed to focus on production and cost reduction goals, and the end result was the death of 11 workers and an unprecedented environmental disaster.

Although role conflict is a source of dissatisfaction, people need to realize that a key challenge for leaders is to successfully achieve seemingly incompatible goals. If the team has only a productivity goal, many leaders are likely to be successful in helping their team to accomplish this goal. If the team has productivity and profitability goals, fewer leaders are likely to be successful. And if the team has productivity, profitability, safety, quality, and customer satisfaction goals, an even smaller subset of leaders will be successful in all of these areas. The fact is that most teams and organizations have more than one goal, and effective leaders are able to get their teams to successfully accomplish all assigned goals. Hiring achievement-oriented team members, setting clear goals, regularly measuring and reporting on goal progress, clearing obstacles, obtaining needed resources, and providing contingent rewards will go a long way toward the successful accomplishment of multiple goals and improved employee satisfaction.

Sources: G. J. Curphy and R. Hogan, *The Rocket Model: Practical Advice for Building High Performing Teams* (Tulsa, OK: Hogan Press, 2012); "Building High Performing Teams," presentation given at the Minnesota Professionals for Psychology Applied to Work, Minneapolis, MN, February 2013; G. J. Curphy, *Applying the Rocket Model to Virtual Teams*, unpublished manuscript, 2013; G. J. Curphy and M. Roellig, *Followership*, unpublished manuscript, 2010.

FIGURE 9.5
Herzberg's Two-Factor Theory

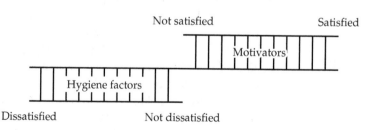
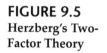

Furthermore, his subjects typically attributed job satisfaction to *their* skill or effort, yet blamed their dissatisfaction on circumstances beyond their control. This sounds suspiciously like the fundamental attribution error described earlier in this book. Despite such limitations, the two-factor theory has provided useful insight into what followers find satisfying and dissatisfying about work.

Organizational Justice: Does Fairness Matter?

Organizational justice is based on the premise that people who are treated unfairly are less productive, satisfied, and committed to their organizations. Moreover, these individuals are also likely to initiate collective action and engage in various counterproductive work behaviors.[141] According to Trevino, organizational justice is made up of three related components. **Interactional justice** reflects the degree to which people are given information about different reward procedures and are treated with dignity and respect. **Distributive justice** concerns followers' perceptions of whether the level of reward or punishment is commensurate with an individual's performance or infraction. Dissatisfaction occurs when followers believe someone has received too little or too much reward or punishment. Perceptions of **procedural justice** involve the process by which rewards or punishments are administered. If someone is to be punished, followers will be more satisfied if the person being punished has been given adequate warnings and has had the opportunity to explain his or her actions, and if the punishment has been administered in a timely and consistent manner.[142] Research has shown that these different components of organizational justice are related to satisfaction with the leader, pay, promotion, the job itself, organizational citizenship behaviors, and counterproductive work behaviors (in instances where perceived injustice was taking place).[31,143–150]

   So what should leaders do to improve follower satisfaction and reduce turnover using organizational justice theory? The underlying principle for organizational justice is fairness; going back to our earlier characters, do Ling Ling or Julie feel that the process in which rewards or punishments are administered is fair? Are the potential rewards commensurate with performance? Do Julie and Ling Ling believe the reward system is unbiased? What would the flight attendants say about whether they were treated with dignity and respect, whether rewards were commensurate with performance, or whether rewards were administered fairly? How about the survivors and those who were laid off during the economic recession of 2008 to 2010? Leaders who want to improve job satisfaction using this approach need to ensure that followers answer yes to these three questions; if not, leaders need to change the reward and punishment system if they want to improve job satisfaction using organizational justice theory. Brockner notes that fairness in the workplace makes intuitive

True patriotism hates injustice in its own land more than anywhere else.

Clarence Darrow, attorney

Business opportunities are like buses, there's always another one coming.

Richard Branson, industrialist

Richard Branson

PROFILES IN LEADERSHIP 9.4

Richard Branson is the chairman of Virgin Industries, which owns such companies as Virgin Airlines, Virgin Records, Virgin Galactic, Virgin Fuels, Virgin Media, Virgin Comics, and Virgin Health Care. An entrepreneur since the age of 16, Branson had his first business success publishing *Student* magazine in 1966. From there he started Virgin Records, which at the time was an audio record mail order business. In 1972 he owned a chain of record stores, Virgin Records, and installed a recording studio. At the time the studio was used by a number of top bands, including Mike Oldfield, the Sex Pistols, and Culture Club.

In the 1980s Branson ventured into the airline industry with the launch of Virgin Atlantic Airways. He expanded his airline holdings to include Virgin Express, a low-cost European carrier, and Virgin Blue, an Asia-Pacific carrier. In 2004 he partnered with Paul Allen and Burt Rutan to launch Virgin Galactic, a space tourism company. His Virgin Fuels business was launched to find more environmentally friendly fuels for automobiles and airplanes.

Having a long history of creating successful companies, selling them, and then using the proceeds to fund other business ventures, Branson sold Virgin Records to EMI for approximately $750,000,000 and sold Virgin Mobile for $1,500,000,000. Virgin Industries currently employs 50,000 people in 30 countries and generates $23,000,000,000 in annual revenues. With a personal net worth of over $4,000,000,000, Branson has turned his attention to more humanitarian causes. Working with the likes of Nelson Mandela, Jimmy Carter, Desmond Tutu, and Bono, Branson is looking to develop peaceful resolutions to long-standing conflicts. He is an active promoter of using entrepreneurship to solve environmental problems. What motivational approach would best describe Richard Branson?

Sources: http://www.solarnavigator.net/sponsorship/richard_branson.htm; http://renewableenergyaccess.com/rea/news/story?id=46071; http://groovygecko.net/anon.groovy/clients/akqa/projectamber/press/The_Elders-Press_Release.pdf; http://www.ft.com/cms/s/0/7f5dd8f32-bfa0-11dc-8052-0000779fd2ac.html; http://virgin.com/richard-branson/autobiography/; http://www.hoovers.com/company/Virgin_Group_Ltd/crjkji-1.html.

sense but is woefully lacking in many organizations. Too many managers play favorites, avoid rather than directly deal with uncomfortable situations, or for legal reasons cannot reveal how certain issues were handled.[36] These instances of perceived unfairness are often the underlying causes of job dissatisfaction in many organizations.

Summary

This chapter has reviewed research concerning motivation, satisfaction, and performance. Motivation was defined as anything that provides direction, intensity, and persistence to behavior. Although motivation is an important aspect of performance, performance and motivation are not the same thing. Performance is a broader concept than motivation; abilities, skills, group norms, and the availability of resources can all affect followers' levels of performance. Job satisfaction is a set of attitudes that people have about work. Although many people are generally satisfied with their jobs, they often have varying levels of satisfaction with different aspects of their jobs, such as pay, working conditions, supervisors, or co-workers.

Many of the approaches to understanding motivation have distinct implications for increasing performance and satisfaction. Therefore, several different theories of motivation were reviewed in this chapter. Maslow's hierarchy of needs assumes that people are motivated to satisfy a universal set of needs. Achievement orientation views motivation as a personality trait and assumes some people are hardwired to be more motivated than others. Goal setting examines motivation from a cognitive perspective. This approach assumes that people make rational, conscious choices about the direction, intensity, and persistence of their behaviors, and generally engage in behaviors that maximize payoffs and minimize costs. The last two theories, empowerment and operant approach, examine motivation from a situational perspective. Leadership practitioners likely will be more effective if they learn to recognize situations where various approaches, or the insights particular to them, may be differentially useful.

Several other theories seem to be more useful for explaining followers' attitudes about work. Some research suggests that individuals vary in the characteristic tenor of their affectivity; some people generally have positive attitudes about work and life whereas others are generally unhappy about work and life. Such differences have a genetic component and may limit the extent to which initiatives by leaders will change follower satisfaction. Leaders may be able to increase satisfaction levels by giving followers more meaningful work and by treating them fairly. Followers (and leaders) are more likely to have positive attitudes about work if they believe that what they do is important and that the reward and disciplinary systems are fair and just.

Key Terms

motivation, *333*
performance, *334*
effectiveness, *334*
job satisfaction, *334*
organizational
  citizenship
  behaviors, *334*
needs, *340*
hierarchy of
  needs, *341*
achievement
  orientation, *343*
goal setting, *346*
Pygmalion effect, *349*
Golem effect, *349*
operant approach, *350*

reward, *350*
punishment, *350*
contingent, *351*
noncontingent, *351*
extinction, *351*
empowerment, *356*
functional
  turnover, *362*
dysfunctional
  turnover, *362*
global
  satisfaction, *366*
facet satisfaction, *366*
hierarchy effect, *366*
life satisfaction, *367*
reference group, *367*

negative
  affectivity, *370*
positive
  affectivity, *371*
two-factor theory, *372*
motivators, *373*
hygiene factors, *373*
role ambiguity, *374*
role conflict, *374*
organizational
  justice, *375*
interactional
  justice, *375*
distributive
  justice, *375*
procedural justice, *375*

Questions

1. Why do you think there are so many different theories or approaches to understanding motivation? Shouldn't it be possible to determine which one is best and just use it? Why or why not?

2. Many good leaders are thought of as good motivators. How would you rate Barack Obama, Rachel Maddow, Meg Whitman, or Rush Limbaugh in terms of their ability to motivate others?

3. What is your own view of what motivates people to work hard and perform well?

4. Do you know of any examples where reward systems are inconsistent with desired behavior? How are personal values related to rewards?

5. What do you find personally satisfying or dissatisfying at work or school? For those things you find dissatisfying, how could you make them more satisfying? What theory of job satisfaction best explains your actions?

Activities

1. Earlier in this chapter you were asked how five motivation approaches could be used to improve the customer service levels of flight attendants. Break into five groups, and have each group discuss how they would design and implement a motivation program using one of these approaches. Each group should then give a 15-minute presentation on their findings. The presentation should include the approach they used, how they would collect any needed additional data, the program design, program implementation, potential barriers to the program, and their evaluation of the effectiveness of their program.

2. Identify two companies you would like to work for and check out their *Indeed* or *Glassdoor* reviews. Would you want to work for these companies? Why or why not?

3. Interview someone in a leadership position who has been through a merger or a downsizing and determine their level of satisfaction before and after these events.

4. People often leave bosses, not organizations. Interview people with 10 to 20 years of work experience and ask them to list the reasons they have left jobs. How many people left because of bad bosses? How did the reasons for leaving relate to the motivation and satisfaction approaches described in this chapter?

5. How would motivating a group of volunteers for a community project differ from motivating a group of employees in a for-profit business or a platoon of soldiers?

Minicase

Initech versus the Coffee Bean

Consider Peter Gibbons, an employee of the fictional Initech Corporation from the movie *Office Space*. Peter has been asked to meet with efficiency experts (Bob and Bob) to discuss his work environment. One of the Bobs is curious about Peter's tendency toward underperformance and confronts him about his lack of attention to office policies and procedures. It seems Peter has been turning in his TPS reports late and without the company-mandated cover sheet:

Peter: You see, Bob, it's not that I'm lazy, it's that I just don't care.

Bob: Don't? Don't care?

Peter: It's a problem of motivation, all right? Now if I work my butt off and Initech ships a few extra units, I don't see another dime, so where's the motivation? And here's another thing, I have eight different bosses right now.

Bob: Eight?

Peter: Eight, Bob. So that means when I make a mistake, I have eight different people coming by to tell me about it. That's my only real motivation, not to be hassled, that and the fear of losing my job. But you know, Bob, that will only make someone work just hard enough not to get fired.

The environment at Initech is an all too familiar one to many office workers. It is an environment in which success is directly proportional to how busy you look, where questioning authority is taboo, and where meticulous attention to paperwork is the only way to get promoted.

Contrast Initech to The Coffee Bean—a chain of gourmet coffee shops. In an effort to boost employee morale and increase productivity, the management team at The Coffee Bean decided to pursue the FISH philosophy. FISH is a management training program that stresses fun in the workplace. It espouses four principles:

Play—"Work that is made fun gets done."

Make Their Day—"When you make someone's day through a small act of kindness or unforgettable engagement, you can turn even routine encounters into special memories."

Be There—"Being there is a great way to practice wholeheartedness and fight burnout."

Choose Your Attitude—"When you learn you have the power to choose your response to what life brings, you can look for the best and find opportunities you never imagined possible."

Stores in The Coffee Bean chain were encouraged to use these principles to make the stores a fun place for employees and customers. The stores have created theme days where employees dress up for themes (NFL day, basketball day, pajama day)—and then give discounts to customers who dress the same. There are also trivia games in which customers who can answer trivia questions get discounts on their coffee purchases. Nancy Feilen, a Coffee Bean store manager, explains, "We tried to come up with something that would help strike up a conversation with guests and engage fun in the stores for team members and guests." In other stores, customers play Coffee Craps. If a customer rolls a 7 or an 11, he gets a free drink. Some stores have used Fear Factor Fridays: if the store sells a certain number of drinks, one of the baristas will agree to some act—in one case a barista ate a cricket.

The results? One store increased the average check by 12 percent in six months; turnover has decreased significantly—general managers typically left after 22 months with the chain but now stay an average of 31 months; and the turnover rate for hourly employees dropped to 69 percent from more than 200 percent over a three-year period.

So where would you rather work?

1. How would you gauge Peter's achievement orientation? What are some of the needs not being met for Peter Gibbons at Initech? What changes might improve Peter's motivation?

2. Would you judge the leaders at Initech as more likely to invoke the Pygmalion or the Golem effect? What about the environment at The Coffee Bean—Pygmalion or Golem effect?

3. Why has The Coffee Bean seen such a significant reduction in its turnover?

Sources: http://www.findarticles.com/p/articles/mi_m3190/is_2_38/ai_112248126; http://www.imdb.com/title/tt0151804/quotes; http://www.charthouse.com/home.asp; http://www.gazettenet.com/business/02242003/3706.htm.

Part End Notes

1. G. Anders, "Management Leaders Turn Attention to Followers," *The Wall Street Journal*, January 24, 2007, p. B3.

2. S. Jones, "The Lost Art of Following," *The Minneapolis Star Tribune*, October 7, 2007, p. AA1–AA5.

3. E. Hollander, *Inclusive Leadership* (New York: Routledge/Taylor and Francis, 2008).

4. B. Shamir, "From Passive Recipients to Active Coproducers: Followers Role in the Leadership Process," in *Follower-Centered Perspectives on Leadership: A Tribute to the Memory of James R. Meindl*, eds. B. Shamir, R. Pillai, M. C. Bligh, M. Uhl-Bien (Greenwich, CT: Inform.Age, 2007).

5. M. Van Vugt, R. Hogan, and R. B. Kaiser, "Leadership, Followership, and Evolution: Some Lessons from the Past," *American Psychologist* 63, no. 3, pp. 182–96.

6. J. M. Burger, "Replicating Milgram: Would People Still Obey Today?" *American Psychologist* 64, no. 1, pp. 1–11.

7. P. Bordia, S. L. D. Restubog, and R. L. Tang, "When Employees Strike Back: Investigating Mediating Mechanisms between Psychological Contract Breach and Workplace Deviance," *Journal of Applied Psychology* 93, no. 5 (2008), pp. 1104–17.

8. A. Zaleznik, "The Dynamics of Subordinacy," *Harvard Business Review*, May–June 1965, pp. 119–131.

9. R. E. Kelley, *The Power of Followership: How to Create Leaders People Want to Follow, and Followers Who Led Themselves* (New York: Doubleday, 1982).

10. I. Chaleff, *The Courageous Follower* (3rd ed.) (San Francisco: Berrett-Koehler, 2009).

11. B. Kellerman, "What Every Leader Needs to Know about Followers," *Harvard Business Review*, December 2007, pp. 84–91.

12. R. Adair, "Developing Great Leaders, One Follower at a Time," in *The Art of Followership: How Great Followers Create Great Leaders and Organizations*, eds. R. E. Riggio, I. Chaleff, and J. Lipman-Blumen (San Francisco: Jossey-Bass, 2008), pp. 137–53.

13. J. C. McCroskey, V. P. Richmond, A. D. Johnson, and H. T. Smith, "Organizational Orientations Theory and Measurement: Development of Measures and Preliminary Investigations," *Communication Quarterly* 52 (2004), pp. 1–14.

14. E. H. Potter III and W. E. Rosenbach, "Followers as Partners: Ready When the Time Comes," in *Military Leadership*, 6th ed. (Boulder, CO: Westview Press, 2009).

15. G. J. Curphy and M. E. Roellig, *Followership*, unpublished manuscript (North Oaks, MN: Author, 2010).

16. U. K. Bindl, S. K. Parker, P. Totterdell, and G. Hagger-Johnson, "Fuel of the Self-Starter: How Mood Relates to Proactive Goal Regulation," *Journal of Applied Psychology* 97, no. 1 (2012), pp. 134–50.

17. E. R. Burris, "The Risks and Rewards of Speaking Up: Managerial Responses to Employee Voice," *Academy of Management Journal* 55, no. 4 (2012), pp. 851–75.

18. D. Mercer, *Follow to Lead: The 7 Principles of Being a Good Follower* (Mustang, OK: Tate Publishing, 2011).

19. E. Holm and J. S. Lublin, "Loose Lips Trip up Good Hands Executive," *The Wall Street Journal*, August 1, 2011, pp. C1, C3.

20. A. L. Blanchard, J. Welbourne, D. Gilmore, and A. Bullock, "Followership Styles and Employee Attachment to the Organization," *The Psychologist-Manager Journal* 12, no. 2 (2009), pp. 111–31.

21. D. Brooks, "The Follower Problem," *The New York Times: The Opinion Page*, June 11, 2012, http://www.nytimes.com/2012/06/12/opinion/brooks-the-follower-problem.html?

22. R. Sutton, "How a Few Bad Apples Ruin Everything," *The Wall Street Journal*, October 23, 2011, http://online.wsj.com/article_email/

Chapter End Notes

1. J. E. Hunter, F. L. Schmidt, and M. K. Judiesch, "Individual Differences in Output Variability as a Function of Job Complexity," *Journal of Applied Psychology* 74 (1990), pp. 28–42.

2. E. Matson and L. Prusak, "The Performance Variability Dilemma," *MIT Sloan Management Review* 45, no. 1 (2003), pp. 38–44.

3. Associated Press, "Democrats Hit Troop Extensions," April 12, 2007, http://www.military.com/NewsContent.

4. M. A. Huselid, "The Impact of Human Resource Practices on Turnover, Productivity, and Corporate Financial Performance," *Academy of Management Journal* 38, no. 4 (1995), pp. 635–72.

5. Sirota Consulting, *Establishing the Linkages between Employee Attitudes, Customer Attitudes, and Bottom-Line Results* (Chicago: Author, 1998).

6. D. J. Koys, "The Effects of Employee Satisfaction, Organizational Citizenship Behavior, and Turnover on Organizational Effectiveness: A Unit-Level, Longitudinal Study," *Personnel Psychology* 54, no. 1 (2001), pp. 101–14.

7. S. D. Pugh, J. Dietz, J. W. Wiley, and S. M. Brooks, "Driving Service Effectiveness through Employee–Customer Linkages," *Academy of Management Executive* 16, no. 4 (2002), pp. 73–81.

8. B. A. S. Koene, A. L. W. Vogelaar, and J. L. Soeters, "Leadership Effects on Organizational Climate and Financial Performance: Local Leadership Effect in Chain Organizations," *The Leadership Quarterly* 13, no. 3 (2002), pp. 193–216.

9. G. A. Gelade and M. Ivery, "The Impact of Human Resource Management and Work Climate on Organizational Performance," *Personnel Psychology* 56, no. 2 (2003), pp. 383–404.

10. J. Z. Carr, A. M. Schmidt, J. K. Ford, and R. P. DeShon, "Climate Perceptions Matter: A Meta-analytic Path Analysis Relating Molar Climate, Cognitive and Affective States, and Individual Level Work Outcomes," *Journal of Applied Psychology* 89, no. 4 (2004), pp. 605–19.

11. I. Smithey-Fulmer, B. Gerhart, and K. S. Scott, "Are the 100 Best Better? An Empirical Investigation of the Relationship between Being a 'Great Place to Work' and Firm Performance," *Personnel Psychology* 56, no. 4 (2003), pp. 965–93.

12. D. B. McFarlin, "Hard Day's Work: A Boon for Performance but a Bane for Satisfaction?" *Academy of Management Perspectives* 20, no. 4 (2006), pp. 115–16.

13. S. A. Hewlett and C. Buck Luce, "Extreme Jobs: The Dangerous Allure of the 70-Hour Work Week," *Harvard Business Review,* December 2006, pp. 48–49.

14. J. C. Rode, M. L. Arthaud-Day, C. H. Mooney, J. P. Near, T. T. Baldwin, W. H. Bommer, and R. S. Rubin, "Life Satisfaction and Student Performance," *Academy of Management Learning & Education* 4, no. 4 (2005), pp. 421–33.

15. J. D. Shaw, N. Gupta, and J. E. Delery, "Alternative Conceptualizations of the Relationship between Voluntary Turnover and Organizational Performance," *Academy of Management Journal* 48, no. 5 (2005), pp. 50–68.

16. K. Birdi, C. Clegg, M. Patterson, A. Robinson, C. B. Stride, T. D. Wall, and S. J. Wood, "The Impact of Human Resources and Operations Management Practices on Company Productivity," *Personnel Psychology* 61, no. 3 (2008), pp. 467–502.

17. A. G. Walker, J. W. Smither, and D. A. Waldman, "A Longitudinal Examination of Concommitant Changes in Team Leadership and Customer Satisfaction," *Personnel Psychology* 61, no. 3 (2008), pp. 547–78.

18. R. B. Kaiser, R. T. Hogan, and S. B. Craig, "Leadership and the Fate of Organizations," *American Psychologist* 63, no. 2 (2008), pp. 96–110.

19. C. Kiewitz, "Happy Employees and Firm Performance: Have We Been Putting the Cart before the Horse?" *Academy of Management Executive* 18, no. 2 (2004), pp. 127–29.

20. B. Schneider, P. J. Hanges, D. B. Smith, and A. N. Salvaggio, "Which Comes First: Employee Attitudes or Organizational Financial and Market Performance?" *Journal of Applied Psychology* 88, no. 5 (2003), pp. 836–51.

21. R. Kanfer, "Motivation Theory in Industrial and Organizational Psychology," in *Handbook of Industrial and Organizational Psychology*, vol. 1, eds. M. D. Dunnette and L. M. Hough (Palo Alto, CA: Consulting Psychologists Press, 1990), pp. 75–170.

22. E. A. Locke and G. P. Latham, "What Should We Do about Motivation Theory? Six Recommendations for the Twenty-First Century," *Academy of Management Review* 29, no. 3 (2004), pp. 388–403.

23. R. M. Steers, R. T. Mowday, and D. L. Shapiro, "The Future of Work Motivation Theory," *Academy of Management Review* 29, no. 3 (2004), pp. 379–87.

24. F. E. Saal and P. A. Knight, *Industrial Organizational Psychology: Science and Practice* (Belmont, CA: Brooks/Cole, 1988).

25. T. A. Judge, C. J. Thoresen, J. E. Bono, and G. K. Patton, "The Job Satisfaction–Job Performance Relationship: A Qualitative and Quantitative Review," *Psychological Bulletin* 127 (2001), pp. 376–407.

26. D. P. Campbell and S. Hyne, *Manual for the Revised Campbell Organizational Survey* (Minneapolis, MN: National Computer Systems, 1995).

27. Health, Education, and Welfare Task Force, *Work in America* (Cambridge, MA: MIT Press, 1973).

28. R. Hoppock, *Job Satisfaction* (New York: Harper, 1935).

29. F. J. Smith, K. D. Scott, and C. L. Hulin, "Trends in Job-Related Attitudes in Managerial and Professional Employees," *Academy of Management Journal* 20 (1977), pp. 454–60.

30. G. L. Staines and R. P. Quinn, "American Workers Evaluate the Quality of Their Jobs," *Monthly Labor Review* 102, no. 1 (1979), pp. 3–12.

31. J. A. Colquitt, B. A. Scott, J. B. Rodell, D. M. Long, C. P. Zapata, D. E. Conlon, and M. J. Wesson, "Justice at the Millennium, a Decade Later: A Meta-Analytic Test of Social Exchange and Affect-Based Perspectives," *Journal of Applied Psychology* 98, no. 2 (2013), pp. 199–36.

32. R. Cropanzano, D. E. Rupp, and Z. S. Byrne, "The Relationship of Emotional Exhaustion to Work Attitudes, Job Performance, and Organizational Citizenship Behaviors," *Journal of Applied Psychology* 88, no. 1 (2003), pp. 160–69.

33. R. Ilies, B. A. Scott, and T. A. Judge, "The Interactive Effects of Personality Traits and Experienced States on the Intraindividual Patterns of Citizenship Behavior," *Academy of Management Journal* 49, no. 3 (2006), pp. 561–75.

34. B. R. Dineen, R. J. Lewicki, and E. C. Tomlinson, "Supervisory Guidance and Behavioral Integrity: Relationships with Employee Citizenship and Deviant Behavior," *Journal of Applied Psychology* 91, no. 3 (2006), pp. 622–35.

35. L. Y. Sun, S. Aryee, and K. S. Law, "High Performance Human Resource Practices, Citizenship Behavior, and Organizational Performance: A Relational Perspective," *Academy of Management Journal* 50, no. 3 (2007), pp. 558–77.

36. J. Brockner, "Why It's So Hard to Be Fair," *Harvard Business Review,* March 2006, p. 122–30.

37. D. S. Whitman, D. L. Van Rooy, and C. Viswesvaran, "Satisfaction, Citizenship Behaviors, and Performance in Work Units: A Meta-Analysis of Collective Construct Relations," *Personnel Psychology* 63, no. 1 (2010), pp. 41–81.

38. http://news.yahoo.com/s/ap/20100105/ap/_on_bi_ge/us_unhappy_workers.

39. "Schumpeter: Overstretched," *The Economist,* May 22, 2010, p. 72.

40. K. B. Paul and C. L. Johnson, "Engagement at 3M: A Case Study," in *The Executive Guide to Integrated Talent Management,* eds. K. Oakes and P. Galahan (Alexandria, VA: ASTD Press, 2011), pp. 133–46.

41. D. Ulrich, "Integrated Talent Management," in *The Executive Guide to Integrated Talent Management,* eds. K. Oakes and P. Galahan (Alexandria, VA: ASTD Press, 2011), pp. 189–12.

42. R. Charan, S. Drotter, and J. Noel, *The Leadership Pipeline: How to Build the Leadership-Powered Company* (San Francisco: Jossey-Bass, 2001).

43. B. N. Pfau, and S. A. Cohen, "Aligning Human Capital Practices and Employee Behavior with Shareholder Value," *Consulting Psychology Journal* 55, no. 3 (2003), pp. 169–78.

44. M. A. Huselid, R. W. Beatty, and B. E. Becker, "'A Players' or 'A Positions'? The Strategic Logic of Workforce Management," *Harvard Business Review,* December 2005, pp. 110–21.

45. G. J. Curphy and M. Roellig, "Followership," working paper, 2010.

46. R. T. Hogan, *Personality and the Fate of Organizations* (Mahwah, NJ: Lawrence Erlbaum Associates, 2007).

47. J. P. Campbell, "The Cutting Edge of Leadership: An Overview," in *Leadership: The Cutting Edge,* eds. J. G. Hunt and L. L. Larson (Carbondale: Southern Illinois University Press, 1977).

48. J. P. Campbell, "Training Design for Performance Improvement," in *Productivity in Organizations: New Perspectives from Industrial and Organizational Psychology,* eds. J. P. Campbell, R. J. Campbell, and Associates (San Francisco: Jossey-Bass, 1988), pp. 177–216.

49. M. T. Iaffaldano and P. M. Muchinsky, "Job Satisfaction and Job Performance: A Meta-analysis," *Psychological Bulletin* 97 (1985), pp. 251–73.

50. E. A. Locke and G. P. Latham, "Work Motivation and Satisfaction: Light at the End of the Tunnel," *Psychological Science* 1 (1990), pp. 240–46.

51. A. H. Maslow, *Motivation and Personality* (New York: Harper & Row, 1954).

52. E. L. Betz, "Two Tests of Maslow's Theory of Need Fulfillment," *Journal of Vocational Behavior* 24 (1984), pp. 204–20.

53. J. W. Atkinson, "Motivational Determinants of Risk Taking Behavior," *Psychological Review* 64 (1957), pp. 359–72.

54. D. C. McClelland, *Power: The Inner Experience* (New York: Irvington, 1975).

55. M. R. Barrick and M. K. Mount, "The Big Five Personality Dimensions and Job Performance: A Meta-analysis," *Personal Psychology* 44 (1991), pp. 1–26.

56. T. A. Judge and R. Ilies, "Relationship of Personality to Performance Motivation: A Meta-analytic Review," *Journal of Applied Psychology* 87, no. 4 (2002), pp. 797–807.

57. R. Hogan, T. Chamorro-Premuzic, and R. B. Kaiser, "Employability and Career Success: Bridging the Gap Between Theory and Reality," *Industrial and Organizational Psychology: Perspectives on Science and Practice* 1, no. 6 (2013), pp. 3–16.

58. G. J. Curphy and K. D. Osten, "Technical Manual for the Leadership Development Survey," *Technical Report No. 93-14* (Colorado Springs, CO: U.S. Air Force Academy, 1993).

59. T. A. Judge and J. D. Kanmeyer-Mueller, "On the Value of Aiming High: The Causes and Consequences of Ambition," *Journal of Applied Psychology* 97, no. 4 (2012), pp. 758–75.

60. R. T. Hogan and J. Hogan, *Manual for the Hogan Personality Inventory* (Tulsa, OK: Hogan Assessment Systems, 1992).

61. D. L. Nilsen, Using Self and Observers' Rating of Personality to Predict Leadership Performance, unpublished doctoral dissertation, University of Minnesota, 1995.

62. S. A. Hewlett, "Executive Women and the Myth of Having It All," *Harvard Business Review,* April 2002, pp. 66–67.

63. G. J. Curphy, *Hogan Assessment Systems Certification Workshop Training Manuals* (Tulsa, OK: Hogan Assessment Systems, 2003).

64. R. Gregory, R. T. Hogan, and G. J. Curphy, "Risk-Taking in the Energy Industry," *Well Connected* 5, no. 6 (June 2003), pp. 5–7.

65. T. W. Britt, "Black Hawk Down at Work," *Harvard Business Review,* January 2003, pp. 16–17.

66. E. A. Locke and G. P. Latham, "Building a Practically Useful Theory of Goal Setting and Task Motivation: A 35-Year Odyssey," *American Psychologist* 57, no. 9 (2002), pp. 705–18.

67. E. A. Locke, "Goal Setting Theory and Its Applications to the World of Business," *Academy of Management Executive* 18, no. 4 (2004), pp. 124–25.

68. G. P. Latham, "The Motivational Benefits of Goal Setting," *Academy of Management Executive* 18, no. 4 (2004), pp. 126–29.

69. E. A. Locke and G. P. Latham, "Has Goal Setting Gone Wild, or Have Its Attackers Abandoned Good Scholarship?" *Academy of Management Perspectives* 23, no. 1 (2009), pp. 17–23.

70. L. D. Ordonez, M. E. Schweitzer, A. D. Galinsky, and M. H. Bazerman, "Goals Gone Wild: The Systematic Side Effects of Overprescribing Goal Setting," *Academy of Management Perspectives* 23, no. 1 (2009), pp. 6–16.

71. S. Kerr and S. Landauer, "Using Stretch Goals to Promote Organizational Effectiveness and Personal Growth: General Electric and Goldman Sachs," *Academy of Management Executive* 18, no. 4 (2004), pp. 139–43.

72. Y. Fried and L. Haynes Slowik, "Enriching Goal-Setting Theory with Time: An Integrated Approach," *Academy of Management Review* 29, no. 3 (2004), pp. 404–22.

73. E. A. Locke, "Linking Goals to Monetary Incentives," *Academy of Management Executive* 18, no. 4 (2004), pp. 130–33.

74. S. B. Sitkin, K. E. See, C. C. Miller, M. W. Lawless, and A. M. Carton, "The Paradox of Stretch Goals: Organizations in Pursuit of the Seemingly Impossible," *Academy of Management Review* 36, no. 3 (2011), pp. 544–66.

75. M. Imai, *Kaizen: The Key to Japan's Competitive Success* (New York: Random House, 1986).

76. D. D. Van Fleet, T. O. Peterson, and E. W. Van Fleet, "Closing the Performance Feedback Gap with Expert Systems," *Academy of Management Executive* 19, no. 3 (2005), pp. 35–42.

77. O. B. Davidson and D. Eden, "Remedial Self-Fulfilling Prophecy: Two Field Experiments to Prevent Golem Effects among Disadvantaged Women," *Journal of Applied Psychology* 83, no. 3 (2000), pp. 386–98.

78. D. Eden, D. Geller, A. Gewirtz, R. Gordon-Terner, I. Inbar, M. Liberman, Y. Pass, I. Salomon-Segev, and M. Shalit, "Implanting Pygmalion Leadership Style through Workshop Training: Seven Field Experiments," *Leadership Quarterly* 11, no. 2 (2000), pp. 171–210.

79. S. S. White and E. A. Locke, "Problems with the Pygmalion Effect and Some Proposed Solutions," *Leadership Quarterly* 11, no. 3 (2000), pp. 389–416.

80. D. B. McNatt, "Ancient Pygmalion Joins Contemporary Management: A Meta-analysis of the Result," *Journal of Applied Psychology* 83, no. 2 (2000), pp. 314–21.

81. R. D. Arvey and J. M. Ivancevich, "Punishment in Organizations: A Review, Propositions, and Research Suggestions," *Academy of Management Review* 5 (1980), pp. 123–32.

82. G. J. Curphy, "What We Really Know about Leadership (But Seem Unwilling to Implement)," presentation given at the Minnesota Professionals for Psychology Applied to Work, Minneapolis, MN, January 2004.

83. L. S. Anderson, *The Cream of the Corp* (Hastings, MN: Anderson Performance Improvement Company, 2003).

84. S. E. Markham, K. D. Scott, and G. H. McKee, "Recognizing Good Attendance: A Longitudinal Quasi-Experimental Field Study," *Personnel Psychology* 55, no. 3 (2002), pp. 639–60.

85. A. D. Stajkovic and F. Luthans, "Differential Effects of Incentive Motivators on Performance," *Academy of Management Journal* 44, no. 3 (2001), pp. 580–90.

86. F. Luthans and A. D. Stajkovic, "Reinforce for Performance: The Need to Go beyond Pay and Even Rewards," *Academy of Management Executive* 13, no. 2 (1999), pp. 49–57.

87. M. Bloom and G. T. Milkovich, "Relationships among Risk, Incentive Pay, and Organizational Performance," *Academy of Management Journal* 41, no. 3 (1998), pp. 283–97.

88. G. D. Jenkins, A. Mitra, N. Gupta, and J. D. Shaw, "Are Financial Incentives Related to Performance? A Meta-analytic Review of Empirical Research," *Journal of Applied Psychology* 83, no. 5 (1998), pp. 777–87.

89. J. L. Komacki, S. Zlotnick, and M. Jensen, "Development of an Operant-Based Taxonomy and Observational Index on Supervisory Behavior," *Journal of Applied Psychology* 71 (1986), pp. 260–69.

90. R. D. Pritchard, J. Hollenback, and P. J. DeLeo, "The Effects of Continuous and Partial Schedules of Reinforcement of Effort, Performance, and Satisfaction," *Organizational Behavior and Human Performance* 16 (1976), pp. 205–30.

91. F. Luthans and R. Kreitner, *Organizational Behavior Modification and Beyond: An Operant and Social Learning Approach* (Glenview, IL: Scott Foresman, 1985).

92. P. M. Podsakoff and W. D. Todor, "Relationships between Leader Reward and Punishment Behavior and Group Process and Productivity," *Journal of Management* 11 (1985), pp. 55–73.

93. P. M. Podsakoff, W. D. Todor, and R. Skov, "Effects of Leader Contingent and Noncontingent Reward and Punishment Behaviors on Subordinate Performance and Satisfaction," *Academy of Management Journal* 25 (1982), pp. 810–25.

94. R. D. Arvey, G. A. Davis, and S. M. Nelson, "Use of Discipline in an Organization: A Field Study," *Journal of Applied Psychology* 69 (1984), pp. 448–60.

95. R. E. Quinn and G. M. Spreitzer, "The Road to Empowerment: Seven Questions Every Leader Should Consider," *Organizational Dynamics*, Autumn 1997, pp. 37–49.

96. S. H. Wagner, C. P. Parker, and N. D. Christiansen, "Employees That Think and Act Like Owners: Effects of Ownership Beliefs and Behaviors on Organizational Effectiveness," *Personnel Psychology* 56, no. 4 (2003), pp. 847–71.

97. A. Srivastava, K. M. Bartol, and E. A. Locke, "Empowering Leadership in Management Teams: Effects on Knowledge Sharing, Efficacy, and Performance," *Academy of Management Journal* 49, no. 6 (2006), pp. 1239–51.

98. S. E. Seibert, S. R. Silver, and W. A. Randolph, "Taking Empowerment to the Next Level: A Multiple-Level Model of Empowerment, Performance, and Satisfaction," *Academy of Management Journal* 47, no. 3 (2004), pp. 332–49.

99. M. Ahearne, J. Mathis, and A. Rapp, "To Empower or Not Empower Your Sales Force? An Empirical Examination of the Influence of Leadership Empowerment Behavior on Customer Satisfaction and Performance," *Journal of Applied Psychology* 90, no. 5 (2005), pp. 945–55.

100. J. Combs, Y. Liu, A. Hall, and D. Ketchen, "How Much Do High Performance Work Practices Matter? A Meta-analysis of Their Effects on Organizational Performance," *Personnel Psychology* 59 (2006), pp. 502–28.

101. L. R. Offermann, "Leading and Empowering Diverse Followers," in *The Balance of Leadership and Followership*, eds. E. P. Hollander and L. R. Offermann, Kellogg Leadership Studies Project (College Park: University of Maryland Press, 1997), pp. 31–46.

102. J. L. Xie and G. Johns, "Job Scope and Stress: Can Job Scope Be Too High?" *Academy of Management Journal* 38, no. 5 (1995), pp. 1288–1309.

103. G. M. Spreitzer, "Psychological Empowerment in the Workplace: Dimensions, Measurement, and Validation," *Academy of Management Journal* 38, no. 5 (1995), pp. 1442–65.

104. J. C. McElroy, P. C. Morrow, and S. N. Rude, "Turnover and Organizational Performance: A Comparative Analysis of the Effects of Voluntary, Involuntary, and Reduction-in-Force Turnover," *Journal of Applied Psychology* 86, no. 6 (2001), pp. 1294–99.

105. J. A. Krug, "Why Do They Keep Leaving?" *Harvard Business Review,* February 2003, pp. 14–15.

106. A. Hewitt, *Trends in Global Employee Engagement*, (Chicago: Author, 2011).

107. G. Curphy, "How You Lead Those You Perceive as Uncommitted? Start by Looking in the Mirror," *Journal of Character and Leadership Integration*, Winter, (2011).

108. D. Rigby, "Look before You Lay Off," *Harvard Business Review,* April 2002, pp. 20–21.

109. D. S. Levine, *Disgruntled: The Darker Side of the World of Work* (New York: Berkley Boulevard Books, 1998).

110. B. E. Litzky, K. E. Eddleston, and D. L. Kidder, "The Good, The Bad, and the Misguided: How Managers Inadvertently Encourage Deviant Behaviors," *Academy of Management Perspectives* 20, no. 1 (2006), pp. 91–103.

111. D. W. Organ and K. Ryan, "A Meta-analytic Review of Attitudinal and Dispositional Predictors of Organizational Citizenship Behavior," *Personnel Psychology* 48 (1995), pp. 775–802.

112. L. A. Bettencourt, K. P. Gwinner, and M. L. Meuter, "A Comparison of Attitude, Personality, and Knowledge Predictors of Service-Oriented Organizational Citizenship Behaviors," *Journal of Applied Psychology* 86, no. 1 (2001), pp. 29–41.

113. R. C. Mayer and M. B. Gavin, "Trust in Management and Performance: Who Minds the Shop While Employees Watch the Boss?" *Academy of Management Journal* 48, no. 5 (2005), pp. 874–88.

114. B. J. Tepper, M. K. Duffy, C. A. Henle, L. Schurer Lambert, "Procedural Injustice, Victim Precipitation, and Abusive Supervision," *Personnel Psychology* 59 (2006), pp. 101–23.

115. G. Strauss, "Workers Hone the Fine Art of Revenge: Acts of Violence, Harassment toward Boss on Rise in Corporate World," *Denver Post*, August 24, 1998, p. 6E.

116. A. E. Colbert, M. K. Mount, J. K. Harter, L. A. Witt, and M. R. Barrick, "Interactive Effects of Personality and Perceptions of the Work Situation on Workplace Deviance," *Journal of Applied Psychology* 89, no. 4 (2004), pp. 599–609.

117. B. Marcus and H. Schuler, "Antecedents of Counterproductive Behavior at Work: A General Perspective," *Journal of Applied Psychology* 89, no. 1 (2004), pp. 647–60.

118. R. P. Tett and J. P. Meyer, "Job Satisfaction, Organizational Commitment, Turnover Intention, and Turnover: Path Analyses Based on Meta-analytic Findings," *Personnel Psychology* 46 (1993), pp. 259–93.

119. G. J. Curphy, "In-Depth Assessments, 360-Degree Feedback, and Development: Key Research Results and Recommended Next Steps," presentation at the Annual Conference for HR Managers at US West Communications, Denver, CO, January 1998.

120. T. Peters, *The Circle of Innovation: You Can't Shrink Your Way to Greatness* (New York: Random House, 1997).

121. S. Schellenbarger, "Investors Seem Attracted to Firms with Happy Employees," *The Wall Street Journal*, March 19, 1997, p. I2.

122. A. G. Bedeian and A. A. Armenakis, "The Cesspool Syndrome: How Dreck Floats to the Top of Declining Organizations," *Academy of Management Executive* 12, no. 1 (1998), pp. 58–63.

123. P. W. Hom and A. J. Kinicki, "Towards a Greater Understanding of How Dissatisfaction Drives Employee Turnover," *Academy of Management Journal* 44, no. 5 (2001), pp. 975–87.

124. P. W. Hom, L. Roberson, and A. D. Ellis, "Challenging Conventional Wisdom about Who Quits: Revelations from Corporate America," *Journal of Applied Psychology* 93, no. 1 (2008), pp. 1–34.

125. D. P. Campbell, G. J. Curphy, and T. Tuggle, *360 Degree Feedback Instruments: Beyond Theory*, workshop presented at the 10th Annual Conference of the Society for Industrial and Organizational Psychology, Orlando, FL, May 1995.

126. P. Morrel-Samuels, "Getting the Truth into Workplace Surveys," *Harvard Business Review*, February 2002, pp. 111–20.

127. http://www.kellyglobal.net/eprise/main/web/us/mykelly/en/careertips_jan13_jobsecurity

128. http://www.strategicstudiesinstitute.army.mil/pubs/summary.cfm?q=912.

129. Associated Press, "Military Pay Soars," April 11, 2007, http://military.com/NewsContent.

130. http://www.armytimes.com/news/2007/09/army_bonuses_070910w/.

131. D. P. Campbell and S. Hyne, *Manual for the Revised Campbell Organizational Survey* (Minneapolis, MN: National Computer Systems, 1995).

132. C. Kleiman, "Survey: Job Satisfaction Can Be Costly to Employers," *Denver Post*, June 22, 1997, p. J–4.

133. T. A. Judge and R. Ilies, "Relationship of Personality to Performance Motivation: A Meta-analytic Review," *Journal of Applied Psychology* 87, no. 4 (2002), pp. 797–807.

134. R. Ilies and T. A. Judge, "On the Heritability of Job Satisfaction: The Mediating Role of Personality," *Journal of Applied Psychology* 88, no. 4 (2003), pp. 750–59.

135. S. Anchor, "Positive Intelligence: Three Ways Individuals Can Cultivate Their Own Sense of Well-Being and Set Themselves Up to Succeed," *Harvard Business Review*, January–February 2012, pp. 100–2.

136. G. Morse, "The Science Behind the Smile: An Interview with Daniel Gilbert," *Harvard Business Review*, January-February 2012, pp. 85-90.

390 Part Three *Focus on the Followers*

137. R. D. Arvey, T. J. Bouchard Jr., N. L. Segal, and L. M. Abraham, "Job Satisfaction: Environmental and Genetic Components," *Journal of Applied Psychology* 74 (1989), pp. 187–92.

138. F. Herzberg, "The Motivation-Hygiene Concept and Problems of Manpower," *Personnel Administrator* 27 (1964), pp. 3–7.

139. F. Herzberg, *Work and the Nature of Man* (Cleveland, OH: World Publishing, 1966).

140. F. Herzberg, "One More Time: How Do You Motivate Employees?" *Harvard Business Review*, January 2003, pp. 87–96.

141. B. H. Sheppard, R. J. Lewicki, and J. W. Minton, *Organizational Justice: The Search for Fairness in the Workplace* (New York: Lexington Books, 1972).

142. L. K. Trevino, "The Social Effects of Punishment in Organizations: A Justice Perspective," *Academy of Management Review* 17 (1992), pp. 647–76.

143. P. A. Siegel, C. Post, J. Brockner, A. Y. Fishman, and C. Garden, "The Moderating Influence of Procedural Fairness on the Relationship between Work–Life Conflict and Organizational Commitment," *Journal of Applied Psychology* 90, no. 1 (2005), pp. 13–24.

144. J. A. Colquitt, "On the Dimensionality of Organizational Justice: A Construct Validation of a Measure," *Journal of Applied Psychology* 86, no. 2 (2001), pp. 386–400.

145. J. A. Colquitt, D. E. Conlon, M. J. Wesson, C. O. L. H. Porter, and K. Y. Ng, "Justice at the Millennium: A Meta-analytic Review of 25 Years of Organizational Justice Research," *Journal of Applied Psychology* 86, no. 2 (2001), pp. 425–45.

146. M. L. Ambrose and R. Cropanzano, "A Longitudinal Analysis of Organizational Fairness: An Examination of Reactions to Tenure and Promotion Decisions," *Journal of Applied Psychology* 88, no. 2 (2003), pp. 266–75.

147. B. J. Tepper and E. C. Taylor, "Relationships among Supervisors' and Subordinates' Procedural Justice Perceptions and Organizational Citizenship Behaviors," *Academy of Management Journal* 46, no. 1 (2003), pp. 97–105.

148. T. Simons and Q. Roberson "Why Managers Should Care about Fairness: The Effects of Aggregate Justice Perceptions on Organizational Outcomes," *Journal of Applied Psychology* 88, no. 3 (2003), pp. 432–43.

149. E. C. Hollensbe, S. Khazanchi, and S. S. Masterson, "How Do I Assess If My Supervisor and Organization Are Fair: Identifying the Rules Underlying Entity-Based Justice Perceptions," *Academy of Management Journal* 51, no. 6 (2008), pp. 1099–116.

150. B. C. Holtz and C. M. Harold, "Fair Today, Fair Tomorrow? A Longitudinal Investigation of Overall Justice Perceptions," *Journal of Applied Psychology* 94, no. 5 (2009), pp. 1185–99.

Chapter 12

The Situation

Introduction

April 16, 2007, was a dark day at Virginia Tech. On that day Cho Seung Hui went on a shooting rampage that killed 32 students and faculty and injured a host of others. There is no doubt that Cho was a villain, if not a deranged one, as he created a situation of terror in Norris Hall. But in that same awful situation, heroes were created. One was Zach Petkewicz.

Zach and his fellow classmates were in a classroom near the one where Cho initiated his massacre. They heard the initial gunshots through the walls and could hear them getting closer. At first everyone experienced fear and hid behind whatever they could find for protection. But it occurred to Zach that "there's nothing stopping him from coming in here. We were just sitting ducks." And that's when Zach and others took action.

Zach grabbed a table and shoved it against the door. Seeing his plan, other students joined him, pinning the table against the cinderblock walls around the door frame. They were just in time. Cho tried to get into their classroom next. Having tried the door handle and then brute force, Cho emptied a clip of ammunition through the door before giving up and moving on to another room.

Days after the assault, Zach Petkewicz was interviewed by Matt Lauer on NBC's *Today Show*. Lauer asked Zach if he could have predicted, before the shooting, how he would react. The young hero, whose first reaction had been fear, said that's not possible for anyone. "There's no way of telling what I would have done until you're put in that situation."

Zach was right about two things. First, as he said, it is difficult to predict anyone's behavior unless you take the situation into account. Second, we are coming to understand that the situation is one of the most powerful variables in the leadership equation. And that is the topic of this chapter. It is important to understand how the situation influences leaders and followers and, furthermore, that the situation is not just a "given" that leaders and followers must adapt to; sometimes, at least, leaders and followers can change the situation and thereby enhance the likelihood of desired outcomes. That's what Zach did: he changed the situation. Of course Zach reacted to a situation he was tragically confronted with, but leaders do not always need to be reactive. Leaders also can use their knowledge of how the situation affects leadership to proactively *change* the situation in order to enhance the likelihood of success. All too often, leaders and followers overlook how changing the situation can help them to change their behavior. This is called **situational engineering.**

Suppose, for example, that a leader received developmental feedback that she needed to spend more time interacting with subordinates. Even with the best intentions, such a goal can prove difficult to achieve, just as numerous New Year's resolutions fail. In both cases an important barrier to success is that the person does not adequately address challenges posed by the situation in which they find themselves. After the holidays, many well-intentioned dieters don't lose weight because they fail to reduce the number of food cues around them. And a leader who may genuinely desire greater interaction with subordinates may nonetheless unwittingly subvert her own goal by continuing to define her tasks in the same way she always had. A better strategy could be to review her own tasks and then delegate some of them to subordinates. This would free up some of the leader's time and also create opportunities to interact with subordinates in ways like mutually setting performance goals and meeting regularly to review their progress.[1]

Highlight 12.1 presents ways in which various versions of a familiar situation may significantly affect your own likelihood of being a "good follower." Highlight 12.2 examines how leaders in dangerous situations might have to adopt different strategies to be successful than they would in more normal situations.

In a book designed to introduce students to the subject of leadership, a chapter about "the situation" poses some challenging obstacles and dilemmas. The breadth of the topic is daunting: it could include almost everything else in the world that has not been covered in the previous chapters! To the typical student who has not yet begun a professional career, pondering the magnitude of variables making up the situation is a formidable request. For one thing, the situation you find yourself in is often seen as completely beyond your control. How many times have you heard someone say, "Hey, I don't make the rules around here—I just follow them"? The subject is made more difficult by the fact that most students have limited organizational experience as a frame of reference. So why bother to introduce the material in this chapter? Because the situation we are in often explains far more about what is going on and what kinds of leadership behaviors will be best than any other single variable we have discussed so far!

In this chapter we will try to sort out some of the complexity and magnitude of this admittedly large topic. First, we will review some of the research that has led us to consider these issues. Then, after considering a

When you've exhausted all possibilities, remember this: You haven't!
Robert H. Schuller

Trying to change individual and/or corporate behavior without addressing the larger organizational context is bound to disappoint. Sooner or later bureaucratic structures will consume even the most determined of collaborative processes. As Woody Allen once said, "The lion and the lamb may lie down together, but the lamb won't get much sleep." What to do? Work on the lion as well as the lamb designing teamwork into the organization. . . . Although the Boston Celtics have won 16 championships, they have never had the league's leading scorer and never paid a player based on his individual statistics. The Celtics understand that virtually every aspect of basketball requires collaboration.
Robert W. Keidel

The College Classroom as Situation

HIGHLIGHT 12.1

One way to appreciate the variety of ways in which the situation affects leadership is to look at one of the most familiar situations to you: the college classroom and its associated work. Let's define the leadership challenge in every case as "getting the best out of you" in terms of your study, your work on assignments, and enhancing the experience of the course for everyone. With those criteria of effective leadership (or followership, if you prefer), reflect on how the challenges you face as a follower are affected by the variations in the series of classroom situations described here:

Situation 1	Situation 2	Situation 3 (in some Cases)
You're in a seminar with 15 other students.	You're in a 200-student lecture hall.	You're taking the course virtually over the Internet.
This is an elective course in your major.	This is a required general education course at your school.	
There's much student autonomy in the course in determining course paper topics.	Highly specific writing assignments are prescribed for you.	
A group project is an important part of your grade, and you're working on it with three good friends who are all good students.	A group project is an important part of your grade, and you're working on it with three strangers who are doing poorly in the course.	
Your class meets at 8 a.m.	Your class meets at 2 p.m.	Your class meets at 7 p.m.
You're a full-time student living in a dorm at your college.	You're a part-time student taking the class at a "commuter college" after you finish your regular day job.	

huge situational change that is now occurring, we will present a model to help us consider key situational variables. Finally, we will take a look forward through an interesting lens. Throughout the chapter, though, our objective will be primarily to increase awareness rather than to prescribe specific courses of leader action.

The appropriateness of a leader's behavior with a group of followers often makes sense only when you look at the situational context in which the behavior occurs. For example, severely disciplining a follower might seem a poor way to lead; but if the follower in question had just committed a safety violation endangering the lives of hundreds of people, the leader's actions might be exactly right. In a similar fashion, the situation may be the primary reason personality traits, experience, or cognitive abilities are related less consistently to leadership effectiveness

Leading in Extremis

HIGHLIGHT 12.2

Colonel Tom Kolditz is head of the Department of Behavioral Sciences and Leadership at the U.S. Military Academy at West Point. He's the author of a book called *In Extremis Leadership*, which looks at leadership in dangerous contexts. In doing research for the book, Kolditz and his colleagues interviewed leaders of SWAT teams, parachuting teams, special operations soldiers, mountain climbing guides, and others who led in dangerous situations. Kolditz identified several characteristics of effective in extremis leaders:

- They embrace continuous learning because dangerous situations demand it.
- They share risks with their followers.
- They share a common lifestyle with their followers.
- They are highly competent themselves in ways specific to the dangerous situation.
- They inspire high competence and mutual trust and loyalty with others.

Source: T. Kolditz, *In Extremis Leadership: Leading as If Your Life Depended on It* (San Francisco: Jossey-Bass, 2007).

The way of the superior is threefold, but I am not equal to it. Virtuous, he is free from anxieties; wise, he is free from perplexities; bold, he is free from fear.

Confucius

than to leadership emergence.[2,3] Most leadership emergence studies have involved leaderless discussion groups, and for the most part the situation is quite similar across such studies. In studies of leadership effectiveness, however, the situation can and does vary dramatically. The personal attributes needed by an effective leader of a combat unit, chemical research and development division, community service organization, or fast-food restaurant may change considerably. Because the situations facing leaders of such groups may be so variable, it is hardly surprising that studies of leader characteristics have yielded inconsistent results when looking at leadership effectiveness across jobs or situations. Thus the importance of the situation in the leadership process should not be overlooked.

Historically, some leadership researchers emphasized the importance of the situation in the leadership process in response to the Great Man theory of leadership. These researchers maintained that the situation, not someone's traits or abilities, plays the most important role in determining who emerges as a leader.[4-6] As support for the situational viewpoint, these researchers noted that great leaders typically emerged during economic crises, social upheavals, or revolutions; great leaders were generally not associated with periods of relative calm or quiet. For example, Schneider[7] noted that the number of individuals identified as great military leaders in the British armed forces during any period depended on how many conflicts the country was engaged in—the higher the number of conflicts, the higher the number of great military leaders. Moreover, researchers advocating the situational viewpoint believed leaders were made, not born, and that prior leadership experience helped forge effective leaders.[8] These early situational theories of leadership tended to be popular in the United States because they fit more closely with American ideals of equality and meritocracy and ran counter to the genetic views of leadership that were popular among European researchers at the time.[9] (The fact that many of these European researchers had aristocratic backgrounds probably had something to do with the popularity of the Great Man theory in Europe.)

More recent leadership theories have explored how situational factors affect leaders' behaviors. In **role theory,** for example, a leader's behavior was said to depend on a leader's perceptions of several critical aspects of the situation: rules and regulations governing the job; role expectations of subordinates, peers, and superiors; the nature of the task; and feedback about subordinates' performance.[10] Role theory clarified how these situational demands and constraints could cause role conflict and role ambiguity.[11] Leaders may experience role conflict when subordinates and superiors have conflicting expectations about a leader's behavior or when company policies contradict how superiors expect tasks to be performed. A leader's ability to successfully resolve such conflicts may well determine leadership effectiveness.[12]

Another effort to incorporate situational variables into leadership theory was Hunt and Osborn's[13] **multiple-influence model.** Hunt and Osborn distinguished between microvariables (such as task characteristics) and macrovariables (such as the external environment) in the situation. Although most researchers looked at the effects tasks had on leader behaviors, Hunt and Osborn believed macrovariables have a pervasive influence on the ways leaders act. Both role theory and the multiple-influence model highlight a major problem in addressing situational factors, which was noted previously: that situations can vary in countless ways. Because situations can vary in so many ways, it is helpful for leaders to have an abstract scheme for conceptualizing situations. This would be a step in knowing how to identify what may be most salient or critical to pay attention to in any particular instance.

One of the most basic abstractions is **situational levels.** The idea behind situational levels may best be conveyed with an example. Suppose someone asked you, "How are things going at work?" You might respond by commenting on the specific tasks you perform ("It is still pretty tough. I am under the gun for getting next year's budget prepared, and I have never done that before"). Or you might respond by commenting on aspects of the overall organization ("It is really different. There are so many rules you have to follow. My old company was not like that at all"). Or you might comment on factors affecting the organization itself ("I've been really worried about keeping my job—you know how many cutbacks there have been in our whole industry recently"). Each response deals with the situation, but each refers to a different level of abstraction: the task level, the organizational level, and the environmental level. Each of these three levels provides a different perspective with which to examine the leadership process (see Figure 12.1).

FIGURE 12.1
An Expanded
Leader–Follower–
Situation Model

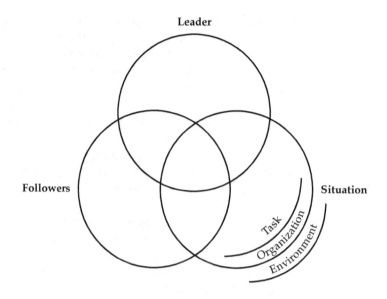

These three levels certainly do not exhaust all the ways in which situations vary. Situations also differ in terms of physical variables like noise and temperature levels, workload demands, and the extent to which work groups interact with other groups. Organizations also have unique "corporate cultures," which define a context for leadership. And there are always even broader economic, social, legal, and technological aspects of situations within which the leadership process occurs. What, amid all this situational complexity, should leaders pay attention to?

The Task

The brain is a wonderful organ; it begins working the moment you get up in the morning and does not stop until you get to the office.

Robert Frost

How Tasks Vary, and What That Means for Leadership

The most fundamental level of the situation involves the tasks to be performed by individuals or teams within the organization. Several ways in which tasks vary are particularly relevant to leadership. Industrial and organizational psychologists spent much of the last half-century classifying and categorizing tasks to better understand how to enhance worker satisfaction and productivity. Some of this research has great relevance to leadership, particularly the concepts of task autonomy, feedback, structure, and interdependence.

Task autonomy is the degree to which a job provides an individual with some control over what he does and how he does it. Someone with considerable autonomy would have discretion in scheduling work and deciding the procedures used in accomplishing it. Autonomy often covaries with technical expertise: workers with considerable expertise will be given more latitude, and those with few skills will be given more instruction and coaching when accomplishing tasks.[14,15] Moreover, responsibility and job satisfaction often increase when autonomy increases.[16]

Another important way in which tasks vary is in terms of **task feedback,** which refers to the degree to which a person accomplishing a task receives information about performance *from performing the task itself.* In this context feedback is received not from supervisors but rather from what is intrinsic to the work activity itself. Driving a car is one example of feedback intrinsic to a task. If you are a skilled driver on a road with a number of twists and turns, you get all the feedback you need about how well you are accomplishing the task merely by observing how the car responds to your inputs. This is feedback from the job itself as opposed to feedback from another person (who in this example would be a classic backseat driver). Extending this example to work or team settings, leaders sometimes may want to redesign tasks so that they (the tasks) provide more intrinsic feedback. Although this does not absolve the leader from giving periodic performance feedback, it can free up some of the leader's time for other work-related activities. Additionally, leaders should understand that followers may eventually become dissatisfied if leaders provide high levels of feedback for tasks that already provide intrinsic feedback.[17–19]

Perhaps the easiest way to explain **task structure** is by using an example demonstrating the difference between a structured task and an unstructured task. Assume the task to be accomplished is solving for x given the formula $3x + 2x = 15$. If that problem were given to a group of people who knew the fundamental rules of algebra, everyone would arrive at the same answer. In this example there is a known procedure for accomplishing the task; there are rules governing how one goes about it; and if people follow those rules, there is one result. These features characterize a *structured task.*

On the other hand, if the task is to resolve a morale problem on a team, committee, or work group, there may be no clear-cut method for solving it. There are many different ways, perhaps none of which is obvious or necessarily best for approaching a solution. Different observers may not see the problem in the same way; they may even have different ideas of what morale is. Solving a morale problem, therefore, exemplifies an *unstructured task.*

People vary in their preferences for, or ability to handle, structured versus unstructured tasks. With the Myers-Briggs Type Indicator (MBTI), for example, perceivers are believed to prefer unstructured situations, whereas judgers prefer activities that are planned and organized.[20] Individuals with high tolerance for stress may handle ambiguous and unstructured tasks more easily than people with low tolerance for stress.[21] Aside from these differences, however, we might ask whether there are any general rules for how leaders should interact with followers as a function of task structure. One consideration here is that while it is *easier* for a leader or coach to give instruction in structured tasks, it is not necessarily the most helpful thing to do.

We can see this by returning to the algebra problem described earlier. If a student had never seen such an algebra problem before, it would be relatively easy to teach the student the rules needed to solve the problem. Once any student has learned the procedure, however, she can solve similar problems on her own. Extending this to other situations, once a subordinate knows or understands a task, a supervisor's continuing instruction (that is, initiating structure or directive behavior) may provide superfluous information and eventually become irritating.[22,23] Subordinates *need* help when a task is unstructured, when they do not know what the desired outcome looks like, and when they do not know how to achieve it. Anything a supervisor or leader can do to increase subordinates' ability to perform unstructured tasks is likely to increase their performance and job satisfaction.[24] Paradoxically, though, unstructured tasks are by nature somewhat ill defined. Thus they often are more difficult for leaders themselves to analyze and provide direction in accomplishing. Nonetheless, reducing the degree of ambiguity inherent in an unstructured situation is a leadership behavior usually appreciated by followers.

Finally, **task interdependence** concerns the degree to which tasks require coordination and synchronization for work groups or teams to accomplish desired goals. Task interdependence differs from autonomy in that workers or team members may be able to accomplish their tasks in an autonomous fashion, but the products of their efforts must be coordinated for the group or team to succeed. Tasks with high levels of interdependence place a premium on leaders' organizing and planning, directing, and communication skills.[25] In one study, for example, coaches exhibiting high levels of initiating-structure behaviors had better-performing teams for sports requiring relatively interdependent effort, such as football, hockey, lacrosse, rugby, basketball, and volleyball; the same leader behaviors were unrelated to team performance for sports requiring relatively independent effort, such as swimming, track, cross-country, golf, and baseball.[26] Thus the degree of task interdependence can dictate which leader behaviors will be effective in a particular situation.

Problems and Challenges

Astronaut Jim Lovell's words during the *Apollo 13* lunar mission, "Houston, we have a problem," launched a remarkable tale of effective teamwork and creative problem solving by NASA engineers working to save the lives of the imperiled crew when two oxygen tanks exploded en route to the moon. The problem they faced was urgent, critical, and novel: no one had ever confronted a problem like this before, no one had even anticipated it, and there were no established checklists, emergency procedures, or backup equipment that could be counted on to reach a viable solution. We might say, of course, that the engineers' task was to devise a solution, but we want to stress a distinction here between the connotation of *task* as it was examined in the preceding section and that of completely novel problems or challenges for which routine solutions do not exist. As we noted earlier, up to this point our treatment of tasks has derived largely from the perspective of industrial and organizational psychology wherein the task dimensions just described (and many others) represent ways to systematically and objectively describe relatively enduring aspects of routine work or jobs. Obviously the situation that the NASA engineers and astronauts faced was anything but routine.

Ronald Heifetz has been studying the leadership implications of problems and challenges like that for many years. He says that often we face problems or challenges for which the problem-solving resources already exist. In general, you can think of these resources as having two aspects: specialized methods and specialized expertise. There are many technical problems that we can solve by applying widely known though specialized methods for solution. A simple example might be determining the gas mileage your car gets on a cross-country trip. The rules are simple to follow, and they always work if you follow them correctly. At other times we may not know the answers, but it may be relatively easy to find the people who do. Maybe we can't fix the rattle coming from the car engine, but we believe the mechanic can do so. We may not know how to fix our ailment, but we believe the physician will know what to do. We may not know how to use a new software system, but we believe we can master it with assistance from an expert. Problems like these are what Heifetz calls **technical problems.** Even though they may be complex, there are expert solutions to them, and experts know how to solve them even if we don't.[27]

But not all problems are like that. Some problems, by their nature, defy even expert solution. Some problems cannot be solved using currently existing resources and ways of thinking. In fact, it's the nature of such problems that *it can be quite difficult even reaching a common definition of what the problem really is.* Solving such problems requires that the systems facing them make fundamental changes of some kind. Heifetz calls these **adaptive problems.** Whereas technical problems can be solved without changing the nature of the social system itself within which they occur, *adaptive problems can only be solved by changing the system itself.*

At work, the most important issue in addressing technical problems is making sure they get to someone with the authority to manage the solution. According to Heifetz, however, most social problems turn out to be adaptive in nature. Almost by definition, then, significant organizational change is at least in part an adaptive challenge. Even a seemingly simpler leadership challenge at work, like getting someone else to take more seriously some constructive feedback, is actually an adaptive challenge rather than a technical one. But here is where the distinction between technical problems and adaptive problems can become blurred. Go back to our earlier example of seeing a physician for a medical problem—but let's assume

Rough waters are truer tests of leadership. In calm water every ship has a good captain.
Swedish proverb

TABLE 12.1
Adaptive and
Technical
Challenges

	What's the Work?	Who Does the Work?
Technical	Applying current know-how.	Authorities.
Adaptive	Discovering new ways.	The people facing the challenge.

it's your elderly parent rather than yourself who is the patient. Let's further assume that the physician correctly solves the technical problem and provides the correct technical solution—a particular medication that has a noticeable but tolerable side effect. Getting your parent to take the medicine if he doesn't want to turns this seemingly simple technical problem into a challenging adaptive one.

How do you know when a challenge is mostly a technical challenge or mostly an adaptive challenge? It's an adaptive challenge either wholly or mostly

- When people's hearts and minds need to change, and not just their standard or habitual behaviors.
- By a process of elimination—if every technical solution you can think of has failed to improve the situation, it is more likely to be an adaptive challenge.
- If there is continuing conflict among people struggling with the challenge.
- In a crisis, which may reflect an underlying or unrecognized adaptive problem.

Some problems are so complex that you have to be highly intelligent and well informed just to be undecided about them.

Laurence J. Peter,
management
consultant

Different leadership approaches are required to solve adaptive problems than are required to solve technical problems. That's because adaptive problems involve people's *values*, and finding solutions to problems that involve others' values requires the active engagement of *their* hearts and minds—not just the leader's. This is what Heifetz calls **adaptive leadership.** The importance of the difference between adaptive and technical problems will become clearer as we look later in the chapter at the organizational and environmental levels of the situation.

To summarize, Table 12.1 shows the relationship between whether a problem or a challenge is mostly technical or adaptive in nature, the kind of work required to effectively address the challenge, and whom should be thought of as the "problem solver."[28]

The Organization

From the Industrial Age to the Information Age

All of us have grown up in the age of industry, but perhaps in its waning years. Starting just before the American Civil War and continuing through the last quarter of the 20th century, the industrial age supplanted the age of agriculture. During the industrial age, companies succeeded according to how well they could capture the benefits from "economies of scale and scope."[29] Technology mattered, but mostly to the extent that companies could increase the efficiencies of mass production. Now a new age is emerging, and in this information age many of the fundamental assumptions of the industrial age are becoming obsolete.

Kaplan and Norton[30] have described a new set of operating assumptions underlying the information age and contrasted them with their predecessors in the industrial age. They described changes in the following ways companies operate.

Cross Functions   Industrial age organizations gained competitive advantage through specialization of functional skills in areas like manufacturing, distribution, marketing, and technology. This specialization yielded substantial benefits, but over time also led to enormous inefficiencies and slow response processes. The information age organization operates with integrated business processes that cut across traditional business functions.

Links to Customers and Suppliers   Industrial age companies worked with customers and suppliers via arm's-length transactions. Information technology enables today's organizations to integrate supply, production, and delivery processes and to realize enormous improvements in cost, quality, and response time.

Customer Segmentation   Industrial age companies prospered by offering low-cost but standardized products and services (remember Henry Ford's comment that his customers "can have whatever color they want as long as it is black"). Information age companies must learn to offer customized products and services to diverse customer segments.

Global Scale   Information age companies compete against the best companies throughout the entire world. In fact, the large investments required for new products and services may require customers worldwide to provide adequate returns on those costs.

Innovation   Product life cycles continue to shrink. Competitive advantage in one generation of a product's life is no guarantee of success for future generations of that product. Companies operating in an environment of rapid technological innovation must be masters at anticipating customers' future needs, innovating new products and services, and rapidly deploying new technologies into efficient delivery processes.

Knowledge Workers   Industrial companies created sharp distinctions between an intellectual elite on the one hand (especially managers and engineers) and a direct labor workforce on the other. The latter group performed tasks and processes under direct supervision of white-collar engineers and managers. This typically involved physical rather than mental capabilities. Now all employees must contribute value by what they know and by the information they can provide.

Growing Up with The Gap

HIGHLIGHT 12.3

The Gap, Inc., is growing up in the information age. The retail company got its start in 1969 when Don and Doris Fisher opened the first Gap store in San Francisco. The Fishers' goal was to appeal to young consumers and bridge "the generation gap" they saw in most retail stores. Their first store sold only jeans and targeted customers mainly in their 20s. As Gap customers have grown up, so has the brand. In 1983 The Gap acquired Banana Republic mainly for its thriving catalog business and evolved the company from its original travel theme to an upscale alternative to the more casual Gap stores. In 1990 Baby Gap was born, appealing to young parents looking for stylish alternatives for their children. In 1994 Old Navy stores were introduced as the Gap looked for ways to appeal to value-oriented shoppers. The Piperline brand was created in 2006, retailing footwear online, and Athleta, a women's athletic wear line was added in 2009. From young adult, to career professional, to parent, to cost-conscious family, to aging baby boomer, The Gap has stuck close to its customers and evolved to offer products that would appeal to their changing needs.

Sources: http://www.sfgate.com/cgi-bin/article.cgi?file=/c/a/2004/08/20/BUG8288V9244.DTL&type=printable; http://www.gapinc.com/financmedia/press_releases.htm; http://www.gapinc.com/about/ataglance/milestones.htm.

One needs only to reflect upon Kaplan and Norton's list of changing operating assumptions to recognize that the situation leaders find themselves in today is different from the situation of 20 years ago. What's more, it is probably changing at an ever-increasing rate. In a real sense, the pace of change today is like trying to navigate whitewater rapids; things are changing so rapidly it can be difficult to get one's bearings. You can see how one well-known company has been trying to navigate these changing waters in Highlight 12.3. To understand how organizations cope with change, it will be helpful to look at two different facets of organizations: the formal organization and the informal organization, or organizational culture.

The Formal Organization

The study of the **formal organization** is most associated with the disciplines of management, organizational behavior, and organizational theory. Nonetheless, many aspects of the formal organization have a profound impact on leadership, and so we will briefly review some of the most important of them.

Level of authority concerns our hierarchical level in an organization. The types of behaviors most critical to leadership effectiveness can change substantially as we move up an organizational ladder. First-line supervisors, lower-level leaders, and coaches spend a considerable amount of time training followers, resolving work unit or team performance problems, scheduling practices or arranging work schedules, and implementing policies. Leaders at higher organizational levels have more autonomy and spend relatively more time setting policies, coordinating activities,

A man may speak very well in the House of Commons, and fail very completely in the House of Lords. There are two distinct styles requisite.
Benjamin Disraeli

and making staffing decisions.[31,32] Moreover, leaders at higher organizational levels often perform a greater variety of activities and are more apt to use participation and delegation.[33,34] A quite different aspect of how level of authority affects leadership is presented in Highlight 12.4.

Organizational structure refers to the way an organization's activities are coordinated and controlled, and represents another level of the situation in which leaders and followers must operate. Organizational structure is a conceptual or procedural reality, however, not a physical or tangible one. Typically it is depicted in the form of a chart that clarifies formal authority relationships and patterns of communication within the organization. Most people take organizational structure for granted and fail to realize that structure is really just a tool for getting things done in organizations. Structure is not an end in itself, and different structures might exist for organizations performing similar work, each having unique advantages and disadvantages. There is nothing sacrosanct or permanent about any structure, and leaders may find that having a basic

---

The Glass Ceiling and the Wall

HIGHLIGHT 12.4

While the past 25 years have been marked by increasing movement of women into leadership positions, women still occupy only a small percentage of the highest leadership positions. Researchers at the Center for Creative Leadership embarked on the Executive Woman Project to understand why.[35]

They studied 76 women executives in 25 companies who had reached the general management level or the one just below it. The average woman executive in the sample was 41 and married. More than half had at least one child, and the vast majority were white.

The researchers expected to find evidence of a "glass ceiling," an invisible barrier that keeps women from progressing higher than a certain level in their organizations *because they are women.* One reason the women in this particular sample were interesting was precisely because they had apparently "broken" the glass ceiling, thus entering the top 1 percent of the workforce. These women had successfully confronted three different sorts of pressure throughout their careers, a greater challenge than their male counterparts faced. One pressure was that from the job itself, and this was

no different for women than for men. A second level of pressure, however, involved being a female executive, with attendant stresses such as being particularly visible, excessively scrutinized, and a role model for other women. A third level of pressure involved the demands of coordinating personal and professional life. It is still most people's expectation that women will take the greater responsibility in a family for managing the household and raising children. And beyond the sheer size of such demands, the roles of women in these two spheres of life are often at odds (such as being businesslike and efficient, maybe even tough, at work yet intimate and nurturing at home).

Resear Researchers identified the "lessons for success" of this group of women who had broken through the glass ceiling, and they also reported a somewhat unexpected finding. Breaking through the glass ceiling presented women executives with an even tougher obstacle. They "hit a wall" that kept them out of the very top positions. The researchers estimated that only a handful of the women executives in their sample would enter the topmost echelon, called senior management, and that none would become president of their corporation.

understanding of organizational structure is not only useful but imperative. Leaders may wish to design a structure to enhance the likelihood of
attaining a desired outcome, or they may wish to change a structure to
meet future demands.

One important way in which organizational structures vary is in terms
of their complexity. Concerning an organizational chart, **horizontal complexity** refers to the number of "boxes" at any particular organizational
level. The greater the number of boxes at a given level, the greater the
horizontal complexity. Typically greater horizontal complexity is associated with more specialization within subunits and an increased likelihood
for communication breakdowns between subunits. **Vertical complexity**
refers to the number of hierarchical levels appearing on an organizational
chart. A vertically simple organization may have only two or three levels
from the highest person to the lowest. A vertically complex organization,
on the other hand, may have 10 or more. Vertical complexity can affect
leadership by impacting other factors such as authority dynamics and
communication networks. **Spatial complexity** describes geographical dis-
persion. An organization that has all its people in one location is typically
less spatially complex than an organization that is dispersed around the
country or around the world. Obviously spatial complexity makes it more
difficult for leaders to have face-to-face communication with subordinates
in geographically separated locations, and to personally administer rewards or provide support and encouragement. Generally all three of these
elements are partly a function of organizational size. Bigger organizations
are more likely to have more specialized subunits (horizontal complexity)
and a greater number of hierarchical levels (vertical complexity), and to
have subunits that are geographically dispersed (spatial complexity).

Organizations also vary in their degree of **formalization,** or degree of
standardization. Organizations having written job descriptions and standardized operating procedures for each position have a high degree of
formalization. The degree of formalization in an organization tends to
vary with its size, just as complexity generally increases with size.[36] Formalization also varies with the nature of work performed. Manufacturing
organizations, for example, tend to have fairly formalized structures,
whereas research and development organizations tend to be less formalized. After all, how could there be a detailed job description for developing a nonexistent product or making a scientific discovery?

The degree of formalization in an organization poses both advantages
and disadvantages for leaders and followers. Whereas formalizing procedures clarifies methods of operating and interacting, it also may constitute
demands and constraints on leaders and followers. Leaders may be constrained in the ways they communicate requests, order supplies, or reward or discipline subordinates.[37] If followers belong to a union, then
union rules may dictate work hours, the amount of work accomplished
per day, or who will be the first to be laid off.[38] Other aspects of the impact

Is There Any Substitute for Leadership?

HIGHLIGHT 12.5

Are leaders always necessary? Or are certain kinds of leader behaviors, at least, sometimes unnecessary? Kerr and Jermier proposed that certain situational or follower characteristics may effectively neutralize or substitute for leaders' task or relationship behaviors. *Neutralizers* are characteristics that reduce or limit the effectiveness of a leader's behaviors. *Substitutes* are characteristics that make a leader's behaviors redundant or unnecessary.

Kerr and Jermier developed the idea of **substitutes for leadership** after comparing the correlations between leadership behaviors and follower performance and satisfaction with correlations between various situational factors and follower performance and satisfaction. Those subordinate, task, and organizational characteristics having higher correlations with follower performance and satisfaction than the two leadership behaviors were subsequently identified as substitutes or neutralizers. The following are a few examples of the situational factors Kerr and

Jermier found to substitute for or neutralize leaders' task or relationship behaviors:

- A subordinate's ability and experience may substitute for task-oriented leader behavior. A subordinate's indifference toward rewards overall may neutralize a leader's task and relationship behavior.

- Tasks that are routine or structured may substitute for task-oriented leader behavior, as can tasks that provide intrinsic feedback or are intrinsically satisfying.

- High levels of formalization in organizations may substitute for task-oriented leader behavior, and unbending rules and procedures may even neutralize the leader's task behavior. A cohesive work group may provide a substitute for the leader's task and relationship behavior.

Source: S. Kerr and J. M. Jermier, "Substitutes for Leadership: Their Meaning and Measurement," *Organizational Behavior and Human Performance* 22 (1978), pp. 375–403.

of formalization and other situational variables on leadership are presented in Highlight 12.5

Centralization refers to the diffusion of decision making throughout an organization. An organization that allows decisions to be made by only one person is highly centralized. When decision making is dispersed to the lowest levels in the organization, the organization is very decentralized. Advantages of decentralized organizations include increased participation in the decision process and, consequently, greater acceptance and ownership of decision outcomes. These are both desirable outcomes. There are also, however, advantages to centralization, such as uniform policies and procedures (which can increase feelings of equity) and clearer coordination procedures.[39] The task of balancing the degree of centralization necessary to achieve coordination and control, on one hand, and gaining desirable participation and acceptance, on the other, is an ongoing challenge for the leader.

The Informal Organization: Organizational Culture

The word that sums up the **informal organization** better than any other is its *culture*. Although most people probably think of culture in terms of very large social groups, the concept also applies to organizations. **Organizational culture** has been defined as a system of shared backgrounds, norms, values, or beliefs among members of a group,[40] and **organizational climate** concerns members' subjective reactions to the organization.[41,42] These two concepts are distinct in that organizational climate is partly a function of, or reaction to, organizational culture; our feelings or emotional reactions about an organization are probably affected by the degree to which we share the prevailing values, beliefs, and backgrounds of organizational members.[43] If a person does not share the values or beliefs of the majority of members, then in all likelihood this person would have a fairly negative reaction about the organization overall. Thus organizational climate (and indirectly organizational culture) is related to how well organizational members get along with each other.[44,45] Also note that organizational climate is narrower in scope but highly related to job satisfaction. Generally, organizational climate has more to do with nontask perceptions of work, such as feelings about co-workers or company policies, whereas job satisfaction usually also includes perceptions of workload and the nature of the tasks performed.

Just as there are many cultures across the world, there are a great number of different cultures across organizations. Members of military organizations typically have different norms, background experiences, values, and beliefs, for example, from those of the faculty at most colleges or universities. Similarly, the culture of an investment firm is different from the culture of a research and development firm, a freight hauling company, or a college rugby team. Cultural differences can even exist between different organizations within any of these sectors. The culture of the U.S. Air Force is different from the culture of the U.S. Marine Corps, and Yale University has a different culture than the University of Colorado even though they are both fine institutions of higher learning. Questions that suggest further ways in which organizational cultures may differ are listed in Table 12.2.

One of the more fascinating aspects of organizational culture is that it often takes an outsider to recognize it; organizational culture becomes so second nature to many organizational members that they are unaware of how it affects their behaviors and perceptions.[46] Despite this transparency to organizational members, a fairly consistent set of dimensions can be used to differentiate between organizational cultures. For example, Kilmann and Saxton[47] stated that organizational cultures can be differentiated based on

TABLE 12.2   Some Questions That Define Organizational Culture

- What can be talked about or not talked about?
- How do people wield power?
- How does a person get ahead or stay out of trouble?
- What are the unwritten rules of the game?
- What are the organization's morality and ethics?
- What stories are told about the organization?

Source: Adapted from R. H. Kilmann and M. J. Saxton, *Organizational Cultures: Their Assessment and Change* (San Francisco: Jossey-Bass, 1983).

Schein's Four Key Organizational Culture Factors

HIGHLIGHT 12.6

Myths and stories are the tales about the organization that are passed down over time and communicate a story of the organization's underlying values. Virtually any employee of Walmart can tell you stories about Sam Walton and his behavior—how he rode around in his pickup truck, how he greeted people in the stores, and how he tended to "just show up" at different times. The Center for Creative Leadership has stories about its founder, H. Smith Richardson, who as a young man creatively used the mail to sell products. Sometimes stories and myths are transferred between organizations even though the truth may not lie wholly in either one. A story is told in AT&T about one of its founders and how he trudged miles and miles through a blizzard to repair a faulty component so that a woman living by herself in a rural community could get phone service. Interestingly enough, this same story is also told in MCI (now Verizon).

Symbols and artifacts are objects that can be seen and noticed and that describe various aspects of the culture. In almost any building, for example, symbols and artifacts provide information about the organization's culture. For example, an organization may believe in egalitarian principles, and that might be reflected in virtually everyone having the same size office. Or there can be indications of opulence, which convey a very different message. Even signs might act as symbols or artifacts of underlying cultural values. At one university that believed students should have first priority for facilities, an interesting sign showed up occasionally to reinforce this value. It was not a road sign, but a sign appearing on computer monitors. When the university's main computer was being overused, the computer was

programmed to identify nonstudent users, note the overload, and issue a warning to nonstudent users to sign off. This was a clear artifact, or symbol, underlying the priority placed on students at that school.

Rituals are recurring events or activities that reflect important aspects of the underlying culture. An organization may have spectacular sales meetings for its top performers and spouses every two years. This ritual would be an indication of the value placed on high sales and meeting high quotas. Another kind of ritual is the retirement ceremony. Elaborate or modest retirement ceremonies may signal the importance an organization places on its people.

Language concerns the jargon, or idiosyncratic terms, of an organization and can serve several different purposes relevant to culture. First, the mere fact that some know the language and some do not indicates who is in the culture and who is not. Second, language can also provide information about how people within a culture view others. Third, language can be used to help create a culture. A good example of the power of language in creating culture is in the words employees at Disneyland or Walt Disney World use in referring to themselves and park visitors. Employees—all employees, from the costumed Disney characters to popcorn vendors—are told to think of themselves as members of a cast, and never to be out of character. Everything happening at the park is part of the "show," and those who paid admission to enter the park are not mere tourists, but rather "the audience." Virtually everyone who visits the Disney parks is impressed with the consistently friendly behavior of its staff, a reflection of the power of words in creating culture. (Of course a strict and strongly enforced policy concerning courtesy toward park guests also helps.)

members' responses to questions like those found in Table 12.2. Another way to understand an organization's culture is in terms of myths and stories, symbols, rituals, and language.[48] A more detailed description of the four key factors identified by Schein can be found in Highlight 12.6.

Here is an example of how stories contribute to organizational culture. A consultant was asked to help a plant that had been having morale and production problems for years. After talking with several individuals at the plant, the consultant believed he had located the problem. It seems everyone he talked to told him about Sam, the plant manager. He was a giant of a man with a terrible temper. He had demolished unacceptable products with a sledgehammer, stood on the plant roof screaming at workers, and done countless other things sure to intimidate everyone around. The consultant decided he needed to talk to this plant manager. When he did so, however, he met an agreeable person named Paul. Sam, it seems, had been dead for nearly a decade, but his legacy lived on.[49]

Leaders must realize that they can play an active role in changing an organization's culture, not just be influenced by it.[50-53] Leaders can change culture by attending to or ignoring particular issues, problems, or projects. They can modify culture through their reactions to crises, by rewarding new or different kinds of behavior, or by eliminating previous punishments or negative consequences for certain behaviors. Their general personnel policies send messages about the value of employees to the organization (such as cutting wages to avoid layoffs). They can use role modeling and self-sacrifice as a way to inspire or motivate others to work more vigorously or interact with each other differently. Finally, leaders can also change culture by the criteria they use to select or dismiss followers.

Changing an organization's culture, of course, takes time and effort, and sometimes it may be extremely difficult. This is especially true in very large organizations or those with strong cultures. New organizations, on the other hand, do not have the traditions, stories or myths, or established rites to the same extent that older companies do, and it may be easier for leaders to change culture in these organizations. Still another way to think about organizational culture change is described in Highlights 12.7 and 12.8.

Why would a leader *want* to change an organization's culture? It all should depend on whether the culture is having a positive or a negative impact on various desirable outcomes. We remember one organization with a very polite culture, an aspect that seemed positive at first. There were never any potentially destructive emotional outbursts in the organization, and there was an apparent concern for other individuals' feelings in all interactions. However, a darker side of that culture gradually became apparent. When it was appropriate to give feedback for performance appraisals or employee development, supervisors were hesitant to raise negative aspects of behavior; they interpreted doing so as not being polite. And so the organization continued to be puzzled by employee behavior that tended not to improve; the organization was a victim of its own culture.

At other times, organizational culture itself can be a victim of changes initially considered to be merely technical. A classic example of this pertains to the coal mining industry in England. For hundreds of years coal was mined by teams of three people each. In England coal is layered in narrow seams, most only a few feet high. In the past the only practical means to get the coal out was to send the three-person teams of miners

Stages of Leadership Culture Development

HIGHLIGHT 12.7

Researchers at the Center for Creative Leadership have been studying different kinds of leadership cultures, which they define as the values, beliefs, and often taken-for-granted assumptions about how people work together in an organization, reflecting its collective approach to achieving direction, alignment, and commitment. While virtually all large organizations include aspects of all three types, often one of these cultures will be most dominant. Furthermore, these types of leadership culture are thought to represent successive stages of culture development, each one better adapted to deal with increasingly complex challenges. An important practical purpose of this work is to help organizations transform their cultures in ways better suited to the organization's current and future challenges.

Dependent leadership cultures are characterized by widespread beliefs and practices that it's primarily people in positions of authority who are responsible for leadership. This assumption may lead to organizations that emphasize top-down control and deference to authority. In general, you can think of dependent cultures as "conforming" cultures. Other characteristics often associated with dependent cultures include these:

- There may be a command and control mind-set.
- Seniority and position levels are important bases of respect.
- There's great emphasis on keeping things running smoothly.
- Most people operate with the philosophy that it's usually safest to check things out with one's boss before taking a new direction.

Independent leadership cultures are characterized by widespread beliefs and practices that leadership emerges as needed from a variety of individuals, based on knowledge and expertise. There's great emphasis on individual responsibility; decentralized decision making; and the promotion of experts, professionals, and individual contributors into positions of authority. In general, you can think of independent cultures as "achievement-oriented" cultures. Other characteristics associated with independent cultures include these:

- The results that leaders achieve, whatever it takes, are an important basis of respect.
- Even during times of stress, there is great pressure not to let performance numbers go down.
- Bold and independent action that gets results is highly prized.
- The organization is successful because of its large number of highly competent and ambitious individuals.

Interdependent leadership cultures are characterized by widespread beliefs and practices that leadership is a collective activity requiring mutual inquiry and learning. There's widespread use of dialogue, collaboration, horizontal networks, valuing of differences, and a focus on learning. In general, you can think of interdependent cultures as "collaborative" cultures. Other characteristics associated with interdependent cultures include these:

- Many people wear several hats at once, and roles change frequently as the organization continually adapts to changing circumstances.
- People believe it's important to let everyone learn from your experience, even your mistakes.
- There's a widely shared commitment to doing what it takes to make the entire organization be successful, not just one's own group.
- Openness, candor, and building trust across departments are valued.

Metaphors of Leadership Culture

HIGHLIGHT 12.8

Highlight 12.7 described a theory of organizational culture based on the idea that different cultures represent different stages of development. In that theory, interdependent cultures represent a higher stage of development than independent cultures, and independent cultures represent a higher stage of development than dependent cultures. In line with the old saying that a picture is worth a thousand words, here are some pictures that represent different metaphors of leadership culture. Try your hand at aligning each picture (thinking of it as a metaphor) with the type of culture it most represents: dependent, independent, or interdependent.

Evangelistic Preachers

Player Coaches

Pool of Sharks

Motivational Coaches

Network of Peers

Nurturing Parents

Answers: evangelistic preachers = dependent culture; player coaches = interdependent culture; pool of sharks = independent culture; motivational coaches = independent culture; network of peers = interdependent culture; nurturing parents = dependent culture.

Source: Copyright © 2008 Center for Creative Leadership. Reprinted by permission.

down into the mines to dig coal from the seam and then haul it to the surface on a tram. These mining teams had extremely high levels of group cohesiveness. A technological development called the long-wall method of coal extraction upset these close relationships, however. In the long-wall method, workers were arrayed all along an entire seam of coal rather than in distinct teams, and the method should have resulted in higher productivity among the miners. However, the breakdown of the work teams led to unexpected decreases in productivity, much higher levels of worker dissatisfaction, and even disruption of social life among the miners' families. Although the long-wall method was technically superior to the three-person mining team, the leaders of the coal-mining companies failed to consider the cultural consequences of this technological advancement.[54]

These examples help make the point that while organizational culture is a powerful aspect of the situation, it can also seem fairly elusive and unresponsive to simple executive orders to change. For those reasons and others changing an organization's culture is usually both difficult and time-consuming, usually taking years in large organizations. To put it differently, it is much easier to change formal aspects of the organization like its structure or policies than it is to change its culture. In our view, however, it is precisely those organizational change efforts that focus solely or primarily on the formal organization that tend to fail. Truly significant organizational change or transformation is unlikely to be successful without addressing organizational culture as well as the formal organization.

Furthermore, a change effort is more likely to be successful if it is based on an established theory of organizational culture, and not merely subjective preferences about what needs to change. Absent a guiding theory, misguided and superficial targets of change may be selected that miss the point and usually create problems rather than produce desired results. For example, efforts to create a more collaborative culture that only target surface behaviors such as "we'll dress and talk less formally" and "we'll spend more time in meetings together" invariably miss the point, waste energy, and breed cynicism.

You may not be surprised to learn that there are a number of theories of organizational culture, and we will not try to summarize or even list them all here. It will be sufficient for our purposes to examine just one to illustrate how culture theories systematically use abstract dimensions to depict the variety of ways in which living and working in one organization can feel so different from another. The theory we will focus on is Cameron and Quinn's **Competing Values Framework**.[55]

A Theory of Organizational Culture

The Competing Values Framework is depicted in Figure 12.2. It derives its name from the fact that the values depicted on opposite ends of each axis are inherently in tension with each other. They represent competing assumptions about the desired state of affairs in the organization. The core

FIGURE 12.2
The Competing Values Framework

Source: K. S. Cameron and R. E. Quinn, *Diagnosing and Changing Organizational Culture* (Reading, MA: Addison-Wesley, 1999), p. 32.

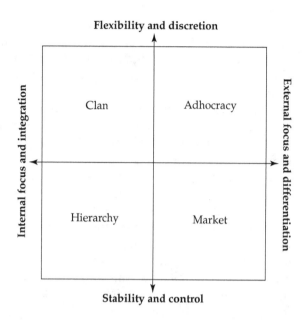

values at one end of each axis or continuum are opposed to the core values at the opposite end. Thus it's impossible that an organization could be both extremely flexible and extremely stable all the time. An organization's culture represents a balance or trade-off between these competing values that tends to work for that organization in its particular competitive environment.

Organizational cultures are not usually designed intentionally. That's one reason we noted earlier in this section that people tend not to be consciously aware of their own organization's culture. In fact, it's usually only when an organization's culture is impeding organizational performance (typically in a changing competitive environment) that people become aware of any need for culture change. It's at just such times that it can be useful for people within an organization to consider something different. The Competing Values Framework was designed to help organizations be more deliberate in identifying a culture more likely to be successful given their respective situations, and in transitioning to it.

As you can see in Figure 12.2, the intersection of the competing values axes creates four quadrants describing four different combinations of values. The distinctive sets of values in these quadrants define four unique organizational cultures.

Organizations that emphasize stability and control, and also focus their attention inward (on how people within the organization interact with each other, on whether internal operating procedures are followed, and so forth), have a **hierarchy culture.** Organizations with a hierarchy culture tend to have formalized rules and procedures; they tend to be highly structured places to work. Following standard operating procedures, or

SOPs, is the rule of the day. The emphasis is on ensuring continuing efficiency, smooth functioning, and dependable operations. Examples of hierarchy cultures are government agencies, fast-food chains, and traditional large manufacturing companies.[56]

Organizations that, like hierarchy cultures, emphasize stability and control but focus their attention primarily on the external environment (outside the organization itself) are called **market cultures.** Their interest is more on interactions with external constituencies like customers and suppliers. Market cultures are competitive and results-oriented, and the results that count most are typically financial measures of success such as profit. To ensure discipline in achieving these ends, there is great emphasis on achieving measurable goals and targets. Fundamentally, what characterizes market cultures is a pervasive emphasis on winning, often defined simply as beating the competition.[57]

Organizations that emphasize having a high degree of flexibility and discretion, and that also focus primarily inward rather than outward, are known as **clan cultures** because in many ways they can be thought of as an extended family. A strong sense of cohesiveness characterizes clan cultures along with shared values and a high degree of participativeness and consensus building. Clan cultures believe their path to success is rooted in teamwork, loyalty, and taking care of people within the organization, including their continuing development. In a real sense clan cultures can be thought of as *relationship* cultures.[58]

Finally, organizations that emphasize having a high degree of flexibility and discretion, and that focus primarily on the environment outside the organization, are called **adhocracy cultures.** In many ways adhocracy cultures represent an adaptation to the transition from the industrial age to the information age described earlier in that this form of organizational culture is most responsive to the turbulent and rapidly changing conditions of the present age. The name *adhocracy* has roots in the phrase *ad hoc,* which means temporary or specialized. Adhocracy cultures are by nature dynamic and changing so as to best foster creativity, entrepreneurship, and staying on the cutting edge. This requires a culture that emphasizes individual initiative and freedom.[59]

In actuality, these four cultures represent idealized forms; no real organization probably exists whose culture can be completely described by just one quadrant. The complexities and necessities of organizational life and survival inevitably require that all cultures include elements from all four of the cultures (that is, all cultures put some value on all the competing values). What differentiates one culture from another, then, is the relative predominance of one culture type over the others. Nonetheless, it should be apparent that quite different approaches to leadership are called for based on which of these four distinctive cultures dominates any organization.

Leadership in hierarchy cultures, for example, emphasizes careful management of information, monitoring detailed aspects of operations, and assuring operational dependability and reliability. In contrast, leadership in market cultures places a premium on aggressiveness, decisiveness, productivity (which is not the same thing as stability or continuity), and outperforming external competitors. Leadership in a clan culture focuses on process more than output, especially as it pertains to minimizing conflict and maximizing consensus. A premium is placed on leadership that is empathetic and caring and that builds trust. And leadership in adhocracy cultures requires vision, creativity, and future-oriented thinking.

An Afterthought on Organizational Issues for Students and Young Leaders

Let us conclude this section by adding an afterthought about what relevance organizational issues may have for students or others at the early stages of their careers, or at lower levels of leadership within their organizations. It is unlikely that such individuals will be asked soon to redesign their organization's structure or change its culture. As noted earlier, this chapter is not intended as a how-to manual for changing culture. On the other hand, it has been our experience that younger colleagues sometimes develop biased impressions of leaders or have unrealistic expectations about decision making in organizations, based on their lack of familiarity with, and appreciation of, the sorts of organizational dynamics discussed in this section. In other words, a primary reason for being familiar with such organizational variables is the context they provide for understanding the leadership process at your own level in the organization. Finally, we have worked with some senior leaders of huge organizations who have been with their companies for their entire careers. They have often been unable to identify *any* of the dimensions of their culture because they have never seen anything else. In these cases we were amazed by how junior managers were far better at describing the culture of the large organization. While these junior people may have had only five to eight years of total work experience, if that experience was obtained in several different organizations, they were much better prepared to describe the characteristics of their new large organization's culture than were the senior executives.

The Environment

The environmental level of the situation refers to factors outside the task or organization that still affect the leadership process. We will focus on two interrelated aspects of these extra-organizational aspects of the situation: (1) the ways in which leaders increasingly confront situations that are unexpected, unfamiliar, complex, and rapidly changing; and (2) the growing importance of leadership across different societal cultures.

Are Things Changing More Than They Used To?

One general aspect of the situation that affects leadership is the degree of change that's occurring. Leading in a relatively stable situation presents different challenges—generally simpler ones—than does leading in a dynamic situation. Many people think things *are* changing more than they used to, and at an increasing pace, but that's not so simple a question as it first might appear. For example, it may seem as though no age could possibly rival ours in terms of the transformative effect technology has had on our lives. On the other hand, an interesting case can be made that technologies introduced to most Americans during the early to mid-20th century like indoor electric lighting, refrigerators, electric and natural gas ovens, and indoor plumbing, changed everyday life to a greater degree than new technologies of the past decade.[60]

Nonetheless, while there's no argument that the generations growing up in the early part of the 20th century experienced profound transformations in life (television, the automobile, air travel, and atomic energy, to name a few), we believe that the nature of challenges facing leaders is changing as never before. Ronald Heifetz argues that leaders not only are facing more crises than ever before but that a new mode of leadership is needed because we're in a *permanent* state of crisis.[61] Thomas Friedman provocatively titled his book *The World Is Flat* to convey how globalization and technology are radically changing how we live and work.[62] And Army General David Petraeus used an oddly anachronistic painting in speaking with the troops he was soon to take command of in what was widely known as "the surge" in Iraq. The painting was *The Stampede*, painted by western artist Frederic Remington in 1908. It depicts a cowboy in the 1800s riding desperately to survive a stampeding herd of cattle panicked by a thunderstorm. As Thomas Ricks tells the story in his account of the surge *The Gamble*, Petraeus used the painting to convey to his subordinates his notion of command. "I don't need to be hierarchical," he explained. "I want to flatten organizations. I'm comfortable with a slightly chaotic environment. I know that it's okay if some of you get out ahead of us. Some of the cattle will get out ahead and we will catch up with them. And some will fall behind and we will circle back and we won't leave them behind. . . . We're just trying to get the cattle to Cheyenne."[63]

To appreciate the significance of what Petraeus was saying, contrast the language and images used here ("don't need to be hierarchical," "some of the cattle will get out") with the stereotypical notions of command and control in the military. Situational changes are being met with new approaches to leadership even within what is often regarded as the epitome of traditional top-down leadership.

We think Heifetz, Friedman, and Petraeus illuminate important ways in which the challenge of leadership is changing. It might be useful, therefore, to introduce a variation of Figure 12.1, which depicted the task, organizational, and environmental levels of the situation. In Figure 12.3 we've

FIGURE 12.3
Contrasting
Different
Environments in the
Situational Level

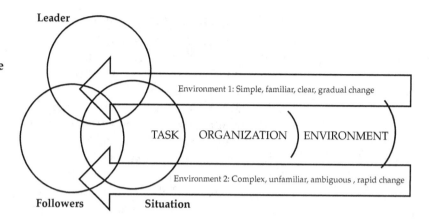

added two vectors to the original diagram to highlight how two contrasting and multidimensional kinds of environments affect leadership. We don't intend the two vectors to imply there's a simple categorization of environments (either simple or complex); we use the representation in the figure to illustrate a range of possible environments. Nonetheless, change has become so fast and so pervasive that it impacts virtually every organization everywhere, and everyone in them. And appropriate to our times, an acronym has been given to this new state of affairs: **VUCA.** Coined by the Army War College, the term *VUCA* describes a world that is volatile, uncertain, complex, and ambiguous.

Another purpose of the vectors in Figure 12.3 is to underscore how different levels of the situation interact. Thus relatively narrow and specific descriptions of job tasks tend to be most common and most appropriate in more formal and highly structured organizations having more hierarchical cultures. This set of situational levels is reasonably aligned to deal with what Heifetz called technical problems. Adaptive or wicked problems, on the other hand, are more likely to be effectively addressed when tasks for individuals and teams are more fluid, in organizations that are less formal, less structured, and more agile and that have adhocracy-like cultures.

Of course we are not saying that once situational variables have been identified as corresponding more closely to the bottom vector, it's a simple matter for a leader to just "turn on" adaptive leadership. The whole point is that such leadership is inherently more than an individual leader or his behavior or skills. Certain kinds of established relationships with followers are vital, and distinctive skill sets on their parts are needed, as is a certain kind of organizational culture.

In addition, Heifetz has described a thorny leadership challenge that can raise its head even after a challenge is recognized as an adaptive one. Followers generally want their leaders to be experts having all the answers (recall that by definition, adaptive problems don't have expert solutions). He said, "When you attain a position of significant authority, people inevitably expect you to treat adaptive challenges as if they were technical—to provide

Workplace Trends

HIGHLIGHT 12.9

In response to increasing competitiveness, uncertainty, globalization, and the pace of change, a number of leadership trends have been identified in how organizations can best face the future:

- Recognize that complex challenges are on the rise, and therefore that new approaches to leadership and leadership development will be required.

- Embrace innovation as a driver of future organizational success.

- Prepare for ever-greater levels of and need for virtual leadership, and that the skills it requires are different than those needed for face-to-face leadership.

- Collaboration across organizational boundaries (across teams, departments, units, regions, and so on) will be essential to organizational success.

- Because trust and respect will be vital, leaders will need to be more authentic in their roles than ever before.

- The next generation of leaders will place new kinds of leadership demands on their organizations.

- A crisis of talent in organizations is coming, and so organizations that have credible and established programs of talent development and succession planning will be at an advantage.

- Ensuring the health and fitness of all employees, leaders included, must become an organizational priority.

Source: A. Martin, *What's Next: The 2007 Changing Nature of Leadership Survey*, CCL Research White Paper (Greensboro, NC: Center for Creative Leadership). Center for Creative Leadership, CCL®, and its logo are registered trademarks owned by the Center for Creative Leadership. © 2007 Center for Creative Leadership. All rights reserved.

I claim not to have controlled events, but confess plainly that events have controlled me.

Abraham Lincoln

---

for them a remedy that will restore equilibrium with the least amount of pain and in the shortest amount of time."[64] Furthermore, leaders themselves easily fall prey to the same expectation. People in positions of authority often take personal pride in being able to solve problems that others can't solve. When facing an adaptive challenge, it can be difficult for them to admit they've come to the limit of their expertise.[65] To put it differently, leadership has never been easy and appears to be growing more difficult. A number of trends driving the changing nature of leadership are listed in Highlight 12.9. And a situational challenge that has always confronted leaders taking over new responsibilities is addressed in Profiles in Leadership 12.1.

Leading across Societal Cultures

A telling illustration of the role societal culture can play in leadership is provided by Malcolm Gladwell in his book *Outliers*. It concerns the role that culture played in a series of airline crashes, including that of Korean Air Flight 801 in 1997, which killed 228 of the 254 people on board. In fact, the loss rate (deaths per number of departing passengers) for Korean Air in the period from 1988 to 1998 was 17 times what it was for a representative American carrier. It may seem initially that the likely cause of such a difference would be deficiencies in the Korean pilots' technical flying expertise or knowledge, but that was not the case—nor is it usually the case. The kinds of errors that cause crashes are almost always errors of teamwork and communication rather than errors of flying skill. Careful

Taking Charge

PROFILE IN LEADERSHIP 12.1

A critical period for any leader often involves those first few moments and days of assuming command. This is a time when first impressions are formed and expectations are set. It is especially challenging when the situation is stressful and the stakes are high.

That was precisely the situation facing Coast Guard Admiral Thad Allen when he took responsibility for overall leadership of the 2005 Hurricane Katrina search-and-rescue recovery efforts. Allen was replacing Michael Brown, then director of the Federal Emergency Management Agency, who had received harsh criticism for mishandling the relief efforts.

The first thing that happened on the day Allen was told of his new responsibility was a joint press conference with his new boss, the Director of Homeland Security, to announce Allen's appointment. The very next thing Allen did was ask to have a meeting with all 4,000 people assigned to the recovery effort. Although they couldn't find a space large enough to hold that many, they did find a place that could accommodate 2,000 of them.

Here is Allen's account of how he handled those critical first moments:

> I got up on a desk, with a loudspeaker, and told everybody that I was giving one order: They were to treat anybody they came into contact with who had been affected by the storm like a member of their own family. Their mother, father, brother, sister, whatever. And I said, "If you do that, two things are going to happen. Number one, if you make a mistake, you're going to err on the side of doing too much, and that's okay. Number two, if somebody has a problem with what you've done, their problem's not with you; their problem's with me."
>
> After I said that, a cheer broke out, because there had been so much stress from the pressure that had been exerted on the response and the perception that it wasn't going well. Just a simple set of core values—a North Star to steer by—was, I think, what they were looking for.

Source: "You Have to Lead from Everywhere," *Harvard Business Review*, November 2010, pp. 76–79.

analysis of those crashes reveals that a root cause was the Korean pilots' customary cultural deep respect for authority. The same factor also played a role in crashes of airliners piloted by crews of other nationalities sharing a similar respect for authority. Respect for authority in itself is neither a good nor a bad thing, but it can be a problem when it interferes with clear and direct communication about an emergency situation. That's just what was happening in these crashes. Strange as it may sound, the crews did not make the criticality of their situations crystal clear to air traffic controllers. Conversing with the controllers as equals, such as by correcting the controllers' understanding of the actual situations, would have seemed disrespectful from the crew's cultural perspective. (As a footnote, Korean Air has corrected its procedures and now has an exemplary safety record.)[66]

This is admittedly a dramatic illustration, and airline crashes are fortunately rare events. The point the story makes, however, applies to leaders of all sorts and in all places: cultural differences—especially when they are not recognized and addressed—can create significant challenges to communication and teamwork. It's no surprise, then, that in recent years an increasing number of empirical studies have examined the challenges of leading across societal cultures. One value of such studies is that their findings can

"... Then it's agreed. As a crowd, we'll be subdued
in innings one through seven, then suddenly become
a factor in innings eight and nine ..."

point out myths, mistaken assumptions, or invalid generalizations people have or make about leadership.

For example, a person regarded as an effective leader in one society may not be perceived as effective in another. That's what one study found in comparing evaluations by supervisors of the leadership effectiveness of female managers in Malaysia with those by supervisors of female managers in Australia. These findings appeared to be based not on an objective appraisal of the female managers' capability but rather on strongly held cultural beliefs about appropriate roles for women in society. There was a clear culturally based readiness by both male and female supervisors in Australia to value equality between the roles of men and women generally and in organizational roles specifically; this was not the case in Malaysia, where more gender-specific stereotypes were held. While these findings were not unexpected, they point out how research findings in Western cultures may not be transferable to developing cultures.[67]

Such findings have a practical importance beyond mere academic or scholarly interest. A survey of executives in the 500 largest corporations in the world showed that having competent global leaders was the most important contributor to business success (as discussed further in Highlight 12.10). What's more, 85 percent of those executives did not think their companies had sufficient numbers of competent global leaders.[68]

Global Leadership

HIGHLIGHT 12.10

There is no doubt about it: the world is getting smaller. Globalization has allowed goods and services to be manufactured, traded, and delivered in places no one thought possible just 10 or 20 years ago. World business leaders, such as Jeffery Immelt of General Electric, Carlos Ghosn of Renault and Nissan Motors, and Steve Ballmer of Microsoft all believe these global trends are irreversible and gaining momentum. But what are the implications of globalization for leadership? It is clear that the ways in which leaders get results through others and build cohesive, goal-oriented teams will vary somewhat from one country to the next. For example, Malaysian leadership culture inhibits assertive, confrontational behavior and puts a premium on maintaining harmony. Effective leaders are expected to show compassion while demonstrating more of an autocratic than participatory leadership style. German leadership culture does not value compassion, and interpersonal relationships are straightforward and stern. Effective leaders in Germany generally value autonomy and participation but have a low team orientation.

So how does one lead in a global economy? Certainly appreciating what different cultures value and how things get done in different countries is an important first step. But do leaders need to do fundamentally different things to build teams or get results through others in India, Zimbabwe, or Estonia? Will leaders of the future need to speak multiple languages or actually live in other countries to be effective? The answers to these questions will depend to some extent on the global orientation of the organization. Some organizations, such as Waste Management or ServiceMaster, operate primarily in Canada and the United States and probably will not need to

have leaders who have lived in other countries or speak multiple languages. Other organizations, such as 3M, Hewlett-Packard, Pfizer, BP, Levono, Nike, Toyota, or the British military have significant manufacturing, marketing, sales, or other operations in multiple countries. These organizations often use a global competency model to outline the expectations for leaders in all countries, and these models tend to vary more by company than by country (see Figure 7.3 for an example of a competency model).

It seems likely that leaders who have spent time in other countries, have applied the action–observation–reflection model to maximize the lessons learned from their expatriot experiences, and can speak multiple languages would be better able to lead international organizations. But currently this is conjecture; more research is needed before we can definitively say whether international experience matters, how much and what kinds of experience are needed, what the key lessons to be learned from these experiences are, and how we should select and develop leaders to successfully lead international organizations. The good news here is that a group of 150 social scientists working on the GLOBE (Global Leadership and Organizational Behavior Effectiveness) project are actively seeking the answers to these questions and will soon be publishing their findings.

Sources: S. Green, F. Hassan, J. Immelt, M. Marks, and D. Meiland, "In Search of Global Leaders," *Harvard Business Review,* August 2003, pp. 38–45; J. C. Kennedy, "Leadership in Malaysia: Traditional Values, International Outlook," *The Academy of Management Executive,* 16, no. 3 (2002), pp. 15–24; F. Brodbeck, M. Frese, M. Javidan, and F. G. Kroll, "Leadership Made in Germany: Low on Compassion, High in Performance," *The Academy of Management Executive* 16, no. 1 (2002), pp. 16–30; GLOBE program: http://mgmt3.ucalgary.ca/web/globe.nsf/index.

Without competent global leaders, misunderstandings and slights can occur when people from different cultures are working together. Here are two specific examples. First consider the historic U.S. emphasis on individualism (the focus on *self*-confidence, *self*-control, *self*-concept, *self*-expression, or the way rugged individualists are heroically portrayed in film, television, and literature) and how it might impact work. Given an individualist perspective, certain management practices and expectations seem self-evident, such as the idea of individual accountability for work. When individual accountability is valued, for example, decision-making authority tends to be delegated to individual managers. What's more, those same managers may be inclined to take personal credit when the job is well done. A different norm, however, applies in industrialized Japan. Decision making is often time-consuming to ensure that everyone who will be affected by a decision has input on it beforehand. Another self-evident principle to the U.S. mind is that individual career progress is desirable and good. In some other cultures, however, managers resist competing with peers for rewards or promotions so as not to disturb the harmony of the group or appear self-interested.

Another example of potential conflict or misunderstanding can be seen in the case of orientation to authority—how people should handle power and authority relationships with others. The United States is a relatively young and mobile country, populated mostly by immigrants. Relative to other countries, there is little concern with family origin or class background. There is a belief that success should come through an individual's hard work and talent, not by birthright or class standing. This all leads to relative informality at work, even among individuals of strikingly different position within a company. Subordinates expect their bosses to be accessible, even responsive in some ways to their subordinates. In some other cultures, however, higher status in a company confers nearly unchallengeable authority, and an expectation as well that most decisions will be referred *up* to them (as distinguished from delegated down to others).

What Is Societal Culture?

Before we look at more specific findings about leading across societal cultures, it will be useful first to clarify what the term *societal culture* means. **Societal culture** refers to those learned behaviors characterizing the total way of life of members within any given society. Cultures differ from one another just as individuals differ from one another. To outsiders, the most salient aspect of any culture typically involves behavior— the distinctive actions, mannerisms, and gestures characteristic of that culture. Americans visiting Thailand, for example, may find it curious and even bothersome to see male Thais hold hands with each other in public. They may react negatively to such behavior because it is atypical to them and laden with North American meaning ("It's okay for women to hold hands in public, but men shouldn't do that"). Salient as such behaviors are, however, they are just the tip of the iceberg. The mass of culture is not so readily visible, just as most of an iceberg lies beneath the water. Hidden from view are the beliefs, values, and myths that provide context to manifest behaviors.[69] A clear implication for business leaders in the global context, therefore, is the need to become aware and respectful of cultural differences and cultural perspectives. Barnum pointed out the importance of being able to look at one's own culture through the eyes of another:

> Consciously or unconsciously they will be using their own beliefs as the yardsticks for judging you, so know how to compare those yardsticks by ferreting out their values and noting where they differ the least and most from yours. For example, if their belief in fatalism outweighs your belief in accountability, there will be conflicts down the road. This is a severe problem in the Middle East, for instance, and affects management styles in companies and even the ability to market life insurance, which is frowned upon in communities where Muslim observances are strong.[70]

The GLOBE Study

I do believe in the spiritual nature of human beings. To some it's a strange or outdated idea, but I believe there is such a thing as a human spirit. There is a spiritual dimension to man which should be nurtured.

Aung San Suu Kyi

GLOBE is an acronym for a research program called the Global Leadership and Organizational Behavior Effectiveness Research Program. It is the most comprehensive study of leadership and culture ever attempted, involving data collected from over 17,000 managers representing 950 companies in 62 countries.[71,72]

Hofstede was one of the pioneers in the study of beliefs and culture, and his seminal work provided some of the early roots of the GLOBE study.[73] He identified five fundamental dimensions of cultural values and beliefs, and these, as well as dimensions drawn from the work of other researchers, became the nine dimensions of societal culture used in the GLOBE study. Because of the number of scales and complexity of findings, we'll look at representative findings from just two of those scales to convey the flavor of some of these cross-cultural findings. We'll look at the dimensions of future orientation and collectivism–individualism. Here's a brief definition of each of them:[74]

> **Future orientation:** The degree to which individuals in organizations or societies engage in future-oriented behaviors like planning and investing in the future.

> **Collectivism:** The degree to which individuals express pride, loyalty, and cohesiveness in their organizations, families, or similar small groups.

Table 12.3 presents some of the representative findings that differentiate cultures high or low on each of these dimensions. Cross-cultural differences on these and the other seven dimensions of culture used in GLOBE constitute a foundation for the GLOBE findings on differences in leadership across cultures.

The heart of the conceptual model in the GLOBE research is what's called **implicit leadership theory.** This theory holds that individuals have implicit beliefs and assumptions about attributes and behaviors that distinguish leaders from followers, effective leaders from ineffective leaders, and moral from immoral leaders. The GLOBE model further posits that relatively distinctive implicit theories of leadership characterize different

TABLE 12.3 Representative Societal Differences on Two GLOBE Dimensions

Societies Higher on Collectivism Tend to	Societies Higher on Individualism Tend to
• Have a slower pace of life. • Have lower heart attack rates. • Assign less weight to love in marriage decisions. • Have fewer interactions, but interactions tend to be longer and more intimate.	• Have a faster pace of life. • Have higher heart attack rates. • Assign greater weight to love in marriage decisions. • Have more social interactions, but interactions tend to be shorter and less intimate.
Societies Higher on Future Orientation Tend to	**Societies Lower on Future Orientation Tend to**
• Achieve economic success. • Have flexible and adaptive organizations and managers. • Emphasize visionary leadership that is capable of seeing patterns in the face of chaos and uncertainty.	• Have lower rates of economic success. • Have inflexible and maladaptive organizations and managers. • Emphasize leadership that focuses on repetition of reproducible and routine sequences.

societal cultures from each other as well as organizational cultures within those societal cultures. GLOBE calls these **culturally endorsed implicit theories of leadership** (CLT).

After detailed analysis of findings, GLOBE researchers identified six dimensions that were determined to be applicable across all global cultures for assessing CLT. Here are those six dimensions and a brief description of each:[75]

- **Charismatic/value-based leadership** reflects the ability to inspire, motivate, and expect high performance from others on the basis of firmly held core values.
- **Team-oriented leadership** emphasizes effective team building and implementation of a common purpose or goal among team members.
- **Participative leadership** reflects the degree to which managers involve others in making and implementing decisions.
- **Humane-oriented leadership** reflects supportive and considerate leadership as well as compassion and generosity.
- **Autonomous leadership** refers to independent and individualistic leadership.
- **Self-protective leadership** focuses on ensuring the safety and security of the individual or group member.

After analyzing the data from all the societies in the study, GLOBE researchers categorized them into 10 different societal clusters (such as Eastern Europe, Nordic Europe, Latin America, Southern Asia, and Anglo). Societies were included in a cluster based on criteria of relative similarity of

TABLE 12.4   **Relative Rankings of Selected Societal Clusters on CLT Leadership Dimensions**

Societal Cluster	Charismatic/ Value-Based	Team-Oriented	Participative	Humane-Oriented	Self-Protective
Eastern Europe	Medium	Medium	Low	Medium	High
Anglo	High	Medium	High	High	Low
Middle East	Low	Low	Low	Medium	High

values and beliefs *within* each cluster, and *differentiation* from other societal clusters. Again, it is beyond our purposes here to present a comprehensive description of all these societal clusters. It will suffice to look at just three of them so you will have a general sense of the nature of the GLOBE findings. Table 12.4 presents the relative rankings (high, medium, or low) for three different societal clusters on each of the six global CLT dimensions.[76]

The considerable variation in views of what constitutes good leadership across different societal clusters evident in Table 12.4 makes it clear that behaving effectively as a leader (and being perceived as effective) requires awareness of the cultural values and practices in the society within which one is working.

A final set of interesting findings coming out of GLOBE concerns the **universality of leadership attributes.** These findings both refine and temper the distinctiveness of societal CLTs exemplified in Table 12.4. They temper the impression we may get that different societies have completely different notions of what constitutes good and bad leadership by demonstrating that actually there is consensus across cultures on a number of desirable leadership attributes as well as consensus on what are considered to be universally negative leadership traits. But these findings also provide further insight into which attributes see much of the variability across cultures. GLOBE researchers identified 22 specific attributes and behaviors that are viewed universally across cultures as contributing to leadership effectiveness.[77] They are listed in Table 12.5. In addition,

TABLE 12.5

Leader Attributes and Behaviors Universally Viewed as Positive

Trustworthy	Positive	Intelligent
Just	Dynamic	Decisive
Honest	Motive arouser	Effective bargainer
Foresighted	Confidence builder	Win–win problem solver
Plans ahead	Motivational	Administratively skilled
Encouraging	Dependable	Communicative
Informed	Coordinator	Team builder
Excellence oriented		

Source: Adapted from House et al., *Cultural Influences on Leadership and Organizations: Project Globe. Advances in Global Leadership*, vol. 1 (JAI Press, 1999), pp. 171–233.

TABLE 12.6   Leader Attributes and Behaviors Universally Viewed as Negative

Loner	Nonexplicit
Asocial	Egocentric
Noncooperative	Ruthless
Irritable	Dictatorial

Source: Adapted from House et al., *Cultural Influences on Leadership and Organizations: Project Globe. Advances in Global Leadership,* vol. 1 (JAI Press, 1999), pp. 171–233.

TABLE 12.7   Examples of Leader Behaviors and Attributes
That Are Culturally Contingent

Ambitious	Logical
Cautious	Orderly
Compassionate	Sincere
Domineering	Worldly
Independent	Formal
Individualistic	Sensitive

Source: Adapted from House et al., *Cultural Influences on Leadership and Organizations: Project Globe. Advances in Global Leadership,* vol. 1 (JAI Press, 1999), pp. 171–233.

the project identified eight characteristics that are universally viewed as impediments to leader effectiveness (see Table 12.6). And GLOBE researchers identified 35 leader characteristics that are viewed as positive in some cultures but negative in others (some of these are listed in Table 12.7). This large set of culturally contingent characteristics apparently accounts for most of the variance across societal cultures.

Implications for Leadership Practitioners

The perspectives and findings presented in this chapter have significant implications for leadership practitioners. Perhaps most important, leadership practitioners should expect to face a variety of challenges to their own systems of ethics, values, or attitudes during their careers. Additionally, values often are a source of interpersonal conflict. Although we sometimes say two people don't get along because of a personality conflict, often these conflicts are due to differences in value systems, not personality traits. Often people on either side of an issue see only themselves and their own side as morally justifiable. Nonetheless, people holding seemingly antithetical values may need to work together, and dealing with diverse values will be an increasingly common challenge for leaders. As noted earlier, interacting with individuals and groups holding divergent and conflicting values will be an inevitable fact of life for future leaders. This does not mean, however, that increased levels of interpersonal conflict are inevitable. Both leaders and followers might be well advised to minimize the conflict and tension often associated with value differences. Leaders in particular have a responsibility not to let their own personal values interfere with professional leader–subordinate relationships unless the conflicts pertain to issues clearly relevant to the work and the organization.

Summary

The situation may be the most complex factor in the leader–follower–situation framework. Moreover, situations vary not only in complexity but also in strength. Situational factors can play such a pervasive role that they can effectively minimize the effects of personality traits, intelligence, values, and preferences on leaders' and followers' behaviors, attitudes, and relationships. Given the dynamic nature of leadership situations, finding fairly consistent results is a highly encouraging accomplishment for leadership researchers.

As an organizing framework, this chapter introduced the concept of situational levels as a way to consider many situational factors. At the lowest level, leaders need to be aware of how various aspects of tasks can affect both their own and their followers' behaviors, and how they might change these factors to improve followers' satisfaction and performance. The organizational level includes both the formal organization and informal organization. The formal organization involves the ways authority is distributed across various organizational levels and how organizational structure impacts the way activities in the organization are coordinated and controlled. The informal organization or the organizational culture can have a profound impact on the way both leaders and followers behave—and may be the least recognizable because it is the water in the bowl where all the fish are swimming. An increasingly important variable at the environmental level is societal culture, which involves learned behaviors that guide the distinctive mannerisms, ways of thinking, and values within particular societies.

Key Terms

situational engineering, *482*
role theory, *485*
multiple-influence model, *485*
situational levels, *485*
task autonomy, *486*
task feedback, *487*
task structure, *487*
task interdependence, *488*
technical problems, *489*
adaptive problems, *489*
adaptive leadership, *490*
formal organization, *492*
level of authority, *492*
organizational structure, *493*
horizontal complexity, *494*
vertical complexity, *494*
spatial complexity, *494*
formalization, *494*

substitutes for leadership, *495*
centralization, *495*
informal organization, *495*
organizational culture, *495*
organizational climate, *496*
myths and stories, *497*
symbols and artifacts, *497*
rituals, *497*
language, *497*
dependent leadership culture, *499*
independent leadership culture, *499*

interdependent leadership culture, *499*
Competing Values Framework, *501*
hierarchy culture, *502*
market culture, *503*
clan culture, *503*
adhocracy culture, *503*
VUCA, *506*
societal culture, *511*
GLOBE, *512*
future orientation, *512*
collectivism, *512*
implicit leadership theory, *512*
culturally endorsed implicit theories of leadership, *513*

charismatic/values-based leadership, *513*
team-oriented leadership, *513*
participative leadership, *513*
humane-oriented leadership, *513*
autonomous leadership, *513*
self-protective leadership, *513*
universality of leadership attributes, *514*

Questions

1. The term *bureaucratic* has a pejorative connotation to most people. Can you think of any positive aspects of a bureaucracy?

2. Think of a crisis situation you are familiar with involving a group, team, organization, or country, and analyze it in terms of the leader–follower–situation framework. For example, were the followers looking for a certain kind of behavior from the leader? Did the situation demand it? Did the situation, in fact, contribute to a particular leader's emergence?

3. Can you identify reward systems that affect the level of effort students are likely to put forth in team or group projects? Should these reward systems be different than those for individual effort projects?

Activity

Your instructor has several exercises available that demonstrate the impact of situational factors on behavior. They are not described here because identifying the situational factors being manipulated in an exercise undercuts the purpose of that exercise.

Minicase

Innovation at IKEA

Redecorating and renovating have become a popular international pastime. In a world facing persistent terrorist alerts and lagging economies, more and more people are opting to stay home and make their homes safe havens. This phenomenon has contributed tremendously to the success of IKEA, the Swedish home furniture giant. In monetary terms alone, that success is measured by sales for the fiscal year ending in 2013 totaling 27.9 billion euros - that's a lot of furniture!

Much of IKEA's success can be attributed to its founder, Ingvar Kamprad. Kamprad used graduation money to start IKEA in the small Swedish village where he was born. He started off selling belt buckles, pens, and watches—whatever residents in the small local village of Agunnaryd needed. Eventually Kamprad moved on to selling furniture. One day in 1952, while struggling to fit a large table in a small car, one of Kamprad's employees came up with the idea that changed the furniture industry forever—he decided to remove the legs. IKEA's flat-pack and self-assembly methodology was born, and it rocketed the company past the competition. "After that [table] followed a whole series of other self-assembled furniture, and by 1956 the concept was more or less systematized," writes Kamprad.

Kamprad is dedicated to maintaining the corporate culture he has helped define over the past 50 years. He is a simple man—his idea of a luxury vacation is riding his bike. He is fiercely cost-conscious and, even though his personal wealth has been estimated in the billions, he refuses to fly first class. He values human interaction above all, and, even though retired, he still visits IKEA stores regularly to keep tabs on what is going on where the business really happens.

The culture at IKEA is a culture closely connected with Kamprad's simple Swedish farm roots. It is a culture that strives "to create a better everyday for the many people." IKEA supports this culture by

- Hiring co-workers (IKEA prefers the word *co-workers* to *employees*) who are supportive and work well in teams.
- Expecting co-workers to look for innovative, better ways of doing things in every aspect of their work.
- Respecting co-workers and their views.
- Establishing mutual objectives and working tirelessly to realize them.
- Making cost consciousness part of everything they do from improving processes for production to purchasing wisely to traveling cost-effectively.
- Complicated solutions—simplicity is a strong part of the IKEA culture.
- Leading by example, so IKEA leaders are expected to pitch in when needed and create a good working environment.
- Believing that a diverse workforce strengthens the company overall.

The IKEA culture is one that resonates for many. The buildings are easy to identify—the giant blue and gold warehouses that resemble oversized Swedish flags are hard to miss. Millions of customers browse through the Klippan sofas and Palbo footstools (Nordic names are given to all IKEA products) in the stark, dimly lit warehouses. The surroundings may not be lavish and the service may be minimal, but customers keep going back not just for the bargains but to experience the IKEA culture as well.

1. Discuss the three input components of the Congruence Model as they apply to the success of IKEA.
2. Consider Schein's four key organizational culture factors as described in Highlight 12.6. What examples can you identify within the IKEA organization that contribute to the company's strong corporate culture?
3. Based on the level of technological complexity and the degree of environmental uncertainty present at IKEA, what type of organizational structure would you expect?

Sources: http://archive.cinweekly.com/content/2004/03/24/0324travelikea.asp; http://www.azcentral.com/home/design/articles/0812ikea12.html; http://strategis.ic.gc.ca/epic/internet/inimr-ri.nsf/en/gr-76894e.html; http://www.geocities.com/TimesSquare/1848/ikea.html; http://www.sustainability.com/news/press-room/JE-teflon-shield-Mar01.asp?popup=1; http://www.benefitnews.com/retire/detail.cfm?id=345.

End Notes

1. T. J. Peters and R. H. Waterman, *In Search of Excellence* (New York: Harper & Row, 1982).
2. R. T. Hogan and J. Hogan, *Manual for the Hogan Personality Inventory* (Tulsa, OK: Hogan Assessment Systems, 1992).
3. G. Yukl, *Leadership in Organizations*, 2nd ed. (Englewood Cliffs, NJ: Prentice Hall, 1989).
4. A. J. Murphy, "A Study of the Leadership Process," *American Sociological Review* 6 (1941), pp. 674–87.
5. H. S. Person, "Leadership as a Response to Environment," *Educational Record Supplement*, no. 6 (1928), pp. 9–21.
6. G. Spiller, "The Dynamics of Greatness," *Sociological Review* 21 (1929), pp. 218-32.
7. J. Schneider, "The Cultural Situation as a Condition for the Condition of Fame," *American Sociology Review* 2 (1937), pp. 480–91.
8. Person, "Leadership as a Response to Environment."
9. B. M. Bass, *Bass and Stogdill's Handbook of Leadership*, 3rd ed. (New York: Free Press, 1990).
10. R. K. Merton, *Social Theory and Social Structure* (New York: Free Press, 1957).
11. J. Pfeffer and G. R. Salancik, "Determinants of Supervisory Behavior: A Role Set Analysis," *Human Relations* 28 (1975), pp. 139–54.
12. A. Tsui, "A Role Set Analysis of Managerial Reputation," *Organizational Behavior and Human Performance* 34 (1984), pp. 64–96.

13. J. G. Hunt and R. N. Osborn, "Toward a Macro-Oriented Model of Leadership: An Odyssey," in *Leadership: Beyond Establishment Views,* eds. J. G. Hunt, U. Sekaran, and C. A. Schriesheim (Carbondale: Southern Illinois University Press, 1982), pp. 196–221.

14. P. Hersey and K. H. Blanchard, *Management of Organizational Behavior: Utilizing Human Resources,* 3rd ed. (Englewood Cliffs, NJ: Prentice Hall, 1977).

15. P. Hersey and K. H. Blanchard, *Management of Organizational Behavior: Utilizing Human Resources,* 4th ed. (Englewood Cliffs, NJ: Prentice Hall, 1984).

16. J. R. Hackman and G. R. Oldham, *Work Redesign* (Reading, MA: Addison-Wesley, 1980).

17. R. J. House and G. Dressler, "The Path-Goal Theory of Leadership: Some Post Hoc and A Priori Tests," in *Contingency Approaches to Leadership,* eds. J. G. Hunt and L. L. Larson (Carbondale: Southern Illinois University Press, 1974).

18. J. P. Howell and P. W. Dorfman, "Substitute for Leadership: Test of a Construct," *Academy of Management Journal* 24 (1981), pp. 714–28.

19. S. Kerr and J. M. Jermier, "Substitutes for Leadership: Their Meaning and Measurement," *Organizational Behavior and Human Performance* 22 (1978), pp. 375–403.

20. I. B. Myers and B. H. McCaulley, *Manual: A Guide to the Development and Use of the Myers-Briggs Type Indicator* (Palo Alto, CA: Consulting Psychologists Press, 1985).

21. Bass, *Bass and Stogdill's Handbook of.*

22. J. D. Ford, "Department Context and Formal Structure as Constraints on Leader Behavior," *Academy of Management Journal* 24 (1981), pp. 274–88.

23. Yukl, *Leadership in Organizations.*

24. M. Siegall and L. L. Cummings, "Task Role Ambiguity, Satisfaction, and the Moderating Effect of Task Instruction Source," *Human Relations* 39 (1986), pp. 1017–32.

25. J. Galbraith, *Designing Complex Organizations* (Menlo Park, CA: Addison-Wesley, 1973).

26. L. Fry, W. Kerr, and C. Lee, "Effects of Different Leader Behaviors under Different Levels of Task Interdependence," *Human Relations* 39 (1986), pp. 1067–82.

27. R. A. Heifetz, *Leadership without Easy Answer* (Cambridge, MA: Belknap, 1998).

28. R. A. Heifetz and M. Linsky, *Leadership on the Line: Staying Alive through the Dangers of Leading* (Boston: Harvard Business School Press, 2002).

29. A. D. Chandler, *Scale and Scope: The Dynamics of Industrial Capitalism* (Cambridge: Harvard University Press, 1990).

30. R. S. Kaplan and D. P. Norton, *The Balanced Scorecard: Translating Strategy into Action* (Boston: Harvard Business School Press, 1996).

31. F. Luthans, S. A. Rosenkrantz, and H. W. Hennessey, "What Do Successful Managers Really Do? An Observational Study of Managerial Activities," *Journal of Applied Behavioral Science* 21 (1985), pp. 255–70.

32. R. C. Page and W. W. Tornow, "Managerial Job Analysis: Are We Any Further Along?" paper presented at a meeting of the Society of Industrial Organizational Psychology, Atlanta, GA, 1987.

33. G. Chitayat and I. Venezia, "Determinates of Management Styles in Business and Nonbusiness Organizations," *Journal of Applied Psychology* 69 (1984), pp. 437–47.

34. L. B. Kurke and H. E. Aldrich, "Mintzberg Was Right! A Replication and Extension of the Nature of Managerial Work," *Management Science* 29 (1983), pp. 975–84.

35. A. M. Morrison, R. P. White, and E. Van Velsor, *Breaking the Glass Ceiling* (Reading, MA: Addison-Wesley, 1987). Morse, G. "Why We Misread Motives," *Harvard Business Review,* January 2003, p. 18.

36. S. P. Robbins, *Organizational Behavior: Concepts, Controversies, and Applications* (Englewood Cliffs, NJ: Prentice Hall, 1986).

37. P. M. Podsakoff, "Determinants of a Supervisor's Use of Rewards and Punishments: A Literature Review and Suggestions for Future Research," *Organizational Behavior and Human Performance* 29 (1982), pp. 58–83.

38. T. H. Hammer and J. Turk, "Organizational Determinants of Leader Behavior and Authority," *Journal of Applied Psychology* 71 (1987), pp. 674–82.

39. Bass, *Bass and Stogdill's Handbook of Leadership.*

40. E. H. Schein, *Organizational Culture and Leadership: A Dynamic View* (San Francisco: Jossey-Bass, 1985).

41. Bass, *Bass and Stogdill's Handbook of Leadership.*

42. S. W. J. Kozlowski and M. L. Doherty, "Integration of Climate and Leadership: Examination of a Neglected Issue," *Journal of Applied Psychology* 74 (1989), pp. 546–53.

43. B. Schneider, P. J. Hanges, D. B. Smith, and A. N. Salvaggio, " Which Comes First: Employee Attitudes or Organizational Financial and Market Performance?" *Journal of Applied Psychology* 88, no. 5 (2003), pp. 836–51. J. Schneider, "The Cultural Situation as a Condition for the Condition of Fame," *American Sociology Review* 2 (1937), pp. 480–91.

44. Bass, *Bass and Stogdill's Handbook of.*

45. Kozlowski and Doherty, "Integration of Climate and Leadership".

46. Bass, *Bass and Stogdill's Handbook of Leadership.*

47. R. H. Kilmann and M. J. Saxton, *Organizational Cultures: Their Assessment and Change* (San Francisco: Jossey-Bass, 1983).

48. Schein, *Organizational Culture and Leadership.*

49. B. Dumaine, "Creating a New Company Culture," *Fortune,* 1990, pp. 127–131.

50. B. M. Bass, *Leadership and Performance beyond Expectations* (New York: Free Press, 1985).

51. J. M. Kouzes and B. Z. Posner, *The Leadership Challenge: How to Get Extraordinary Things Done in Organizations* (San Francisco: Jossey-Bass, 1987).

52. Schein, *Organizational Culture and Leadership.*

53. N. M. Tichy and M. A. Devanna, *The Transformational Leader* (New York: John Wiley, 1986).

54. F. E. Emery and E. L. Trist, "The Causal Texture of Organizational Environments," *Human Relations* 18 (1965), pp. 21–32.

55. C. S. Cameron and R. E. Quinn, *Diagnosing and Changing Organizational Culture* (Reading, MA: Addison-Wesley, 1999).

56. Ibid.

57. Ibid.

58. Ibid.

59. Ibid.

60. M. Lind, "The Boring Age," *Time*, March 22, 2010, pp. 58–59.

61. R. Heifetz, A. Grashow, and M. Linsky, "Leadership in a (Permanent) Crisis," *Harvard Business Review*, July–August 2009, pp. 62–69.

62. T. Friedman, *The World Is Flat: A Brief History of the Twenty-First Century* (New York: Farrar, Straus and Giroux, 2005).

63. T. Ricks, *The Gamble* (New York: The Penguin Press, 2009).

64. R. Heifetz, "An Interview with Ronald A. Heifetz: Interview by James Nelson," http://www.managementfirst.com/management_styles/interviews/heifetz .htm, accessed June 5, 2006.

65. Ibid.

66. M. Gladwell, *Outliers* (New York: Little, Brown and Company, 2005).

67. U. D. Jogulu and G. J. Wood, "A Cross-Cultural Study into Peer Evaluations of Women's Leadership Effectiveness," *Leadership & Organization Development Journal* 29, no. 7 (2008), pp. 606–16.

68. M. Javidan and R. J. House, "Cultural Acumen for the Global Manager: Lessons from Project GLOBE," *Organizational Dynamics* 29 (2001), pp. 289–305.

69. L. R. Kohls, *Survival Kit for Overseas Living* (Boston: Intercultural Press, 2001).

70. D. F. Barnum, "Effective Membership in the Global Business Community," in *New Traditions in Business*, ed. J. Renesch (San Francisco: Berrett-Koehler, 1992), p. 153.

71. R. House, P. Hanges, M. Javidan, P. Dorfman, and V. Gupta (ed.), *Culture, Leadership and Organizations: The GLOBE Study of 62 Societies* (Thousand Oaks, CA: Sage, 2004).

72. J. S. Chhokar, F. C. Brodbeck, and R. J. House (eds.), *Culture and Leadership around the World: The GLOBE Book of In-Depth Studies of 25 Societies* (Mahwah, NJ: Lawrence Erlbaum, 2007).

73. G. Hofstede, *Cultural Consequences: Comparing Values, Behaviors, Institutions and Organizations across Nations*, 2nd ed. (Thousand Oaks, CA: Sage Publications, 2001).

74. J. S. Chhokar, F. C. Brodbeck, and R. J. House, "Introduction," in *Culture and Leadership around the World: The GLOBE Book of In-Depth Studies of 25 Societies*, eds. J. S. Chhokar, F. C. Brodbeck, and R. J. House (Mahwah, NJ: Lawrence Erlbaum, 2007), pp. 1–6.

75. P. W. Dorfman, P. J. Hanges, and F. C. Brodbeck, "Leadership and Cultural Variation: The Identification of Culturally Endorsed Leadership Profiles," in *Culture, Leadership and Organizations: The GLOBE Study of 62 Societies*, eds. R. House, P. Hanges, M. Javidan, P. Dorfman, and V. Gupta (Thousand Oaks, CA: Sage, 2004), pp. 669–719.

76. Ibid.

77. R. House, House, R. J., Hanges, P. J., Ruiz-Quintanilla, S. A., Dorfman, P. W., Javidan, M. and Dickson, M. W. *Cultural Influences on Leadership and Organizations: Project Globe. Advances in Global Leadership*, vol. 1 (JAI Press, 1999), pp. 171–233.

Chapter 3

Skills for Developing Yourself as a Leader

One reason any person can improve his or her leadership effectiveness is that part of leadership involves skills, and skills can be practiced and developed. A further advantage of looking at leadership skills is that most people are less defensive about deficits in skills (which can be improved) than about suggested deficits in, say, personality. We will present a chapter about leadership skills following each of the four parts of the book, looking at skills that seem particularly relevant to various facets of our interactional framework. And because these skills chapters are quite different in purpose than the other chapters in the text, their format will be correspondingly different. Specifically, there will not be all the same closing sections found in the other chapters.

Not surprisingly, this first segment deals with some of the most fundamental, immediate, and yet in other ways most enduring challenges you will face as a leader. Key among these challenges is continuing to learn as a leader what you need to know now to be successful, and how to keep learning and developing throughout your life and career. The skills in this chapter will help in that effort. By the way, it might be useful to say more here about development planning, the last skill addressed in this chapter. Generally speaking, development planning would be considered an advanced leadership skill because it typically involves a leader developing her or his subordinates or followers. It's included with other skills in this introductory section so that you might think how to apply some of the ideas about development planning *to yourself*.

Here are the leadership skills we'll cover in this chapter:

- Your First 90 Days as a Leader
- Learning from Experience
- Building Technical Competence
- Building Effective Relationships with Superiors
- Building Effective Relationships with Peers
- Development Planning

Your First 90 Days as a Leader

People often find moving into a new leadership position to be a highly stressful work experience. Often these promotions involve relocations, working for new organizations and bosses, leading new teams, and being responsible for products or services that may be outside their immediate areas of expertise. Whether the move is from individual contributor to first-line supervisor or into senior executive positions, the stresses and strains of the first 90 days are both real and acute. Although the first three months give leaders unique opportunities to make smooth transitions, paint compelling pictures of the future, and drive organizational change, far too many new leaders stumble during this critical time period. This is unfortunate—these early activities often are instrumental to a leader's future success or failure. Many of these early mistakes are avoidable, and what follows is a road map for helping people make successful transitions into new leadership positions. It is important to note that the onboarding road map developed by Roellig and Curphy[1] is focused on external hires—those outside an organization who have been brought in to leadership positions. (See Figure 3.1.) Some of the steps in the onboarding road map can be ignored or need to be modified for individuals who have been promoted from within.

Before You Start: Do Your Homework

In all likelihood people wanting to move into a leadership role with another organization have already done a considerable amount of preparation for the interview process. Candidates should have read as much as

FIGURE 3.1
New Leader Onboarding Road Map

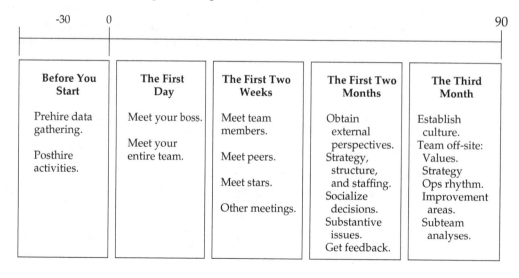

Before You Start	The First Day	The First Two Weeks	The First Two Months	The Third Month
Prehire data gathering.	Meet your boss.	Meet team members.	Obtain external perspectives.	Establish culture.
Posthire activities.	Meet your entire team.	Meet peers.	Strategy, structure, and staffing.	Team off-site: Values.
		Meet stars.	Socialize decisions.	Strategy Ops rhythm.
		Other meetings.	Substantive issues.	Improvement areas.
			Get feedback.	Subteam analyses.

they can about the organization by reviewing its website, annual reports, press releases, and marketing literature. They should also use Facebook, LinkedIn, Plaxo, and other social networking sites to set up informational interviews with people inside the organization. These informational interviews will help candidates learn more about the organization's history and culture and provide additional insight about the vacant position. Sometime during the interview process candidates should also seek answers to the following five questions:

- Why is the organization looking for an outside hire for the position?
- What can make the function or team to be led more effective?
- What is currently working in the function or team to be led?
- What is currently not working in the function or team to be led?
- What about the function or team is keeping interviewers awake at night?

Once candidates have landed new positions, they should seek additional information about their new jobs as well as set up some of the activities that need to take place during their first two weeks at work. New hires should check with their bosses to see if they can get copies of the results or metrics pertaining to the group to be led, any presentations predecessors made about the group or department, budget information, contact information for their direct reports, and so forth. They should also ask their new bosses what they need to do to set up access cards and e-mail, office, and cell phone accounts, as being able to get into the facility and having functional computers and phones at the start is crucial to a smooth beginning. Prior to arrival, a new hire should also set up one-hour meetings with the boss and with the entire team on the first day and follow-up two- to three-hour one-on-one meetings with each team member during the first two weeks on the job.

The First Day: You Get Only One Chance to Make a First Impression

New leaders have two critical tasks the first day on the job: to meet their new boss and their new team. The first meeting should happen in the boss's office and be about an hour long. Here are some key topics to discuss in this meeting:

- Identifying the team's key objectives, metrics, and important projects.
- Understanding the boss's view of team strengths and weaknesses.
- Working through meeting schedules and communication styles. (How, when, and on what does the boss want to be kept informed?)
- Sharing plans for the day and the next several weeks.

New hires should end the discussion by arranging a follow-up meeting with their bosses to review progress and to ask whether weekly or monthly one-on-one meetings would be helpful.

New leaders should also meet with their entire teams the first day on the job. Depending on the size of the team, this meeting could be held in a small conference room or it could be in a large auditorium with Webcasts or conference calls to remote sites. It usually takes new leaders about an hour to share their backgrounds, the attributes and values they feel are important to success, expectations for themselves and employees, work habits and preferred ways of interacting, family and recreational activities, and what they plan on doing over the next few weeks. After sharing this information new leaders should ask team members whether they have any questions but should not expect many takers. Because team members do not know new leaders well, these initial meetings tend to have more one-way communication than interactive dialogue.

The First Two Weeks: Lay the Foundation

New leaders should spend the first two weeks meeting with many people both inside and outside the team. The key objectives for these meetings are to (1) learn as much as possible, (2) develop relationships, and (3) determine future allies. New leaders need to be particularly mindful about what they say or write in these meetings because they have no idea in whom they can confide. They also need to be aware of the fact that some of the people they are meeting with, for whatever reason, are not happy about their arrival and may not want them to succeed.

During the first two weeks new leaders will want to have one-on-one meetings with key team members. If the team has fewer than 15 people, new leaders should meet individually with everyone on the team; if the team is larger, new leaders should meet one-on-one with direct reports during the first two weeks and have small group or individual meetings with everyone else on the team sometime during the first 90 days. The one-on-one meetings usually last from two to three hours, and some of the critical questions to ask include these:

- *What is the team member working on?* New leaders should ask about major projects and where people are spending their time because this will help identify the critical issues facing the team.
- *What are the team member's objectives?* This is an important question that needs to be asked after the previous question. Often team members spend their time and energy working on projects that are completely unrelated to their work objectives, and new leaders need to understand what these gaps are and why they are occurring.
- *Who are the "stars" a level or two down in the organization?* This question may be omitted if new leaders are in charge of groups consisting of fewer than 15 people. But if groups are significantly larger, it is important for new leaders to know who their top performers are. In all likelihood direct reports will name many of the same people as stars, and

these high-performing individuals can play critical roles during the first 90 days of a new leader's tenure.

- *What are the people issues on the team?* This can be a difficult question to ask—new leaders don't want team members to think they are asking them to disparage others. However, it is important for new leaders to find out who is displaying inappropriate behavior or is difficult to work with. Once properly identified, new team leaders will need to address these people issues within the first 60 days in order to make clear who is in charge and to show what type of behavior will and will not be tolerated on the team.

- *What can the team do better?* Team members' answers to this question can help new leaders develop ideas for improving team performance. These answers also indicate whether team members are capable of thinking about, accepting, and driving change.

- *What advice do team members have for the new leader, and what can the new leader do to help team members?* New team leaders should close their meetings with these two questions and pay particular attention to what they can do to help their direct reports be successful. New leaders should avoid making any immediate promises but commit to closing the loop on those requests they will or will not fulfill sometime during the next two months.

Although new leaders should start building rapport during these one-on-one meetings, they should minimize their personal interactions with direct reports during their first two months on the job. Business lunches and team get-togethers are fine, but meeting with families and spouses during the first 60 days can make later structure and staffing decisions more difficult. New leaders need to make personnel decisions with team performance, not personal friendships, in mind.

During the first two weeks on the job, new leaders should also schedule one-on-one meetings with all their peers. These meetings should last about an hour and take place in peers' offices; this will give new leaders opportunities to build rapport by observing office décor, diplomas, family pictures, awards, and so on. New leaders should discuss the following issues with peers:

- Their peers' objectives, challenges, team structure, and the like.
- Their perspectives on what the new leader's team does well and could do better.
- Their perspectives on the new leader's team members.
- How to best communicate with the boss.
- How issues get raised and decisions made on their boss's team.

New leaders should make it clear that they want and appreciate their peers' help. Scheduling regular meetings with their peers will build relationships and help new leaders stay ahead of potential conflicts or work issues. Unlike more personal meetings with direct reports, it is perfectly acceptable to socialize with peers and their families during the first 60 days. And because the boss will likely ask peers how the new leader is doing, meeting with peers on a regular basis becomes even more important.

If the team being led is fairly large, new leaders should also meet with their stars during the first two weeks on the job. Stars will be full of ideas for improving team performance, and these individuals are likely candidates for direct report positions should the new leader decide to change the structure of the team. If chosen for promotion, stars are likely to be loyal and well respected by others because they were widely recognized as being among the top performers on the team.

During the first two weeks new leaders should also try to meet with individuals who were once part of the team but have taken positions in other parts of the organization. These individuals can offer unique insights into the history of the team and team members, and this source of information should not be overlooked. The two other pieces of information new leaders should gather during the first two weeks are what the organization sees as the critical roles on the team and if there were any internal candidates for the team leader position. This information can be gathered from the boss, peers, former team members, the human resources representative, or the like. New leaders need this information to ensure they have the best talent filling key roles and to see if anyone on the team may be hoping they fail.

The First Two Months: Strategy, Structure, and Staffing

After their initial round of meetings with the boss, peers, and direct reports, new leaders need to spend the next six weeks gathering more information, determining the direction, and finalizing the appropriate structure and staffing for the team. Some of the tasks to be performed during this time include gathering benchmarking information from other organizations, meeting with key external customers and suppliers, and if appropriate, meeting with the former team leader. This additional information, when combined with the information gleaned from bosses, peers, direct reports, and stars, should help new team leaders determine the proper direction for their teams. This direction, or vision, may be more or less the same as what is already in place, or it may represent a significant change in direction. In either case, new leaders need to be able to articulate where the team has been and where it needs to go over the next one to three years, what it needs to accomplish, what changes will be needed to make this happen, and their expectations for team members. Depending on the new leader's vision, some of these changes may involve changing the team's structure and membership. In making these changes, new leaders need to remember that team strategy (vision and goals) should drive team structure, which in turn should drive team staffing decisions. Leaders who alter the strategy–structure–staffing sequence risk building dysfunctional, underperforming teams.

Although the first 90 days on the job provide a unique window for driving change, new leaders need to "socialize" their strategy, structure, and staffing ideas with their boss and peers before making any personnel decisions. Gathering input and working through potential disruptions with these two groups before moving ahead should improve buy-in and support for any change decisions. Once the proposed changes have been agreed to, new leaders need to have one-on-one meetings with all team members affected by any strategy, structure, and staffing decisions. During these meetings new leaders need to describe their vision and rationale for the changes and clarify roles and expectations for affected team members.

Although gathering additional information, developing the team's vision, and socializing key changes with affected parties take a considerable amount of time, new leaders must remember to stay focused on team performance. Team leaders may have less leeway to make needed changes if team performance drops precipitously during their first 60 days because dealing with day-to-day team issues will take up so much time that there will be little time left to drive change. Although it will be hard to obtain, new leaders should also seek feedback from others during their first two months with the organization. Possible sources for feedback include peers and recruiters. Recruiters have vested interests in seeing their placed candidates succeed and often tap their contacts within organizations to give new leaders feedback.

The Third Month: Communicate and Drive Change

At this point in a new leader's tenure, he or she has developed a vision of the future and can articulate how the team will win; identified the what, why, and how of any needed changes; and defined a clear set of expectations for team members. The two major events for the third month are meeting with the entire team and meeting off-site with direct reports (if the team is large). The purpose of the first team meeting is for the new leader to share what he or she learned from whom during the information gathering process, his or her vision of the future, the new team structure and staffing model, his or her expectations for team members, and the rationale for any team changes. New leaders need to tie their changes to the attributes and values they shared during their first day on the job. Change is not about a new leader's PowerPoint presentation or the posters put up, but instead involves the tangible actions taken. And the actions team members pay the most attention to are the hiring, firing, promotion, restructuring, and staffing decisions made by new team leaders. One of the fastest ways to change the culture and norms of a team is to change the people in it.

If the group being led is large, the new leaders will want to have a separate second meeting with direct reports. This meeting may be from one to two days long and should be held off-site to minimize interruptions. The key issues to work through off-site include these:

- *Get agreement on the critical attributes and values of team members.* Although new leaders will have clear ideas about the values and attributes they are looking for in team members, they cannot be sure direct reports have fully bought into this set of attributes. New leaders should set aside time during the off-site meeting to finalize and clearly define the positive and negative behaviors for all the attributes and values they want to see in team members.

- *Create a team scorecard.* The new leader will paint a vision and some overall objectives for the future, but the direct report team needs to formulate a set of concrete, specific goals with timelines and benchmarks for measuring success.

- *Establish an operating rhythm.* Once the direction and goals have been clarified, the team will need to work on its meeting cadence and rules of engagement. The new leader and the direct report team need to determine how often they will meet, when they will meet, the purpose and content of the meetings, meeting roles and rules (sending substitutes to meetings, showing up to meetings on time, taking calls during meetings, and the like). This new meeting schedule should be published in a one-year calendar and sent to everyone in the group.

- *Establish task forces to work on key change initiatives.* In all likelihood a number of issues will need to be addressed by the team. Some of these issues can be discussed and resolved during the off-site meeting, whereas task forces might be a better venue for resolving other issues. The task forces should be staffed by stars, which will both improve the odds that good recommendations are made and allow the new leader to see the stars in action.

After finalizing team structure and staffing, creating a team scorecard, and establishing a new operating rhythm, new leaders should be well on the way to success. As stated at the beginning of this section, the first 90 days give new leaders a unique opportunity to put in place many of the components needed to drive long-term change in their teams. Thus they need to use this time wisely.

Learning from Experience

Leadership practitioners can enhance the learning value of their experiences by (1) creating opportunities to get feedback; (2) taking a 10 percent stretch; (3) learning from others; (4) keeping a journal of daily leadership events; and (5) having a developmental plan.

Creating Opportunities to Get Feedback

It may be difficult for leaders to get relevant feedback, particularly if they occupy powerful positions in an organization. Yet leaders often need feedback more than subordinates do. Leaders may not learn much from their leadership experiences if they get no feedback about how they are doing. Therefore, they may need to create opportunities to get feedback, especially from those working for them.

Leaders should not assume they have invited feedback merely by saying they have an open-door policy. A mistake some bosses make is presuming that others perceive them as open to discussing things just because they say they are open to such discussion. How truly open a door might be is in the eye of the beholder. In that sense, the key to constructive dialogue (that is, feedback) is not just expressing a policy but also being perceived as approachable and sincere in the offer.

Some of the most helpful information for developing your own leadership can come from asking for feedback from others about their perceptions of your behavior and its impact on your group's overall effectiveness. Leaders who take psychological tests and use periodic surveys or questionnaires will have greater access to feedback than leaders who fail to systematically solicit feedback from their followers. Unless leaders ask for feedback, they may not get it.

Taking a 10 Percent Stretch

Learning always involves stretching. Learning involves taking risks and reaching beyond one's comfort zone. This is true of a toddler's first unsteady steps, a student's first serious confrontation with divergent worlds of thought, and leadership development. The phrase *10 percent stretch* conveys the idea of voluntary but determined efforts to improve leadership skills. It is analogous to physical exercise, though in this context stretching implies extending one's behavior, not muscles, just a bit beyond the comfort zone. Examples could include making a point of conversing informally with everyone in the office at least once each day, seeking an opportunity to be chair of a committee, or being quieter than usual at meetings (or more assertive, as the case may be). There is much to be gained from a commitment to such ongoing "exercise" for personal and leadership development.

Several positive outcomes are associated with leaders who regularly practice the 10 percent stretch. First, their apprehension about doing something new or different gradually decreases. Second, leaders will broaden their repertoire of leadership skills. Third, because of this increased repertoire, their effectiveness will likely increase. And finally, leaders regularly taking a 10 percent stretch will model something valuable to others. Few things send a better message to others about the importance of their own development than the example of how sincerely a leader takes his or her own development.

One final aspect of the 10 percent stretch is worth mentioning. One reason the phrase is so appealing is that it sounds like a measurable yet manageable change. Many people will not offer serious objection to trying a 10 percent change in some behavior, whereas they might well be resistant (and unsuccessful) if they construe a developmental goal as requiring fundamental change in their personality or interpersonal style. Despite its nonthreatening connotation, though, an actual 10 percent change in behavior can make an enormous difference in effectiveness. In many kinds of endeavors the difference between average performers and exceptional performers is 10 percent. In baseball, for example, many players hit .275, but only the best hit over .300—a difference of about 10 percent.

Learning from Others

Leaders learn from others, first of all, by recognizing that they *can* learn from others and, importantly, from *any* others. That may seem self-evident, but in fact people often limit what and whom they pay attention to, and thus what they may learn from. For example, athletes may pay a lot of attention to how coaches handle leadership situations. However, they may fail to realize they could also learn a lot by watching the director of the school play and the band conductor. Leaders should not limit their learning by narrowly defining the sorts of people they pay attention to.

Similarly, leaders also can learn by asking questions and paying attention to everyday situations. An especially important time to ask questions is when leaders are new to a group or activity and have some responsibility for it. When possible, leaders should talk to the person who previously had the position to benefit from his or her insights, experience, and assessment of the situation. In addition, observant leaders can extract meaningful leadership lessons from everyday situations. Something as plain and ordinary as a high school car wash or the activities at a fast-food restaurant may offer an interesting leadership lesson. Leaders can learn a lot by actively observing how others react to and handle different challenges and situations, even common ones.

Keeping a Journal

Another way leaders can mine experiences for their richness and preserve their learning is by keeping a journal.[2] Journals are similar to diaries, but they are not just accounts of a day's events. A journal should include entries that address some aspect of leaders or leadership. Journal entries may include comments about insightful or interesting quotes, anecdotes, newspaper articles, or even humorous cartoons about leadership. They may also include reflections on personal events, such as interactions with bosses, coaches, teachers, students, employees, players, teammates, roommates, and so on. Such entries can emphasize a good (or bad) way somebody handled something, a problem in the making, the differences between people in their reactions to situations, or people in the news, a book, or a film. Leaders

Sample Journal Entries

HIGHLIGHT 3.1

I went skiing this weekend and saw the perfect example of a leader adapting her leadership style to her followers and situation. While putting on my skis, I saw a ski instructor teaching little kids to ski. She did it using the game "red light, green light." The kids loved it and seemed to be doing very well. Later that same day, as I was going to the lodge for lunch, she was teaching adults, and she did more demonstrating than talking. But when she talked she was always sure to encourage them so they did not feel intimidated when some little kid whizzed by. She would say to the adults that it's easier for children, or that smaller skis are easier. She made the children laugh and learn, and made the adults less self-conscious to help them learn too. . . .

Today may not exactly be a topic on leadership, but I thought it would be interesting to discuss. I attended the football game this afternoon and could not help but notice our cheerleaders. I was just thinking of their name in general, and found them to be a good example (of leadership). Everyone gets rowdy at a football game, but without the direction of the cheerleaders there would be mayhem. They do a good job of getting the crowd organized and the adrenaline pumping (though of course the game is most important in that too!). It's just amazing to see them generate so much interest that all of the crowd gets into the cheering. We even chant their stupid-sounding cheers! You might not know any of them personally, but their enthusiasm invites you to try to be even louder than them. I must give the cheerleaders a round of applause. . . .

I've been thinking about how I used to view/ understand leadership, trying to find out how my present attitudes were developed. It's hard to remember past freshman year, even harder to go past high school. Overall, I think my father has been the single most important influence on my leadership development—long before I even realized it. Dad is a strong "Type A" person. He drives himself hard and demands a great deal from everyone around him, especially his family and especially his only son and oldest child. He was always pushing me to study, practice whatever sport I was involved in at the time, get ahead of everybody else in every way possible.

should also use their journals to "think on paper" about leadership readings from textbooks or formal leadership programs or to describe examples from their own experience of a concept presented in a reading.

There are at least three good reasons for keeping a journal. First, the process of writing increases the likelihood that leaders will be able to look at an event from a different perspective or feel differently about it. Putting an experience into words can be a step toward taking a more objective look at it. Second, leaders can (and should) reread earlier entries. Earlier entries provide an interesting and valuable autobiography of a leader's evolving thinking about leadership and about particular events in his or her life. Third, journal entries provide a repository of ideas that leaders may later want to use more formally for papers, pep talks, or speeches. As shown in Highlight 3.1, good journal entries give leaders a wealth of examples that they may use in speeches, presentations, and so on.

Having a Developmental Plan

Leadership development almost certainly occurs in ways and on paths that are not completely anticipated or controlled. That is no reason, however, for leaders to avoid actively directing some aspects of their own development. A systematic plan outlining self-improvement goals and strategies will help leaders take advantage of opportunities they otherwise might overlook. This important skill is addressed in greater detail in the last part of this chapter.

A leader's first step in exercising control over his or her personal development is to identify some actual goals. But what if a leader is uncertain about what he or she needs to improve? As described earlier, leaders should systematically collect information from a number of different sources. One place a leader can get information about where to improve is through a review of current job performance, if that is applicable. Ideally, leaders will have had feedback sessions with their own superiors, which should help them identify areas of relative strength and weakness. Leaders should treat this feedback as a helpful perspective on their developmental needs. Leaders also should look at their interactions with peers as a source of ideas about what they might work on. Leaders should especially take notice if the same kind of problem comes up in their interactions with different individuals in separate situations. Leaders need to look at their own role in such instances as objectively as they can; there might be clues about what behavioral changes might facilitate better working relationships with others. Still another way to identify developmental objectives is to look ahead to what new skills are needed to function effectively at a higher level in the organization, or in a different role than the leader now has. Finally, leaders can use formal psychological tests and questionnaires to determine what their relative strengths and weaknesses as a leader may be.

On a concluding note, there is one activity leaders should put in their developmental plans whatever else might be included in them: a program of personal reading to broaden their perspectives on leadership. This reading can include the classics as well as contemporary fiction, biographies and autobiographies of successful leaders, essays about ethics and social responsibility, and assorted self-improvement books on various leadership and management issues. A vital part of leadership development is intellectual stimulation and reflection, and an active reading program is indispensable to that. Leaders might even want to join (or form) a discussion group that regularly meets to exchange ideas about a book everyone has read.

Building Technical Competence

Technical competence concerns the knowledge and repertoire of behaviors one can bring to bear to successfully complete a task. For example, a skilled surgeon possesses vast knowledge of human anatomy and surgical techniques and can perform an extensive set of highly practiced surgical procedures; a skilled volleyball player has a thorough understanding of the rules, tactics, and strategies of volleyball and can set, block, and serve effectively. Individuals usually acquire technical competence through formal education or training in specialized topics (such as law, medicine, accounting, welding, or carpentry), on-the-job training, or experience,[3] and many studies have documented the importance of technical competence to a person's success and effectiveness as both a leader and a follower. This section describes why technical competence is important to followers and leaders; it also provides ideas about how to increase readers' own technical competence.

There are many reasons why followers need to have a high level of technical competence. First, performance is often a function of technical competence.[4,5] Relatedly, research has shown that technical expertise plays a key role in supervisors' performance appraisal ratings of subordinates.[6,7] Second, followers with high levels of technical competence have a lot of expert power and at times can wield more influence in their groups than the leader does.[8,9] Third, individuals with high levels of technical competence may be more likely to be a member of a leader's in-group[10] and are more likely to be delegated tasks and asked to participate in decisions. Conversely, supervisors are more likely to use a close, directive leadership style when interacting with subordinates with poor technical skills.[11–14] Similarly, Blau[15] noted that organizations with relatively high numbers of technically competent members tended to have a flatter organizational structure; organizations with relatively fewer qualified members tended to be more centralized and autocratic. Thus, if followers wish to earn greater rewards, exert more influence in their groups, and have greater say in decisions, they should do all they can to enhance their technical competence.

There are also many reasons why it benefits leaders to have high levels of technical competence. First, technical competence has been found to be consistently related to managerial promotion rates. Managers having higher levels of technical competence were much more likely to rise to the top managerial levels at AT&T than managers with lower levels of technical competence.[16,17] Second, having a high level of technical competence is important because many leaders, particularly first-line supervisors, often spend considerable time training followers.[18] Perhaps nowhere is the importance of technical competence in training more readily apparent than in sports coaching; little is as frustrating as having a coach who knows less about the game than the team members. Third, leaders with high levels of technical competence seem to be able to reduce the level of role ambiguity and conflict in their groups,[19,20] and followers are generally more satisfied with leaders who have high rather than average levels of technical competence.[21,22] Finally, leaders who have a high level of technical competence may be able to stimulate followers to think about problems and issues in new ways, which in turn has been found to be strongly related to organizational climate ratings and followers' motivation to succeed.[23,24] Given these findings for both leaders and followers, we next discuss some practical advice for improving technical competence.

Determining How the Job Contributes to the Overall Mission

The first step in building technical competence is to determine how one's job contributes to the overall success of the organization. By taking this step, individuals can better determine what technical knowledge and which behaviors are most strongly related to job and organizational success. Next, people should evaluate their current level of technical skills by seeking verbal feedback from peers and superiors, reviewing past performance appraisal results, or reviewing objective performance data (such as test scores, team statistics, or the number of products rejected for poor quality). These actions will help individuals get a better handle on their own strengths and weaknesses, and in turn can help people be certain that any formal education or training program they pursue is best suited to meet their needs.

Becoming an Expert in the Job

Becoming an expert in one's primary field is often the springboard for further developmental opportunities. There are a number of ways in which individuals can become experts in their field, and these include enrolling in formal education and training programs, watching others, asking questions, and teaching others. Attending pertinent education and training courses is one way to acquire technical skills, and many companies pay the tuition and fees associated with these courses. Another way to increase expertise in one's field is by being a keen observer of human behavior. Individuals can learn a lot by observing how others handle work coordination problems, achieve production goals, discipline team members, or help team members with poor skills develop. However, merely observing how others do things is not nearly as effective as observing and reflecting about how others do things. One method of reflection is trying to explain others' behaviors in terms of the concepts or theories described in this book. Observers should look for concepts that cast light on both variations and regularities in how others act and think about why a person might have acted a certain way. Additionally, observers can develop by trying to think of as many different criteria as possible for evaluating another person's actions.

It is also important to ask questions. Because everyone makes inferences regarding the motives, expectations, values, or rationale underlying another person's actions, it is vital to ask questions and seek information likely to verify the accuracy of one's inferences. By asking questions, observers can better understand why team practices are conducted in a particular way, what work procedures have been implemented in the past, or what really caused someone to quit a volunteer organization. Finally, perhaps nothing can help a person become a technical expert more than having to teach someone else about the equipment, procedures, strategies, problems, resources, and contacts associated with a job, club, sport, or activity. Teachers must thoroughly understand a job or position to effectively teach someone else. By seeking opportunities to teach others, individuals enhance their own technical expertise as well as that of others.

Seeking Opportunities to Broaden Experiences

Individuals can improve their technical competence by seeking opportunities to broaden their experiences. Just as a person should try to play a variety of positions to better appreciate the contributions of other team members, so should a person try to perform the tasks associated with the other positions in his or her work group to better appreciate how the work contributes to organizational success. Similarly, people should visit other parts of the organization to understand its whole operation. Moreover, by working on team projects, people get to interact with members of other work units and often can develop new skills. Additionally, volunteering to support school, political, or community activities is another way to increase one's organization and planning, public speaking, fund-raising, and public relations skills, all of which may be important aspects of technical competence for certain jobs.

Building Effective Relationships with Superiors

As defined here, superiors are individuals with relatively more power and authority than the other members of the group. Thus superiors could be teachers, band directors, coaches, team captains, heads of committees, or first-line supervisors. Needless to say, there are a number of advantages to having a good working relationship with superiors. First, superiors and followers sharing the same values, approaches, and attitudes will experience less conflict, provide higher levels of mutual support, and be more satisfied with superior–follower relationships than superiors and followers having poor working relationships.[25,26] Relatedly, individuals having good superior–follower relationships are often in the superior's in-group and thus are more likely to have a say in decisions, be delegated interesting tasks, and have the superior's support for career advancement.[27] Second, followers are often less satisfied with their supervisors and receive lower performance appraisal ratings when superior–follower relationships are poor.[28,29]

Although the advantages of having a good working relationship with superiors seem clear, one might mistakenly think that followers have little, if any, say in the quality of the relationship. In other words, followers might believe their relationships with superiors are a matter of luck: either the follower has a good superior or a bad one, or the superior just happens to like or dislike the follower, and there is little the follower can do about it. However, the quality of a working relationship is not determined solely by the superior, and effective subordinates do not limit themselves to a passive stance toward superiors. Effective subordinates have learned how to take active steps to strengthen the relationship and enhance the support they provide their superior and the organization.[30,31]

Wherever a person is positioned in an organization, an important aspect of that person's work is to help his superior be successful, just as an important part of the superior's work is to help followers be successful. This does not mean followers should become apple polishers, play politics, or distort information to make superiors look good. However, followers should think of their own and their superior's success as interdependent. Followers are players on their superior's team and should be evaluated on the basis of the team's success, not just their own. If the team succeeds, both the coach and the team members should benefit; if the team fails, the blame should fall on both the coach and the team members. Because team, club, or organizational outcomes depend to some extent on good superior–follower relationships, understanding how superiors view the world and adapting to superiors' styles are two things followers can do to increase the likelihood their actions will have positive results for themselves, their superiors, and their organizations.[32]

Understanding the Superior's World

Followers can do a number of things to better understand their superior's world. First, they should try to get a handle on their superior's personal and organizational objectives. Loyalty and support are a two-way street, and just as a superior can help subordinates attain their personal goals most readily by knowing what they are, so can subordinates support their superior if they understand the superior's goals and objectives. Knowing a superior's values, preferences, and personality can help followers understand why superiors act as they do and can show followers how they might strengthen relationships with superiors.

Second, followers need to realize that superiors are not supermen or superwomen; superiors do not have all the answers, and they have both strengths and weaknesses. Subordinates can make a great contribution to the overall success of a team by recognizing and complementing a superior's weaknesses and understanding his or her constraints and limitations. For example, a highly successful management consultant might spend over 200 days a year conducting executive development workshops, providing organizational feedback to clients, or giving speeches at various public events. This same consultant, however, might not be skilled in designing and making effective visual aids for presentations, or she might dislike having to make her own travel and accommodation arrangements. A follower could make both the consultant and the consulting firm more successful through his own good organization and planning, attention to detail, computer graphics skills, and understanding that the consultant is most effective when she has at least a one-day break between engagements.

A similar process can take place in other contexts, such as when subordinates help orient and educate a newly assigned superior whose expertise and prior experience may have been in a different field or activity.

In an even more general sense, subordinates can enhance superior–follower relationships by keeping superiors informed about various activities in the work group or new developments or opportunities in the field. Few superiors like surprises, and any news should come from the person with responsibility for a particular area—especially if the news is potentially bad or concerns unfavorable developments. Followers wishing to develop good superior–follower relationships should never put their superior in the embarrassing situation of having someone else know more about her terrain than she does (her own boss, for instance). As Kelley[33] maintained, the best followers think critically and play an active role in their organizations, which means followers should keep their superiors informed about critical information and pertinent opinions concerning organizational issues.

Adapting to the Superior's Style

Research has shown that some executives fail to get promoted (that is, are derailed) because they are unable or unwilling to adapt to superiors with leadership styles different from their own.[34] Followers need to keep in mind that it is their responsibility to adapt to their superior's style, not vice versa. For example, followers might prefer to interact with superiors face-to-face, but if their superior appreciates written memos, then written memos it should be. Similarly, a follower might be accustomed to informal interactions with superiors, but a new superior might prefer a more businesslike and formal style. Followers need to be flexible in adapting to their superiors' decision-making styles, problem-solving strategies, modes of communication, styles of interaction, and so on.

One way followers can better adapt to a superior's style is to clarify expectations about their role on the team, committee, or work group. Young workers often do not appreciate the difference between a job description and one's role in a job. A job description is a formalized statement of tasks and activities; a role describes the personal signature an incumbent gives to a job. For example, the job description of a high school athletic coach might specify such responsibilities as selecting and training a team or making decisions about lineups. Two different coaches, however, might accomplish those basic responsibilities in quite different ways. One might emphasize player development in the broadest sense, getting to know her players personally and using sports as a vehicle for their individual growth; another might see his role as simply to produce the most winning team possible. Therefore, just because followers know what their job is does not mean their role is clear.

Although some superiors take the initiative to explicitly spell out the roles they expect subordinates to play, most do not. Usually it is the subordinate's task to discern his or her role. One way followers can do this is to make a list of major responsibilities and use it to guide a discussion with the superior about different ways the tasks might be accomplished and the relative priorities of the tasks. Followers will also find it helpful to talk to others who have worked with a particular superior.

Finally, followers interested in developing effective relationships with superiors need to be honest and dependable. Whatever other qualities or talents a subordinate might have, a lack of integrity is a fatal flaw. No one—superior, peer, or subordinate—wants to work with someone who is untrustworthy. After integrity, superiors value dependability. Superiors value workers who have reliable work habits, accomplish assigned tasks at the right time in the right order, and do what they promise.[35]

Building Effective Relationships with Peers

The phrase *influence without authority*[36] captures a key element of the work life of increasing numbers of individuals. More and more people are finding that their jobs require them to influence others despite having no formal authority over them. No man is an island, it is said, and perhaps no worker in today's organizations can survive alone. Virtually everyone needs a co-worker's assistance or resources at one time or another. Along these lines, some researchers have maintained that a fundamental requirement of leadership effectiveness is the ability to build strong alliances with others, and groups of peers generally wield more influence (and can get more things done) than individuals working separately.[37] Similarly, investing the time and effort to develop effective relationships with peers not only has immediate dividends but also can have long-term benefits if a peer ends up in a position of power in the future. Many times leaders are selected from among the members of a group, committee, club, or team; and having previously spent time developing a friendly rather than an antagonistic relationship with other work group members, leaders will lay the groundwork for building effective relationships with superiors and becoming a member of superiors' in-groups. Given the benefits of strong relationships with peers, the following are a few ideas about how to establish and maintain good peer relationships.

Recognizing Common Interests and Goals

Although Chapters 4 through 8 describe a variety of ways people vary, one of the best ways to establish effective working relationships with peers is to acknowledge shared interests, values, goals, and expectations.[38] In order to acknowledge shared aspirations and interests, however, one must know what peers' goals, values, and interests actually are. Establishing informal communication links is one of the best ways to discover common interests and values. To do so, one needs to be open and honest in communicating one's own needs, values, and goals, as well as being willing to acknowledge others' needs, aspirations, and interests. Little can destroy a relationship with peers more quickly than a person who is overly willing to share his own problems and beliefs but unwilling to listen to others' ideas about the same issues. Moreover, although some people believe that participating in social gatherings, parties, committee meetings, lunches, company sport teams, or community activities can be a waste of time, peers with considerable referent power often see such activities as opportunities to establish and improve relationships with others. Thus an effective way to establish relationships with other members of a team, committee, or organization is to meet with them in contexts outside normal working relationships.

Understanding Peers' Tasks, Problems, and Rewards

Few things reinforce respect between co-workers better than understanding the nature of each other's work. Building a cooperative relationship with others depends, therefore, on knowing the sorts of tasks others perform in the organization. It also depends on understanding their problems and rewards. With the former, one of the best ways to establish strong relationships is by lending a hand whenever peers face personal or organizational problems. With the latter, it is especially important to remember that people tend to repeat behaviors that are rewarded and are less likely to repeat behaviors that go unrewarded. A person's counterproductive or negative behaviors may be due less to his personal characteristics ("He is just uncooperative") than to the way his rewards are structured. For example, a teacher may be less likely to share successful classroom exercises with others if teachers are awarded merit pay on the basis of classroom effectiveness. To secure cooperation from others, it helps to know which situational factors reinforce both positive and negative behaviors in others.[39] By better understanding the situation facing others, people can determine whether their own positive feedback (or lack thereof) is contributing to, or hindering the establishment of, effective relationships with peers. People should not underestimate the power of their own sincere encouragement, thanks, and compliments in positively influencing the behavior of their colleagues.

Practicing a Theory Y Attitude

Another way to build effective working relationships with peers is to view them from a Theory Y perspective (see Chapter 5 for more about Theory Y and a contrasting approach called Theory X). When a person assumes that others are competent, trustworthy, willing to cooperate if they can, and proud of their work, peers will view that person in the same light. Even if one practices a Theory Y attitude, however, it may still be difficult to get along with a few co-workers. In such cases it is easy to become preoccupied with the qualities one dislikes. This should be resisted as much as possible. A vicious cycle can develop in which people become enemies, putting more and more energy into criticizing each other or making the other person look bad than into doing constructive work on the task at hand. The costs of severely strained relationships can extend beyond the individuals involved. Cliques can develop among other co-workers, which can impair the larger group's effectiveness. The point here is not to overlook interpersonal problems, but rather to not let the problems get out of hand.

Practicing Theory Y does *not* mean looking at the world through rose-colored glasses, but it *does* mean recognizing someone else's strengths as well as weaknesses. Nevertheless, sometimes peers will be assigned to work on a task together when they don't get along with each other, and the advice "Practice a Theory Y attitude" may seem too idealistic. At such times it is important to decide whether to focus energy first on improving the relationship (before addressing the task) or to focus it solely on the task (essentially ignoring the problem in the relationship).

Cohen and Bradford[40] have suggested several guidelines for resolving this problem. It is best to work on the task if there is little animosity between the parties, if success can be achieved despite existing animosities, if group norms inhibit openness, if success on the task will improve the feelings between the parties, if the other person handles directness poorly, or if you handle directness poorly. Conversely, it is best to work on the relationship if there is great animosity between the parties, if negative feelings make task success unlikely, if group norms favor openness, if feelings between the parties are not likely to improve even with success on the task, if the other person handles directness well, *and* if you handle directness well.

Development Planning

Development planning is the systematic process of building knowledge and experience or changing behavior. Two people who have done a considerable amount of cutting-edge research in the development planning process are Peterson and Hicks.[41–43] These two researchers believe development planning consists of five interrelated phases. The first phase of development planning is identifying development needs. Here leaders identify career goals, assess their abilities in light of career goals, seek feedback about how their behaviors are affecting others, and review the organizational standards pertaining to their career goals. Once this information has been gathered, the second phase consists of analyzing these data to identify and prioritize development needs. The prioritized development needs in turn are used to create a focused and achievable development plan, the third phase of this process. The fourth phase in development planning is periodically reviewing the plan, reflecting on learning, and modifying or updating the plan as appropriate. As you

Change before you have to.

Jack Welch, former General Electric CEO

might expect, the action–observation–reflection (AOR) model, described in Chapter 2, is a key component during this phase of the development planning process. The last phase in development planning is transferring learning to new environments. Just because a leader can successfully delegate activities to a three-person team may not mean he will effectively delegate tasks or use his staff efficiently when he is leading 25 people. In that case the leader will need to build and expand on the delegation skills he learned when leading a smaller team. These five phases are well grounded in research—several studies have shown that approximately 75 percent of the leadership practitioners adopting these phases were successful in either changing their behaviors permanently or developing new skills. Because these five phases are so important to the development planning process, the remainder of this section will describe each phase in more detail.[44-46]

Conducting a GAPS Analysis

The first phase in the development planning process is to conduct a GAPS (goals, abilities, perceptions, standards) analysis. A GAPS analysis helps leadership practitioners to gather and categorize all pertinent development planning information. A sample GAPS analysis for an engineer working in a manufacturing company can be found in Figure 3.2. This individual wants to get promoted to a first-line supervisor position within the next year, and all of the information pertinent to this promotion can be found in her GAPS analysis. The specific steps for conducting a GAPS analysis are as follows:

- *Step 1: Goals.* The first step in a GAPS analysis is to clearly identify what you want to do or where you want to go with your career over the next year or so. This does not necessarily mean moving up or getting promoted to the next level. An alternative career objective might be to master one's current job—you may have just gotten promoted, and advancing to the next level is not important at the moment. Other career objectives might include taking on more responsibilities in your current position, taking a lateral assignment in another part of the company, taking an overseas assignment, or even cutting back on job responsibilities to gain more work–life balance. This last career objective may be appropriate for leaders who are starting a family or taking care of loved ones who are suffering from poor health. The two most important aspects of this step in the GAPS analysis are that leadership practitioners will have a lot more energy to work on development needs that are aligned with career goals, and in many cases advancing to the next level may not be a viable or particularly energizing career goal. This latter point may be especially true in organizations that have been recently downsized. Management positions often bear the brunt of downsizing initiatives, resulting in fewer available positions for those wishing to advance.

FIGURE 3.2
A Sample GAPS Analysis

Goals: Where do you want to go? *Step 1:* Career objectives: Career strategies:	Abilities: What can you do now? *Step 2:* What strengths do you have for your career objectives? *Step 3:* What development needs will you have to overcome?
Standards: What does your boss or the organization expect? *Step 5:* Expectations:	Perceptions: How do others see you? *Step 4:* 360-degree and performance review results, and feedback from others: • *Boss* • *Peers* • *Direct reports*

Sources: D. B. Peterson and M. D. Hicks, *Leader as Coach* (Minneapolis, MN: Personnel Decisions International, 1996); G. J. Curphy, *Career and Development Planning Workshop: Planning for Individual Development* (Minneapolis MN: Personnel Decisions International, 1998).

- *Step 2: Abilities.* People bring a number of strengths and development needs to their career goals. Over the years you may have developed specialized knowledge or a number of skills that have helped you succeed in your current and previous jobs. Similarly, you may also have received feedback over the years that there are certain skills you need to develop or behaviors you need to change. Good leaders know themselves—over the years they know which strengths they need to leverage and which skills they need to develop.

- *Step 3: Perceptions.* The perceptions component of the GAPS model concerns how your abilities, skills, and behaviors affect others. What are others saying about your various attributes? What are their reactions to both your strengths and your development needs? A great way of obtaining this information is by asking others for feedback or through performance reviews or 360-degree feedback instruments.
- *Step 4: Standards.* The last step in a GAPS analysis concerns the standards your boss or the organization has for your career objectives. For example, your boss may say you need to develop better public speaking, delegation, or coaching skills before you can get promoted. Similarly, the organization may have policies stating that people in certain overseas positions must be proficient in the country's native language, or it may have educational or experience requirements for various jobs.

When completing a GAPS analysis you may discover that you do not have all the information you need. If you do not, then you need to get it before you complete the next step of the development planning process. Only you can decide on your career objectives; but you can solicit advice from others on whether these objectives are realistic given your abilities, the perceptions of others, and organizational standards. You may find that your one-year objectives are unrealistic given your development needs, organizational standards, or job opportunities. In this case, you may need to either reassess your career goals or consider taking a number of smaller career steps that will ultimately help you achieve your career goal. If you are lacking information about the other quadrants, you can ask your boss or others whose opinions you value about your abilities, perceptions, or organizational standards. Getting as much up-to-date and pertinent information for your GAPS analysis will help ensure that your development plan is focusing on high-priority objectives.

Identifying and Prioritizing Development Needs: Gaps of GAPS

As shown in Figure 3.3, the goals and standards quadrants are future oriented; these quadrants ask where you want to go and what your boss or your organization expects of people in these positions. The abilities and perceptions quadrants are focused on the present: what strengths and development needs do you currently have, and how are these attributes affecting others? Given what you currently have and where you want to go, what are the gaps in your GAPS? In other words, after looking at all the information in your GAPS analysis, what are your biggest development needs, and how should these development needs be prioritized? You need to review the information from the GAPS model, look for underlying themes and patterns, and determine what behaviors, knowledge, experiences, or skills will be the most important to change or develop if you are to accomplish your career goals.

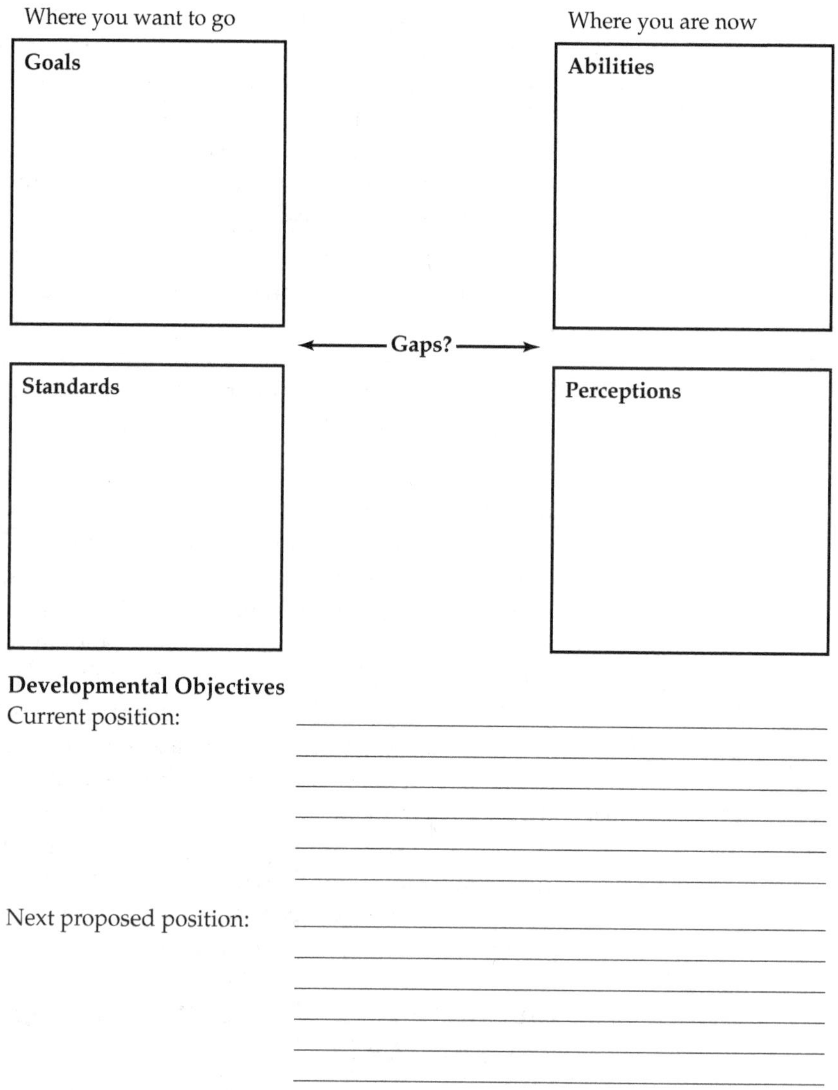

108   Part One   *Leadership Is a Process, Not a Position*

FIGURE 3.3
A Gaps-of-the-GAPS Analysis

Sources: D. B. Peterson and M. D. Hicks, *Leader as Coach* (Minneapolis, MN: Personnel Decisions International, 1996); G. J. Curphy, *The Leadership Development Process Manual* (Minneapolis, MN: Personnel Decisions International, 1998).

Where you want to go

Goals

Where you are now

Abilities

◄——— Gaps? ———►

Standards

Perceptions

Developmental Objectives
Current position: _____
_____
_____
_____
_____
_____
_____
_____

Next proposed position: _____
_____
_____
_____
_____
_____

Bridging the Gaps: Building a Development Plan

A gaps-of-the-GAPS analysis helps leadership practitioners identify high-priority development needs, but it does not spell out what leaders need to do to meet these needs. A good development plan is like a road map: it clearly describes the final destination, lays out the steps or interim checkpoints, builds in regular feedback to keep people on track, identifies where additional resources are needed, and builds in reflection time so people can periodically review progress and determine whether an alternative route is needed. (See Figure 2.4 on page 70 for a sample development plan.) The specific steps for creating a high-impact development plan are as follows:

- *Step 1: career and development objectives.* Your career objective comes directly from the goals quadrant of the GAPS analysis; it is where you want to be or what you want to be doing in your career a year or so in the future. The development objective comes from your gaps-of-the-GAPS analysis; it should be a high-priority development need pertaining to your career objective. People should be working on no more than two to three development needs at any one time.

- *Step 2: criteria for success.* What would it look like if you developed a particular skill, acquired technical expertise, or changed the behavior outlined in your development objective? This can be a difficult step in development planning, particularly with "softer" skills such as listening, managing conflict, or building relationships with others.

- *Step 3: action steps.* The focus in the development plan should be on the specific, on-the-job action steps leadership practitioners will take to meet their development need. However, sometimes it is difficult for leaders to think of appropriate on-the-job action steps. Three excellent resources that provide on-the-job action steps for a variety of development needs are two books, *The Successful Manager's Handbook*[47] and *For Your Improvement*,[48] and the development planning and coaching software *DevelopMentor*.[49] These three resources can be likened to restaurant menus in that they provide leadership practitioners with a wide variety of action steps to work on just about any development need.

- *Step 4: whom to involve and when to reassess dates.* This step in a development plan involves feedback—whom do you need to get it from, and how often do you need to get it? This step in the development plan is important because it helps keep you on track. Are your efforts being noticed? Do people see any improvement? Are there things you need to do differently? Do you need to refocus your efforts?

- *Step 5: stretch assignments.* When people reflect on when they have learned the most, they often talk about situations where they felt they were in over their heads. These situations stretched their knowledge and skills and often are seen as extremely beneficial to learning. If you know of a potential assignment, such as a task force, a project management team, or a rotational assignment, that would emphasize the knowledge and skills you need to develop and accelerate your learning, you should include it in your development plan.

- *Step 6: resources.* Often people find it useful to read a book, attend a course, or watch a recorded program to gain foundational knowledge about a particular development need. These methods generally describe the how-to steps for a particular skill or behavior.

- *Step 7: reflect with a partner.* In accordance with the action–observation–reflection model of Chapter 2, people should periodically review their learning and progress with a partner. The identity of the partner is not particularly important as long as you trust his or her opinion and the partner is familiar with your work situation and development plan.

Reflecting on Learning: Modifying Development Plans

Just as the development plan is a road map, this phase of development planning helps leaders to see whether the final destination is still the right one, if an alternative route might be better, and whether there is need for more resources or equipment. Reflecting on your learning with a partner is also a form of public commitment, and people who make public commitments are much more likely to fulfill them. All things considered, in most cases it is probably best to periodically review your progress with your boss. Your boss should not be left in the dark with respect to your development, and periodically reviewing progress with your boss will help ensure there are no surprises at your performance appraisal.

Transferring Learning to New Environments

The last phase in development planning concerns ongoing development. Your development plan should be a "live" document: it should be changed, modified, or updated as you learn from your experiences, receive feedback, acquire new skills, and meet targeted development needs. There are basically three ways to transfer learning to new environments. The first way is to constantly update your development plan. Another way to enhance your learning is to practice your newly acquired skills in a new environment. A final way to hone and refine your skills is to coach others in the development of your newly acquired skills. Moving from the student role to that of a master is an excellent way to reinforce your learning.

End Notes

1. M. Roellig and G. J. Curphy, *How to Hit the Ground Running: A Guide to Successful Executive On-Boarding* (Springfield, MA: Author, 2010).

2. M. Csikszentmihalyi, *Flow: The Psychology of Optimal Experience* (New York: Harper & Row, 1990).

3. G. Yukl, *Leadership in Organizations,* 2nd ed. (Englewood Cliffs, NJ: Prentice Hall, 1989).

4. G. J. Curphy, "Leadership Transitions and Succession Planning," in *Developing and Implementing Succession Planning Programs,* ed. J. Locke (chair). Symposium conducted at the 19th Annual Conference for the Society of Industrial and Organizational Psychology, Chicago, April 2004.

5. F. L. Schmidt and J. E. Hunter, "Development of a Causal Model of Job Performance," *Current Directions in Psychological Science* 1, no. 3 (1992), pp. 89–92.

6. W. C. Borman, L. A. White, E. D. Pulakos, and S. A. Oppler, "Models Evaluating the Effects of Rated Ability, Knowledge, Proficiency, Temperament, Awards, and Problem Behavior on Supervisor Ratings," *Journal of Applied Psychology* 76 (1991), pp. 863–72.

7. J. Hogan, "The View from Below," in *The Future of Leadership Selection*, ed. R. T. Hogan (chair). Symposium conducted at the 13th Biennial Psychology in the Department of Defense Conference, United States Air Force Academy, Colorado Springs, CO, 1992.

8. D. E. Bugental, "A Study of Attempted and Successful Social Influence in Small Groups as a Function of Goal-Relevant Skills," *Dissertation Abstracts* 25 (1964), p. 660.

9. G. F. Farris, "Colleagues' Roles and Innovation in Scientific Teams," Working Paper No. 552-71 (Cambridge, MA: Alfred P. Sloan School of Management, MIT, 1971).

10. D. Duchon, S. G. Green, and T. D. Taber, "Vertical Dyad Linkage: A Longitudinal Assessment of Antecedents, Measures, and Consequences," *Journal of Applied Psychology* 71 (1986), pp. 56–60.

11. H. D. Dewhirst, V. Metts, and R. T. Ladd, "Exploring the Delegation Decision: Managerial Responses to Multiple Contingencies," Paper presented at the Academy of Management Convention, New Orleans, LA, 1987.

12. C. R. Leana, "Power Relinquishment vs. Power Sharing: Theoretical Clarification and Empirical Comparison of Delegation and Participation," *Journal of Applied Psychology* 72 (1987), pp. 228–33.

13. A. Lowin and J. R. Craig, "The Influence of Level of Performance on Managerial Style: An Experimental Object-Lesson in the Ambiguity of Correlational Data," *Organizational Behavior and Human Performance* 3 (1968), pp. 68–106.

14. B. Rosen and T. H. Jerdee, "Influence of Subordinate Characteristics on Trust and Use of Participative Decision Strategies in a Management Simulation," *Journal of Applied Psychology* 59 (1977), pp. 9–14.

15. P. M. Blau, "The Hierarchy of Authority in Organizations," *American Journal of Sociology* 73 (1968), pp. 453–67.

16. A. Howard, "College Experiences and Managerial Performance," *Journal of Applied Psychology* 71 (1986), pp. 530–52.

17. A. Howard and D. W. Bray, "Predictors of Managerial Success over Long Periods of Time," in *Measures of Leadership*, ed. M. B. Clark and K. E. Clark (West Orange, NJ: Leadership Library of America, 1989).

18. K. N. Wexley and G. P. Latham, *Developing and Training Human Resources in Organizations* (Glenview, IL: Scott Foresman, 1981).

19. P. M. Podsakoff, W. D. Todor, and R. S. Schuler, "Leadership Expertise as a Moderator of the Effects of Instrumental and Supportive Leader Behaviors," *Journal of Management* 9 (1983), pp. 173–85.

20. T. G. Walker, "Leader Selection and Behavior in Small Political Groups," *Small Group Behavior* 7 (1976), pp. 363–68.

21. B. M. Bass, *Leadership and Performance beyond Expectations* (New York: Free Press, 1985).

22. D. D. Penner, D. M. Malone, T. M. Coughlin, and J. A. Herz, *Satisfaction with U.S. Army Leadership,* Leadership Monograph Series, no. 2 (U.S. Army War College, 1973).

23. B. J. Avolio and B. M. Bass, "Transformational Leadership, Charisma, and Beyond," in *Emerging Leadership Vista,* ed. J. G. Hunt, B. R. Baliga, and C. A. Schriesheim (Lexington, MA: D. C. Heath, 1988).

24. G. J. Curphy, "An Empirical Examination of Bass' 1985 Theory of Transformational and Transactional Leadership," PhD dissertation, University of Minnesota, 1991.

25. D. Duchon, S. G. Green, and T. D. Taber, "Vertical Dyad Linkage: A Longitudinal Assessment of Antecedents, Measures, and Consequences," *Journal of Applied Psychology* 71 (1986), pp. 56–60.

26. D. A. Porter, "Student Course Critiques: A Case Study in Total Quality in the Classroom," in *Proceedings of the 13th Biennial Psychology in Department of Defense Conference* (Colorado Springs, CO: U.S. Air Force Academy, 1992), pp. 26–30.

27. G. Yukl, *Leadership in Organizations,* 2nd ed. (Englewood Cliffs, NJ: Prentice Hall, 1989).

28. E. D. Pulakos and K. N. Wexley, "The Relationship among Perceptual Similarity, Sex, and Performance Ratings in Manager-Subordinate Dyads," *Academy of Management Journal* 26 (1983), pp. 129–39.

29. H. M. Weiss, "Subordinate Imitation of Supervisor Behavior: The Role of Modeling in Organizational Socialization," *Organizational Behavior and Human Performance* 19 (1977), pp. 89–105.

30. J. J. Gabarro, and J. P. Kotter, "Managing Your Boss," *Harvard Business Review* 58, no. 1 (1980), pp. 92–100.

31. R. E. Kelley, "In Praise of Followers," *Harvard Business Review* 66, no. 6 (1988), pp. 142–48.

32. Gabarro and Kotter, "Managing Your Boss."

33. Kelley, "In Praise of Followers."

34. M. W. McCall Jr. and M. M. Lombardo, "Off the Track: Why and How Successful Executives Get Derailed," Technical Report No. 21 (Greensboro, NC: Center for Creative Leadership, 1983).

35. J. M. Kouzes and B. Z. Posner, *The Leadership Challenge: How to Get Extraordinary Things Done in Organizations* (San Francisco: Jossey-Bass, 1987).

36. A. R. Cohen and D. L. Bradford, *Influence without Authority* (New York: John Wiley, 1990).

37. G. J. Curphy, A. Baldrica, M. Benson, and R. T. Hogan, *Managerial Incompetence,* unpublished manuscript, 2007.

38. A. R. Cohen and D. L. Bradford, *Influence without Authority* (New York: John Wiley, 1990).

39. Cohen and Bradford, *Influence without Authority.*

40. Ibid.

41. D. B. Peterson and M. D. Hicks, *Professional Coaching: State of the Art, State of the Practice* (Minneapolis, MN: Personnel Decisions International, 1998).

42. D. B. Peterson and M. D. Hicks, "Coaching across Borders: It's Probably a Long Distance Call," *Development Matters,* no. 9 (1997), pp. 1–4.

43. D. B. Peterson and M. D. Hicks, *Leader as Coach: Strategies for Coaching and Developing Others* (Minneapolis, MN: Personnel Decisions International, 1996).

44. J. F. Hazucha, S. A. Hezlett, and R. J. Schneider, "The Impact of 360-Degree Feedback on Management Skills Development," *Human Resource Management* 32 (1993), pp. 325–51.

45. D. B. Peterson, "Skill Learning and Behavioral Change in an Individually Tailored Management Coaching and Training Program," unpublished doctoral dissertation, University of Minnesota, 1993.

46. S. A. Hezlett and B. A. Koonce, "Now That I've Been Assessed, What Do I Do? Facilitating Development after Individual Assessments," paper presented at the IPMA Assessment Council Conference on Public Personnel Assessment, New Orleans, LA, June 1995.

47. B. L. Davis, L. W. Hellervik, and J. L. Sheard, *The Successful Manager's Handbook*, 3rd ed. (Minneapolis, MN: Personnel Decisions International, 1989).

48. M. M. Lombardo and R. W. Eichinger, *For Your Improvement: A Development and Coaching Guide* (Minneapolis, MN: Lominger, 1996).

49. Personnel Decisions International, *DevelopMentor: Assessment, Development, and Coaching Software* (Minneapolis, MN: Personnel Decisions International, 1995).

Subject Index

CPSIA information can be obtained
at www.ICGtesting.com
Printed in the USA
FSHW04n2243270318
46095FS